IN THE SHADOW
OF THE HOLOCAUST
AND THE INQUISITION

IN THE SHADOW OF THE HOLOCAUST AND THE INQUISITION

Israel's Relations with Francoist Spain

RAANAN REIN

Department of History, Tel Aviv University

Translated by Martha Grenzeback

FRANK CASS
LONDON • PORTLAND, OR

First Published in 1997 in Great Britain by
FRANK CASS & CO. LTD.
Newbury House, 900 Eastern Avenue
London, IG2 7HH

and in the United States of America by
FRANK CASS
c/o ISBS, 5804 N.E. Hassalo Street
Portland, Oregon, 97213-3644

British Library Cataloguing in Publication Data:

Rein, Raanan
  In the shadow of the holocaust and the inquisition:
  Israel's relations with Francoist Spain
  1. Israel – Foreign relations – Spain   2. Spain – Foreign
  relations – Israel – 20th century
  I. Title
  327.5'694'046

  ISBN 0 7146 4796 9 (cloth)
  ISBN 0 7146 4351 3 (paper)

Library of Congress Cataloging-in-Publication Data:

Rein, Raanan, 1960–
  [Be-tsel ha-Sho'ah yeha-Inḵvizitsyah. English]
  In the shadow of the Holocaust and the Inquisition : Israel's
relations with Francoist Spain / Raanan Rein : translated by Martha
Grenzeback.
     p.   cm.
  Includes bibliographical references and index.
  ISBN 0-7146-4796-9 (cloth). -- ISBN 0-7146-4351-3 (pbk.)
  1. Israel--Foreign relations--Spain.   2. Spain--Foreign relations-
-Israel.   I. Title.
DS119.8.S68R45   1997
327.4605694--dc21   96-53973

Typeset by Regent Typesetting, London
Printed in Great Britain by
Bookcraft (Bath) Ltd, Midsomer Norton, Avon

To my parents, Nehama and Shlomo

Contents

Introduction

On 19 January 1986, two days after the formal declaration of diplomatic ties between Madrid and Jerusalem, the Prime Minister of Israel, Shimon Peres, met with his Spanish counterpart, Felipe González, at the state guest-house of the Dutch government. After the meeting, they announced to the many journalists waiting outside that a new chapter was beginning in Hispano-Israeli relations. Both leaders stressed that a historical link had been restored in the relations between their nations, a link broken some 500 years previously. González spoke of correcting the historical mistake of expelling the Jews from Spain and severing the fruitful connection between the two Mediterranean peoples. Peres emphasized that, in Israel's view, its relations with Spain were unlike its relations with any other country. He mentioned the 'Golden Age' of the Jews of Spain and the distinguished figures whose names are associated with that period, such as Maimonides, Yehuda Halevy, and others; but he stressed: 'We also carry in our hearts the memory of the expulsion of the Jews from Spain.'[1] The Israeli media were enthusiastic about the meeting, and described the two leaders as men who had 'inscribed their names on the pages of history and [who had] reconnected a chain that was broken five hundred years ago.'[2]

All these declarations contained a certain measure of exaggeration and distortion. Political leaders and the mass media both tend to glorify political moves and attribute a dramatic and historical dimension to them. It is difficult, however, to find any real link between the order of expulsion issued by the Catholic rulers Ferdinand and Isabella at the end of the fifteenth century and the relationship between two sovereign states, Spain and Israel, in the second half of the twentieth century. If Spain had a moral obligation or a historical debt, it was not to the political entity represented by the state of Israel, but rather to the Jewish people. Indeed, from the end of the nineteenth century on, Spain began, slowly and hesitantly, to accept its Jewish heritage.[3] Gradually, long before the establishment of a Jewish state, Jews began to settle in Spain again, and Madrid opened its arms to them. Much later, during the mid-1980s, Spain's decision makers were not influenced by notions of moral obligation so much as they were by political and economic issues and by a concern for the country's international image.

Peres and González were in fact closing a circle with a much smaller radius – one that had begun when the newly declared state of Israel had chosen to adopt a hostile attitude towards the régime of the dictator Francisco Franco. Israel's resolute policy against Spain was fuelled not by the memory of the expulsion of the Jews and the persecutions of the Inquisition, but rather by a series of complex images, positions, and decisions. The factors that shaped the Israeli policy included recent memories of the Francoist régime's evident support for the Nazi régime during the Second World War; the understandable personal and ideological anti-Francoist commitment that many officials in the Foreign Ministry and the political adminis-tration had harbored since the days of the Spanish Civil War; pragmatic foreign policy considerations; and concern about inter-national public opinion and the views of political parties at home.

The situation was similar in Spain. Madrid did not court Israel's favour in the first years of its existence out of a desire to do penance for the 'historical wrong' done to the Jews, but primarily for manifest motives of *realpolitik*. After three years of a very bloody civil war, Franco had ascended to power with the support of Hitler and Mussolini, and he had adopted a policy of friendly neutrality towards the Axis in the Second World War; he was well aware that establish-ing ties with Israel, the Jewish state, would help him differentiate his régime from Italian Fascism and German Nazism, which were associated with anti-Semitism and racism.

In the years after the Second World War – years that were critical for his régime – Franco turned to Peronist Argentina for economic aid, namely food to feed his people (at least some of whom were nearly starving) and to prevent food riots that would endanger his government. He also tried to mend fences with the United States, seeking strategic support for his anti-communist régime in that period when the Cold War was developing rapidly. What he wanted from Israel was the moral legitimation that would help him break through the international boycott imposed on him and expedite an agreement with the United States.

Spain, trying to rehabilitate its image in the West, did not overlook either the potential moral impact of establishing ties with Israel or the influence of Jews around the world, particularly Jews in the United States. This desire for moral legitimacy in the West was also a central motive behind the Francoist régime's declared policy of tolerance and even sympathy for the Jews of Spain. Franco could not afford to treat the little Jewish community in his country in any way that might give rise to anti-Spanish propaganda in sister communities throughout the Jewish world.

This book seeks to present, for the first time, a thorough analysis of the relations between Spain and Israel, focusing on the years 1948–56 but examining them against the background of both nations' historical memories. Israel's Spanish policy and Madrid's attitude towards the Middle East are studied here within the general context of Israeli foreign policy, Francoist foreign policy, and Spain's position in the international arena in those years. How did Nationalist Spain, ruled as it was by a conservative military dictatorship that showed fascist leanings at the end of the 1930s and the beginning of the 1940s, see Jews, the State of Israel, and Zionism? How did Israel see Catholic Spain and General Franco's régime? How far was Spain committed to defending Christianity's holy places and to supporting the Vatican's policy towards the state of Israel? When did the unofficial pro-Francoist lobby that called for normal relations with Madrid begin to develop in Israel, and what groups comprised it? These are some of the questions this work seeks to answer.

The book begins with the day on which the new state of Israel was declared. On that day, Israel announced its birth to the vast majority of the states around the world, and requested diplomatic recognition from them. Spain, however, 'which welcomed, accepted, congratulated and upheld the prospect of Nazi supremacy in Europe and the world',[4] was sent no announcement at the time. Israel was not interested in having any contact with it. At this point, as mentioned, it was actually Francoist Spain that wanted diplomatic ties with Israel and which was already showing interest in the new state a few months after it was founded.

Within a few years, however, each of the two countries had undergone a *volte-face* in its policy towards the other. Spain, initially so eager to press its suit, began to give Israel the cold shoulder, whereas Israel, which had begun by rejecting Franco's régime, in time discovered that its own interests dictated a rapprochement with Spain. The first half of the 1950s saw the beginnings of an internal struggle within the Israeli Foreign Ministry regarding policy towards Spain;

ambassadors and the directors of various departments began to call for a change in that policy, while the senior Ministry officials tried to curb such initiatives. The pressure from below gradually increased, and was supported by the activities of the pro-Francoist lobby that sought to rehabilitate the Spanish dictatorship in the eyes of Israeli public opinion and to bring about the establishment of Hispano–Israeli relations.

The main body of the present study ends with the spring of 1956, when Israel's formal request for full diplomatic relations with Spain, tendered through its embassy in Paris, was categorically rejected. By that time, Israel was interested in establishing ties with Madrid, but it was too late. Now it was Madrid's turn to snub Israel. Spain no longer needed such ties – on the contrary, it feared that relations with Jerusalem might damage the close ties it had developed with the Arab world. An analysis of the processes that led to the reversal in Madrid's and Jerusalem's policies is central to this work.

The book focuses on the years 1948–56 because this period constituted a distinct phase in the relations between Israel and Spain, for several reasons. First, those years saw the formation of the attitudes that each country was to maintain towards the other for the next 20 or even 30 years – at least up to General Franco's death at the end of 1975. The second reason is that a number of influential people in the Foreign Ministry, whose personal views helped shape the hostile Israeli position *vis-à-vis* Franco's Spain, were in office throughout these years, being replaced shortly after the end of the period in question. The most important of these officials was Israel's first Minister of Foreign Affairs, Moshe Sharett, who left the government in June 1956, and was replaced by Golda Meir. Another powerful influence was the first Director-General of the Foreign Ministry, Walter Eytan, who was appointed as Israel's ambassador to Paris at the end of 1959.

The third reason for selecting this period is that the year 1956 was also a milestone in Spain's Middle Eastern policy since, in April of that year, Spain recognized Morocco's independence, thereby freeing itself to a great extent from the colonial burden that had weighed on its relations with the Arab world. Less than a year later, as in Israel, changes took place in the upper echelons of Spanish diplomacy: Alberto Martín Artajo, having completed almost a dozen years as Foreign Minister, was replaced, in February 1957, by Fernando María Castiella.

Finally, my decision to focus on the 1940s and 1950s was dictated by the main primary sources available. Documents from this period were open to researchers in all the archives I consulted in Israel, Spain, the United States, and Britain, but this was not the case for documents dating from the 1960s onward; and it would seem impossible to publish any significant research in this field without the use of contemporary documents.

It has been said of Franco's Middle Eastern policy that 'the adoption of an uncompromisingly anti-Israeli attitude was ultimately a fairly low price that Spain could afford to pay in order to strengthen its friendship with the Arab world.'[5] This assessment is correct only in respect to the period from the mid-1950s onward – certainly not before 1953. Similarly, it can be said that at the end of the 1940s and the beginning of the 1950s Israel's hostile policy on Spain and the absence of relations with Madrid were not a heavy price for Israel to pay in order to project the image, at home and abroad, of a state that gave moral considerations special weight in its international policy.

In Israel's first years of existence, Spain, still isolated from the international community, was not of much interest to the new state. Israel was more concerned with preserving its good name in the international community, particularly in liberal and socialist circles in Europe and the United States, and in the Third World. The non-aligned policy that Israel had opted for initially began to deteriorate rapidly in the course of the Korean War, and as the Cold War intensified, Israel's conduct in international affairs became increasingly identified with the Western camp. If Israel had been prepared for relations with Franco's Spain at the beginning of the 1950s, its international image would have suffered in the eyes of many – or such was the view in the Israeli Foreign Ministry. The government would have faced public criticism at home on yet another aspect of its foreign policy. This was already a difficult period for the Israeli government in many ways: a period of withdrawal from the non-aligned policy, a proceeding criticized by the left-wing opposition; the period of the first contacts with the Federal Republic of Germany and the signing of the reparation agreement with Bonn which aroused a public storm in Israel and laid the government open to attack from both the Left and the Right; and the period when diplomatic relations were established with undemocratic régimes in the Third World and with states like Austria and Japan, which had fought alongside Nazi Germany in the Second World War. At such a conjuncture, Israel's Spanish policy became, perhaps unintentionally, a kind of moral fig leaf for the young state's foreign policy.

Changes in Spain's international situation took place very rapidly in the first half of the 1950s, against the backdrop of the Cold War. The fascism–democracy dichotomy that had characterized the years of the Second World War quickly gave way in the Western countries to a new – or renewed – dichotomy that pitted communism against democracy. Under these circumstances, the Western democracies, led by the United States, were willing to co-operate with any régime as long as it was anti-communist. And Franco's régime, of course, was conspicuously anti-communist. Its propagandists declared that General Franco had perceived back in the 1930s what the leaders of the Western democracies did not realize until more than a decade later: that the main danger to Western civilization lay in communism and Soviet imperialism. Franco's régime thus began to extricate itself from its international isolation, to gain admission to various international organizations, and to win recognition and legitimation from a growing number of states.

If Israel committed a political error it was due to a tardy adaptation to the changing reality of the international arena. Israel amended its policy on Spain only by degrees, lagging behind most of the Western nations, and by the time it made a formal application to the Madrid government, at the beginning of 1956, it was already too late. Israel had lost its importance for Francoist Spain. The latter's ties with the Arab world were too important to Spain, both economically and politically. After all, the international boycott against Franco's régime had been lifted some time earlier. Since December 1955, Spain had been a full member of the United Nations, and Israel's vote in the international organization no longer had a decisive importance for the Spaniards. Spain's interest in establishing normal diplomatic relations with Israel dwindled considerably.

Moreover, the timing of the official application to Spain, at the beginning of 1956, was disastrous. At that time, the chances that Spain would accept were especially slim; the Israeli initiative was virtually doomed to failure from the outset. The nationalist ferment in Morocco was at its peak, and Franco's régime faced the painful necessity of deciding the future of Spanish Morocco. It was not a propitious time to negotiate relations between Spain and Israel. A few months later, both the French and the Spanish sectors of Morocco achieved independence, but by then the friendly relations between Spain and the Arabs had reached a new high in the context of the tension between Nasser's Egypt and Britain and France – a tension that resulted in the Sinai campaign. For Franco, this was an additional opportunity to present his country as a potential mediator between the European states and the Arabs and he did not want to miss it.

Chapter 5 of this book examines a number of central issues in the relations between the two states in the years 1956–75, the period that ended with the death of the Caudillo. During this time, Israel did not succeed in breaking down the wall of Spanish hostility. The subjects analysed in this chapter include Spain's position in the Sinai war (1956), the Six-Day War (1967), and the Yom Kippur War (1973); Francoist Spain's aid to Jews of Spanish origin in Egypt and to Moroccan Jewish emigrants to Israel at the end of the 1950s and the beginning of the 1960s, and the consolidation of the Jewish communities in Spain. The book's epilogue describes Hispano-Israeli relations in the period of Spain's transition from dictatorship to democracy, ending with 1986 and the establishment of full diplomatic relations between Madrid and Jerusalem.

In writing this book I have relied mainly on primary sources, since the subject of Hispano-Israeli relations has not yet received much attention from researchers of either Israeli or Spanish history. These sources include documents from archives in Jerusalem, Madrid, Washington, and London; press clippings from the archives of daily newspapers in Israel and Spain, and interviews with some of the Israelis who helped shape foreign policy in those years. I would like to thank the staff of these archives, as well as the veteran diplomats who gave me their time.

In the course of researching and writing this work, I enjoyed useful conversations with many people, a number of whom read various versions of the manuscript and offered important comments and suggestions. Others directed me to documents or books I might otherwise have missed, or offered encouragement. I would like to thank them all, notably my colleagues at Tel Aviv University, Shlomo Ben-Ami, Miri Eliav-Feldon, Natan Lerner, and Tzvi Medin; Haim Avni and Leonardo Senkman from the Hebrew University of Jerusalem; Amikam Nachmani from Bar-Ilan University; Ignacio Klich from the University of Westminster, London, and my Spanish colleagues, Manuel Espadas Burgos, Lorenzo Delgado, Florentino Portero, and María Dolores Algora Weber.

The completion of my research and Martha Grenzeback's faithful translation were made possible by the assistance of the Yad Hanadiv Fellowship of the Rothschild Foundation, Jerusalem. Like my first book (on the Franco–Perón alliance and relations between Spain and

Argentina during the period 1946–55), this work also owes a great deal to my wife, Mónica, and her immense help at various stages of writing and editing.

1

The Israeli Refusal (1948–49)

Republicans and Nationalists vie for Israel's recognition

A few hours after the end of the ceremony declaring Israel as an independent state on 14 May 1948, Moshe Sharett arrived at the new Foreign Ministry, which had taken up temporary quarters in the 'Red House' on the Tel Aviv coast. Sharett spent the evening composing telegrams to announce the establishment of the state of Israel to capitals around the world – an announcement that also constituted, in the rules of international relations, an implicit request for diplomatic recognition. At the same time, his two aides were busy drawing up the list of states to which telegrams should be sent. Generally speaking, this list included all the countries that were then members of the United Nations Organization, and all the Western and Eastern European countries that had not yet joined that organization.[1] It excluded the Arab states and Germany, as well as Franco's Spain – 'for reasons which appeared clear at the time'.[2] Thus, on its very first day, the state of Israel adopted an inimical attitude to the tyrannical régime of General Francisco Franco.

A short time later, the new-born state found itself being courted by both the exiled Republican government of Spain and the Francoist dictatorship. Both Spanish governments were then pursuing intensive diplomatic efforts to improve their respective international positions. The Republicans were worried by what seemed to be the beginning of a process of Western reconciliation with the government that had arisen in Madrid at the end of the Civil War, while Franco's Spain was making herculean attempts to rejoin the family of nations by engineering the cancellation of the United Nations boycott that had been imposed on it in December 1946. The establishment of the State of Israel and the assumption that it would soon join the United Nations necessarily aroused interest in Madrid, as well as among the Republican exiles and the members of the underground democratic parties in Spain itself.

Republican exiles were in contact with representatives of the Jewish Agency even before the birth of the state. In May 1945, for example, Eliahu Elath, an emissary to the United States from the Agency's political department, met with Spanish exiles who were lobbying among friendly delegations at the United Nations founding convention in San Francisco in order to safeguard their rights and prevent Francoist Spain from joining the United Nations. In the fall of 1947, Elath had more significant meetings with representatives of the Republican government-in-exile who were present at Lake Success during the meeting of the United Nations General Assembly; once again they were trying to persuade the various delegations to withhold recognition from the Franco régime and to deny it membership in the United Nations. Elath maintained contact with Dr. Juan Negrín, the Republican Prime Minister during the last two years of the Civil War, and especially with Julio Alvarez del Vayo, the last Foreign Minister in Negrín's government. Among other things, Elath used his connections in Washington to introduce some of the Republican exiles to Congress members and journalists in order to help them create public sympathy for the Spanish Republicans' anti-Francoist campaign.[3]

In November 1948, the anti-Francoist opposition sent letters to governments and political parties all over the world, including the government of Israel and the Israeli workers' party, *Mifleget Poalei Eretz Yisrael* (MAPAI), asking for assistance in its struggle against Franco's dictatorship.[4] The letter said that since 90 per cent of the Spaniards endorsed this struggle, not supporting Franco did not in any way constitute a hostile step against Spain; on the contrary, it would help the Spaniards to regain the power to influence the course of events in their country. Meanwhile, the Republican government-in-exile was also sounding out representatives of Paris-based Zionist parties on the possibility of obtaining Israel's recognition. The chairman of the General Zionists in Paris, who was in contact with representatives of the Republican government, sent a telegraph on the subject to Foreign Minister Sharett, but the answer was negative.[5]

Francoist Spain, surprisingly enough, did not lag behind its opponents. From just before Israel's war of independence until it ended, the Spanish media – which were completely controlled by the government – displayed evident sympathy for the Arab position, although Franco himself and his Foreign Minister, Alberto Martín Artajo, refrained from taking a public stand on the issue. The press provided broad coverage of Arab views concerning the Jews' 'barbarous acts' during the war.[6]

Spain's suspicious attitude towards Israel can be explained in part by its fear that the new state would become a centre of communist and Soviet influence in the Middle East. This fear was based on the facts that the USSR had supported the establishment of the state; the dominant party, MAPAI, was social-democratic; and waves of immigrants from communist-controlled Eastern Europe were expected to make their way to Israel. It should be remembered, too, that the Spanish right wing had characteristically tended to identify Jews as communists since at least the 1930s. These old fears were being given expression in Spanish newspaper articles, which warned that the 'Zionist state' would be a Bolshevik stronghold. The Falange organ *Arriba* and the Catholic daily *Ya* were prominent proponents of this line of thinking.

The Spanish press also helped disseminate accusations that the Jews had desecrated Catholic places of worship, destroyed sacred objects and religious buildings, and humiliated members of the clergy.[7] Such reports reached their peak with a furious attack by the Bishop of Teruel which was published in the local paper on 12 January 1949 and was quoted the next day by the Madrid press. The headline and subheading speak for themselves: 'Jews Perpetrate Vile Sacrileges in the Holy Places. Arabs Nobly Defend Christianity'.[8] Bishop León Villuendas's strong words should not necessarily be considered representative of the views of the entire Spanish Church, and he was not a spokesperson for the Francoist régime. None the less, under the Spanish dictatorship, with the censor's alert eye on every publication, such an article could probably not have been published unless the authorities concurred with it to some degree. Thus, the Spaniards clearly took the part of the Arabs in the Israeli war of independence – although even at the time it was known in the Santa Cruz Palace (the seat of the Spanish Foreign Ministry), that these accusations were gross distortions of reality. One of the Spanish diplomats in Jerusalem reported:

> Although it is true that a few fanatic elements among the Jewish forces have taken advantage of the circumstances of war to plunder and even profane certain holy places within the fighting zones, the Jewish authorities, from the minute the hostilities began, have been openly eager to show their respect for the interests of the different denominations [. . .] One cannot help noting that [. . .] the religious communities established in

Nazareth have been able to live in greater freedom since the city was occupied by the Jews than they did when it was occupied by the Arab forces [. . .].[9]

Apparently, Spanish officials even authorized the shipment, through indirect channels, of small quantities of arms from Spain to Arab hands. In June 1949, the Foreign Ministry in Madrid instructed the Consul-General in Jerusalem to issue an official denial of all the reports of alleged sales of arms to the Arabs, whether direct or indirect but a few arms shipments did indubitably leave the Iberian Peninsula bound for the Arab countries, whether motivated by political sympathy or a desire to obtain the foreign currency that the Spanish treasury needed so badly at the time.[10] The Arabs attached great importance to every shipment of this kind, since an embargo imposed by the British and United States governments on the supply of military matériel to the Middle East during 1948 and the beginning of 1949 kept them short of arms and ammunition.

Nevertheless, once the outcome of Israel's war of independence was clear, Franco's Spain began to make its first tentative efforts to investigate the possibility of establishing diplomatic relations with the Jewish state. Its interest in Israel was great enough to allow it to overlook the conspicuously chilly attitude that Israel had shown towards Spain from the start. In the years 1949 and 1950, Spain worked through no fewer than four channels of communication to convey its intentions to the new state. One conduit was the informal contacts between Spanish diplomats and their Israeli counterparts in various capitals of the world. Another gambit involved encouraging Jews in Spain, Spanish Morocco, and other places to urge Israel to establish relations with Madrid. The third channel was the Spanish consulate in Jerusalem, which had been operating since the mid-nineteenth century. This channel became especially important after Madrid changed its representative in Israel, replacing him as Consul-General in the summer of 1949 with the Duke of Terranova, who was known for his warm attitude toward the Jewish people. The fourth medium was the special emissary who arrived in Tel Aviv in April 1949 where he met with the Director-General of the Foreign Ministry, Walter Eytan.

On 15 February 1949, Eliahu Elath, who was by then Israel's first ambassador to the United States, sent a telegram from Washington to the Foreign Minister, Moshe Sharett, reporting a Spanish overture that had reached him through Robert Nathan, a Jewish-American businessman who served as economic advisor to the Jewish Agency in Washington (he was later an advisor to the Israeli Embassy there as well). Francoist Spain's representatives had requested an informal meeting with Elath to discuss the possibility of establishing diplomatic relations between the two states. Apparently Elath did not see a refusal as axiomatic, since he turned to Sharett for guidance, asking him whether such a meeting was advisable. Sharett immediately instructed Elath not to meet with the Spanish representatives.[11]

At the same time, Meir Fingerhut, the director of the Jewish Agency office in Paris, wrote to the Israeli Foreign Ministry saying: 'A few days ago my brother [Miguel Jaime] in Barcelona, Spain, informed me by telephone that there is a possibility of establishing diplomatic ties with Spain, and he wants to know if we are interested.' The reply that Gershon Avner (Hirsch) sent Fingerhut from the West European division of the Foreign Ministry stated explicitly: 'During the last weeks many official and semi-official hints have been reaching us from various world centres to the effect that Spain is willing to establish diplomatic ties with us.'[12] This indicates that approaches to Elath or other Israelis or Jews were not isolated, unofficial contacts but part of a much broader Spanish campaign.

The Israeli response to all these openings was negative. At the time, Israel had no interest at all in diplomatic relations with Spain. 'We discussed it in the Foreign Ministry', wrote Avner, 'and the decision was to hint to them that for us this was not the right moment for establishing these ties [. . .] We are certain to discuss this matter again in the future.'

Avner wrote a similar letter to Eliahu Eliachar, a member of the Constitutive Assembly and later a Knesset member for the Sephardi List, which worked energetically to persuade the Foreign Ministry to establish ties with Spain. Eliachar showed the Director-General of the Foreign Ministry, Walter Eytan, a letter that he had received from his cousin, François Barukh, a Jerusalem-born Jew who, being a French subject, had left the city when Turkey entered the First World War. At the end of the 1940s, he had transferred his business to Spain, and by the beginning of the 1950s he headed the Jewish community of Madrid and was a willing tool in the service of the Francoist propaganda machine. His letter ran as follows:

1. The Government of Spain views Israel's success with composure.

2. It is especially interested in the friendship and prosperity of the Sephardic Jews.

3. If Israel wants to be recognized and to exchange representatives, it must send an accredited representative.

4. A commercial treaty will also be welcomed, after study by the economic ministries of both states [. . .] so if the foreign minister sends an accredited representative, preferably a Sephardic Jew, he will achieve immediate success.

Barukh also offered to assist in presenting Israel's ambassador to the Spanish authorities and to support his activities.

Avner replied within a few days. He explained to Eliachar that after a series of discussions, the Foreign Ministry had decided to 'postpone the establishment of such ties for a while'.[13] The phrasing of his reply at this point did not convey an absolute rejection of the possibility of establishing ties with Franco's régime, but merely a postponement of any decision in the matter.

Concurrently with the 'hints' it sent to Israel during those months, the Franco régime also made certain gestures towards the Jews in Spain, who at the time numbered only a few thousand. Similarly, it showed tolerance for the Jews of the Spanish protectorate in Morocco – as well as in the coastal cities of Melilla and Ceuta, which had been in Spanish hands since the end of the fifteenth and seventeenth centuries, respectively.[14] These gestures were in large part intended to improve the Franco régime's image in the Western democracies and Israel. Among other things, the régime wanted to whitewash the manifestations of anti-Semitism that had been evident in the Nationalist camp since the 1930s, when both the Falangists and the clergy had warned against 'Jewish–communist cooperation against Christian civilization', or when they identified Jews with all the ideologies and ways of life against which Nationalist Spain was rebelling: materialistic communism, secular liberalism, exploitative capitalism, and masonic atheism.[15]

One measure that was taken concerned the Sephardic Jews living in Egypt and Greece who were under Spain's protection. Under the treaties that Spain had concluded with Egypt and Greece back in the mid-1930s – treaties which themselves expressed the Republican government's sympathetic attitude towards Jews – such Jews were due to lose Spanish consular protection in 1949. Before that deadline, Franco published a decree permitting these protected Jews (descendants of those Jews expelled from Spain in 1492 who appeared in Spain's population census or consular or diplomatic records) to apply to one of the Spanish legations for the status of 'Spanish subjects abroad'.[16] This decree – which benefited only a few hundred Jews – was signed at the end of December 1948, and on 11 February 1949 the Spanish Foreign Ministry sent instructions regarding its implementation to its embassies in Cairo and Athens.[17] At the same time, the Spanish authorities lost no time in urging Sephardic Jews (the Jews of Tangiers, for example) to convey their gratification at this measure. All expressions of gratitude were then passed on to the foreign press in Madrid in order to achieve maximum propaganda value – and they largely succeeded. The régime tried to create the deceptive impression that Spanish citizenship was being extended to all Jews of Spanish descent, rather than merely to certain families who already enjoyed Spain's consular protection. Moreover, some of those on the list for Greece had perished in the Holocaust and were consequently unable to benefit from Spain's gesture.

An article of semi-official commentary published in Madrid had this to say: 'This decree proves once more Spain's elevated international conduct, to which racism is unknown.'[18] This statement must be viewed, of course, within the context of the never-ending effort to emphasize the difference between the Franco régime and its former allies, defeated in the Second World War. Around the same time the Spanish authorities published an official document entitled *El Sefardismo* (Spanish Jewry), which sought to underline the importance the Franco régime attributed to the existence of Jewish communities of Spanish descent throughout the world. The aim was to enlist these Jews' assistance somehow in promoting Spain's interests and improving its image in the international arena.[19] Interestingly, the document reflected an ambivalent but not completely hostile attitude towards Zionism, merely expressing a fear that the latter might damage the cultural and linguistic heritage of Sephardic Jews.

It should be stressed that from the 1920s onward – and particularly in the Franco period – the Spanish leadership and diplomatic corps made a distinction between Sephardic Jews, whom they regarded with fundamental, albeit faintly suspicious, approval, and Ashkenazic Jews, on whom they pinned all their negative stereotypes: the Jew as the enemy of Christianity in general and Catholic Spain in particular, the Jew as traitor, and the Jew as materialistic money-grubber. Even the attitude towards Sephardic Jews, however, was always utilitarian at best. Among other things, the Spanish authorities hoped to use the Jews to expand Spain's economic and commercial ties, and to strengthen its diplomatic status and international prestige. Yet at the same time, they never lost their strong aversion to the idea of Jews immigrating to Spain, fearing the creation of a new 'Jewish problem' – the same problem that the Catholic sovereigns Isabella and Ferdinand had 'known so wisely how to solve' at the end of the fifteenth century.

The Republican exiles, worried that the Francoist propaganda would achieve its purpose, sought to uncover what they considered to be the true motives behind the dictatorship's initiatives. Notable in this respect was an attack by the former Foreign Minister, Alvarez del Vayo, who described the decree on behalf of protected Jews as 'an intelligent gesture', but explained to United States public opinion that it should be seen primarily as a propagandist attempt to break through the wall keeping Spain out of the United Nations and to win friendship in North America. 'Knowing the great influence exercised by the Jewish community [in the United States]', said Alvarez del Vayo, '[Franco] made a gesture of propitiation.' The Republican statesman advised the Sephardic Jews, 'whom we Spanish Republicans have always regarded as our compatriots', to 'renounce with thanks' the consular protection Franco offered them. According to him, they would be better advised to wait until liberty returned to Spain and a government arose that would welcome their participation in efforts to rehabilitate and develop their homeland.[20]

Another gesture on Franco's part was granting authorization to open a new synagogue in Spain's capital, where only some 200 Jews resided at the time. The previous synagogue – opened in 1917 and named after Yitzhak Abarbanel – had closed down during the Civil War, when most of the Jews who used to attend it left the city. The new synagogue opened at the beginning of January 1949 (ironically enough, on the street named after Cardinal Cisneros, Queen Isabella's advisor and confessor at the time the Jews were expelled from Spain). The inaugural ceremony was attended by representatives of the government and of the Jews of Barcelona and Tangiers.[21] Despite this fanfare, however, many more years were to pass before the dictatorship granted official authorization for an organized Jewish community to operate.

In Barcelona, where the Jewish community was older and larger, a synagogue had been reopened earlier, in December 1945. The Nationalist authorities had closed down this synagogue – built during the First World War – after the city fell into their hands in 1939, despite Franco's explicit declaration two years earlier, at the height of the Civil War, that the Nationalists would show religious tolerance and permit 'mosques and synagogues to stand open in accordance with the spirit of the Christian State'.[22] When World War II ended, the Jews of Barcelona requested permission to reopen the synagogue, but the mayor refused. The representative of the World Jewish Congress (WJC) in Portugal, Yitzhak Weissman, took the matter to Nicolás Franco, the Caudillo's older brother, who was serving as his country's ambassador in Lisbon, and who had helped Weissman rescue Jews during the Second World War. Nicolás Franco spoke with the Spanish leadership, and the mayor of Barcelona was instructed not to pose any obstacle to the reopening of a Jewish place of worship in the Catalonian capital.[23] At the end of 1949, official recognition was accorded to the Jewish community in Barcelona and to the institutions that governed it.[24]

In any case, the synagogues were quartered in private houses, with no outward sign to indicate that they were places of worship. The reason for this was the prohibition on public non-Catholic religious ceremonies contained in the Spanish Bill of Rights (*Fuero de los Españoles*) of July 1945. This set of laws, published only a few weeks after the end of the Second World War, must be seen in the context of the Franco régime's efforts to adjust to the new international circumstances prevailing since the defeat of fascism and to create a more liberal impression. On the surface, the *Fuero* appeared to guarantee the citizens of Spain a series of democratic liberties. These rights had no real substance, however, since they were reserved for those who did not oppose the 'fundamental principles of the [Nationalist] state and the spiritual, national, and social unity of the country'. The charter gave the government the right to suspend various liberties in times of emergency – a right that it naturally did not hesitate to exercise frequently.[25] The Catholic religion was set down as the official state religion and the Church's position was guaranteed in various spheres. The charter also provided, however, that no one was to be harassed on account of his or her religious beliefs, and that non-Catholic religious worship was not to be hindered as long as it was performed alone and in private. Only members of the Catholic religion were allowed to hold public ceremonies and display other external manifestations of their faith. The Catholic Church's privileged status and the inferior status of religious minorities such as Jews and Protestants in Nationalist Spain were reconfirmed by the Concordat that Spain signed with the Vatican in August 1953. The primate of Spain, Cardinal Enrique Plá y Deniel, stressed that non-Catholic public religious ceremonies were forbidden in Spain because of the danger that some political minority might try to take advantage of such ceremonies to disseminate its propaganda.[26] In comparison to the Republican constitution of 1931, the *Fuero* represented a real regression.

Under the Second Republic, the Jews had enjoyed the most favourable status they had ever had in Spain since the expulsion at the end of the fifteenth century. The leading figures of the Republic, including President Niceto Alcalá Zamora, Prime Minister (later President) Manuel Azaña, and Prime Minister Alejandro Lerroux, had already manifested their sympathy for the Jews back in the 1920s. The Republican constitution gave the Jews (and the Protestants) full equal rights, stating that 'the Spanish state has no official religion'. It guaranteed 'freedom of conscience and the right to profess and freely practice any religion [. . .]', and emphasized that 'religious affiliation shall not affect civil or political status'.[27]

The successive governments of the Republic showed their friendly attitude towards Jews and Zionism on various occasions. In October 1932, while visiting Madrid, Chaim Weizmann, one of the leaders of the Zionist movement and subsequently the first President of the State of Israel, met with the Socialist Education Minister, Fernando de los Ríos, who told him that the Republican government was in favour of the idea of a national homeland for the Jews in Palestine. In May 1933, Spain's representative in the League of Nations, Luis de Zulueta, supported a petition sponsored by the Jews of Upper Silesia against Nazi anti-Jewish legislation. The Jews claimed that this legislation constituted a violation of treaties signed between Germany and Poland at the beginning of the 1920s – treaties by which Germany had undertaken to guarantee equal rights for the minorities in the region. As a result of the petition presented to the League of Nations, the Jews of Upper Silesia enjoyed equal rights until 1937. The Spanish representative defended his position on the grounds of the importance of the principle of defending minority rights, the lesson Spain had learned from the expulsion of the Jews, and the sympathy it felt for the descendants of those Jews who had retained the Spanish language and customs. In the fall of that year, another representative of Republican Spain, Salvador de Madariaga, used the League of Nations as a platform from which to defend persecuted Jews.

Two years later, in March 1935, festivities were held in the city of Córdoba to mark the 800th anniversary of the birth of Maimonides (the Rambam). The celebrations were initiated and organized by the government, and representatives of Jewish Palestine took part in them. That was the year in which Germany adopted the Nuremberg laws, and some of the speakers at the event in Córdoba expressed the hope that the commemoration would convey a message to those states that continued to persecute their Jewish inhabitants. Although the strong impact on Spain of the world economic crisis made the successive governments of the Republic unwilling to see their country become a refuge for Jews, between 1 March 1933 and January 1935, some 3,000 Germans, mostly Jews, found shelter there.[28]

In any case, the Bill of Rights that the Franco régime published in the summer of 1945 was not enough to stop the erosion of Spain's international status at the time; nor was the promise of limited democracy in the local authorities, or the changes Franco made in the composition of his cabinet. In the new government, the Falange – that element in the government most closely identified with fascism – was less prominently represented, whereas the Catholic contingent was strengthened, especially the part represented by Acción Católica in the person of the new Foreign Minister, Alberto Martín Artajo. Years later, one of the régime's apologists was to write of this new government that it reflected a 'typical Francoist methodology, where something changes so that everything will remain the same'.[29] In July 1945, Franco even pledged to reinstitute the monarchy, after a transition period to consolidate the achievements and ideals that had triumphed in the Civil War; and in September, the régime abolished the Fascist salute it had adopted in April 1937. In the West, however, all these measures were perceived as merely cosmetic changes, insufficient to alter the ugly face of the dictatorship.[30]

In April 1949, there was manifest competition between the rival Republican and Francoist governments to obtain Israel's recognition. On 22 April at 3.30 p.m., the Director-General of the Israeli Foreign Ministry, Walter Eytan, received Rafael Soriano, special envoy and plenipotentiary minister of the Franco government. Only a few minutes after he had left the Director-General's office it was entered by Julio de Huici, special envoy and plenipotentiary minister of the Republican government of Spain in Sofia. Each of these men had come to Israel for the same sole purpose: to make an official request to the Israeli authorities that they apply to his own particular government for recognition. Each promised, in the name of his government, that a reciprocal recognition of Israel would be extended immediately. The Francoist envoy appeared particularly eager, and explained that Franco 'regrets very much that [Israel] did not ask him to recognize [it], and thinks that it is due to a misunderstanding!' At the conclusion of his conversation with Eytan, Soriano asked hopefully, 'Have you nothing to say that I can convey to my government as a message from the government of Israel?'[31]

Thus, on that day Israel was called upon to decide unequivocally what its policy on Spain was. Up until then, it had preserved a frosty demeanour towards the Franco régime without ever really clarifying, either at home to the Israeli public or abroad, the question of whether Israel had a Spanish policy, and, if so, in exactly what it consisted. The Foreign Ministry rose to the challenge presented to it that day, but without giving any explanation for its decision. It was not until three weeks later, when Abba Eban raised his hand in the United Nations General Assembly to oppose the cancellation of the international diplomatic ban on Francoist Spain, that the official grounds for Israel's hostile policy towards Madrid were presented. In April, however, Eytan merely gave Soriano a short, cool reply: 'For the time being, no', he said. 'If we ever have anything to say to your government, I am sure we will find a way to convey it.'[32] The formula 'if we ever' indicates a more explicit refusal than 'we are certain to discuss this matter again in the future', as the Foreign Ministry had written in response to Spain's earlier approaches through Jewish intermediaries. Eytan wrote to Foreign Minister Moshe Sharett: 'I suggest that we do not request recognition from either of these governments, and in my view, if one of the Spanish envoys requests an interview with you, you should refuse.'[33] Eytan was strongly anti-Francoist but he also opposed diplomatic ties with the Spanish Republican government:

> We turned the Republicans down because it wasn't serious. It was clear that this government was somehow managing to keep going but was not really serious. Why should Israel establish diplomatic relations with a government that was in fact a pretend government?[34]

Indeed, in 1949 the Republican government headed by Alvaro de Albornoz represented a divided and fragmented Republican camp. Its influence was limited and it was unable to present a viable alternative to the Franco régime. Even in 1946, when there still seemed to be some possibility of a Republican restoration in Spain, the government-in-exile was officially recognized by only 10 states: four Latin American governments and six communist governments in Eastern Europe. Of those 10, only two – Mexico and Yugoslavia – maintained formal diplomatic recognition until the end of the Francoist régime. The government-in-exile survived merely as a democratic, anti-Francoist symbol which contributed to the delegitimization of the dictatorship in various sectors of international public opinion up until the first democratic elections, held in Spain in June 1977.[35]

The Republicans, who strongly hoped for recognition from Israel, chose to send Julio de Huici to Tel Aviv because he was acquainted with many Bulgarian Jews, some of whom he said he had helped emigrate to Israel, and because he was an expert on Spanish–Jewish folklore and the Jewish literature that had flourished in medieval Spain. Huici, who was apparently slated to be Republican Spain's representative in Israel, even lectured on these subjects at the Hebrew University in Jerusalem during his stay.[36] The Republican representative remained in Israel for more than two weeks, waiting for an official reply. On 8 May he sent a message to Sharett suggesting a *de jure* recognition of Israel by the Republican government. The Spanish envoy asked whether Israel would consent to accept such recognition and requested a prompt reply before he left the country. The Foreign Ministry, which had provided Julio de Huici with an escort during his stay, chose to dodge the issue; Huici received no answer to his missive.[37]

Rafael Soriano's visit to Israel – in the framework of a three-month trip through the Middle East to assess the functioning of Spain's legations in the region – apparently led the Arabs to suspect that Madrid was secretly trying to establish relations with the new state. Since Soriano did not achieve his purpose in Israel, the Spaniards were able to explain that their country was not inclined to exchange diplomatic representatives with Israel and that Spanish envoys were visiting Palestine merely 'to assess the situation of Spanish citizens [and of Spanish assets] in the Arab part of Palestine and in Israel'.[38] As long as Franco was uncertain about the possibility of establishing diplomatic relations with Israel, he did not want to endanger his relations with the Arabs needlessly. Outwardly, Spain's official policy continued to be that Madrid had no intention of recognizing Israel and establishing diplomatic ties with it.

Spain's international isolation

On 11 May 1949, Israel was accepted as a member of the United Nations Organization.[39] For a few months the Franco régime did everything it could to delay Israel's admission to the United Nations, both because it was worried about how Israel would vote on matters pertaining to Spain, and because Madrid, as will be seen, unreservedly supported the Vatican's call to internationalize Jerusalem. Spain – which in April had expressed, through Rafael Soriano, its willingness to recognize Israel without any preconditions – was trying at the same time to exercise its influence on the Catholic countries, especially in Latin America, to persuade them to make their recognition of Israel and support for its admission to the United Nations conditional on the prior internationalization of Jerusalem in order to protect the Christian holy places. The results were disappointing from Madrid's point of view. During the first half of 1949, almost all the Catholic countries recognized Israel, while in the United Nations vote 18 out of the 20 Latin American delegations favoured Israel's admission. El Salvador and Brazil, which called on Israel to respect the United Nations' resolutions concerning Jerusalem, abstained.[40]

Its admission to the United Nations naturally increased Israel's value in the eyes of Francoist Spain, which at the time was fighting for its international position. The General Assembly was debating the 'Spanish question' just then, and was about to decide whether to continue the diplomatic boycott it had imposed on the Spanish dictatorship two-and-a-half years previously. The first important test of foreign policy that Israel faced in the United Nations was, accordingly, its attitude towards Spain; it had to define its position quickly, before the vote in the General Assembly.

Before any discussion of Israel's vote – why it voted the way it did and the implications that vote was to have for relations between Israel and Spain in the years to come – some general background is needed on Spain's international status during the Second World War and the process by which the Franco régime was pushed into an isolated corner of the international arena in the years 1945–47. Without this international background it is impossible to analyse Spain's relations with any state at the end of the 1940s.

The Franco régime was born of a military uprising against the Second Republic – an uprising that developed into a prolonged civil war (from 1936 to 1939) claiming hundreds of thousands of victims. Although the origins of the war were specific to Spain, German and Italian intervention on the side of the Nationalist forces contributed considerably to the Francoist victory.[41] In the minds of many, this established a connection between Franco's new régime and the régimes of Hitler and Mussolini. Franco himself contributed to this impression by affirming, in July 1940, that the Nationalist struggle in Spain was merely 'the first battle of the New Order [in Europe]'.[42]

Only five months after the Civil War officially ended and the Caudillo established his government in Madrid, the Second World War began. Immediately upon the outbreak of hostilities, Franco hurried to declare Spain's official neutrality, but his sympathy for the Axis countries was an open secret.[43] In fact, until the beginning of 1944 Franco continued to believe, with greater or lesser conviction, that the Third Reich would emerge victorious from the war. None the less, throughout the war years he maintained a cautious policy dictated less by his own views on the conflict in Europe than by a series of objective constraints. The Spanish leader knew that, at the time, so soon after the Civil War, his country was economically, socially, militarily, and psychologically exhausted. He wanted to enter the war, but only in its final stages, in the hope of enjoying the fruits of the Fascist victory.[44] After France fell in June 1940, Spain took one more step toward the battlefield when it moved from neutrality to the status of non-belligerent and occupied the international zone of Tangiers – violating treaties it had signed in the past. Unlike Mussolini's Italy, however, it went no further than this; Britain's success in withstanding the German offensive kept Franco circumspect.

In the early stages of the war, the Spanish leaders entertained the delusion that an Axis victory would lead to the re-establishment of a Hispanic empire: Spain would again rule over Gibraltar (lost at the beginning of the eighteenth century), as well as sections of the French empire in North and west Africa; it would occupy French Morocco and the Oran region in Algeria, and extend its control in the Spanish Sahara and Spanish Guinea.[45] These were some of the demands put forward by the régime's representatives in their negotiations with Germany over the conditions for Spain's entering the war on the side of the Axis. The Spaniards even hoped to increase their influence in Palestine and strengthen their hold on the places sacred to Christianity, something which, of course, would have suited the interests of the Catholic Church.[46] When Franco realized, however, that the war would last longer than he had expected and that Germany could not satisfy his territorial demands or meet Spanish needs for food, fuel, or arms, he decided to avoid direct involvement in the conflict. A more generous attitude towards Spain on Hitler's part might well have persuaded Franco to enter the war – but German obstinacy and arrogance prevented this. The Führer, who expected Britain's imminent surrender, did not think it worthwhile to pay a high price for something which, although desirable, was not, in his view, essential for a German victory.

Britain and the United States monitored the Caudillo's activities with concern. They hoped to take advantage of the régime's economic difficulties as it tried to rehabilitate a country in which entire regions, devastated by the Civil War, were half-starved and suffering terrible hardship. To prevent Spain from entering the war on the Axis side and to limit economic ties and co-operation between the two, the Allies were obliged to adopt a policy of extreme caution in their relations with Franco's régime, despite their disapproval of its character and outlook. Gibraltar's significance for control of the Mediterranean Sea and the plan to invade North Africa were two particularly important considerations underlying Allied strategy concerning Spain. Accordingly, Spain was offered various inducements in the form of economic aid, shipments of raw materials and essential food products (oil and grain were the most important), credit, and navicerts (transit permits) for ships carrying major grain shipments from Argentina to Spain – all to make Franco dependent on the Allies.[47]

This remained Allied strategy throughout the war, despite the occasional upset or crisis. General Franco was thus obliged to manoeuvre between his clear natural sympathy for the Axis and his economic dependence on the Allies, pressed on the one hand by the Germans, who had been encamped on the other side of the Pyrenees since the occupation of southern France, and on the other by his fear that the Allies would try to bring down his government. In these circumstances, the fortunes of war dictated the extent to which Spain inclined to support one warring camp or the other, depending on which seemed to have the upper hand.

Hitler, naturally, was angry with the man he called 'the Latin charlatan' and 'the Moroccan carpet dealer' for sitting on the fence without definitely committing himself to either side. On one occasion, the Führer likened Franco's policy to that of 'a Jew who wants to do business with the most sacred values of humanity',[48] and accused him of selling Spain to the Allies for a handful of wheat. Fortunately for Spain, Hitler soon lost interest in both Spain and the possibility of taking over neighbouring Gibraltar. Spain's importance in Germany's overall strategy decreased noticeably once preparations began for the German invasion of the Soviet Union ('Operation Barbarossa').[49]

Many researchers, and of course Franco's propagandists, have claimed that from the outset Franco never planned to join the combatants and consequently posed conditions he knew Hitler could not accept. These views, being based on what Winston Churchill wrote after the war (that Spain held the key to all British activity in the Mediterranean Sea and that it had never, even in its darkest hours, turned its back on Britain), exaggerated the degree to which he supposedly co-operated with the West.[50] It should be kept in mind that the Spanish media expressed enthusiastic support for the Axis throughout the war years ('Europe presents arms in honour of its great son, Adolf Hitler', wrote one of the papers after Germany's surrender and Hitler's suicide); that Spain permitted German intelligence operations on its home territory and in its possessions in North Africa; that German ships used Spanish ports for provisioning and maintenance; that Spanish workers were sent to assist in the war industry of the Reich; that the Spanish police was greatly influenced by the Gestapo; and that in the summer of 1941, following the German invasion of the Soviet Union – at the height of pro-German fervour in Francoist Spain – the Spanish government organized the Blue Division, a volunteer force numbering some 18,000 men, and sent it off to fight on the eastern front alongside the Wehrmacht.[51] Given all these circumstances, it is doubtful if Spain's position in the war can really be described as neutral. If neutrality was ever approximated, it was only in the first months of the war, when the battle picture was not yet clear, and in the final months, by which time even Madrid could see that the Axis' fate was sealed.

From about the beginning of 1943, Franco gradually became more amenable to co-operation with the Allies. The Axis' defeats in North Africa and Stalingrad and the removal of Mussolini obliged Madrid to re-examine its own position, and doubtless played a part in Spain's return to neutrality (instead of 'non-belligerence') in October 1943, and its decision to call the Blue Division home – almost in secret and without the fanfare that had accompanied its departure. This process of rapprochement with the Allies accelerated from 1944 to 1945, as the Allies advanced.

As the war neared its end, however, public opinion in Britain and the United States began to press for a firmer policy toward Spain than the countries' leaders favoured and than their economic and strategic interests would dictate. Now it was claimed that since there was no longer any need to keep Spain neutral for the sake of the war, steps should be taken against a régime that had been established with the aid of Nazi Germany and Fascist Italy. The general feeling was that, when the war ended, the Allies would no longer need to show restraint in their relations with the tyrannical régime in Madrid, and would take steps to eliminate this anachronistic vestige of the

Fascist world that had gone up in flames. This encouraged Franco's opponents, who in 1944 and 1945 believed on many occasions that the end of the Francoist régime was already in sight, approaching in tandem with the anticipated Allied victory. They expected that outside pressure combined with the internal agitation, born of economic hardship and political repression, would bring down the régime.

At the founding convention of the United Nations, held in San Francisco from 25 April to 26 June 1945, the Mexican delegate, Luis Quintanilla, proposed denying membership in the organization not only to the Axis powers, but also to those régimes established with the aid of the Axis military forces. This was a direct reference to Spain, the involvement of Fascist Italy and Nazi Germany in the Civil War on the side of the Francoist forces, and the sympathy Franco had shown toward the Axis during World War II.[52] Not by chance was it the Mexican delegate who proposed such a resolution. Together with the Soviet Union, Mexico had been the only country to offer any active assistance to the Republicans during the Civil War. It had also taken in many Republican exiles after the Republic's defeat, and it maintained a clearly anti-Francoist stand for years afterward. Quintanilla's draft resolution – which did not specifically mention Spain – was unanimously approved by the conference plenum. Not a single demurring voice was heard, nor a word in favour of the Franco régime.

A month later, the leaders of the three great powers met in Potsdam, and at the beginning of August they confirmed the ban on Spain. However, Britain and the United States did not accept Stalin's suggestion that concrete measures be taken against Spain on the grounds that the régime constituted a threat to world peace and security.[53] Churchill and Truman held that such steps might merely strengthen the Franco régime, and that it was up to Spain to solve its problems by itself. Obviously both men, despite their disapproval of the dictatorship, saw Franco as preferable to any alternative that might endanger their strategic and economic interests on the Iberian Peninsula. The communiqué issued by the three leaders censured Franco's régime and indicated that it should effect changes in Spain, but mentioned no possibility of concrete action against it. It asserted that the three world powers would not support any application for United Nations membership submitted by the Spanish régime.[54]

In July 1945, the Labour Party won the elections in Britain. This was presumably a blow for Spain, since the Labour Party had sided with the Republic in the Civil War and, during the election campaign, had attacked the Conservatives for their conciliatory attitude toward Franco.[55] The election results in Britain and the Potsdam declaration caused 'great concern' in Spain and, according to the press attaché at the British embassy in Madrid, the internal situation in Spain had not been so critical since the end of the Civil War.[56]

Two additional sources of concern for the Francoist régime in those days were the increasing power of the Socialists and the Communists in France and the establishment of the Republican government-in-exile in Mexico following the convening of the Republican Cortes (parliament). Although the exiled government did not represent a real threat to the Franco régime, since it brought out dissension rather than unity in the Republican camp, it did serve as an instrument for mobilizing support among anti-Francoists all over the world. A few weeks later the United States' ambassador left Madrid, and for five years American interests were represented by a diplomat of lower rank.

In February 1946, at its inaugural meeting in London, the United Nations General Assembly adopted Panama's proposal to ratify the decisions concerning Spain that had been taken in San Francisco and Potsdam. The new resolution added that the General Assembly advised its members to take into account both the letter and spirit of the aforementioned decisions in their future relations with Spain. Forty-six states voted in favour of the resolution and only two against it (El Salvador and Nicaragua), with three abstentions.[57]

France, which in the period from 1945 to 1947 was the Western power most hostile to Spain, urged the Security Council to discuss breaking off diplomatic and economic ties with the Franco régime and warned that Spain was concentrating troops on their common border.[58] London, which had an economic interest in maintaining relations with Spain (it needed Spanish raw materials and agricultural products), advocated a more moderate position and was supported by the United States, where more and more people, reacting to the initial stages of the Cold War, were calling for cooperation with General Franco's anti-communist régime. The result was a compromise in the form of the Tripartite Note, published on 4 March 1946, which stated that although friendly relations with the Franco régime were impossible, the United States, Britain, and France had no intention of intervening in Spain's internal affairs. The three countries merely expressed the hope that Spain would pardon its political prisoners, dissolve the Falange, and hold free elections.[59]

At the same time as the Tripartite Note, the State Department published the *White Book* on Spain, a collection of documents concerning the Franco régime's ties with Nazi Germany and Fascist Italy between the summer of 1940 and the end of 1943. A series of letters, telegrams, and memoranda found in archives in Berlin documented the comprehensive Hispano-German ties, the Spanish conditions for entering the war on the Axis side, Spain's agreement to allow Germany's ships to refuel in its harbours, and more.[60]

In April, Poland warned the United Nations that Spain was concentrating troops in the Pyrenees with aggressive intent and allowing German scientists to develop atomic weapons on Spanish territory. The Polish delegate asserted that Spain represented a threat to world peace and that the international community must not settle for moral condemnation but must take concrete steps against it. Britain and the United States continued to oppose any intervention in Spain, claiming that Poland's accusations were exaggerated and unfounded. The atmosphere of suspicion toward Spain was such, however, that in the end the members accepted Australia's proposal to appoint a subcommittee that would examine the situation in Spain and decide whether Spain indeed represented a danger to world peace and security and a source of international strife. The subcommittee presented its conclusions at the beginning of June: the Francoist régime was a fascist régime that constituted a 'potential' threat to world peace. The subcommittee advised the Security Council to pass on these findings to the General Assembly, together with the recommendation that if the Franco régime remained in power and democratic liberties were not safeguarded in Spain, the members of the United Nations should sever diplomatic relations with Madrid.[61]

In this difficult climate of international hostility, Franco's régime tried to cope with its problems in several ways. It continued the iron-fist policy at home, benefiting from the Spanish Church's legitimization, and continuing to exploit memories of the Civil War to promote fear of another fratricidal war. At the same time it attempted to convey a number of messages to the West. First, it made much of its anti-communist character and tried to instill in Western public opinion the belief that in Spain the only alternative to the existing government was chaos and communist takeover. Second, it maintained that Spain had remained truly neutral throughout the Second World War, and if it had taken steps that could be interpreted as supportive of the Axis, this was because the German threat to Spain had left it no choice. Again and again officials quoted the words Churchill had spoken before the British Parliament in May 1944, when he emphasized the importance of Spanish neutrality to the Allies during the critical stages of the war.[62] Third, emphasis was placed on the unique nature of the régime, which 'had nothing to do with fascism'. By the end of 1944, Franco was maintaining in a newspaper interview that 'Spain could never be joined to other governments that did not hold to Catholicism as a first principle'. In his words, his régime was nothing other than 'a true democracy', 'an organic democracy', based on religion, family, syndicates, and local authorities.[63]

In its domestic propaganda, the régime portrayed international opposition as one more chapter in the 'black legend', the chain of attacks and libels from which Spain had suffered since the sixteenth century; and as such, it was no cause for alarm. Shrugging off all responsibility, the régime stressed that the international opprobrium was not a campaign against the present government, but rather against Spanish essence and tradition and Christian civilization in general. For the most part, criticism of Spain was attributed to communists, freemasons, or the 'red' exiles, who, although defeated, were trying to fight Spain from abroad.[64]

When the régime realized what a heavy price the Americans and the British were demanding in exchange for improved relations – the elimination of the Falange, for example – it decided to bide its time. The Spanish leadership interpreted international developments correctly. It realized that in a polarized world, characterized by rivalry between the West and the Soviet Union, the day could not be far off when the United States would recognize the validity of the anti-communist path taken by the Franco government and welcome Spain back into the fold. Until then, the Francoists would have to wait patiently.[65]

At the same time, the régime worked at nurturing its relations with the two blocs it hoped would help it to break through the international blockade: Latin America and the Arab world. In both cases Madrid emphasized the special relations that had developed through history with these states. In its dealings with Latin America, the régime stressed the policy of 'Hispanidad', which extolled the ties of a shared history, blood, culture, language, and religion that linked Spain to its former American colonies. It tried to enlist the support of the Arabs – as will be seen later – by presenting Spain as a country that, by virtue of its history, well understood the interests of the Moslem world and could serve as a bridge between Islam and Europe.

On 12 December 1946, the United Nations General Assembly resolved to expand the original boycott it had imposed on Spain. This resolution stated that the origin, character, structure, and conduct of the Franco régime rendered it ineligible to participate in the United Nations, its institutions, or the organizations connected with it. The resolution called upon United Nations members to withdraw their ambassadors and plenipotentiary ministers from Madrid, and it recommended that the Security Council consider additional measures if a democratic government were not established in Spain within 'a reasonable time'.[66] Thirty-four states voted in favour of the diplomatic sanctions. Six Latin American states, led by General Perón's Argentina, opposed it, while 13 abstained and one was absent.[67] Notable among the abstainers was the bloc of Moslem states: Egypt, Lebanon, Saudi Arabia, Syria, Afghanistan, and Turkey.

At the time this resolution was passed, most United Nations members either had no diplomatic relations at all with the Franco régime, or else had no ambassador or plenipotentiary minister in Madrid.[68] In the wake of the resolution, the British ambassador and the ministers of the Netherlands and Turkey left the Spanish capital, followed later by the ministers of El Salvador and the Dominican Republic. Italy, although not a member of the United Nations, felt obliged to implement the resolution, and withdrew its ambassador from Madrid as well. The accredited diplomatic corps in Madrid was thus reduced to the papal nuncio, the ambassador of Portugal, the ministers of Switzerland and Ireland (countries which were not members of the United Nations), and diplomats of lower rank in the missions of the other countries that continued to maintain diplomatic relations with Spain. Peronist Argentina was the conspicuous exception to the rule since it actually hurried to fill the vacancy in its embassy in Spain. Less than 24 hours after the United Nations resolution recommending the withdrawal of diplomatic-mission heads, the decision to send a new ambassador to Madrid was announced in Buenos Aires.[69]

During 1947, the representatives of the communist bloc in the United Nations pushed for an intensification of the ostracism of Spain and for the imposition of economic sanctions. In September Poland called for a reaffirmation of the resolutions of December 1946, and for Security Council action to rectify the situation in Spain, as a 'reasonable time' had already passed since the General Assembly resolution and no real change had been effected in the Spanish régime. Yugoslavia also called for an economic boycott of Spain. Another proposal by five Latin American countries called for a reaffirmation of the December resolutions but stopped short of demanding heavier sanctions.[70]

On 18 November, the General Assembly voted separately on each of the provisions of a draft resolution similar to the one proposed by the five Latin American countries. When the vote was counted for the second and most important provision, the one reaffirming the resolutions of December 1946, it was discovered that this time the necessary two-thirds majority had not been attained. Only 29 states had voted in favour, with 16 against – including the United States, which had voted for the boycott the previous year – and eight abstentions: Egypt, Iraq, Lebanon, Pakistan, Saudi Arabia, Syria, Turkey, and Yemen. In the other provisions of the resolution, which were adopted by a large majority, the General Assembly expressed confidence that the Security Council would exercise its authority the moment it considered the situation in Spain to warrant its intervention.

In Francoist Spain the results of the vote were greeted with jubilation – except by the régime's opponents, who were disappointed by what they perceived as their final abandonment by the Western democracies.[71] The Spanish press burst into a joyful paean to Spain's victory, emphasizing that Spain would demand satisfaction from the United Nations members for the wrong inflicted on it until now, and radiating the belief that Spain was soon to be released from its isolation; not only would the foreign ambassadors return to the Spanish capital, but Spain could expect to be integrated into frameworks such as the Marshall Plan. It was soon clear, however, that this euphoria was premature. The United Nations vote was indeed important in that it symbolized the end of the supposed agreement between the Western democracies and the Soviet bloc with respect to Spain; but despite the Spaniards' inferences, the December 1946 resolution remained technically in force, since it had not been officially revoked – although the reduction of the majority supporting it challenged its validity politically. Three more years would pass before a two-thirds majority was achieved in the General Assembly for a formal cancellation of the diplomatic ban.

Thus, although a trend toward improving relations with Madrid was visible in several Latin American countries, Spain's isolation continued, notwithstanding a more definite hope that its end was now not far off. Now more than ever, the Spanish dictatorship had only to wait patiently.

Israel and the United Nations vote

In May 1949, just at the time that Israel was admitted to the United Nations, four Latin American countries – Brazil, Peru, Colombia, and Bolivia – proposed a resolution lifting the diplomatic sanctions imposed on Spain in 1946. Franco's régime invested great effort in an attempt to get the diplomatic boycott abolished at last. From the beginning it was clear that the issue would be decided on the strength of a few votes. Accordingly, every vote mattered to the Spaniards – especially the vote of a state like Israel, which at the time enjoyed a special moral status in the international community.[72]

Israel, as we have seen, however, had shown animosity toward Francoist Spain from the day it was founded, and during the following months it rejected various Spanish initiatives aimed at the establishment of formal ties. These initiatives had all been diplomatic moves carried out behind the scenes; now Israel had to take a public stand on the 'Spanish question' and justify it to domestic and foreign public opinion.

Spain tried to exert pressure on Israel to prevent it from joining the régime's opponents in the United Nations. Three days after Israel's admission to the organization, Rafael Soriano – the same Spanish diplomat who had visited Israel in April to try to bring about the establishment of diplomatic ties between the two countries – sent urgent telegrams from Madrid to the Foreign Ministry in Tel Aviv, asking the Ministry to instruct Israel's United Nations delegation to vote in favour of lifting the diplomatic ban on Spain, or at least to abstain from the vote.[73] His petitions were to no avail, however. Although Israel had not been a member in the United Nations when the previous debates on the 'Spanish question' had taken place, on 13 May Foreign Minister Moshe Sharett, who was staying at the United Nations centre with the Israeli delegation, decided that Israel should vote against any proposal that would allow Francoist Spain to rejoin the international community. Sharett saw the vote on Spain as a moral test of the young state's international policy.[74]

On the eve of the vote, the Foreign Minister was faced with a moral dilemma when he received telegrams sent from the Jewish communities in Spanish Morocco, which, encouraged by the Foreign Ministry in Madrid, urged Israel to support Spain. The Jews of

Tangiers – the Moroccan port town facing the shores of Gibraltar and an international free zone for many years (up until 1956), although strongly influenced by Spain – explicitly asked Israel not to vote against Franco's Spain, since such a vote might endanger the well-being of the Jews in both Spain and Spanish Morocco. This 'Jewish consideration' was counterbalanced by disapproval of the dictatorial régime which had collaborated with Hitler. The latter consideration seemed more important to Sharett than the interests of a small Jewish community, and this tipped the scales.[75] A year later, the Franco régime launched a more extensive propagandist effort, and Israel received many requests from Sephardic Jewish communities all over the world calling upon it – mostly in recognition of Spanish aid to the Jews during the Holocaust – to vote for Franco's Spain in the United Nations. On that occasion, too, Israel rejected their requests.

Sharett knew well who figured on the list of the principal advocates of lifting the diplomatic ban on Spain. The Latin American countries' position, to which Israel attributed great importance at the time, was not uniform. Brazil, Colombia, Bolivia, and Peru were the initiators of the draft resolution. Countries friendly to Israel, such as Guatemala and Uruguay (ruled during that period by liberal régimes), opposed it. It was known that the United States intended to abstain from voting, and that the USSR, the Eastern European countries, and Australia meant to oppose the resolution. The resolution's sponsors knew that they had to obtain a two-thirds majority in the General Assembly in order to abolish the resolution of 1946. Israel's vote was considered to be very important by both the supporters and the opponents of the resolution. Franco's representatives in New York believed that if Israel voted against it, the resolution was almost certain to fail.[76] At their urging, some of the Latin American countries – particularly Argentina – exerted pressure on Israel.

Under the leadership of President Juan Domingo Perón, Argentina had become one of Francoist Spain's most prominent allies during those years of international isolation and it provided Nationalist Spain with key economic, political, and diplomatic aid. Throughout the second half of the 1940s, Argentina's representatives defended Spain in the United Nations and its subsidiary organizations, in pan-American conferences and other international frameworks, and tried to persuade other states to oppose the continuation of the international boycott on Spain and to normalize their relations with Madrid.[77] In anticipation of the United Nations vote of May 1949,

Spain's ambassador in Buenos Aires, José María de Areilza, asked Perón to urge Israel to support the abolition of the ban. Subsequently, Israel's representative, Dr Carlos M. Grünberg, was indeed called to a meeting with the Argentine Foreign Minister, Juan Atilio Bramuglia, who conveyed to him 'a strong request from the President [Perón] that Israel support Spain's position'.[78]

According to some reports, the members of the Israeli delegation to the United Nations were divided as to the position they should take concerning Spain, but Sharett's opinion was the decisive one: Israel would vote against any step signifying a rehabilitation of the Franco régime. Sharett explained to the Prime Minister, David Ben-Gurion, that, in his view, if Israel abstained from voting, it would arouse the ire of the socialist states and those Latin American countries that had led the campaign in favour of Israel's admission to the United Nations only a few days previously. An abstention would also turn liberal opinion against Israel.

Equally important here were considerations of domestic policy and fears of public reaction at home, as we shall see more fully in the next chapter. MAPAI, it should be remembered, had been hostile to Francoism since the days of the Civil War, and the parties of the left-wing opposition, led by the Zionist–Marxist MAPAM (United Workers' Party), even more so. This hostility was clearly reflected in most of the daily newspapers in Israel at the time. In reports on Spain that were published in the months April and May 1949, just before the United Nations vote on the 'Spanish question', *Davar*, the newspaper affiliated with the *Histadrut* (the General Federation of Jewish Labour in Eretz Yisrael), *Al Hamishmar*, the MAPAM organ, and, of course, the Communist *Kol Ha'am* more than once used expressions such as 'the hangman of Madrid', 'the fascist dictator', and 'Franco's gang'.[79] 'The radio and the press [here] are patently hostile to us', the Spanish Consul in Jerusalem complained to Madrid. He reported that the Israeli media criticized Spain's pro-Arab policy and its alleged arms sales to Israel's enemies during and after the War of Independence, as well as the Franco régime's relations with the Axis countries during the Second World War and the fact that the decree expelling the Jews in 1492 was technically still in force, never having been revoked.[80]

On 16 May the United Nations General Assembly debated the Latin American proposal to abolish the ban on General Franco's régime and to permit those United Nations members who desired it to re-establish full diplomatic relations with Spain. In the course of the debate, Israel's ambassador to the United Nations, Abba Eban, asked permission to make a speech – a speech which was to have an immediate and extended influence on relations between Israel and Spain. This was the first time that Israel publicly and explicitly explained the motives for its animosity towards the Franco régime. As this speech was so important, its main points are quoted here:

> [. . .] the United Nations arose out of the sufferings of a martyred generation, including six million Jewish dead. In the terrors of Nazism one million of our children were thrown like useless rubbish into furnaces and gas chambers. If the history of Israel lasts for countless generations, we shall never for a single moment allow ourselves to forget that most frightful episode of organized inhumanity. This memory is for us decisive. We do not for a moment assert that the Spanish régime had any direct part in that policy of extermination; but we do assert that it was an active and sympathetic ally of the régime which was so responsible and thus contributed to the effectiveness of the alliance as a whole.
>
> In defining our position on this resolution, we do not address ourselves to the detailed question relating to diplomatic representation. We do not imply any criticism of the Spanish people. Israel, itself, is firmly attached to parliamentary democracy, but we have not come here to criticize another régime, alien as it is to all our conceptions. For us the central and inescapable point is the association of this régime with that Nazi–Fascist alliance which corroded the moral foundations of civilized life and inflicted upon the human race its most terrible and devastating ordeal. Of that coalition, the only surviving expression is the Spanish régime which welcomed, accepted, congratulated and upheld the prospect of Nazi supremacy in Europe and the world.
>
> We are aware that had that supremacy been established, not only would the State of Israel not have existed and the Jewish people and its ancient civilization have perished from the earth, but the United Nations itself would not have come into existence, and all democracy, all progress in every country, would have gone down in irrevocable ruin. These are therefore the most compelling reasons – both universal and particular – why Israel must in all conscience and responsibility vote against the draft resolution.[81]

In his speech, Eban said nothing critical of the origins of the Franco régime, its dictatorial nature, or its unsavoury record on human rights, but merely stressed Spain's support for Nazi Germany during the Second World War.

When the moment came, Israel voted against the resolution, together with 14 other states – Australia, New Zealand, Norway, Uruguay, Guatemala, Mexico, Panama, India, Yugoslavia, and the Soviet bloc countries. Twenty-six states voted in favour, among them the Latin American countries and a bloc of Arab (Egypt, Iraq, Lebanon, Saudi Arabia, Syria, and Yemen) and Moslem (Turkey and Pakistan) countries. There were 16 abstentions, including the United States, France, Britain, Iran, and Afghanistan, and two absences.[82] Two opposing votes prevented the mandatory two-thirds majority required to change previous General Assembly resolutions, and so the resolution failed. Israel's vote did not make the difference but it carried considerable weight. If Israel and just one other country had abstained – as Francoist Spain had hoped up to the very last moment – the resolution would have passed.[83]

In 1947 the boycott's supporters, while not obtaining enough votes to reaffirm the resolution of December 1946, had nevertheless still enjoyed a majority; but now the tide was turning. Although a majority of the members of the General Assembly now supported changing the resolutions against Spain, they still did not total the two-thirds majority required. The change was impressive, however: whereas a total of six states had opposed sanctions in 1946, this figure had increased to 16 in 1947 and 26 in 1949. In the vote on another resolution, proposed by Poland, which called for the introduction of new penalties against Spain, the opponents of Francoism were defeated by a large majority. Forty states opposed the resolution, and only the six states of the Soviet bloc voted in its favour. Seven other states, including Israel, preferred to abstain. The 1946 United Nations resolutions therefore remained in force, without changes or amendments.

When Israel joined the ranks of those opposing the annulment of the boycott on Spain, its position was accepted with understanding in most of the capitals of the world. France privately expressed its appreciation. The United States, which at no point had pressured Israel to vote differently, expressed no disapproval. Argentina, however, was another matter. Yitzhak Navon reported from Montevideo to the Foreign Ministry in Tel Aviv that 'our vote against Spain's admission to the United Nations despite Perón's requests has made him very angry, and he has not refrained from curses and abuse against "the treacherous bastards"; he was not satisfied even when told that his request came late'.[84] The Republican exiles, in contrast, were overjoyed. The opponents of the Franco régime, who in those days oscillated between hope and despair over the chances of engineering the fall of the régime, were delighted by Israel's vote. The Foreign Minister of the Republican government-in-exile approached Israel's representative in Paris, Maurice Fischer, to convey thanks to the Israeli government. Letters of appreciation streamed in from Republican exiles in many countries. The Basque government-in-exile also sent Eban, through its representative in the United States, Jesús Galíndez, a letter of 'frank appreciation' for the stand the Israeli delegation had taken in the United Nations 'in defence of the democratic cause against the Spanish dictator Franco. Your moving and just statements reached the hearts of all men who have been fighting Hitler's ally for 13 years.'[85]

The representative of the government-in-exile in Chile, Antonio de Lama, sent the Israeli consul in Santiago, Shmuel Goren, an emotional letter:

> The Jewish people, whose independence and victory fill our hearts with joy as if on our own account, began its activity in the United Nations by voting against a dictatorial régime, filled with fanatical social hate. In this way, it not only reiterated its love for freedom and democracy, but it also repaid all its old suffering and tribulation at Spain's hands with generosity and friendship [. . .] Please [. . .] convey to your government our gratitude and good wishes for Israel's prosperity and well-being.[86]

The letter emphasized that the Republican exiles would never forget the blood that Jewish volunteers had spilled when they went to fight in defence of freedom and the Republic in the International Brigades. The anti-Francoist Catalonians in Argentina also thanked the government of Israel for its 'noble gesture' towards the Spanish Republic. In July 1949, the Spanish League of Human Rights in Paris sent a thank-you letter to the office of the Prime Minister, David Ben-Gurion, for Israel's vote in the United Nations, which had strengthened the Republican exiles and given them hope.[87]

The Israeli Left was pleased by Eban's United Nations vote. In the first political debate held in the first Knesset, on 15 June 1949, Ya'akov Riftin, one of the leaders of MAPAM and Hashomer Hatza'ir, explained that Israel must fight in the United Nations Organization against every manifestation of fascism, for the sake of the Jewish nation's historical interests and the progressive image it wanted to establish for itself. He praised Israel's unequivocal vote against the resolution to allow normal relations with the Franco régime or to allow such a régime to join the United Nations.[88] Riftin expressed a broader opposition to the Franco régime than Eban did; it was the nature of the régime itself, and not merely its past connection with Nazi Germany, that made any relations with it unthinkable.

In Francoist Spain, the results of the United Nations vote in general, and the way Israel had voted in particular, aroused great anger. In demonstrations organized with government encouragement against the United Nations decision, some of the demonstrators carried placards which were anti-Israeli, or even anti-Semitic: 'Israel has again sold itself for 30 pieces of silver'. The Falange organ *Arriba* accused Israel of having 'knifed [Spain] in the back, with unprecedented rancour and an ingratitude unknown in history', of having pushed Uruguay into voting against Spain as well, and of having misled the Latin American states by promising them it would vote in favour of canceling the boycott. The Arab countries, in contrast, were praised for the 'noble stand' they had taken in the United Nations. Madrid radio also criticized Israel's vote in anti-Semitic terms.[89] Franco himself, according to his biographers, felt personally wounded by Israel's vote and by the claim that his cooperation with Hitler had injured the Jews.[90]

The Jews of Spain, who feared the régime would respond to Israel's vote by making life difficult for them, hurried to distance themselves from Israel's position and Eban's speech. The leader of the Jewish community in Madrid, Ignacio Bauer, wrote to the head of the Instituto de Cultura Hispánica (Institute of Hispanic Culture), one of the Spanish Foreign Ministry's principal propaganda channels, as follows:

> Many of us – not to say all of us – feel sincere regret that the delegate A. Eban did not at least abstain from the vote in the United Nations [. . .] [in that vote] a great and senseless injustice was done, but I am certain that this will not harm Spanish Jews, who love Spain as always, and are willing to prove it, too.[91]

The Spanish Foreign Ministry, for its part, began a barrage of propaganda intended to reveal the 'truth' concerning Spain's attitude towards the Jews. This included a 50-page booklet entitled *España y los judíos* (Spain and the Jews), published in Madrid as a rebuttal to the speech Eban had made ascribing Israel's support for the diplomatic boycott on Spain to memories of the Holocaust. The booklet –

disseminated in many countries in Spanish, English, and French – provided an exaggerated account of Francoist Spain's contribution to the rescue of Jews during the Holocaust,[92] and described Israel's ungrateful behaviour towards Spain, which had done much more to save the Jews of Europe than the Western democracies had. The first of the booklet's three sections began with a quotation from Eban's speech, and was devoted to criticism of the position the Israeli delegation had adopted in the United Nations during the debate on the Spanish question. It claimed that Israel's vote had determined the fate of the resolution. This section quoted a letter that one of the heads of the WJC, Rabbi Maurice Perlzweig, had sent during the war to the Spanish ambassador in Washington, expressing that organization's gratitude for the refuge that the Spanish government had offered Jews who managed to escape from the German-occupied countries, and for Spain's efforts to obtain exit visas permitting Jewish children to leave the territories under Nazi control. 'The Jews are a race that possesses a great memory', Perlzweig wrote. 'They will not forget easily the opportunity that has been given [by Spain] to save the lives of thousands of their brothers.'

The second section discussed in detail Spain's assistance to Sephardic Jews during the Second World War, adducing various documents and other evidence. Stress was laid, for example, on the Spanish government's intervention on behalf of Sephardic Jews in Pétain's France, at a time when the United States, still maintaining relations with the Vichy government, had not done anything of the kind to protect American Jews in France. The booklet also compared Spain's sympathetic treatment of Jewish refugees with England's policy, which at the time did not permit emigration to Palestine. Interestingly, this section of the book also took the opportunity to try to soften a historical memory 450 years old, stating: 'The expulsion from Spain in 1492 was the only possible option in terms of Spain's internal affairs.' Moreover, it went on, this expulsion

> was described in exaggerated and distorted terms by various historians, but compared with what has happened over the last years, such an expulsion certainly cannot be termed a 'pogrom', or be said to have been particularly cruel.

The final section of the pamphlet extolled the Franco government's treatment of the Jews of Spain and Spanish Morocco, who enjoyed complete religious freedom. Among other things, the booklet repeated the canard that the Madrid synagogue had been desecrated and plundered by the Communists during the Civil War, and that it was only thanks to the help of Catholic clergy that the Tora scrolls were saved, since they had been deposited for safekeeping in a convent in Murcia. The truth was that most of the Jews of Madrid had left the capital in the first months of the Civil War, and in the summer of 1938 the synagogue beadle transferred the holy scriptures to Murcia. Just before he left Spain, he entrusted them to the local museum.[93] The booklet published by the Foreign Ministry described at length the opening ceremony of the new synagogue in Madrid and mentioned that another synagogue, damaged during the Civil War, had been repaired with the help of a grant from the Spanish government. On the subject of the Jews of Spanish Morocco, the booklet said that they enjoyed the same rights and duties as the other local inhabitants. Unlike the Jews of French Morocco, against whom the Vichy government discriminated, many of the Jews of Spanish Morocco had been successfully integrated into the economic and cultural life of the protectorate. The booklet ended by repeating the claim concerning the imbalance between Spain's 'noble' treatment of the Jews and the Israeli delegation's 'unjustified and ungrateful' stand in the United Nations.

The extent of Francoist Spain's assistance to Jews during the Second World War – the subject of the first section of the Spanish propaganda booklet – merits clarification before examining the reactions to Israel's vote in the United Nations in May 1949.[94] It should be remembered, first of all, that following the subjugation of a large part of Europe by the Germans and the transformation of several states into satellites of the Third Reich, only five states on the continent remained neutral and therefore able to serve as bases for operations to rescue Jews, or as transit stations on the way to safe havens in the free world. Those five states were Switzerland, Sweden, Turkey, and the two Iberian nations, Spain and Portugal. The behaviour of these last two towards the Jews in those years came as a surprise. Eliahu Dobkin, a Jewish Agency envoy who was active on the Iberian Peninsula during the years 1943–44 in attempts to save Jews, commented:

> When we mention Spain or Portugal, the words 'dictatorship' and 'fascism' come to mind, but I must admit that in those fateful days for the Jewish people, when the Nazis ruled most of Europe, it was in fact those countries which not only gave us hope, but concrete help in saving Jews.[95]

How many Jews were saved thanks to Spain's help? Estimates vary. Most sources give figures ranging from 40,000 to 60,000, although the press published various unfounded claims that the government of Spain directly aided in the rescue of up to a quarter of a million Jews.[96] Between the outbreak of the war and the summer of 1942, more than 30,000 Jews passed through Spain's territory, with or without a transit permit, on their way to Portugal, whence they embarked for various havens beyond the ocean. After France fell in mid-1940, droves of refugees arrived in Spain. Initially, the Spaniards were very generous in issuing transit permits. In the ensuing months, however, they changed their policy a number of times, intermittently opening and closing their border with France.

In any case, at that time Germany did not yet oppose the emigration of Jews, so the Spanish policy did not pose any risk of conflict with Berlin. Moreover, Spain took care to ensure that most of the refugees left the country, being unwilling to grant them asylum for any extended period. Those who did remain in Spain during that period were concentrated in refugee camps. The representatives of Jewish aid organizations were not permitted to set up offices in Spain. However, no anti-Jewish legislation was introduced in Spain, Spanish Morocco, or Tangiers, which Spain took over in 1940. Similarly, Jews were not generally discriminated against in the issue of transit passes. The fact that there was no racist legislation in Spain during the Second World War – although anti-Semitic pronouncements were heard with some regularity in the Nationalist camp during and after the Civil War, mostly from prominent figures in the Church and the Falange – helped the Francoist régime, after Germany's defeat, to emphasize the differences between itself and Italian Fascism and German Nazism, which were tainted with racism and anti-Semitism.

In the summer of 1942, the Vichy government stopped issuing exit passes and the route through the Pyrenees became illegal. Nevertheless, Spain continued, in most cases, to grant asylum to the refugees who entered its territory. Thus, between July 1942 and the end of 1944, over 7,500 more Jews arrived in Spain. During this period the Spanish government alternately hardened and softened its stand, the main influencing factor being its estimation of the opposing sides' respective chances of winning the war. For example, the treatment of the Jews staying in Spain steadily improved in parallel to the victories that the Allies began to chalk up against the Third Reich.

Rumours have long persisted to the effect that General Franco was of Jewish descent and that this was the reason Spain helped save Jews. Spain's ambassador in Washington during the war, Juan Cárdenas, once explained to his friend Rabbi Maurice Perlzweig that if the Nuremburg laws had been introduced in Spain, they would have included the Generalissimo himself. Franco's grandfather, claimed the Spanish ambassador, had been a Portuguese Jew who married a Spanish Catholic and converted. A letter sent in the summer of 1950 to the Israeli Prime Minister, David Ben-Gurion, by a Jew from London said that, while still an officer in Morocco, Franco had boasted of being descended from a family of *marranos* (Jews converted to Christianity by force). Some have claimed that the names Franco, Bahamonde, and Andrade (his mother's family name) were all of Spanish Jewish origin;[97] but, in fact, almost every Spanish family that is not of Basque extraction can lay claim to a certain measure of Jewish blood. Anyone with pretensions to racial purity would have great difficulty proving them. In any case, there is no evidence that Franco ever gave his alleged Jewish ancestry a thought, and it is unlikely that considerations of this kind influenced Spanish policy.

Among the Jews helped by Spain were a few thousand, most of them Sephardic, who were saved by means of passports and safe-conduct passes given to them by Spanish representatives in countries under German occupation. The Franco régime based this proceeding on a decree – published in December 1924, by the Primo de Rivera dictatorship – which permitted those Jews who had hitherto enjoyed Spanish protection to receive Spanish citizenship without residing in Spain. On this basis, Spanish diplomats worked on behalf of Sephardic Jews in France, Romania, Greece, Bulgaria, Hungary, and French Morocco – with varying degrees of success.

Despite Spain's efforts to repatriate them, however, these Jews, too, were treated the same way as the others: they were not allowed to remain in Spain for long. As the Spanish Foreign Minister, Francisco Gómez Jordana, told the War Minister, Carlos Asensio, at the end of 1943:

> the possibility of bringing them in groups of about 100 people each was considered, and when one group had left Spain, *passing through our country as light passes through glass, without leaving traces*, a second group would be brought in and then moved on to enable others to come. This being the system, obviously we will under no circumstances allow these Jews to remain in Spain.[98]

Certainly many more could have been saved by means of a firm, decisive Spanish policy, particularly with respect to rescuing Sephardic Jews from Greece and France and transferring them to Spain. Madrid, however, set rigid criteria for determining a person's right to Spanish citizenship. The Spaniards, of course, were also faced with an objective difficulty; they feared a flood of refugees which would put a strain on their economy, still floundering after the Civil War.

Madrid's policy underwent frequent mutations and reversals. In many cases the Spanish authorities wavered visibly in everything to do with rescue operations, their hesitation allowing the Germans to send even Jews with Spanish citizenship to their deaths; on a number of occasions Spain refused to admit Jews to its territory and sent Jewish refugees back to France. However, more than once Spain's representatives in other countries did not wait for instructions from their government, but worked on their own initiative to save Jews.

There were also other reasons why Spain's potential for saving Jews was not fully realized. Although at the end of 1939 Dr Nahum Goldmann had already suggested to the Jewish Agency that a centre for emigration and refugee assistance should be established in Lisbon, in co-operation with the Joint (American Jewish Joint Distribution Committee), the Agency directors did not discuss such proposals until three years later, in November 1942. It was only after another year-and-a-half, in April 1944, when Perez Leshem (Fritz Lichtenstein) was authorized to open an Agency office in Lisbon.[99] Leshem worked, together with Eliahu Dobkin and Yitzhak Weissman (the Lisbon representative of the WJC) to save children and adults from France, Greece, and Hungary. The rescue operations they managed to organize in the last year of the war, however, were of limited scope.[100] Moreover, the disputes between the Joint and the WJC (described by Weissman in his memoirs) also made implementation of rescue plans difficult.

None the less, in view of the fact that most of the countries of the world stood by and did nothing while the Jews of Europe were led to the gas chambers, even if Spain's actions were motivated in large part by the desire to project a positive image to the Allies, Francoist Spain's policy, with all its ups and downs, deserves recognition. We should not, however, be misled by Francoist propaganda, which greatly exaggerated the extent of the rescue operations and described them as a systematic, consistent government policy.

The Spanish Foreign Ministry booklet *España y los judíos* and other, similar pamphlets were disseminated in many countries for a few months.[101] Copies of it were also sent to Israel's embassies in Europe and America. It was distributed again in the summer of 1950, perhaps in the framework of Spain's renewed efforts to win Israel's support in the next debate on the Spanish problem, which was to take place a few months later in the United Nations General Assembly. The Israeli Foreign Ministry judged, at the time, that Israel was witnessing 'a Spanish propaganda campaign intended to buy our sympathy for the present régime in Spain, or to prove, at least outwardly, how morally unjust our antipathy is'.[102]

But Spain did not stop there. A short time after Israel's vote in the United Nations, the Franco régime was given the opportunity to pay Israel back in its own coin. In June 1949, the Diplomatic Conference of Geneva, convened at the urging of the Red Cross, debated a Geneva Convention amendment tabled by Israel that would have allowed it to use the star of David instead of the red cross as the internationally recognized symbol of its national relief society, as the Moslems had been authorized to use the red crescent. The Israeli delegate asked his Spanish colleague – that same Rafael Soriano who had received a cool reception from Walter Eytan a few weeks earlier – to abstain from the vote. Foreign Minister Martín Artajo instructed Spain's delegate to vote against the use of the star of David. In a secret vote, Israel's amendment was defeated, with 22 states voting against and only 21 voting in favour. As a result, Israel was unable to qualify for membership in the Red Cross Movement.[103]

The Spanish propaganda had a certain impact in Latin America, but as Avraham Darom was to say years later, in no case did any Latin American state exert overt pressure on Israel to establish relations with Spain. Occasionally Latin American countries would use the absence of relations with Spain as an excuse for not establishing diplomatic ties with Israel or for not improving relations with it, but this was never a significant factor.[104] For example, when Moshe Tov, one of the senior officials of the Latin American division in the Israeli Foreign Ministry, visited Brazil, some months after Israel's vote in the United Nations, the Brazilian Foreign Minister, Raúl Fernandes, mentioned Israel's vote on the Spanish question as one of the reasons that Brazil did not establish diplomatic ties with Israel. This, however, was not a serious obstacle in the relations between the two countries. By the beginning of 1950, Ya'akov Tsur and the Foreign Minister of the new Brazilian government were already signing letters of agreement authorizing the establishment of diplomatic relations between Brazil and Israel.[105] The President of Argentina, as mentioned, did not like the way Abba Eban voted. None the less, the issue did not disrupt Israeli–Argentinian relations in those years.

For years afterwards, many of Franco's supporters and opponents remembered the way Israel had voted. Spanish diplomats reminded Israeli representatives they met of Israel's hostile votes in the United Nations in 1949 and 1950. Examples are numerous, and I will mention no more than two of them here. A few months after Israel's first anti-Spain vote in the United Nations, the Spanish ambassador in Buenos Aires said that 'his government responded with great regret to [Israel's] United Nations vote concerning the renewal of diplomatic ties with Franco'. He added that 'the General himself is a warm friend of the Jews, and has showed himself to be one many times in the past, too [. . .]'. At the end of 1955, the Spanish ambassador in Paris, who himself had been involved in operations to help Jews during the Second World War, explained to Ya'akov Tsur that his country's coolness towards Israel could be attributed to

> strong disappointment due to [Israel's] vote in the United Nations in 1950. He said that Spain was one of the few countries in Europe that saved Jews during the war. And as soon as a Jewish state appeared on the horizon, its first act was an attack on Spain's sovereignty. This grudge, he added, still existed today, and was difficult to uproot from the hearts of Spain's rulers.[106]

In perhaps the most pro-Francoist biography of Franco ever published in English, Sidney Coles pathetically expressed the feeling that prevailed in Spain at the time, that after Franco had helped the Jews in the Second World War, Israel paid him back a few years later with ingratitude:

> how unjust that a brand-new State, only brought into being through the dispossession of the Arab inhabitants of land on which they had been settled for a millennium and more and over which they were promised sovereignty by Lawrence of Arabia in the name of the Allied Powers in return for the invaluable services they rendered towards victory in the first World War, how unjust, I say, that this State should be enabled to cast a vote against membership of the 'United Nations' of a key European people of twenty-nine millions, the foremost of all in the defence of that Western Christendom for which they had suffered and bled [. . .] How unjust indeed that a State that had turned a blind eye to the pirate-hanging by the

Stern gang of unoffending British soldiers in deserted olive groves and to the assassination in its chosen capital of a special Delegate of the same United Nations, the almost saintly Count Folke Bernadotte [. . .] how unjust, how tragic and how farcical that such a State should have the power to vote against Spain![107]

In Israel, too, MAPAI's right-wing opposition and those who favoured relations with Franco viewed with disapproval what they saw as a 'venomous speech' against Spain, as

ingratitude, patent, tasteless arrogance – like a child pushing his way in front of everyone – and as a desire to win the sympathies of those classist and party circles in Israel and the world who have put the good of party and social class before the good of the nation as a whole and of the reborn state of Israel.[108]

In contrast, Franco's opponents generally recalled the Israeli vote with approval for many years afterwards. Eban recalls that at the beginning of the 1980s, before leading the Socialist Party to power in Madrid, Felipe González praised Israel's anti-Francoist stand, and mentioned it as one of the factors that disposed him to promote the establishment of diplomatic ties with Israel.[109] In 1984, during a debate in the Cortes (the Spanish Parliament), the former Spanish Foreign Minister, Fernando Morán, explained that the absence of relations between his country and Israel was due to Israel's refusal to recognize the Franco régime in 1949, and – to the surprise of some observers – he claimed that Israel's position was 'justified', in view of the type of régime then governing Spain.[110]

In his memoirs, Eban linked his vote with the views of other social-democratic states on the same subject:

Within a few days we were voting on international issues, some of them delicate. The first concerned a proposal by a Latin American group led by Peru to remove the ban on the admission of Franco Spain to the United Nations. Since all the democratic socialist countries [. . .] felt that the memories of the alliance with Hitler and Mussolini were too fresh, I saw no course but to join with them in solidarity. Nothing could have been more absurd than for Israel to show less concern than did other countries with the tormenting memories of the Hitler epoch. It was not logical for Israelis in later years to regret, as they did, a vote in which their representatives had no element of choice.[111]

When diplomatic relations were finally established between Israel and Spain, 37 years later, Eban sought once again to clarify why he had voted as he did, emphasizing that Israel was obliged to vote with those states which, only a few days before, had led the effort to get Israel admitted to the United Nations. These states consisted of the Soviet bloc, European socialist states, and Latin American states such as Mexico and Guatemala, which held clear anti-Francoist views. In answer to the claims that Israel could have voted differently in the General Assembly, Eban wrote: 'Whoever suggests that option, even in retrospect, is recommending political and moral insanity.'[112]

An isolated Consul

In 1949, despite Israel's hostile vote in the United Nations and Spain's anti-Israel vote at the Diplomatic Conference of Geneva, the Franco régime had not yet given up hope of coming to an understanding with Israel. Besides its tolerant attitude towards the small Jewish community in Spain, it also permitted a certain amount of Zionist activity. Although Zionist activists in Barcelona complained of the many restrictions hampering their attempts to hold assemblies and public lectures and to establish official organizational frameworks, restrictions of this sort were the lot of all Spanish citizens under the Francoist dictatorship. In fact, as Dr Shimshon Glanzmann of Barcelona remarked during a visit to Israel in the fall of 1949, 'The authorities are not strict, and they turn a blind eye to Zionist activity, which in fact is illegal [. . .].'[113]

In the ensuing months, the Spanish government invested much effort in developing the three channels of communication with Israel already mentioned: first, assistance for Spanish Jews, whom it encouraged to offer themselves to Israel as intermediaries or 'bridges' between the two countries; second, the close relations which Spanish ambassadors in capitals all over the world fostered with Israeli representatives; and third, increased exertions on the part of the Spanish consulate in Jerusalem. By chance, the consulate-general of Spain had been set up in the western part of Jerusalem in the middle of the previous century, so that when Israel was created and the city was divided, a Spanish consulate-general was already present in the capital of Israel, even though the two states did not formally recognize each other.

An example of an attempt to expand the first type of communication channel was the visit that Ignacio Bauer, one of the leaders of the

Jewish community in Madrid, paid to Maurice Fischer, Israel's representative in Paris, in September 1949. Bauer was a scion of one of the wealthiest Jewish families in Spain, a family of Austrian origin which represented the Rothschild interests in Spain and had enjoyed, since the end of the nineteenth century, good relations with people in high society, political leaders, and prominent intellectuals. Bauer was, in fact, one of the founders of the Jewish community in Madrid and its first president, and the licence to erect the first synagogue in the Spanish capital, in 1917, bore his name. In 1920, he was one of the founders of the Spanish Zionist Federation. During the Civil War, Bauer lived abroad and was active in Zionist affairs, at one point spending time in Jewish Palestine to get to know the country and its problems. At the end of 1939, he returned to Spain.

Fischer was impressed by Bauer's personality, and attached importance to his visit. Bauer told him about Spain's efforts to draw closer to Israel, attributing these efforts to Spain's desire to remain involved in the Middle East and to protect Catholic interests in Israel.[114] Bauer claimed to be on good terms with the Spanish diplomatic establishment and with the Franciscan order, and said that the Spanish Foreign Ministry had suggested to him that it would look favourably upon Bauer's appointment as Consul-General of Israel in Spain.[115] In the Israeli Foreign Ministry – at the time still located in Tel Aviv – officials did not like the private initiatives of individual Jews that were a recurring feature during this period, and had no intention, at least at that point, of changing their policy towards Spain. The head of the West European Division answered Israel's Minister in Paris promptly and unequivocally: Israel was not interested in relations of any kind with Spain, and did not intend to appoint Bauer or anyone else as Consul-General there. In its reply, the Foreign Ministry emphasized its esteem for Ignacio Bauer, but pointed out the conflict between his interests as head of the Jewish community in Madrid and Israel's policy.[116]

Several Jews arrived from Spain during those same months to visit Israel, and all of them raised the issue of relations with Spain. One of them was Enrique Benarroya, a Jew of Turkish descent who had moved from France to Spain during the Second World War and had become the president of the Jewish community in Barcelona. Benarroya had energetically enlisted in the Francoist propaganda campaign to rehabilitate the Spanish dictatorship in the eyes of the world. In the spring of 1950, José Sebastián de Erice, the second in command at the Spanish Foreign Ministry, characterized him as a man 'very devoted to Spain, who has served us admirably on a number of occasions' – a rather dubious compliment, coming from one of the heads of Francoist diplomacy.[117] One of Benarroya's main objectives was to improve relations between Spain and Israel.[118] Behind Benarroya's initiative, like those of other Spanish Jews, a whole series of motives was discernible. Such enterprises were undertaken to please a rigid, authoritarian régime in hopes of guaranteeing that the dictatorship's tolerant treatment of the Jewish communities in Spain and Spanish Morocco would continue; to promote personal interests; or, as we shall see, to safeguard the Sephardic identity, which was threatened in the new Israel by Ashkenazic hegemony. Benarroya did not find an attentive ear in Israel either. Only much later, when Israel was showing interest in ties with Spain, would the Foreign Ministry examine the possibility of enlisting the services of local Jews but it was never enthusiastic about this, preferring to work through its own people.

The way in which Spanish ambassadors sounded out Israeli representatives is exemplified by the relations that were established between Ya'akov Tsur, Israel's ambassador to Argentina, and his Spanish counterpart in Buenos Aires, despite the Tel Aviv Foreign Ministry's initial injunctions against such ties. 'The ambassador of Spain, who is considered one of his country's great diplomats, was courting Israel assiduously at the time', wrote Tsur in his memoirs.[119] José María de Areilza, Count Motrico, was an important political figure in Franco's Spain, despite his relative youth and monarchist tendencies. Areilza, a lawyer and an engineer, had the benefit of experience in the field of economics (he had previously served as Director-General of the Ministry of Industry), and had joined the Falange during the Civil War. His skills earned him his appointment, in 1947, as ambassador to Perón's Argentina, Francoist Spain's most important ally during the second half of the 1940s.

In those years, Buenos Aires was a major intersection of Spanish diplomacy, and the post of ambassador there became a key position in Francoist foreign and economic policy. From Argentina it was also possible to work at increasing Spain's influence in all of Latin America and to weaken the influence of the 'red' exiles on the continent. Of equal importance, however, during the second half of the 1940s, was that the Embassy in Argentina opened a window between Spain and the hostile world outside. Lacking representatives in many countries, in sympathetic Buenos Aires the Francoist régime was able to make contact with diplomats from various countries, such as

Israel, which did not have relations with Spain, but which did maintain diplomatic missions in Argentina. With good reason, Areilza
described his mission in Argentina as that of 'a submarine periscope
that permits a clear view of the panorama outside'.[120]

In a report to his Foreign Ministry, Tsur wrote: 'During the
courtesy call that I made on the ambassador of Spain here, I was
received with an eager friendliness and greater warmth than I had
met in my visits to other members of the diplomatic corps.' The two
men had a long conversation about the chances of rapprochement
between the two states. Areilza claimed that in his government's view
the matter was not only political but moral. Spain, he said, wanted to
renew its ties with the Jewish culture, which had played an important
part in the creation and shaping of the Spanish culture.[121]

The two ambassadors met frequently, the Spanish diplomat showing a friendly attitude towards Israel. Once he even suggested that the
two embassies co-operate in organizing an evening dedicated to the
'golden age' of the Jews of Spain. Foreign Ministry policy forced Tsur
to sidestep this proposal. Areilza tried at the same time to develop
close ties with the Sephardic community in Buenos Aires, and with
other Jews.[122] At the end of that same year, however, in the context of
the crisis in relations between Madrid and Buenos Aires, Areilza was
obliged to terminate his work in Argentina and return to Spain.

The most striking manifestation of Francoist Spain's efforts to find
the way to Israel's heart during this period, however, was the
appointment of Antonio de la Cierva y Lewita, Count Ballobar and
Duke Terranova, to the post of Consul-General of Spain in
Jerusalem. The duke was sent to Israel in 1949, and his appointment
was by no means fortuitous; it was the Spanish government's way of
indicating to Israel that its policy would not be anti-Israeli in any
way. In fact, the nomination of a diplomat who had already served in
Jerusalem in the past was a sign of cordiality towards Israel. At the
same time, Foreign Minister Martín Artajo wanted to make clear to
the Arab countries that, despite the reports published by the French
news agency, the appointment of the duke was not a step towards the
establishment of diplomatic relations between the two countries.
Rather, Spain was merely replacing the previous Consul-General,
Gonzálo Diéguez, who had been appointed as Spain's plenipotentiary
minister to Amman; the appointment simply reflected Spain's desire
to continue safeguarding the holy places, explained Spain's representatives in Cairo, Amman, Beirut and Baghdad to the governments to
which they were accredited.[123]

Terranova had been appointed as Consul-General in Jerusalem back in 1914, at the onset of the First World War, by the king of Spain, Alfonso XIII. At the time, the king ordered him to protect Sephardic Jews from oppression by the Turkish régime.[124] The Consul's mother had apparently been a Jew who had converted to Catholicism after her marriage. In Jerusalem, Terranova maintained close relations with old Spanish families such as the Valeros, the Manis, and the Meyuhases, as well as with Rabbi Uziel and Dr Feigenbaum, Rabbi Yosef Meyuhas's son-in-law. In the winter of 1916, his negotiations with the Ottoman authorities were instrumental in getting a large quantity of food, sent to the Jews of Palestine by Jewish organizations in the United States, released from Jaffa port.[125]

In the first years of the war, American diplomats played a central role in protecting the Jews of Palestine, but when the United States declared war on Germany and its allies in the spring of 1917, they could no longer provide this protection and it was the consul of Spain who filled the vacuum they left. For example, during 1917 the Spanish consulate in Jerusalem operated an aid fund fed by American funds through Denmark and Turkey. Eliezer Hoffein, head of the *Yishuv*'s aid committee, came to an early understanding with the Spanish representative according to which aid to the Jews, then suffering from economic distress or harassment by the Turks, would be administered by a special department in the consulate building. The Spanish diplomat ensured that the consular clerks did not make difficulties for Jews, especially Sephardic Jews, who applied for Spanish passports or other documents.

The blows that the British dealt Turkey in Egypt and southern Palestine led the Ottomans to begin driving thousands of Jews northward out of Jaffa and Tel Aviv towards Syria, on the grounds that many of them were spying for Britain. It was feared that the Jews of Palestine were facing a fate similar to that suffered by the Armenians. A telegram sent by King Alfonso XIII to the German Kaiser Wilhelm, and protests by Spain's representatives in Berlin, Vienna, and Constantinople contributed to a change in Turkey's policy, and in June of the same year the Jews of Jaffa and Tel Aviv were allowed to return to their homes.

At the beginning of November 1917, Jerusalem was in danger of being occupied, and all the foreign consuls left the city, except for Antonio de La Cierva. Not a few Jews welcomed the Spanish Consul's decision to remain in the city and to offer the residents his protection. A month later, a few days before leaving the city, the Turks expelled a few central figures of the Jewish *Yishuv* to Damascus. At least three such leaders, however, were saved from exile with the help of the Spanish Consul, who used all his diplomatic connections to prevent their expulsion: Dr Ya'akov Thon, Director of the Jewish Palestine office; Eliezer Hoffein; and Yosef Meyuhas.[126] In December, the British entered Jerusalem, and the Spanish diplomat's role in helping the Jews came to an end. The Jewish city council of Jerusalem sent a letter of thanks to the king of Spain for the help his country had given the Jews of Palestine. The letter, signed by the president of the council, David Yellin, and his deputy, Yosef Meyuhas, said:

> The Jews of Jerusalem and all Palestine, who were in deep trouble and who had no contact with their generous brothers abroad, found help and protection from the political and consular representatives of your country. These representatives managed to sweeten the bitterness of their fate by bringing them the material aid and the news they needed from their brothers abroad.[127]

From the end of 1917 to September 1918, Palestine was divided between the British administration – from the Yarkon River southward – and the Turkish administration – in the area north of the Yarkon. During that period, the Spanish Consul in Jerusalem was unable to help those Jews who had already been expelled northwards but, at his instigation, the Spanish consulate in Damascus worked on their behalf. The Duke of Terranova served as Consul in Jerusalem until the summer of 1920, when he was recalled to Spain. In November of that year, he was appointed Consul of Spain in Tangiers; there, too, he established good relations with the Jewish community.

The Spanish Consul's activities in Jerusalem must be viewed in the wider context of the friendly policy that monarchist Spain showed towards the Jews in the years of the First World War. Once again we see the gap between Spain's negative image in the eyes of many Jews, and the reality of a neutral country that offered assistance to Jews This gap was reflected in a 1916 article in Hebrew, 'Spanish Surprise', written by Max Nordau, a Zionist leader who was a direct descendant of Jews who had been expelled from Spain in 1492.[128] Nordau, whose Austrian citizenship forced him and his family to leave Paris during the First World War and seek refuge in neutral

Spain, also bore witness to the contribution of Avraham Shalom Yahuda (another descendent of exiled Spanish Jews) who had been appointed to the chair of Hebrew language and literature at the Central University of Madrid and who also did much to persuade the Spanish authorities to extend a helping hand to the Jews.

In Spain, Professor Yahuda directed a wide-ranging propaganda campaign and succeeded in convincing the authorities to act on behalf of the Jews of Palestine and those Jews in danger in the belligerent states. Such aid was given to Sephardic Jews with Turkish citizenship who lived in France, Italy, and Portugal, to Jews with Russian citizenship in Berlin, and, as mentioned, to Palestinian Jews, who were in danger from Jemal Pasha, the head of the Turkish military administration in Palestine. Thus, the First World War saw the beginning of a Spanish tradition of coming to the aid of Jews in distress, a tradition that was continued during the Second World War and after the establishment of the state of Israel, when Spain began to help Jews in the Arab countries.

In 1949, when Francoist Spain was trying to establish some kind of relationship with the state of Israel, the Foreign Minister, Martín Artajo, chose to replace the Consul-General in Jerusalem with Terranova who, at the time, was the director of the Africa division in the Spanish Foreign Ministry. Martín Artajo probably hoped that the Duke would be warmly received in Israel, and would be able to turn to advantage some of the contacts he had made in Jerusalem during the First World War. 'As far as I know', the director of the division of Christian communities in the Israeli ministry of religion wrote four years later,

> the appointment of the abovementioned was not by chance; the Spanish authorities purposely sent to Jerusalem a man who had distinguished himself by his sympathetic approach to the Jews when he was consul of Spain in Jerusalem during World War I.[129]

The Spanish Consul did indeed meet a number of his friends in Israel, including the mayor of Jerusalem at the time, Daniel Auster, but ran into many obstacles. First, it was difficult to operate in a divided city in which the Spanish consulate was also divided – some of the consulate's furniture, equipment, and files were in the Arab part of Jerusalem. The necessity of making frequent forays between the two parts of the city became a burden, since passes were required from the authorities of both sides. The fact that all the government ministries and the diplomatic corps were located in Tel Aviv did not make the work of the Spanish Consul in Jerusalem any easier. In addition, the consul's position depended on Israel's good will, since the Spanish authorities had refrained from requesting an Israeli exequatur for him, fearing that such a request would be interpreted as signifying acceptance of Israeli sovereignty in Jerusalem and/or as indirect recognition of the state of Israel.[130]

Terranova's main problem, however, was the hostility he met with on the official level, from the government ministries and the media, and he frequently complained of this in his reports to Madrid. During the more than three years he served as Consul-General in Jerusalem, up to the end of 1952, all his endeavours to bring about the establishment of diplomatic relations between the two states failed. He never even managed, despite all his efforts, to meet with the Foreign Minister, Moshe Sharett, or with the Director-General of the Foreign Ministry, Walter Eytan. Madrid forbade the consul to attend any meetings in the Foreign Ministry in Tel Aviv, since the countries did not recognize each other, so the consul tried to organize an unofficial meeting. One of his messages to Sharett was conveyed by Aryeh Tartakover, of the Hebrew University and the World Jewish Congress (WJC). Tartakover wrote to Sharett:

> He asked if I couldn't speak with you unofficially and ask if you would be willing to meet with him over a cup of tea in some private home in Jerusalem for a short conversation [. . .] on the matter of relations between Israel and Spain in general.

Tartakover hastened to apologize for conveying the request to Sharett at all, and noted in his letter:

> Of course I do not think for a moment of trying to persuade you, especially since first of all I had to persuade myself [to agree to convey the request]. Do as you wish, according to your humane, socialist conscience.

Sharett's reply was brief: 'As you guessed, my answer is negative. I suggest that you tell him the response was: "The time has not yet come".'[131] And the time did not come for as long as the Duke served in Jerusalem. During the entire term of his appointment, the Foreign Ministry treated him with suspicion, and recoiled from almost all contact with him. In contrast, Eliahu Eliachar, one of the leaders of the Sephardic community, arranged meetings in his own home between the Duke and leaders of the General Zionists – Israel Rokah, Peretz

Bernstein, Yosef Sapir, and Yosef Serlin – in the hope that they would be able to promote the idea of Hispano-Israeli relations in the Knesset.[132] This was the nucleus of the pro-Francoist lobby that began to take form in Israel and to call for normalizing relations with Madrid.

The Consul-General did not despair and channeled vigorous efforts in various directions. He laboured in the belief that, since most of the countries of the world recognized Israel, Spain should too. As the Consul working with him, Pío de las Cásares, wrote, he believed it was impossible not to recognize a state which was already a *fait accompli* – particularly since the state had a tremendous potential. Both Consuls felt cultural activity to be particularly essential in Israel, so that Spain would not 'be hated here forever'.[133] Under Terranova's leadership, accordingly, the consulate showed great interest in developing social and cultural relations with the Jewish population, particularly with the Sephardic community.[134]

During his years in Jerusalem, Terranova managed to sow in various minds the idea of setting up Israel–Spain friendship associations. Efforts to establish such organizations were actually made in 1953. In the summer of that year, the lawyer Rafael Mani founded the Israel–Spain Friendship League in Tel Aviv. In the speech he made at the inauguration ceremony, Mani extolled Spain's efforts to save Jews in the two world wars, praising in particular the deeds of his friend the Duke of Terranova during the First World War. 'We are interested', declared Mani,

> in creating a league to promote cultural rapprochement and closer relations with the state of Spain and the Spanish people; and perhaps our action and educational efforts will lead the Israeli government to reconsider and to reflect, and to recover from its previous confusion and recognize the Franco government as soon as possible.

The Foreign Ministry, however, did not encourage such efforts at the time, and they never succeeded in making any impression on relations between the two countries.[135]

The Spanish Consul also tried to make contacts in the Hebrew University, the Jewish Agency, and commercial circles, believing that the development of trade relations should precede the beginning of political ties; and he prepared a list of products that Spain could buy from Israel, and another list of merchandise that it could sell to Israel.[136] Given Spain's difficult economic situation, however – a large part of the population was still living in great poverty, and foreign currency reserves were meagre – as well as Israel's limited foreign trade in those days, this approach was unlikely to lead to a speedy establishment of diplomatic relations. Moreover, at the end of 1949 the Arab countries began to pressure Spain not to develop commercial relations with Israel. For example, when the Egyptian embassy found out that an Israeli trader by the name of Avraham Alalouf had paid a visit to Spain, it quickly informed the Spanish Foreign Ministry of its displeasure over the possibility of any trade between the two states.[137]

The Consul also presented ideas for promoting cultural relations between Spain and Israel to Haim Wardi, the adviser on Christian affairs in the Ministry of Religion, and to Dr Avraham Biran, who was in charge of the Jerusalem district in the interior ministry and the Foreign Ministry's representative in the city. A short time before, an exhibition of Spanish art had been held in Cairo, and Terranova suggested writing to the relevant authorities in Madrid to find out whether such an exhibition could be held in Israel as well. He told Haim Wardi about a forthcoming visit by Spanish dancers to Israel and about his plans to organize lectures on Spain and Spanish culture. Within a few days, the adviser in the religion ministry was warned to tread cautiously in his relations with the Spanish Consul, for

> while non-binding contact with him is desirable, it is nonetheless very important that none of us, while representing a government ministry, respond to this consul's plans and initiatives. You probably know that we are avoiding any official initiative to encourage ties with Spain, and are being careful not to respond to initiatives from the other side'.[138]

The Spanish Foreign Ministry, too, shrank from the consul's cultural initiatives, fearing their potential political significance and that they would damage Spain's growing ties with the Arab countries.[139] The Duke, for his part, demonstrated his willingness to lend himself to any Israeli request – whether it was to work for the release of a Jewish prisoner from a Spanish prison in the summer of 1950, to recommend a Spanish government scholarship for one of the professors at the Hebrew University, or anything else.

The Consul invested great energy in trying to change the negative attitude of the Israeli press towards Francoist Spain. Difficulties in communicating with the editors of the Hebrew press, together with easy access to the editorial boards of papers in other languages, led him to concentrate his efforts on the English- and French-language press. In a report to Madrid, the Consul took pride in the fact that within a few months he had managed to soften the patently anti-Francoist views of *The Jerusalem Post* and to get sympathetic reports on Spain published in the *Journal de Jerusalem*, *L'Echo d'Israel*, and *L'Aurore*.[140] *The Jerusalem Post*, however, continued to maintain a hostile attitude towards Franco's Spain, while the French-language newspapers had a limited circulation and little influence on Israeli public opinion. The editor of *L'Aurore*, Raoul Ami, frequently published news and features in his paper that were favourable to Spain, and even made a tour of that country – apparently at the Spaniards' expense. He later published a book on the subject which gave a sympathetic portrayal of the Nationalist régime and its treatment of Jews.[141] Ami became an important source of information for the Spanish consulate in Jerusalem, given the consulate's lack of good relations with the government ministries. In 1950 most of the Hebrew press was still hostile to the Franco régime. The change was to begin gradually in the months that followed – first in the organs of Herut and the General Zionists, and only several years later in the newspapers controlled by MAPAI.

Throughout his term of service, the Consul tried to engineer normal diplomatic ties between Israel and Spain, but he was doomed to disappointment. Each time that an issue concerning Spain was about to be raised in the United Nations, he did his best to find out how Israel was going to vote, and emphasized to any Israeli he chanced to meet 'how eager the government of Spain is that Israel should not vote against this resolution [to accept Spain as a member of the United Nations]'. At the same time, the consulate maintained its constant protection over the Christian institutions under Spanish influence (in such places as Jerusalem, Haifa, Nazareth). A considerable part of the routine work of the Spanish consulate in Jerusalem was devoted to obtaining transit passes for Spanish priests and monks who frequently crossed the border between the two parts of Jerusalem. The consulate maintained excellent relations with the division for Christian communities in the Ministry of Religion.[142]

None the less, despite all Spain's attempts to establish contact with Israel through various channels, Israel continued to adhere – for the time being – to the same position it had presented in May 1949, through the medium of Abba Eban in the United Nations General Assembly. In December 1949, the United Nations returned to the subject of Spain, by chance, in the course of a debate in the organization's legal committee about inviting non-member states to subscribe to the convention on the prevention and punishment of the crime of genocide. One proposal was to invite only states which were 'active members' of at least one of the United Nations agencies, while Lebanon wanted to eliminate the word 'active'. Lebanon's proposal, which apparently entitled Spain to accede to the convention, was accepted. An unofficial initiative from the Israeli delegate reopened the debate, however, and a repeat vote defeated Lebanon's proposal; the original proposal was passed, leaving Spain out.[143]

2

In the Shadow of a Collective Memory

Franco's sympathy for Nazi Germany

The official reason for Israel's hostile position on Francoist Spain, as presented by Abba Eban in the United Nations General Assembly, was the connection between that régime and the Nazi–Fascist alliance, and the fact that Franco's régime was 'an active and sympathetic ally of the régime which had been responsible for [the policy of extermination]'. This argument was repeated, in similar terms and on many occasions, to Spanish representatives, the international public, and critics at home who called for the establishment of relations with Madrid. Again and again Israel emphasized that its policy was not a reaction against the régime's tyrannical nature, or its foreignness to Israel's political culture. Thus, for example, Ambassador Ya'akov Tsur reported a conversation with his Spanish counterpart in Buenos Aires, José María de Areilza, in the fall of 1949:

> I said that we do not usually take a position regarding the type of régime adopted in one country or another. Moreover, we know that the government of Spain did what it could during the war to help the Jewish refugees in Europe. But he must understand that Jews have not yet recovered from the bleeding wound of losing a third of their people in the Nazi massacre. The time has not yet come to forget. Whereas [the Spanish] government was, for a certain time, the ally – even if only on paper, as he says – of that government that bears the responsibility for that massacre [. . .] This is not, then, directed against Spain and its government, but against the Nazi régime, which still casts a shadow over our relations with this country [Spain].[1]

Six years later, while serving as Israel's ambassador to Paris, Tsur was obliged to explain once again why Israel had taken an inimical stand against Spain in its first years of statehood. Tsur told the Spanish ambassador that Israel's vote at the United Nations in 1949 had to be considered in the context of the atmosphere prevailing in the Jewish state such a short time after the horrors of the Holocaust.[2]

When Israel again voted in the United Nations against lifting the diplomatic boycott on Spain at the end of 1950, exactly the same justifications were given, this time by Shmuel Eliashiv, Israel's representative on the United Nations' *ad hoc* committee at the time. The Israeli diplomat justified the 1946 General Assembly resolution on the grounds that the Franco régime had been established with the assistance of Hitler and Mussolini, who sought to 'establish Nazi and Fascist régimes throughout the world and to liquidate freedom and democracy [. . .] and destroy the Jewish people'.[3] At the beginning of 1953, the Foreign Minister, Moshe Sharett, was still rejecting proposals to change the policy on Spain, using the same arguments:

> The main consideration with regard to Spain is that the Franco régime was the faithful ally of Nazism and Fascism – that is, it hoped for their victory and saw its future in a world order built on the graves of the Jewish people, among other things, and soaked in their blood.

Sharett dismissed the argument proffered by advocates of ties with Spain that Israel's recognition of Italy, Austria, and Japan – and certainly its contacts with Germany – justified relations with Franco's Spain. According to Sharett, there were no grounds for such a comparison, since each of these countries had instituted a new régime which repudiated – publicly, at least – the criminal past of the previous régime. In Spain, by contrast, the régime had remained intact without any change in its nature or internal policy. In states like Germany, Austria, and Italy, the line of succession had been cut; in Spain it had not.[4]

Sharett's remarks were particularly significant since they were not designed to justify Israel's policy for the benefit of foreign and domestic public opinion but rather were made in the course of an internal Foreign Ministry debate as a rejoinder to those demanding a change in the position on Spain. Yet Sharett used almost the same arguments that were voiced publicly by Israel's representatives. The most evident difference was that while diplomats like Abba Eban took care in their speeches to stress that Israel was not criticizing the Franco régime *per se*, Sharett's comments deviated from the usual focus on Nationalist Spain's co-operation with the Third Reich.

Personal anti-Francoist commitment

The Franco régime's evident sympathy for Nazi Germany undoubtedly had a decisive influence on the formulation of Israel's hostile policy towards Spain. It was the basis for both Israel's central motive and its principal ideological justification for opposing Francoist Spain. It is true that this was also an example of what has been called more than once 'the influence of the Jewish factor on Israeli foreign policy', or, more grandly, 'considerations of Jewish conscience' which affected the formation of Israel's positions in the international arena;[5] but there were also other motives that were not included in the repertoire of ideological justifications produced by the heads of the Foreign Ministry and the ruling party, MAPAI, for critics at home and abroad. Conversely, certain arguments that *were* used by government spokespersons did not actually carry much weight in the shaping of Israel's Spanish policy. This chapter will examine them all.

A central role must be attributed, for example, to the personal anti-Francoist commitment of a number of decision-makers in the top ranks of the Israeli Foreign Ministry, who formed their views in the 1930s, even before the Holocaust and the outbreak of the Second World War. Official documents make only one explicit reference to this motivating factor. At the beginning of 1951, the head of the Western European division in the Israeli Foreign Ministry, Gershon Avner, wrote to the Israeli ambassador in Brussels, Michael Amir, in response to the latter's claim that political logic demanded the establishment of relations with Madrid:

> The problem is difficult, because logic is mostly on your side, while in fact there are complications working strongly in the opposite direction. You remember our position in the [United Nations General] Assembly; we said that Franco was actually Hitler's ally and we cannot forgive [. . .] Nevertheless, there is an additional factor here, the domestic factor [. . .] The central complication [. . .] derives from the fact that all the leaders of our country are members of MAPAI – in the government, in the upper ranks of the administration, in the Histadrut, and in the Knesset – and were, in the past, themselves denouncers of Franco's régime. In 1936, they collected money for the Republicans. At conferences in Israel and abroad, they censured that régime. Today it is difficult for them to overcome these personal feelings and to make any move that would mean coming to terms with the current situation. While it is true that our political policy is not

usually determined by the form of government in a country, our leadership is personally committed to its long-standing opposition to this régime, and that is why changing [the policy] is so difficult.[6]

The Spanish Civil War had indeed aroused a wide reaction in the Jewish *Yishuv* in Palestine. Right-wing groups showed notable sympathy for Spain's Nationalist rebels, a sympathy reflected in their various publications. A typical example of their position appears in an article that was published in the fall of 1936 in *Hayarden*, the organ of the Revisionist Zionists in Palestine. The article said, in part:

> There is no doubt that the Spanish revolt is a phenomenon that is natural and necessary to that country. This revolt is aimed at the elimination of the communist régime that tried to take over one of the most important shores of the Mediterranean Sea [. . .] Franco is not antisemitic [. . .] Jews have suffered from the rebels, it is true – but those Jews are communists [. . .] Not only every honest Spaniard, but every honest Zionist must wish them, the rebels, a complete victory.[7]

Haboker, the organ of the Union of General Zionists, also attacked the Spanish Republic and the Popular Front that led it.

Public opinion, however, was manifestly sympathetic to the Republican cause, which was perceived as a struggle to halt the turbid wave of fascism that threatened to engulf all of Europe. The central committee of MAPAI, the dominant party in the Jewish community in Palestine, issued an appeal to the workers of *Eretz Yisrael* (the 'Land of Israel'), calling on them to go 'to the aid of Spain, weltering in its own blood in its war – a war of the working class against reaction, against anti-Semitic fascism, against the danger of world slaughter'.[8] The *Histadrut* took part in the international campaign to help the workers of Spain, its executive committee calling upon all the members of the organization to contribute to the cause of the workers struggling on the Iberian peninsula.[9] Various workers' councils organized rallies of solidarity with Republican Spain, and solidarity with the workers of Spain was one of the main themes of the May Day celebrations in Palestine.

Parties and organizations to the left of MAPAI – for example, *Hashomer Hatza'ir* ('The Young Guard') and *Poalei Tzion* ('Workers of Zion') – displayed an even greater moral commitment to the Republican cause. *Hakibbutz Ha'artzi*, the left wing of the kibbutz movement, sent the following telegram to the workers of Spain:

From the trenches whence we defend socialist Zionism against the attack of the forces of reaction, we send this fervent, brotherly salutation to the Spanish proletariat, who are paving with their blood the road to the future of socialism. The need of the hour – immediate united action by the proletariat through all its international organizations to help the workers of Spain.[10]

The Palestinian Communist Party (PCP) – which operated outside the law in those days, publishing its organ, *Kol Ha'am* ('The Voice of the People'), clandestinely – took an active stand in favour of the anti-Fascist struggle in Spain. Like many communist parties in the world, the PCP tried to turn its defence of that struggle, which was a popular cause in the *Yishuv*, into a means of mobilizing support and sympathy for the party even in non-communist circles.

Prominent intellectuals in the *Yishuv* – most of them, of course, associated with the Left Wing – worked through the Association to Aid the Victims of Fascism and Antisemitism (ANTIFA) to enlist support for the struggle against the Francoist forces. The activists in the Association – which at the time had counterparts all over the world – included Martin Buber, Yehuda L. Magnes, Akiva Ernest Simon, Shmuel N. Eisenstadt, Shmuel Sambursky, Avigdor Hameiri, Mordechai Avi-Shaul, Alexander Penn, and others.[11]

Solidarity with the beleaguered Republic was not confined to the Left, however. The liberal daily *Ha'aretz* showed consistent support for the Republic and denounced the Anglo-French policy of non-intervention, a policy that in fact served the interests of the Nationalist rebels. The paper regularly attacked the policy of appeasement that the London and Paris governments had adopted towards the extortionary behaviour of Italy and Germany.[12]

Despite these expressions of solidarity with the Republic, almost every group in the *Yishuv*, including the various gradations of the Zionist Left, opposed sending youths from Palestine to join the volunteers in the International Brigades. Those days were the days of the rebellion of the Palestine National Movement, the Arab anti-Jewish riots of 1936–39, and the establishment of the 'stockade and watchtower' line of settlements. The usual arguments were that 'the *Yishuv* is fighting for its life no less than the Spanish Republic', and 'Hanita [a frontier kibbutz] comes before Madrid'. As a result, only 160–300 volunteers left Palestine for Spain, most of them Communist Party members.[13] These volunteers, buoyed by faith and a sense of purpose, set off as pioneers of the anti-Fascist struggle –

even though some of them in fact only joined the International Brigades after they had been thrown out of Palestine by the British authorities. One volunteer told the League of Nations commission of inquiry that went to Spain how the British secret police in Palestine had forced him to volunteer for the war in Spain:

> I spent eight months in jail in Palestine, and the English police's detective, S., came into my cell and threatened that if I didn't go to Spain, they'd keep me in jail for years. He prepared the papers and gave me money for my travel expenses.[14]

The relationship between Jews and Spanish Republicans continued even after the Francoist victory of 1939. In the course of the Second World War, they found themselves together more than once in concentration camps, or fighting side-by-side against the Nazis. During the struggle to bring Holocaust survivors to British-controlled Palestine, Spanish Republicans manned a number of the ships that carried illegal immigrants – two prime examples being the ships *Pan York* (renamed *Atzma'ut*, or 'independence') and San Filipe (*Moledet*, or 'homeland'). The captain of the *Pan York* was Esteban Hernández ('Captain Steve') who, after the establishment of Israel, continued to serve in the new state's merchant marine. On the eve of the War of Independence, the *Hagana* tried to make use of Spanish Republicans to smuggle arms to Israel from France.[15]

None the less, the argument that personal anti-Francoist commitment was an important factor in the formulation of Israel's Spanish policy requires more evidence than the statement by the head of the Israeli Foreign Ministry's Western European division that 'all the leaders of our country [. . .] were, in the past, themselves denouncers of Franco's régime'. The extent to which the senior decision-makers in the Ministry of Foreign Affairs were essentially hostile to the Francoist régime must be examined. We will not discuss here the negative views of Nationalist Spain held by many other senior officials, such as the first president of the country, Chaim Weizmann.[16] Exhaustive research and a series of interviews with several veteran Foreign Ministry officials support the assumption that many senior decision-makers did indeed hold fierce anti-Francoist views back in the years of the Civil War. Of course, when the State of Israel was founded and these individuals joined the Foreign Ministry, most of them pragmatically abandoned their ideological commitment to the Republican cause. For some of them, however, the process of relinquishing their strong moral stand against the Franco régime was slow and painful, as evidenced by their attitude during the internal debate on Israel's Spanish policy. Three notable examples will suffice here: Abba Eban, Ambassador to the United Nations at the time of the May 1949, vote and later Ambassador to Washington; Avraham Darom, from 1949 to 1953 Director of the Foreign Ministry's Latin American division, which for linguistic reasons was also responsible for Spanish affairs; and Walter Eytan, Director-General of the Foreign Ministry from 1949 to 1959.

Abba Eban was undoubtedly comfortable with Israel's official position on Spain as he presented it in the United Nations General Assembly, since it matched his own views, held since the 1930s. While studying at Cambridge he had opposed Chamberlain's appeasement policy and had called for 'collective resistance' to Franco, Hitler and Mussolini.[17] At the beginning of 1937, Eban was stunned when a close friend of his, John Cornford, was killed on the Córdoba front while fighting with the Republicans against the Nationalist forces. According to a biography of Eban published in the early 1970s, this death had a profound impact on him. In the ensuing two years, Eban denounced the British government's policy of non-intervention a number of times in the Cambridge Union, and even organized meetings in support of the Spanish Republic. When he called, in 1938, for active opposition to Germany and Italy, he declared fervently that 'Spain is the key to the situation. A victory of the Spanish [Republican] government would mean strengthening the forces working for peace in the world.'[18]

Avraham Darom had similar feelings. When he joined the Ministry of Foreign Affairs in the summer of 1949, his views were strongly anti-Francoist. In October 1936, while still living in Chile, Darom had wanted to volunteer for the International Brigades in order to fight for the Spanish Republic against Franco and the Nationalists but, by then, the agreement of the Non-Intervention Committee was in force, and the Santiago government, which had ratified it, would not allow volunteers to leave for Spain. Darom therefore remained in Chile but, decades later, in the 1980s, he had still not abandoned 'my faithful duty to the Republic'.[19]

It should be recalled that between 4,000 and 8,000 Jews volunteered to defend the Republic by fighting in the International Brigades.[20] It is difficult to form a more precise estimate, since they were scattered among the various national units – except for those who fought in the company named after Naftali Botwin, a

Jewish–Polish communist who was executed by the Pilsudski government in 1925. Many of these volunteers were internationalists, and
the idea of emphasizing their Jewish identity was alien to them. Most
of them sought to use their own bodies to halt Nazism and the Fascist
storm that threatened to engulf the European continent. It is clear,
however, that the proportion of Jews among the volunteers from
each particular country was in most cases far greater than their
representation in the general population of that country, and that a
considerable proportion of the war-long total of 40,000 – if not
more[21] – Brigade volunteers were Jews. This was one of the reasons
why the Spanish Nationalists commonly equated Jews and
Bolsheviks, a link that was frequently made in the Spanish Falange's
publications during those years.

Walter Eytan was almost the last senior official in the Foreign
Ministry to reconcile himself to the changes in Franco's international
status, and to the necessity, dictated by considerations of *realpolitik*,
of establishing relations with the régime. Eytan evinced a marked
emotional opposition to the Francoist régime – more so than most
of the other Foreign Ministry officials. In a letter to the Israeli representative in Tokyo at the beginning of 1954, Eytan described the
development of contacts between Israel and Spain and expressed his
personal reservations. 'From time to time, thoughts have been aired
here about an effort to arrange some sort of rapprochement. It was
not easy to get used to this idea', Eytan confessed. 'For me, at least,
Franco is still a man who reached power with the help of Hitler, and
who would never have attained power had it not been for that help.'
For this reason, Franco seemed to him to belong to a different moral
category from that of other dictators with whom Israel maintained
relations. To his regret, however,

> many dismiss this as pure sentimentality, and point to Spain's growing
> importance in Europe as a bastion of western defense at a time when,
> of course, the acceptance of reparations from Germany itself somehow
> weakens everyone's opposition to contacts with Franco. As a result of
> much thought and debate, we decided (almost over my dead body, since by
> the end I was in a minority of one) to take a first step towards rapproche-
> ment by opening a consulate in Barcelona.[22]

Many years later, when asked to explain his resistance to establishing
relations with Franco during the early years of the state, Eytan was
no less explicit in revealing his deep emotional attachment to Spain:

For people of my generation, those years, 1936–1939, were a real trauma. The Civil War in Spain was something that horrified us all [. . .] In every free society, everyone [. . .] sided with the Republicans [. . .] It wasn't enough that there was a Fascist régime in Italy and a Nazi régime, a régime like that had to come to power in Spain? This was perceived as terrible in itself, but also as a real threat, a threat to Europe in the form of another, third, Fascist state [. . .] We still remember Franco as a kind of monster, the darkest thing you can imagine. Obviously, this influenced people in MAPAI, people in MAPAM, in fact, every liberal person in the *Yishuv*. After World War II, Franco's régime was the only one of all those helped by Hitler that had survived. Hitler established all sorts of puppet régimes in the Balkans and in central Europe, and there was the Vichy government in France, too; all those disappeared at the end of the war. Only one remained, Franco. And his régime was, in our eyes, a symbol of what was left of Hitler [. . .] and that was the reason for Israel's negative view of Franco.[23]

Eytan, who during the Civil War years was still a university lecturer in England, had a strong personal attraction towards Spain. As a student, he had taken almost every possible opportunity to spend holidays in Spain and he developed a great love of the country. Having visited Spain for the first time in 1926, as a youth of 16, he returned many times – until the advent of the Franco régime.

When Franco came to power, I simply stopped visiting Spain, and I didn't go there again until after he died. I just couldn't bring myself to do it. Just as I never went to Germany – except on unavoidable official missions – or to Austria, I did not go to Spain either, although I loved the place very much. Since Franco's death, I have returned there, and now I enjoy it again.

The Spanish Republic always retained a special place in Eytan's heart, even though from the beginning he advised against establishing formal relations with the Spanish government-in-exile, well aware that it had lost its importance. Nevertheless, in 1955 he still took it for granted that Israel's representatives in Mexico would attend the reception organized there to commemorate the anniversary of the founding of the Republic.[24] After retiring from his post as Director-General of the Foreign Ministry in 1959, Eytan was appointed Israeli ambassador to Paris, where he maintained personal contact with Republican representatives.

In short, the anti-Francoist feelings that barred the way to friendly relations with the Franco régime in most Western countries affected Israel's foreign policy designers for even longer, impeding the establishment of relations with Madrid.[25]

Memories of the Inquisition and the expulsion of the Jews

In contrast to the definitively important memories of the recent past (the 1930s and 1940s) and the personal anti-Francoist commitment of certain key decision-makers in the Foreign Ministry, the more distant past had virtually no influence on the formulation of the anti-Francoist policy. The persecutions that had begun with the Spanish Inquisition and continued for hundreds of years, the expulsion of the Jews in 1492, and the long years of their estrangement from Spain were scarcely mentioned in the Foreign Ministry's internal discussions of policy. Any mention of the events of the late fifteenth century was incidental or mere lip service; no one at the Ministry ever used them as serious arguments against establishing relations with Spain. In a letter from the Israeli Embassy in Paris to the Foreign Ministry in Tel Aviv in mid-1950 concerning possible justifications for the Israeli refusal to recognize the government of Spain, the First Secretary, Shlomo Kedar, wrote:

> The year 1492 indeed remains a shameful blot on the pages of Spanish history, but at the same time it does not seem to me good political sense to nurse a grudge forever. If Israel wanted to maintain relations only with those states which, throughout their histories, had never persecuted Jews, I doubt that any could be found, except perhaps those where Jews have never lived.[26]

A year later, the Israeli representative in Brussels, Michael Amir, advised the Foreign Ministry to establish ties with Franco's Spain. 'I ask what Spain did to us', he wrote, 'not Ferdinand and Isabella's Spain, but Franco's Spain.'[27] In other words, Amir made a distinction between the two. The Spain of the Catholic sovereigns seemed to him irrelevant to the debate, and in the rest of his letter he spoke only of the Franco régime and its treatment of Jews during the Second World War and afterwards, making no further mention of fifteenth-century Spain. Years later, Joel Barromi, who had dealt with matters pertaining to Latin America and the Iberian Peninsula since the early 1950s, said: 'I imagine that it [references to the Inquisition and the expulsion] was really only for form's sake. It was only after the political decision against Franco had been made that the medieval past was added as Jewish and historical justification, a sort of insurance policy.'[28]

Nevertheless, the historical memory of the 1492 expulsion did leave some residue of hostility or mistrust towards Spain which cannot be completely discounted. In fact, in the hundreds of years since the expulsion, many believed there was a ban on Spain and the Jews who settled there, although there was actually nothing in literary or halachic sources to substantiate such a belief.[29] In retrospect, Darom believed that this factor did carry some weight:

> Don't forget that at the time all the leaders of the Zionist movement and of the state of Israel were Ashkenazim, and the ban on Spain was very strong among European Jews; all of us – even I myself in Chile, who was of Lithuanian descent – grew up with that tendency not to get too close to the Spaniards, at least up until the time of the Republic. So I imagine that was a background influence – that is, that we criticized Francoist Spain more sharply than we did Fascist Italy in the years 1936–1939 [. . .] because we did not have this sort of residual feeling about Italy. About Spain we did. I am certain that at bottom, perhaps instinctually, we were more critical of Spain than of any other country.[30]

Remarkably, most Sephardic Jews felt very differently – even though they might have been expected to nurse a greater sense of hostility towards the country that had expelled their forefathers four-and-a-half centuries earlier. In latter generations at least, nostalgia for Spain has apparently overridden the feelings of alienation and acrimony suffered by Jews of the first generations after the expulsion. It must be emphasized that the term 'the holocaust of 1492', used by some researchers, has no basis[31] – certainly not in the consciousness of Sephardic Jews. The Spanish Jews were not exterminated but expelled from the country. Although the Catholic sovereigns, Ferdinand and Isabella, indeed sought a 'final solution' to the Jewish problem, they did not see annihilation as that solution. The expelled Jews suffered a great deal, but they were able to preserve their lives either by converting to Catholicism or by leaving Spain, and most of the Jews who chose to leave succeeded in rehabilitating themselves in the various countries where they were allowed to settle.[32]

The expulsion of the Jews from Spain was undoubtedly one of the most tragic episodes in the chronicles of Israel, since it put an end to the largest and most important Jewish society of the time. It destroyed a Jewish community that over hundreds of years had integrated itself successfully in all spheres of life in its adopted country, from political and economic affairs to creative and cultural endeavours. None the less, this was not the first time Jews had been expelled from a European country, and the Jews of Spain perceived the expulsion as simply one more link in the chain of persecutions and harsh edicts from which the Jewish people had suffered since being forced from their own land. The expulsion was not seen as an extraordinary event marking the end of a period in Jewish history or the beginning of a new epoch in the annals of Israel.[33] Before long, the expelled Jews and their descendants even began to show a tendency to idealize the past, forgetting the steady deterioration in the Jews' situation in the years preceding the expulsion and instead conjuring up the rosy picture of a glorious heritage established over many generations. The country of their origin, rather than their expulsion from it, became a source of pride and a central element in their sense of group identity. There is an interesting distinction here between community memory and a pan-Jewish 'national' memory. While a yearning for Spain remained in the community memory, the 'national' Jewish memory focused on the expulsion, the Inquisition, and the other persecutions. Accordingly, the greater the distance from the original Sephardic community, the greater was the resentment towards Spain.

Y. R. Molko has written about the

> pleasant memories from the distant past, during which we Jews lived in the Iberian Peninsula and occupied a significant position in cultural, political, and economic life for many generations. The traces of that communal life and our presence in it keep reappearing [and] we value them, clinging to and yearning for them.[34]

In a speech delivered in the summer of 1953, at the founding ceremony of the Israel–Spain Friendship League, Rafael Mani, the founder, said:

> It is true that we have old accounts to settle with the Spanish people, foul deeds from hundreds of years ago, and in what other country were we not persecuted? But it cannot be denied that many lights brightened the skies of the diaspora in Spain, so much so that history calls that period 'the Golden Age'. In the culture of Spanish Jewry – there blossomed the original Hebrew culture in its full splendor and created its eternal works of

art. The traveler in Spain today will find at every step traces of the glorious Jewish past.[35]

As mentioned earlier, Sephardic Jews maintained close ties with the Duke of Terranova during both his terms as Spanish Consul-General in Jerusalem, the first during the First World War and the second in the years 1949–52. Eliahu Eliachar, a member of the Constituent Assembly and the provisional government, and later a Knesset member for the Sephardi List, tried to persuade the senior political echelon and the heads of the Foreign Ministry that diplomatic relations should be established with Spain, reminding them that the Franco régime had helped save thousands of Jews during the Second World War. In a speech to the Knesset, Eliachar also asserted that Franco's régime was no more repugnant than those of Perón in Argentina, Stalin in the Soviet Union, or Tito in Yugoslavia, all states with which Israel maintained formal relations.[36]

The appeals Israel received in 1949 and 1950 from Sephardic communities throughout the world calling for a change in its policy towards Madrid were, although in many cases promoted by the Spanish authorities, still indicative of Sephardic Jews' special feeling for Spain. Their sympathy was so evident, in fact, that early in 1953 Avraham Darom proposed it as one of the factors that could be instrumental in changing Israel's Spanish policy: 'The immigration of Sephardic Jews from Bulgaria, Greece, North Africa, etc., has increased the number of people in Israel who sympathize with Spain.'[37]

Although Israeli Foreign Ministry officials seldom mentioned medieval relations between Spain and the Jews to their Spanish colleagues or in internal discussions, Spanish diplomats often did. Spain's ambassador in Buenos Aires, for example, while speaking to Ya'akov Tsur, lauded the Jewish contribution to Spain, discoursing at length on the ties between Spain and the Jews, on the Jewish blood flowing through the veins of most Spanish policymakers, on the Jews' role in Hispanic culture, and on the connection with Sephardic communities around the world.[38]

Frequent mention was also made of the special scientific activity that had begun in Spain during the Second World War. In 1939, the Consejo Superior de Investigacaciones Científicas (High Council of Scientific Research) was founded in Spain, and one of the first research institutes set up under its auspices was the Benito Arias Montano Institute for the study of the Hebrew language and Jewish culture. This institute – which was named after a prominent sixteenth-century Spanish intellectual who served King Felipe II and prepared a revised edition of Cardinal Cisneros's polyglot Bible – was established at the height of the Second World War, just when Nazi Germany had the upper hand. In 1941 the Institute began to publish a periodical called *Sefarad*, as well as studies on Jewish history and a series of translations from Jewish–Spanish literature. The Institute, which was praised by Jewish scholars in Palestine and abroad, boasted a library for Jewish studies, and during the Second World War the Institute's publications were already being sent to Jerusalem.[39]

It is not particularly surprising that Spanish representatives should have mentioned this distant past to their Israeli counterparts. There is a growing recognition in Spain of the special ties between Judaism and Christianity that were established in the country during the Middle Ages, of the contribution that Spanish Jewry's 'Golden Age' made to the formation of Spanish culture, and of the damage that the expulsion of the Jews caused to Spain's development. Many Spaniards are also aware of their own descent from Jewish or *marrano* families.[40] Moreover, there were in fact no Jews in Spain from the end of the fifteenth century until the nineteenth century, and until the Second World War the Jewish community there was minuscule. Thus, apart from the rescue operations of the Second World War, any evocation of a Spanish–Jewish connection necessarily had to reach back several centuries, to the Middle Ages.

The dictatorial nature of the Franco régime

The Spanish régime's patently dictatorial nature was not, in itself, a central reason for Israel's deep-seated resistance to establishing diplomatic ties, but it undoubtedly helped reinforce that resistance. Claims that when the new state of Israel requested international recognition in 1948 it purposely omitted Spain and Portugal because they were 'fascist dictatorships' would appear to be exaggerated, as does the theory that Israel's refusal to establish ties with Spain reflected foreign policy decisions based on 'socialist idealism'.[41] After all, Israel's policy was, in principle, to establish relations with as many countries as possible, regardless of their internal régime. In 1952 Ben-Gurion wrote explicitly that Israel sought to 'establish normal relations with all countries, their governments, and their peoples, without inquiring too closely into the form of their internal régimes'.[42]

Within a short time, Israel began to make a distinction between Spain and Portugal. The latter was ruled by a dictatorship for 48 years, beginning in 1926, and in 1933 it had adopted a corporative, authoritarian constitution. In March 1949, while still hostile towards Franco's Spain, Israel notified Antonio de Oliveira Salazar's Portugal of its foundation, the election of its parliament and president, and the establishment of its first government – to all intents and purposes extending a request for Portugal's recognition.[43] Similarly, Israel did not balk for an instant at establishing relations with the Argentina of Juan Perón, whose populist régime was considered fascist by liberals and socialists as well as by many American Jews. There were other undemocratic régimes with which Israel did not hesitate to establish diplomatic ties, notably the 'people's democracies' of Eastern Europe.

Even at the outset, certain people both in and outside the Foreign Ministry were already seeking to avoid a dichotomous division of régimes into democratic or dictatorial, preferring instead to position them along a continuous line, some of them closer to the democratic pole and others closer to the dictatorial pole. On this scale, some of the régimes with which Israel maintained friendly relations, particularly in Eastern Europe, were just as close to the dictatorial pole as the Franco régime. In the case of Spain, the revulsion felt by decision-makers and certain sectors of the public combined with other motives for hostility to produce Israel's strong resistance to any notion of accepting this régime. As Joel Barromi remarked,

> There was a mixture of various ideological bases that merged together: the Francoist régime's connection with the Nazis – as Abba Eban explained in 1949 – as well as its extreme rightwing fascism, which Israel, a socialist state at the time, saw as loathsome, both because of its nature and because of the Civil War. After all, in spirit the entire Jewish *Yishuv* had sided with the Republicans, and the Francoist victory was perceived as a disaster.[44]

Pragmatic considerations

Other, more pragmatic factors also played a part, of course; and when certain officials in the Foreign Ministry began to call for a change in the policy on Spain, it was precisely such factors that in fact delayed that change, even though they never formed part of the repertoire of ideological justifications offered publicly by Israeli spokespersons to explain the position on Spain. The most important of these factors was the inevitable link between domestic politics and foreign policy.

Rivalries between and within parties over various ideological and political issues influenced the foreign policy of the young state to no small degree. One factor was the concern over 'Jewish public opinion in the world and in Israel, which undoubtedly opposes any change in our attitude towards Franco'.[45] This argument was sometimes put forward in more specific terms, as when concern was expressed over 'worsening relations with MAPAM', or over the possibility that reconciliation with Spain would serve as 'pre-election propagandist material for extremists'.[46]

It should be remembered that MAPAM was perceived as a serious rival to MAPAI. In the January 1949 Knesset elections, MAPAM (which at the time included, besides *Hashomer Hatza'ir, Achdut Ha'avodah-Poalei Zion*) won 19 seats, and in the elections to the *Histadrut* assembly held at the end of May in the same year it won 172 delegates, compared with MAPAI's 286. As Uri Bialer correctly emphasizes, however, the danger posed by MAPAM was not merely electoral but also ideological. Addressing MAPAI's political committee in September 1951, Prime Minister Ben-Gurion dismissed most of the other parties as ideologically empty institutions designed merely to promote the interests of certain sectors; but he did not include MAPAM in this category.[47] MAPAM was, on the contrary, an ideological rival that threatened to draw off MAPAI supporters and therefore had to be combated. Care had to be taken, moreover, to avoid providing its propaganda machine with additional ammunition for attacks on the ruling party. In mid-1950, MAPAM's views took a more radical turn and it began to espouse a neutral foreign policy with greater vigour. Accordingly, it sharpened its criticism of any step tending to incorporate General Franco's anti-communist stronghold into the United States-led Western camp.

The development of relations between Israel and the Federal Republic of Germany during the years 1951–53 and the signing of the reparations agreement between them in September 1952 aroused a storm of debate in Israel and provoked attacks on the government from both the Left and the Right.[48] The Knesset debate held on the subject at the beginning of 1952 was one of the most turbulent the Israeli parliament had ever known, and was punctuated by extreme disturbances by the *Herut* movement. On the eve of the debate the opposition parties convened protest rallies. *Herut*'s leader, Menachem Begin, declared a civil revolt, and threatened to push the country to the brink of civil war. At one point, he asserted:

> When you fired on us with your cannon [on the ship *Altalena*, in June
> 1948], I gave the order: No! Today I give the order: Yes! This will be a war
> of life and death.

Speaking from the Knesset podium, he said:

> This may be my last speech in the Knesset [. . .] There are things more
> precious than life, and this is something for which people are willing to
> leave their families and go to war. There will be no negotiation with
> Germany! Nations have gone to the barricades for less! [. . .] We are ready
> for anything, to stop this thing [. . .] There are things worse than death
> itself [. . .] This is one of the things for which we will give our souls, for
> which we will be ready to die.[49]

The General Zionists, who at the time were the second largest faction
in the Knesset (23 seats), rejected the claim that the money was vital
for building the country, and described the acceptance of reparations
as a moral and spiritual blow to the State of Israel. MAPAM (15
seats) saw the government proposal as both a manifestation of
Israel's efforts to join the Western camp and the latter's anti-Soviet
defence system, and a ratification of West Germany's admission to
that bloc. *Herut* (8 seats) and the Communists (5 seats) also fiercely
opposed reparations and any negotiation with Germany, each party
for its own reasons. During the debate, thousands tried to force their
way into the Knesset building, and in the course of violent clashes
with the police, dozens of people were injured. Some of the stones
thrown at the Knesset building penetrated the assembly hall, one of
them wounding a MAPAM Knesset member, Hanan Rubin, in the
head. At the end of a stormy, tension-filled debate, the government's
proposal was indeed passed (by 61–50) but under the circumstances
the drafters of foreign policy preferred not to invite public debate on
another controversial issue such as relations with Franco's Spain.[50]

   In its first two years of independence, Israel tried to pursue a policy
of non-alignment, and to avoid involvement in the worsening
struggle between the two superpowers. The Foreign Minister, Moshe
Sharett, attributed great importance to this policy, announcing to the
Knesset in June 1949:

> The basic line of Israel's foreign policy has been and always will be to keep
> faith with the United Nations, to be diligent in the fortification of peace
> [. . .] and on no account to identify ourselves with one of the major world
> blocs against the other.[51]

Supporting Francoist Spain in those years could have been interpreted as a hostile step against the Soviet bloc, something Israel wanted to avoid. It should not be forgotten that the Soviet Union had had a decisive influence on the formulation of the United Nations partition resolution in November 1947, the resolution that ended the British Mandate and led to the establishment of a Jewish state in Palestine. The Soviet Union was also the first state to extend full, formal recognition to the State of Israel; it strongly denounced the invasion of Israeli territory by the Arab armies in 1948 and, through Czechoslovakia, it provided Israel with important military aid. Moreover, the Soviet Union firmly supported Israel's application for admission to the United Nations.

In 1949, then, Israel was trying not to alienate the Soviet bloc, in respect to which it was still conducting a policy of non-alignment; nor did it want to lose the broad support it enjoyed in the United Nations – support based in large part on the Soviet bloc and on liberal states in Europe and Latin America, which were sensitive to any move towards reconciliation with a régime tainted with Fascism and Nazism.[52]

The intensifying Cold War, however, eroded Israel's position of non-alignment. The establishment of NATO in April 1949 completed the process of dividing Europe between the two blocs. The Communist victory in the Chinese civil war in September of that year was perceived in the US as one more episode in the contest between the 'free world' and the 'Red peril'; and the Korean conflict brought the Cold War to a new peak, with both Washington and Moscow pressuring their allies to 'stand up and be counted'. From mid-1950 onwards, Israel gradually abandoned its neutral – or semi-neutral – orientation, and threw in its lot with the United States – another step that led left-wingers to criticize the government for joining the 'imperialists' and 'warmongers'.[53] MAPAM and MAKI waged a propaganda campaign against the government, and a heated debate raged over the issue in the Knesset and the press.

Although the Korean War can be seen as a watershed in Israel's non-alignment policy – the point at which Israel really joined the Western camp – up until the end of 1952 MAPAI was still reluctant to adopt a strong anti-communist stance publicly. Its reluctance was compounded by a feeling of responsibility for the Jewish communities in Eastern Europe and the hope that the Jews of the communist bloc would be allowed to emigrate to Israel. Even when MAPAI finally did adopt an openly hostile policy towards the Soviet

Union and communism, it was largely under pressure created by Soviet enmity. The Prague trials contributed to this turning-point in Israel's declared policy; and the 'doctors' trials', reported in January 1953, followed by the temporary severing of diplomatic relations between Israel and the Soviet Union, expedited the process.[54]

The decision to support the United States in the Korean War was not easy, Joel Barromi explained many years later, and it was made more difficult by MAPAM's fierce opposition to abandoning the non-alignment policy. In Barromi's words, Spain was 'a much harder pill to swallow' than Korea, since, after all, Korea was far away in Asia, whereas contacts with Francoist Spain evoked associations with Hitler and the Civil War. A greater length of time was required, accordingly, to accept Franco.[55] However, the improving relations with the United States obviously obliged Israel to abandon any firm anti-Francoist stance in order to avoid conflict with Washington, which at the beginning of the 1950s had very quickly relented towards Spain. General Franco became an ally in the anti-communist struggle, and by the autumn of 1953 the Americans were already signing a military and economic agreement with Madrid which allowed the United States to set up military bases on Spanish territory.

Turning from the analysis of Israel's overall foreign policy in those years to an examination of more specific political and economic interests, it is clear that at the end of the 1940s Spain, which had not yet emerged from the 'black night of Francoism', had very little to offer Israel. Still suffering from the international boycott, Spain was not a member of the United Nations or other international organizations, and Israel was therefore unlikely to sustain any substantial political damage by not maintaining relations with it. Spain's shattered economy ruled out any possibility of significant economic and commercial ties between the two countries.

The Civil War had devastated the Spanish economy.[56] Besides the terrible toll in human lives – hundreds of thousands killed in the war and the waves of terror that followed it, hundreds of thousands of exiles, invalids, and political prisoners – direct economic loss caused by the war should not be underestimated. It is true that most of the essential industries were not hurt, since they fell into Nationalist hands early in the war, and aerial bombings were never as severe as those suffered by the rest of Europe during the Second World War.[57] However, many populated areas had been hit; the transportation system – roads, railway tracks, locomotives – was badly damaged;

many goods and raw materials were unobtainable since, for three years, both sides of the conflict had given priority to the import of tools of destruction; livestock had been sadly depleted, and in 1949 was still less than it had been before the war; much farmland lay untended, and fertilizer imports had ceased almost completely. Agricultural production had accordingly plummeted, bringing wide sectors of the Spanish population to the brink of starvation.[58]

The years of the World War that broke out only a few months after the end of the Civil War were not conducive to economic recovery in Spain. Thus, in 1945 Spain was still a 'land without bread', to quote the title of the celebrated film that Luis Buñuel made in the early 1930s. The severe droughts that struck the agricultural sector in the second half of the 1940s were particularly devastating for the grain crops.[59] The authorities were forced to reduce food rations still further. In the first months of 1949, for example, the bread ration was cut back to a low 150 grams per person per day – this in a country where bread was a major component in the diet of most of the population. In large cities, the water supply to consumers was cut off every day from 5 o'clock in the afternoon until 8 o'clock the next morning to save water. The water shortage even led the authorities to consider evacuating part of the population from Madrid. There were similar restrictions on the electricity supply. Industry, which depended heavily on hydro-electric power, was increasingly paralysed. The problem of the drought was compounded by an inept economic policy characterized by inefficiency, excessive intervention, a corrupt bureaucracy, a booming black market (in which high-ranking officials were involved) and a lack of social sensitivity.

The drafters of Israel's economic and foreign-trade policy thus had no reason to look towards the Iberian Peninsula. They presided over a small economy which, at the beginning of the 1950s, was itself suffering severe hardship, barely managing to cope with the absorption of hundreds of thousands of new immigrants. The drought of 1950–51 obliged the government to enact an even more stringent programme of austerity and rationing. Economic relations with Spain would not have helped Israel to meet these challenges. Nor was Spain a potential source for the arms so urgently needed by the newly created State of Israel, which, just recovering from its war of independence, was still at war with its Arab neighbours. In those years, no major power showed any inclination to act as Israel's benefactor with respect to arms and security, and

Israel was looking into every possible supply source for military equipment.

In general, Israel's foreign policy was not dogmatically ideological as much as pragmatic. It was a *Realpolitik* that constantly strove towards the goal of 'national security'. 'To the best of my knowledge, the command passed on to us by the victims of the Holocaust is to rebuild, reinforce, and promote Israel and insure its security', Ben-Gurion told the Knesset in the summer of 1959. 'To that end, we need friends, especially friends who are able and willing to guarantee our existence [. . .], but if we demonize Germany or any other state, we will receive no arms.'[60]

When the benefits Israel would reap from a reparations agreement with Germany became clear, this pragmatism opened the way to direct talks with Germany. The same approach led to the conclusion of military supply arrangements with West Germany at the end of the 1950s. Israel also abandoned its non-alignment policy fairly quickly, once it recognized the importance of close ties with the West, especially the United States, from which it hoped to obtain raw materials, capital investments, arms, military training, and political support. By the summer of 1955, Ben-Gurion was even advocating a defence alliance with the United States as a means of reinforcing Israel's security.

Spain, in contrast, was, as mentioned, in no position at the time to offer Israel significant assistance in any field – political, economic, or military. Moreover, a hostile attitude towards the Franco régime gave Israel a positive image and enhanced its prestige in the eyes of liberals and socialists in Europe and the United States, countries whose support Israel needed. Even in the Third World countries – a bloc that had only just made its appearance on the international stage – Israel's stand won respect, especially in Asia.[61] At the beginning of 1952, Eytan was invited to India to discuss the possibility of establishing diplomatic relations between the two countries.

> Of all the arguments in favour of India establishing diplomatic relations with us, there were two that impressed Nehru. One was that we were among the first states to recognize the People's Republic of China [. . .] That made a strong impression on him. And the second was that we refused to establish relations with Franco, and that impressed him very much.[62]

Not having any vital interests related to Spain, Israel could afford the luxury of a policy in which moral criteria played a major part. In other words, the absence of relations with Madrid was at the time a relatively low price that the Israeli government paid unhesitatingly in order to preserve its image and prestige in the eyes of broad sectors of public opinion at home and abroad, in the West, in the communist bloc, and in the Third World. Thus, Israel's position on Spain was shaped by a mixture of moral and ideological concerns, laced with personal feelings; but it was influenced at least as much by pragmatism, which in this case was expressed in the decision not to extend diplomatic recognition. And that, after all, is the nature of politics: a blend of ideals and selfish interests.

3

The Beginning of a Change in Israel's Policy (1950–52)

Advantages and disadvantages of Israel's policy

At the beginning of 1950, the Foreign Ministry in Tel Aviv again received reports that the Franco régime might recognize Israel. The Spaniards were still making overtures to Israel, apparently interested in establishing relations between the two countries despite Israel's vote against Spain in the United Nations. At the beginning of January, Rafael Soriano – the same Spanish diplomat who had visited Israel and met with Walter Eytan a few months earlier – went to see Maurice Fischer, Israel's representative in Paris. Soriano, on his way to Italy, seized the opportunity to give Fischer a few messages for Israel. Introducing himself as a fervent proponent of establishing diplomatic relations between the two states, he suggested that commercial ties would make a good starting point. Among other ideas, Soriano mentioned the possibility of arranging for Spanish commercial vessels to dock in Israeli ports.[1] The Franco régime's intensive propaganda highlighting Spain's good treatment of Jews, and international press reports of a possible Spanish initiative concerning Israel[2] led Israeli Foreign Ministry officials to surmise that Spain was preparing for a renewal of negotiations between the two governments, or even for unilateral recognition of Israel as a direct gesture by the Francoist régime. According to one report, Spain had offered to persuade Catholic countries to withdraw their support for the internationalization of Jerusalem if Israel would establish relations with it.[3]

Under these circumstances, Avraham Darom, head of the Latin American division in the Foreign Ministry, perceived an urgent need to define Israel's policy on Spain, to avoid surprises that might necessitate improvising off-the-cuff responses. Accordingly, he prepared a confidential memorandum which at the beginning of April

1950 was distributed to the Director-General of the Ministry and a few senior officials. This memo constituted a first attempt to analyse Israel's Spanish policy in depth;[4] and the very fact of putting a political problem involving emotional and ideological commitment into writing, with the concomitant necessity of reviewing all aspects of that problem – including the erosion of international hostility against Franco's régime – was, in my view, the starting-point for the process that would eventually change Israel's inimical attitude towards Spain.

Darom's seven-page memorandum was in fact a profit-and-loss analysis of the policy on Spain. It began with a description of the United Nations' attitude towards Franco's Spain from 1945 onwards, noting the way Israel had voted on the 'Spanish question' during its first year of membership in that organization. The discussion of United Nations–Spanish relations ended with an emphasis on the fact that the international boycott of Spain was losing steam; the Franco régime was gradually emerging from the isolation imposed on it a few years previously. The memorandum commented that despite the unequivocal United Nations policy, a number of states were ignoring the December 1946 resolutions and, at the beginning of February 1950, the diplomatic corps in Madrid included – besides the representatives of the Vatican, Portugal, Ireland, Switzerland, and Transjordan – ambassadors from Argentina, Peru, the Dominican Republic, Bolivia, Egypt, and Brazil, and envoys from El Salvador, Iceland, Nicaragua, Syria, Lebanon, Iraq, Haiti, Costa Rica, Paraguay, and Venezuela.[5]

This breakdown shows clearly that Franco's foreign policy in that period depended primarily on two main blocs of nations: the Latin American countries and the Arab countries. Franco sought to develop Spain's relations with these two blocs, both of which he portrayed as having a special connection with Spain. Some years later, the Caudillo explained the basis of his foreign policy to the American senator Margaret Chase Smith:

> Spain, which is part of Europe and bordered by the Mediterranean Sea and the Atlantic Ocean, has close ties with the North African and Hispanic American worlds. [Spain] does not evade the obligations and responsibility that derive from its geography and history.[6]

The next subsection of the memo was devoted to the United States' approach to Francoist Spain – specifically, to the rapid crumbling of the hostile attitude expressed by President Roosevelt some years earlier, at the end of his life. The opinions of the country that had won the World War and which was now extending its hegemony over both Western Europe and Latin America were, of course, critical for Francoist Spain's international status.

> As the Cold War intensified, public opinion, Congress, and the state department began to take a more favourable view of Franco, [speaking] of the need to include Spain in the Atlantic Treaty and the war against communism.

Since the end of the Second World War the State Department had indeed been divided between those who advocated using international pressure to change the régime in Madrid and those who wanted to accept the status quo in view of Spain's geo-strategic importance and the régime's anti-communist character. This debate also pitted the State Department against other bodies in the administration, such as the Pentagon, which was unanimously in favour of beginning co-operation with the Franco régime as soon as possible.[7]

In October 1947, the United States administration's policy-planning staff – headed by George Kennan, one of the architects of the Cold War – recommended changing the policy on the Iberian Peninsula:

> In the National interest the time has come for a modification of our policy toward Spain with a view to early normalization of U.S.–Spanish relations, both political and economic [. . .] irrespective of wartime ideological considerations or the character of the régime in power.[8]

This recommendation was quickly accepted by the National Security Council and President Truman.[9] United States public opinion, however, as well as the views of Washington's European allies (particularly Britain and France), imposed caution on the Truman administration, forcing it to implement the desired policy change slowly and gradually.

In the second half of 1949, the pro-Francoist lobby in Washington increased its pressure to normalize relations with Spain and co-operate with General Franco. This lobby included Catholics, anti-communists, members of the military establishment, opponents of Truman, and the representatives of various economic interests.[10] At the same time, a whole series of Congress representatives, senators, and businessmen from the United States visited Spain. One of the most notable visits was that of a military delegation headed by Senator Chan Gurney, who, having met with Franco, declared upon his return to the United States that Spain should be admitted to the United Nations without delay. In September, an American naval squadron cast anchor at El Ferrol, in the first visit of this kind to a Spanish port since the Civil War. Its commander, Admiral Conolly, also met with the Generalissimo, and after returning to Washington he told the House of Representatives that the United States needed military bases in Spain.

Darom's memorandum laid special emphasis on a letter that the American Secretary of State, Dean Acheson, wrote to the Chairman of the Senate Foreign Relations Committee, Tom Connally, in January 1950, saying that from the beginning he had doubted the wisdom and efficacy of the United Nations boycott on Spain and that experience since 1946 had shown that this policy would not lead to any change of régime in Madrid but instead merely strengthened it, since the régime exploited the boycott by presenting it as foreign intervention in Spain's internal affairs. In the letter, which summed up the internal debates that had divided the State Department throughout 1948 and 1949, Acheson explained that his country would support the United Nations draft resolution lifting the diplomatic sanctions on Spain and leaving the organization's members free to decide whether to appoint ambassadors or other representatives to Spain. The American Secretary of State based his arguments on the assumption that the Francoist régime was stable and that no real alternative to the régime was anywhere in sight. Many who would have preferred a different sort of régime in Spain feared that changing the status quo would plunge the country into chaos.[11]

The memorandum then went on to review the general policies on Spain pursued by Britain, the British Commonwealth, and France, and concluded that they did 'not promise a stubborn adherence to the anti-Francoist position, especially after America's change of heart'. Clearly no change in the Eastern bloc's views could be expected in the foreseeable future but the Latin American states, in contrast, showed an obvious inclination to ignore the United Nations resolutions and establish relations with Franco's Spain. By April 1950, 11 of the 20 Latin American states already had full diplomatic representation in Madrid and the prediction was that, of the nine remaining states, at least four would join the camp recognizing Franco's régime, either to make common cause with the rest of the continent or as a result of

United States pressure. The memorandum described Spain's consistent policy of strengthening its relations with the Arabs. By the spring of 1950, four of the six Arab states belonging to the United Nations – Egypt, Syria, Lebanon, and Iraq – had full diplomatic missions in Madrid, while Transjordan maintained an envoy there. Egypt demonstrated the importance of its relations with Spain by appointing as ambassador to Madrid its former Foreign Minister, and considering the possibility of King Farouk visiting Spain, following King Abdallah's successful visit there.

In this exhaustive, in-depth memo, notable for its clear perception of the complex international situation that governed relations with Franco's régime, Darom also examined Spain's attitude towards Jews. He mentioned the abundant Spanish propaganda emphasizing the aid extended to Sephardic Jews during the Second World War, and added:

> The truth is, Franco's régime openly defended Sephardic Jews in the countries occupied by the Nazis, particularly in France and Greece. Franco revived Primo de Rivera's 1924 declaration recognizing Sephardic Jews as subjects of Spain. Despite the formal difficulties, Spanish representatives intervened on behalf of Jews on the grounds that they were Spanish citizens. Franco was tolerant towards the activities of the Joint and the World Jewish Congress, which aided the Jewish refugees who arrived in Spain or passed through it during the war.

The memorandum also noted that a permanent Jewish community numbering a few thousand was again living in Spain, and that the Jews there had set up synagogues in Madrid and Barcelona for the first time since the expulsion from Spain.[12] Darom further stressed that after the State of Israel was established, Spain did not prevent emigration there from Tangiers and Spanish Morocco.

Concluding his discussion of this subject, Darom stated:

> Franco's régime shows no signs of antisemitism. The Spanish press's unfriendly attitude must be attributed to the clergy's propaganda, and should be seen as a reaction to Israel's vote on the question of Franco.

Here, in fact, Darom's view appears to be overly charitable. Certainly the régime did not at any stage implement an anti-Semitic policy, but it should not be forgotten that various elements of the Spanish right wing made use of anti-Semitic slogans more than once during the

1930s and 1940s. The *Protocols of the Elders of Zion* and Henry Ford's pamphlets enjoyed a wide readership. During the Civil War, anti-Semitic articles appeared in most of the newspapers published in the Nationalist zone. These articles called on readers to fight against 'the international conspiracy of the communists, freemasons, and Jews' which threatened Spain. In Spanish Morocco, where the uprising against the Republic began, Jews suffered harsher treatment than other sectors of the population.[13] In August 1936, *Arriba*, the Spanish Falange organ, called on the public in the name of God and the Homeland to drive out Judaism, masonry, Marxism, and separatism, and to destroy and burn their periodicals, books, and propaganda materials. Cardinal Gomá explained that the Jews and the freemasons poisoned the Spanish national spirit with absurd doctrines, while Franco himself, in a speech made on the *Día de Victoria* ('Day of Victory') on 19 May 1939, warned his followers:

> Let us not delude ourselves; the Jewish spirit that has made so many pacts with the anti-Spanish revolution cannot be extirpated in one day, and it flutters in many hearts.[14]

The anti-Semitic tendency was particularly evident in the first stages of the Second World War, when it appeared that the Reich armies were about to engulf all of Europe. The Caudillo justified those nations that wanted – as he saw it – to root out from their midst the mercenary races that undermined their stability and hindered them from fulfilling their historic destiny.[15] The media – particularly those which enjoyed direct aid from the German embassy, such as the daily *Informaciones* – were effusive in their praise of Nazi Germany. Luis Carrero Blanco, Franco's right-hand man for some 30 years, held blatantly anti-Semitic views, and later espoused strong anti-Zionist and anti-Israeli opinions as well. In a book first published in 1941, he wrote that Christian civilization had to wage total war against Judaism, portraying it as a struggle between light and darkness, good and evil, truth and falsehood. At the end of 1973, while serving as Prime Minister shortly before his assassination, he would still browse through the *Protocols of the Elders of Zion*, a work which he took perfectly seriously.[16] The school books used in Francoist Spain of the 1940s and 1950s were also tinged with anti-Semitism, including praise of the 'Catholic sovereigns', Ferdinand and Isabella, for their vision and the thorough way they had resolved the 'Jewish question' in their country.[17] In 1948, Spain banned Elia

Kazan's *Gentlemen's Agreement*, an American film that showed anti-Semitism in a negative light and supported the struggle against it. The censor's office, which in Franco's Spain was controlled mostly by the Church, refused to authorize distribution of the film, claiming that it showed Christians and Jews as equal, something which aroused unjustified pride in the Jews.

Despite all this, however, Darom's memorandum shows clearly that in the late 1940s the Francoist régime did not treat the Jews of Spain any worse because of Israel's anti-Francoist views. On the contrary, the more the chances of establishing diplomatic relations between the two states appeared to dwindle over the years, the more the régime tried to emphasize its good treatment of the small Jewish community in Spain. At the beginning of the 1950s, the régime's spokespersons could claim that the Jews enjoyed complete religious freedom, even though Judaism's legal status in Spain was inferior to that of Catholic Christianity.[18]

Only after completing the review of Spain's international situation and its treatment of Jews did the memorandum address Israel's policy on Spain. To begin with, Darom pointed out that Israel had not informed Spain of its creation, nor asked it for recognition:

> On the contrary, on repeated occasions Franco offered to recognize Israel as soon as we requested it. This was the orientation of Spain's consul in Jerusalem, those members of the Jewish community in Spain who visited here, and, last year, a direct representative of Franco who met with the Director-General. Our response was always negative.

Mention was also made, of course, of Eban's speech in the United Nations, which had been the most comprehensive formulation of Israel's policy on Franco's Spain prior to the memorandum. The head of the Latin American division predicted that at the next United Nations General Assembly session, in the fall of 1950, the 'Spanish question' would again come up on the agenda, and that the number of states favouring the abolishment of the 1946 resolutions would grow. The Spaniards, for their part, would do their best to achieve the two-thirds majority required to cancel those resolutions; and in such circumstances, Israel's vote was apt to carry special weight. According to Darom, the same reasoning might have led Franco to begin a diplomatic campaign in the hope that he would thereby win an additional vote in favour of abolishing the diplomatic boycott – or at least an Israeli abstention.

Darom suggested three possible courses of action for Israel to take in the United Nations:

1. If the United States changed its own position to support abolishing the boycott but did not press its friends to do the same, Israel should vote with the liberal states, as far as possible in agreement with its Latin American friends, who still disapproved of the Franco régime – in other words, vote no or abstain.
2. If the Americans brought pressure to bear but did not manage to persuade France, Benelux, the Scandinavian countries, and the 'progressive states' of Latin America, Israel should vote with the liberal countries – that is, vote no or abstain.
3. If the United States turned the vote into a Cold War, East–West conflict, 'our non-alignment policy will mean abstaining'.

Ultimately, as will be seen, at the end of that year Israel again voted against cancelling the diplomatic ban on Spain, even though the United States led the Western states in supporting the elimination of the sanctions.

Moving beyond the specific problem of the United Nations vote to focus on the wider spectrum of general bilateral relations, the memorandum attempted to list in orderly fashion, for the first time the advantages and disadvantages that would accrue to Israel from establishing relations with Spain. The memo enumerated four possible advantages, all of which it represented as being of limited significance. The first two concerned the status of Jerusalem, which was very important to Israel at the time, since the United Nations resolutions on the subject were sharply at variance with the city's centrality in the national Jewish consciousness.

In November 1947, along with the division of Palestine between Jews and Arabs, the United Nations General Assembly recommended that the city of Jerusalem be recognized as a separate entity under a special international administration governed by the United Nations. In December 1948 – and, to Israel's great surprise, in December 1949, as well – the General Assembly again voted, by a great majority, for the territorial internationalization of the city. Israel defiantly decided, on 11 December 1949, to move the seat of its government to Jerusalem.[19] The Arab countries opposed the partition plan, and some of them, led by Jordan, vehemently opposed the plan to internationalize Jerusalem, too. They claimed that the city was Arab by reason of its population and its history – since the days of the

Jebusites and the Babylonians, as the mayor of Arab Jerusalem said in December 1950 – and that for hundreds of years the Moslems had watched over the holy places of the three major monotheistic religions. The Jordanians were also worried about the possibility that only the Old City, which was under their control and in which most of the holy places were located, would be under international supervision, while the New City, which was controlled by Israel, would remain under Israeli sovereignty.[20]

Another factor in the issue of Jerusalem's status was the Vatican's hostile attitude towards Israel. The Holy See had viewed the establishment of the Jewish state with disfavour, for both theological and political reasons. Publicly, the Vatican remained neutral in the Arab–Israeli conflict, but its policy clearly leaned towards the Arab countries, partly out for concern for the position of Catholics in those countries. From October 1948, Pope Pius XII had displayed firm, unequivocal support for a complete territorial internationalization of Jerusalem in order to protect Christianity's holy places. This position included a demand for the return to Israel of the many Christian Arab refugees who had fled during Israel's war of independence, the goal being to rehabilitate the Catholic communities in the country. Neither internationalization nor the return of the refugees was acceptable to Israel, of course.[21]

In the following months, the papacy used all the means at its disposal to marshal international support for these positions, including the mobilization of Catholic communities around the world. The UN General Assembly resolution of December 1949 to internationalize Jerusalem – which was passed with the mandatory two-thirds majority – was perceived as a great achievement for Vatican policy. Foreign Minister Sharett, unprepared for the results of the vote – which had forged an unlikely union between Arab, Catholic, Moslem, and communist countries – was blamed for the failure of Israel's policy on Jerusalem, and he decided to resign. Ben-Gurion rejected his resignation, however, and Sharett continued in his post.[22]

The plan to internationalize Jerusalem was never implemented, and the 1948 war established the status quo in Jerusalem and its division between a Jordanian administration in the Old City and an Israeli administration in the New City, the situation that prevailed until 1967. However, the General Assembly resolution on the internationalization of Jerusalem was not cancelled, and in the early 1950s there was some concern in Israel that the issue might arise again.

Accordingly, Darom's memorandum itemized the advantages Israel might gain with respect to Jerusalem by establishing relations with Madrid. First, Spain, as a Catholic country, could press the Vatican to accept a solution to this delicate issue that would be more favourable to Israel. Similarly, Franco could also use his influence in several Latin American countries (such as Colombia, El Salvador, Peru, Bolivia, and Brazil), most of which – largely influenced by the Holy See – favoured internationalizing Jerusalem.[23] Darom may not have known how fully the Madrid government identified with the Vatican's position on Jerusalem, and how diligently Spain tried to help promote the Pope's initiative to internationalize Jerusalem and its surroundings. Nor may he have been sufficiently aware of Spain's ideological–diplomatic line of development, which necessarily required papal legitimation. Of all the ideological assets that Franco had accumulated in the course of his dubious past, at the beginning of the 1950s Catholicism remained one of the few resources he could use in his efforts at reconciliation with the West. As the head of a national-Catholic régime in which the Church was a central pillar (in those years even supplanting the Falange, which had been pre-eminent), Franco had to show interest in the fate of the Christian holy places. This duty was taken no less seriously by his Foreign Minister, Alberto Martín Artajo, one of the leaders of the Spanish Acción Católica.

From the late 1940s, the Caudillo had tried to improve relations with the Vatican, which since the end of the Second World War had evidenced a certain degree of cautious suspicion concerning the Spanish dictatorship. The man appointed to serve as ambassador to the Vatican was Joaquín Ruiz Giménez, who had been president of the organization Pax Romana as well as a member of Acción Católica. Ruiz Giménez was supposed to persuade the Holy See that the Francoist régime was a faithful supporter of the Church and wished to co-ordinate its policy with the Vatican in various international matters, particularly those concerning the Holy Land. In addition, he was to prepare the ground for a concordat between Spain and the Vatican. The latter, in turn – once it had realized how firm a hold the régime had on Spain – was interested in winning an important ally in Western Europe, and believed that Madrid would be able to influence the Latin American states.[24]

During the first quarter of 1949, Spain's representatives in the capitals of Latin America tried to persuade the countries of that continent to condition their recognition of Israel on the prompt internationalization of Jerusalem and Nazareth. They also sought to convince the Latin American governments that Catholic countries which were not then United Nations members, such as Spain, Portugal, Italy, and Ireland, should be represented on the proposed international supervisory committee for Jerusalem. This Francoist initiative failed completely. Most of the states on the American continent had already recognized Israel unconditionally.[25] Nevertheless, Spain would long continue its campaign to internationalize the holy places, even though in April of that year, as we have already seen, it explicitly proposed mutual recognition and the establishment of diplomatic relations with Israel, without any pre-conditions.

Spanish newspapers were filled with articles stressing Spain's involvement in the Holy Land since the end of the Middle Ages and its role in protecting the holy places through the medium of the Franciscan order, mentioning in addition that Ferdinand the Catholic and his heirs had been given the title 'Kings of Jerusalem' by Pope Julius II in a papal decree published in July 1510.[26] Bishop Teruel's calls for a new crusade to defend the holy places, issued in May 1948 and January 1949, have already been mentioned. The bishop belonged to the Franciscan order, to which the Church had entrusted the custodianship of the Holy Land.

In May 1949, a ceremony was organized in which young Catholics swore to obey the Pope's orders and do everything they could to achieve the internationalization of the holy places. In August, the government of Spain decided to promote the rehabilitation of those Spanish religious institutions and monasteries (in Ramle, Jaffa, and Ein Karem) which had been damaged during the war in Palestine, as a contribution to 'the Holy See's effort to normalize and strengthen Catholic life in Palestine'.[27] Franco – who in the series of articles against freemasons that he published under the pseudonym of Jakim Boor had accused the masons of 'the hypocritical surrender of Jerusalem and the Holy Places to the fanatic deicides' – also set up the 'Spanish Committee for the Holy Places' to defend Catholic interests in Palestine. Meanwhile, the heads of the Spanish Church rallied to the cause of the internationalization of Jerusalem and called on the leaders of the United States Catholic Church to lobby the Washington administration in the matter.[28] The Spanish Foreign Ministry archives contain reports on extensive diplomatic activity in Europe and Latin America concerning the holy places, as well as letters from universities, mayors, various organizations, and Acción

Católica activists demanding that the United Nations, the Pope, or Franco take action to have Jerusalem declared as an international city owing allegiance to no state.

Another potential advantage that Israel stood to gain from relations with Spain was an economic one. Mutual recognition could facilitate export of Israel's citrus fruits and olive oil, products in which the two countries competed. At the time, however, this benefit was of limited significance. Israel had no difficulty in exporting the relatively small quantities of oranges it produced, and its oil exports were modest. Economic relations between the two countries were negligible in 1950, and Spain's economic situation was not such as to make economic considerations very relevant.

The fourth and last point related to the possibility that a formal relationship between the two states would improve the situation of the Jewish community in Spain and permit the expansion of Zionist activity there. This advantage was also considered to be of minor importance, since it was clear to everyone that Franco could not afford to show any signs of anti-Semitism just when he was trying to win the support of the West; and in any case the community was a small one.

Against these minor benefits, the memorandum listed four possible drawbacks to relations with Spain. First, the government would be a target for embarrassing criticism from the Israeli public, especially from the left-wing opposition parties led by MAPAM. Second, recognizing Franco's Spain would invite denunciation from the countries of the Eastern bloc, with which Israel was still striving to maintain good relations. Third, such recognition would also have a negative impact on liberal public opinion in the world, particularly in the West European democracies and those Latin American countries that were anti-Francoist. Fourth, Israel's moral standing in the United Nations would be weakened, since a foreign policy change of this kind would be interpreted as opportunism.

After examining the advantages and disadvantages of recognizing the Franco régime, Darom made three recommendations. First, if Spain 'spontaneously recognized' Israel, without any previous negotiations, Israel should briefly acknowledge receipt of the letter of recognition, without directly or indirectly committing itself to anything, 'and also without showing any special gratitude'. Second, Israel should not initiate negotiations with Franco's Spain, since 'direct negotiations between us and him will increase his prestige in the world'. On the other hand, 'more or less spontaneous recognition on Franco's part, without any previous negotiations with us, [would constitute] a clear victory for our diplomacy', and would not commit Israel to anything. Third, if the Spaniards initiated negotiations, Israel should refrain from responding to their initiative until it knew exactly what they intended to propose.

The importance of Avraham Darom's document lay not so much in its conclusions as in the debate it aroused among the heads of the Foreign Ministry. A few weeks later, the ambassador to Argentina, Ya'akov Tsur, contributed a few facts and observations to this debate. Tsur described the United States' pressure on Uruguay to make it stop its active resistance to an arrangement with the Franco régime and abstain when the debate on the 'Spanish question' was reopened in the United Nations. He also considered that other Latin American countries, such as Guatemala and Chile, might not oppose lifting the diplomatic ban on Spain. He judged that only a few countries – like Brazil, Argentina, and Colombia – attached great importance to the matter of Spain, and Israel's position in the opposing camp on this issue could create difficulties in relations with them. Tsur argued that circumstances obliged Israel to abstain from voting on the 'Spanish question' at the next United Nations session. Accordingly, he recommended that Israel should not 'take such an abstention as an edict imposed upon [it] at the last minute', but rather ' "sell" [its] abstention in exchange for Spain's support, particularly in the matter of Jerusalem'.[29]

The Director-General of the Foreign Office, Walter Eytan, who was wholeheartedly in favour of continuing the hostile policy towards the Franco régime, was rather concerned by the debate that was developing on the subject, and tried to put a stop to it. 'It is still too early to define the line we will take in the United Nations General Assembly this year if the question of Spain comes up', Eytan wrote to Tsur. 'Our basic attitude towards Franco has always been clear, and it is unlikely that we will deviate from it under pressure from America.' At the same time, Eytan gave Tsur the green light to continue maintaining friendly relations with Spanish representatives in South America. In fact, in most of the Western capitals where Israel was represented, correct and friendly relations were maintained between Israeli representatives and their Spanish counterparts, so there was certainly no reason to prevent Tsur from doing the same.[30]

However, the exchange of views in the upper ranks of the Ministry did not cease, and gradually it began to create cracks in the wall of opposition to relations with the Franco régime. A conversation between Shlomo Kedar, First Secretary in Israel's embassy in Paris, and the Ambassador, Maurice Fischer, gave rise to a letter to the Israeli Foreign Ministry stressing the urgency of defining Israel's position on Spain before the upcoming United Nations General Assembly meeting. The letter said that only two principles could be adduced to justify opposition to Israeli recognition of the Spanish government. The first principle concerned Spain's treatment of the Jews. Kedar emphasized that bearing a grudge against Spain for the 1492 expulsion was unjustified and he countered that memory with the recollection of Spain's assistance in saving Jews during the Second World War. The second justification related to the nature of Franco's régime:

> I am one of those whose souls are repelled by any absolute régime. Nevertheless, I believe that it is an internal matter in every state to establish the régime that it wants. In my opinion, recognition of one country or another should not be conditional on the régime ruling there. If we were to make a practice of maintaining relations only with those states in which the internal régime is to the liking of most of the Israeli population, we would be unable to have relations with many other states. As long as we maintain reasonably friendly relations with states in which – under the existing régime – a Jew with a national Jewish consciousness is considered a criminal, there is no justification for eschewing relations with a state ruled by a régime we do not like for general ideological reasons.

Kedar suggested taking advantage of the fact that the Spaniards were interested in Israeli recognition to propose that Madrid, in exchange for such recognition, should exert its influence with the Vatican and the Latin American states to promote Israel's views on the future of Jerusalem.[31]

In 1950 the debate on the line to be taken with Spain was still in its infancy and powerless at that stage to prompt a change in Israel's policy, but it was to expand considerably during the years 1951–53. Gradually the lower echelons of diplomacy – from secretaries and envoys to ambassadors and division heads – began to exert pressure on the Ministry's senior officials. By the end of 1950, Eliahu Ben-Horin of the West European division was expressing discomfort with Israel's policy. He wrote to Israel's representatives in Rome that he was not at all happy with Israel's behaviour concerning Spain.[32] The Foreign Ministry Director-General and the Minister himself, together with a few other officials, although initially adamant against

Francoist Spain, eventually would bow to pressure, as well as to the changing international circumstances.

Spain as a bridge to the Arab world?

One of the main reasons for the gradual erosion of Israel's hostile position on Franco's régime was the concern felt by Foreign Ministry officials over the increasingly close relations between Spain and the Arab countries. Although one of the pillars of the Franco régime was the Catholic Church, and the Spanish authorities spoke much of the battle to protect Christian civilization from the trends of secularization, liberalization, and socialism that appeared all over the Western world, this did not prevent the régime from developing its relations with the Arab countries for foreign-policy purposes and to strengthen its international status.

Nor was this the only apparent contradiction in Francoist Spain's relations with the Moslem world. While it eulogized the 'Catholic sovereigns', Isabella and Ferdinand, it also tried to appropriate the achievements of the Jewish and Moslem cultures which flourished in Spain during the Middle Ages until Isabella and Ferdinand took steps to extirpate them from Spanish soil. By manipulating the medieval history of his country, the Caudillo was able to present Spain as a bridge and a mediator, a meeting-point between East and West, between the Atlantic and the Mediterranean cultures, between the Latin race and the Arab-Semitic race, between Christianity and Islam. Of the many and lengthy struggles that the Christian rulers of Spain pursued with the Moslems, both on the Iberian peninsula and elsewhere, the spokespersons of the Franco régime preferred to say nothing in their contacts with Arabs. Similarly, while his country continued to hold colonial possessions in North Africa, Franco wrapped himself in the mantle of a defender of Islam and an enemy of colonialism and European imperialism.

During the Civil War, the Nationalists were already emphasizing the 'shared interests' of Spain and North Africa. Spanish Morocco was the Nationalists' starting point and main base in the first stages of the uprising against the Second Republic. Franco, who had spent a considerable portion of his military career in the Maghreb, had wide support in those days in the Moroccan territory under Spanish control, and used hundreds of thousands of hired Moroccan mercenaries in his army, although his campaign was described as a Christian crusade against the 'Red, atheist Republic'.[33] The first use ever made of the Moroccan forces on Spanish soil had been to suppress the revolutionary uprising of the Asturias miners in October 1934. It was General Franco's idea, and this attempt served as an opportunity to examine and assess the effectiveness of these forces. Their success in the mission made them an important element in the Nationalist forces rising up against the Republic.

A mixture of pressure and incentives led many Moroccans – 60,000–70,000 – to join the ranks of the rebels, and, during the Civil War, to cross the straits dividing North Africa from the Iberian Peninsula with them. They were motivated mainly by the severe economic distress then prevailing in the protectorate and the hope of earning good wages and some food. To this were added the techniques of forced enlistment by means of oppression and terror, bolstered by propaganda, which the rebels employed among the various tribes. That propaganda called on the Moroccans to join the campaign against the faithless, for the greater glory of God, even though the religion in whose name Franco fought was anathema to those religious Moslems. It should be noted, too, that the Republic elicited no sense of loyalty in the local tribes, since it had not had time to implement any substantial reforms in the protectorate. During the Civil War, Franco used the Moroccan soldiers as cannon-fodder and psychological weapons. The atrocities perpetrated by these troops, encouraged by their Spanish commanders, wreaked terror and demoralization in the Republican camp.

At the same time, the rebel leaders appointed Colonel Juan Beigbeder as High Commissioner of the Protectorate of Morocco. Beigbeder had considerable administrative experience in Morocco and spoke Arabic. He was well acquainted with the area and with the local leaders, and strove to implement a pro-Arab policy by permitting autonomy in all religious matters and allowing the local nationalist parties a certain measure of freedom.[34] In 1938, a delegation of Syrian journalists visited Spanish Morocco and subsequently published articles lauding the Franco régime's policy and its contribution to the development of the region. All the same, however, during that period when maintaining order and stability in the area and ensuring the population's co-operation were so vital, Franco showed no readiness to make any real concessions or to accede to the Moroccan nationalists' demands for permission to set up an independent administration – in short, he would not do anything that might endanger or loosen Spain's grip on the place.

During the Second World War, Franco tried to exploit the Axis' first victories to strengthen his own country's hold on North Africa. In June 1940, after France fell into German hands, his forces took over the international zone of Tangiers – a commercially prosperous port city of strategic importance – and incorporated it into the administrative system of the Spanish protectorate in Morocco. Caution led Franco to characterize this proceeding as nothing more than a temporary administrative step motivated by the war. Since three of the major powers supervising Tangiers – France, Great Britain, and Italy – were at war with each other, the Spanish government maintained that this was the only way Spain could guarantee the neutrality of the region and of its protectorate. The Falange greeted the move with enthusiasm, declaring that Tangiers would remain Spanish forever. In 1945, however, when the Allies' victory was complete, an international conference met in Paris to discuss Tangiers' future – a conference to which Spain was not even invited. The conference decided that Spain must leave the city by October, and Franco was ignominiously forced to withdraw his forces from Tangiers.[35]

In the ensuing years of international isolation imposed on his régime, Franco deliberately and systematically strove to move closer to the Arab countries. In the Arab world, he found, for the most part, conservative leaders and traditional, monarchic régimes that abhorred godless communism and secular Western liberalism. The Caudillo sought to benefit from the power of the Arabs' vote in the international forum; to secure, through their friendship, Spain's position and interests in North Africa; and to open the markets of Islam to Spanish exports. Accordingly, Franco portrayed his country as a friend to the Arabs, ready to help defend their interests.[36]

He succeeded in this, although Spain still controlled Arab territory. At the beginning of the 1950s, Spain's possessions in Morocco still included the protectorate in the north that had been assigned to it by the accord it had signed with France in 1912. This consisted primarily in the Rif region, which was important to Spain as a line of defence from the south, as a source of iron ore, and as evidence that Spain was still a major European power and should be respected as such. (Throughout the twentieth century Spain has had trouble accepting the loss of its empire and its own demotion to a third-ranking power.) Spain also saw in the protectorate a new theatre for its military operations, having lost the remains of its empire in America and the Philippines in 1898. In addition to the protectorate, which was theoretically ruled by the Sultan of Morocco, Spain had enjoyed complete sovereignty over the two coastal cities of Melilla and Ceuta since the early modern period – the former having been wrested from the Moslems in 1497 and the latter taken from the Portuguese in 1688. Spain continues to hold both these enclaves to this day. In southern Morocco Spain ruled over the small territory of Ifni, and, still further south, the desert colony of Río de Oro.

Spain's growing ties with the Arab states at the end of the 1940s can be partly explained by the animosity that both Spain and the Arabs felt – although for different reasons – towards the Western countries, particularly Britain and France. Relations between Spain and France were tense and had gone through many crises in modern times, beginning with Napoleon's invasion of the Iberian Peninsula at the beginning of the nineteenth century and continuing up to the hostile policy of the Fourth Republic, which made it the Western power most inimical to Franco's régime. The division of Morocco into French and Spanish spheres of influence was an additional source of misunderstandings and friction. Spain always fretted that it was the loser by this partition; after all, no other European state was closer to the Maghreb geographically, ethnically, historically and culturally. The relations between Spain and Britain were of course overshadowed by the latter's control of Gibraltar since the beginning of the eighteenth century. For the Spanish Nationalists this was an open wound; and at the beginning of the Civil War, Franco was already calling for the return of the Rock of Gibraltar. The Arab nationalists had many reasons to criticize French and British imperialism in the Middle East and North Africa, as well as what they saw as encouragement of the Zionist movement.

Thus, a mutual grudge against the Western powers, a shared fear of communism, and the Arab countries' dispassionate attitude towards fascism – the Arab world showed a notorious lack of sensitivity to the Jewish Holocaust and the horrors of Nazism – all made Hispano-Arab co-operation possible. The Arab countries also hoped to benefit from Spain's influence with the Vatican and in Latin America to promote their own interests. One instance of this was the Lebanese Foreign Ministry's appeal to Spain's representative in Beirut to try to change Argentina's position on the Palestinian conflict, which, he claimed, bordered on neutrality and might injure Arab interests. Only Franco's direct intervention, insisted one of the heads of Lebanese diplomacy, was likely to change Perón's attitude.[37]

Another factor that facilitated the relationship was that the Arab countries, having just attained full political independence, wanted to display their sovereignty by developing a network of diplomatic, commercial, and cultural relations with as many states as possible, including Spain. A certain solidarity had arisen as well from a growing feeling in both Spain and the Arab countries that they had been badly treated by the United Nations, in one case through the international boycott imposed on the Franco régime, and in the other through the resolutions that permitted the establishment of a Jewish state in Palestine and Israel's admission to the United Nations. On more than one occasion at the end of the 1940s, Arab and Spanish diplomats discussed the possibility that Madrid might try to mobilize the Latin American countries to support the Arabs and their demands for the return of the Palestinian refugees, as well as implement a liberalization programme in Spanish Morocco; in return, the Arab countries were supposed to support the proposal to lift diplomatic sanctions on Madrid. In addition to these political factors, Franco's years in Morocco and what he had picked up of the Arabic language may have given him a certain nostalgic sympathy for the Arabs.[38]

In 1945, Franco had already proposed cultural co-operation to the Arab League (in public ceremonies he frequently appeared with his Moslem guard), and asked the Arab countries to take a friendly line towards Spain in the United Nations and other international frameworks. In June of that year, the Instituto de Estudios Africanos (Institute of African Studies) was established under the auspices of the Consejo Superior de Investigaciones Científicas to promote research and publications on African subjects, particularly those pertaining to the Maghreb. Similar institutes, focusing on Hispano–Arab relations, were subsequently founded in Spanish Morocco as well.[39] In 1946, Franco amended a few aspects of his policy in Spanish Morocco in order to ensure Arab support. Although in February of the same year the representatives of the Arab states supported the United Nations resolution censuring Spain, by December, when most of the United Nations General Assembly voted in favour of imposing a diplomatic ban on Spain, the Arab states had changed their position; most of the Arab and Moslem delegates abstained. In Arab capitals, newspaper articles stressed that Spain constituted no threat to world peace and that its political system was its own business. In November 1947, when the General Assembly again debated the 'Spanish question', the same voting pattern repeated itself; Egypt, Iraq, Lebanon, Pakistan, Saudi Arabia, Syria, Turkey, and Yemen abstained. Madrid saw this as an important achievement.

Six of the Latin American states voted against imposing the ban on

Spain in December 1946, increasing to eight the following year. Franco realized that Hispanic America and the Arab world represented his opportunity to break down the barriers of international isolation that had been imposed on Spain, and he said so in a speech to the Spanish parliament.[40] The Caudillo invited the Secretary-General of the Arab League to Madrid and began to make overtures to the Arab countries about establishing diplomatic relations and signing cultural agreements. To this end, the Foreign Minister, Alberto Martín Artajo, enlisted the aid of an expert on Arab affairs, Emilio García Gómez, who prepared a great deal of background material for the ministry and, at the beginning of 1947, led a cultural delegation on a tour of Egypt, Iraq, Jordan, Syria, and Lebanon. This delegation was supposed to expand cultural relations and turn them into a tool with which to promote political ties with the Arabs.[41] The Spanish press, which was completely under the control and close supervision of the régime, was full of interviews with Arab political and diplomatic figures, and editorials praising Hispano-Moslem relations.[42] Notable examples were the dailies *Informaciones* and *Arriba*, the Falange organ. The easiest place to demonstrate good will towards the Moslem world was, of course, Spanish Morocco, where Madrid could display an autonomous policy different from that of France. In April 1947 the Spanish High Commissioner, José Enrique Varela, met in Arcila with Sultan Mohammed V, and in September of the same year he inaugurated the Great Mosque of Melilla, taking the opportunity to affirm Spain's friendship for Islam.[43]

This policy of amity with the Arabs even had a special name in those days: '*Mozarabidad*', a word which in Iberian medieval history referred to those Christians who, living under Moslem control, adopted the Arabic language and customs but retained their own religious faith. None the less, despite all Spain's goodwill gestures in Morocco, Spanish rule there was a stumbling block to rapprochement and the establishment of trust between Madrid and the Arab League states. Many North African exiles were concentrated in Cairo, including – notably – Abd-el Krim, the leader of the Rif war against Spain during the 1920s, and the Moroccan nationalist Abd-el Khalek Torres. These exiles set up the 'Committee for the Liberation of North Africa', which, although mostly occupied with anti-French propaganda, also directed some of its barbs at Spain. An additional sore point was Spain's support for the internationalization of the holy places in Jerusalem, Bethlehem, and Nazareth, which conflicted with the policies of some of the Arab countries.

Franco found a warm friend in Jordan. By the summer of 1947 the two states had already established diplomatic relations, and King Abdallah declared that he was 'impressed by what General Franco [had] done for his country – the way he [had] routed the communist monster and maintained Spain's neutrality in the last war'.[44] In November, Spain established diplomatic relations with Iraq and Lebanon. Just before Israel's war of independence, Spain was displaying sympathy for the Arabs. Although the arms shipments that left the ports of Spain and ended in Arab hands were not large, they represented the beginning of Spain's arms-supply connection with the Arab countries, especially Egypt. By the 1950s, Spanish arms sales to the Middle East were already more significant. Israel's hostile attitude and its support for the United Nations diplomatic boycott in May 1949 merely facilitated the increasingly close relations between the Franco régime and the Arabs – although at that stage the Spaniards had not yet given up trying to make friends with Israel. Immediately after the attempt in the United Nations to eliminate the boycott on Spain in May 1949, the establishment of diplomatic relations with Syria and the exchange of ambassadors between the two countries were announced in Madrid. A few months later relations were also established with Saudi Arabia.

In May 1949, as seen earlier, the Arab states changed their position from abstention to support for Franco's Spain, when – unlike Israel – they voted in the UN General Assembly to cancel the ban on Spain. During that period, at least, the Arab League placed more importance on the 'Palestine question' – an issue on which Spain appeared to favour the Arab position – than on the 'North African question'. The members of the Arab League therefore decided to support Spain, and did so again in the United Nations votes on Spain in the autumn of 1950.

At the beginning of September 1949, when Spain was still suffering from international ostracism, the King of Jordan made an official visit to Spain. The Hashemite ruler had in fact been invited back in 1947, but the war in Palestine, uneasiness in Egypt over the planned visit, and pressure from Moroccan exiles all led the King to postpone the trip.[45] Nevertheless, Abdallah was still the first head of a foreign country to go to Spain on an official visit since the outbreak of the Civil War in 1936, and General Franco took pains to welcome him with impressive ceremonies and a show of magnificence far in excess of the Hashemite monarch's reception in London, which he had visited on his way to Spain.[46] His visit was not as important as a visit from the American Secretary of State would have been, of course; but the King of Jordan was greeted at the La Coruña port with a military salute and ship sirens, a band and thousands of people waving the flags of both nations. The Francoist propaganda machine had already had a great deal of experience in mobilizing great crowds to cheer a wanted guest, getting the media to sing the guest's praises, and preventing any expression of criticism or reservation.[47] Despite its dire economic situation, Spain spent huge sums on the Jordanian king's two-week visit. Franco's efforts to enhance the visit's importance were spurred by the fact that, at the time, an American squadron was visiting the port of El Ferrol – the first official visit by American battleships to Spain since the Second World War – while the debates in the United Nations General Assembly were just beginning at Lake Success.[48] The Spanish general wanted to show the world that the ban on his régime was crumbling.

Franco made sure that the King was taken to see the relics of Moslem Spain, wanting to show his guest that Spain could serve as a connecting link between the Moslem world and the Christian world. Abdallah was not invited, however, to visit Spanish Morocco, where the methods employed by the High Commissioner, General Varela, were provoking Arab criticism. Franco in fact granted various concessions to the Moroccan nationalist movement while most of its protests were directed against French rule; but every time the Moroccan nationalists seemed to be endangering Spanish interests their freedom of operation was reduced and strong measures were taken against them. The King of Jordan was allowed to meet in Granada with the Caliph, the Sultan's representative in Spanish Morocco, but only in the presence of General Varela – just to be on the safe side.[49] At the end of Abdallah's visit, a joint Spanish–Jordanian communiqué was issued, saying 'there is complete understanding between King Abdallah and Franco with regard to Middle Eastern affairs, the communist threat, the Spanish administration in Morocco, and the future of Jerusalem and the holy places'.[50] For its part, the Spanish government announced a few gestures meant to benefit the inhabitants of Spanish Morocco. It agreed to provide airplanes for those desiring to make a pilgrimage to Mecca, and to offer financial assistance to pilgrims who had trouble meeting the expense of the journey.[51]

The King's visit increased Franco's prestige in the Arab world and was followed by visits from other Arab dignitaries: the Regent of Iraq, the King of Libya, the son of the Sultan of Morocco, Lebanese and Egyptian ministers, and a whole series of political figures, administrative officials, and journalists from all over the Middle East and from the Arab League. These visits were a great boon to Spain's propaganda in both domestic and international quarters since, in the decade 1945–55, few such visitors came to the country. They added sparkle to the régime's limited foreign relations in those years, and managed to create an appearance of extensive foreign relations and, for Franco, the image of a leader of international stature.[52]

In May 1949, the month when Israel voted against the Franco régime and just before Abdallah's visit to Spain, Spain announced to the government of Jordan its readiness to take in 1,000 Palestinian refugee children: 500 Moslems in Spanish Morocco, and 500 Christians in Spain itself. These children, explained Spain, would be able to go to school there 'until they were given the opportunity to return to their homeland'.[53] By September of the same year, several hundred refugee children in Jordan, Syria, and Lebanon had been registered for the programme, and a special Spanish envoy went to the Old City of Jerusalem to co-ordinate the operation. Ultimately, however, the plan fell through for various reasons. One of them was the opposition of Arab and North African nationalists, who did not want the children to be educated in conquered Moslem territory such as the Spanish protectorate in Morocco. There was also, however, a more concrete reason. Every child of Palestinian refugees received a food ration from the United Nations, which usually helped eke out the family budget; because of this, the refugees did not want to send their children to Spain. The Arab governments' reaction to the Spanish program left Madrid with the impression that the Moslem states 'were not overly fond of the Arabs of Palestine'.[54] However, Spain made other humanitarian gestures for the Palestinian Arabs that could be exploited for political and propagandistic purposes. In July 1949, for example, a shipment of medicines arrived in Beirut and was distributed to Palestinian refugees by the Spanish Consul in Jerusalem. A month later, the ship *Plus Ultra* landed a cargo of clothing, medicine, and food in Port Said, Egypt, 'from Spanish Morocco to the refugees of Palestine'.

Cultural and friendship agreements helped cement the amity fostered by the state visits, the exchange of medals between Franco and various Arab leaders (the most notable example being the Order of Isabella the Catholic, which was awarded to King Farouk of Egypt, and the Order of Fuad I, given to the Generalissimo),[55] the pro-Spanish votes in the United Nations, and the expansion of diplomatic relations (even before the United Nations lifted the diplomatic ban on Spain most of the Moslem countries already maintained full diplomatic relations with the Madrid government). Spain concluded accords of this kind with Lebanon in March 1949, a year after diplomatic relations had been established. It should be noted that the Catholic Maronites' dominant position in Lebanon contributed to the connection with Catholic Spain. Lebanon also hoped to benefit from Spain's influence in Latin America, where a considerable portion of its population had emigrated. The fact that thousands of emigrants returned from Latin America to Lebanon with a good grasp of the Spanish language, and that Spain itself had a fair-sized Lebanese community (particularly in the Canary Islands and Spanish Morocco) also helped strengthen the relationship.[56] Lebanese ministers came to visit Madrid and, in Spain, the Maronite College was established for Lebanese students who came to complete their studies on the Iberian Peninsula.

During the second half of the 1940s Madrid directed special effort towards Cairo, which had become a centre for Spanish activity in the Middle East. At the time, it was also a centre of operations for North African and Middle Eastern nationalists, and the Arab League had established its headquarters there. The Egyptians themselves encouraged these activities as a means of winning a leading position in the Arab world. The Spanish delegation in Cairo accordingly focused on a wider field of endeavour than the relations on the Spain–Egypt axis; one of its goals was to establish contacts with other Arab states and organizations, primarily in the hope of enlisting support for Spain's position in the United Nations and other international forums, such as the Universal Postal Union. At the beginning of 1947, Spain did its best to defeat France's intention of preventing it from joining the Universal Postal Union, which was scheduled to open in May in Paris. Madrid asked the United States administration to intervene with the French government on its behalf but met with refusal. It accordingly focused its efforts on mobilizing support in the Latin American countries, especially Argentina, and in the Arab world, particularly Egypt. Despite the sympathy of these countries, Spain was still not invited to the Paris conference. The international enmity against the Franco régime was then at a peak.

Spain's good relations with Egypt were reflected by the inauguration of the Farouk I Institute of Islamic Studies in Madrid by the Egyptian Education Minister in November 1950.[57] Friendship and cultural agreements were also signed with Jordan (1950), Iraq

(1951), Yemen (1952), Iran (1952), and Syria (1953). Spain also tried to improve its relations with Saudi Arabia, in view of the latter's importance in the Moslem world and the necessity of regular arrangements to allow the Moslems of the Spanish protectorate in Morocco to make the pilgrimage to Mecca.

Spain's economic relations with the Arab world developed along with strengthening political ties. Until the Civil War, the volume of Hispano-Arab trade had been negligible. In fact, until then Spain had significant commercial ties with only four Arab states: Egypt, Saudi Arabia, Persia, and Libya.[58] During the Civil War and, subsequently, the Second World War, Spain's trade with the Middle East ceased almost completely. From 1946 onwards, however, Spain began to show great interest in economic co-operation with the Arab world, and this field indeed expanded steadily, although the political and propagandist aspect was the central element of Spain's relations with the Arab countries. Spain primarily imported cotton from Egypt and oil from Saudi Arabia and Iran. In the five years from 1948 to 1953, the Middle East's share in total Spanish imports approached 10 per cent, but Spain's trade balance with the Islamic countries was negative; only 1.7–2.7 per cent of total Spanish exports found their way to the markets of the Middle East.[59]

On the list of Spain's principal trading partners in 1950, Saudi Arabia was sixth among the states from which Spain imported goods (61.7 million gold pesetas), climbing to fourth place the following year (91.2 million gold pesetas), where it was surpassed only by the United States, France, and Great Britain. Iran was in fifth place (62.9 million), but in 1951 dropped to ninth place (44.4 million). Egypt only ranked 21 on the list in 1950 (9.2 million gold pesetas), but rose to fourteenth place a year later (31.6 million). The list of Spain's export destinations in those years, in contrast, shows a rather different pattern. Iran and Saudi Arabia did not figure at all on the list of the 25 principal states to which Spain exported goods in 1951, but Egypt was – again – in fourteenth place. Tangiers was in ninth place, and French Morocco was number 24 on the list.[60]

In 1950, despite their growing relations with the Arab world, the Spaniards had still not given up hope of forging a link with Israel. Spain's ambassador in Buenos Aires was quick to assure Ya'akov Tsur:

> The visit [of the Jordanian king] has nothing to do with Spain's policy in the Middle East. Franco planned it for one purpose: to strengthen Spain's

position in Spanish Morocco. According to him, a nationalist awakening is underway in Morocco. Its main instigator is the Riffian leader, Abd-el Krim, who resides in Cairo and is supported by foreign powers [. . .] Franco wanted, therefore, to reinforce his position in Morocco, and, taking advantage of the friendly relations he has enjoyed with Abdallah for so long, to set the Hashemites' influence up as a counterforce against the destructive influence of Abd-el Krim [. . .] The ambassador emphasized several times that Franco did not plan to intervene in Middle Eastern conflicts or to support the Arabs in their war against Israel.[61]

Francoists, anti-Francoists, and Israeli policy

Israel's foreign policy, including the stance it took against the Francoist dictatorship, was influenced, as mentioned, by Jewish and Israeli public opinion. At the beginning of the 1950s a tug-of-war was evident between the various groups in Israel and abroad that tried to influence Israel's Spanish policy. Although there was normally no real co-ordination of action between different pro-Spain or anti-Spain groups, for the purpose of analysing and assessing these influences we can speak of an anti-Francoist lobby on the one hand, which operated in Israel and drew encouragement from resolutions against Spain passed by Jewish organizations in various countries, and, on the other hand, a pro-Francoist lobby, which urged Israel's policy-makers to make decisions favouring the establishment of ties with the Franco régime.

Generally speaking, the anti-Francoist lobby consisted of the left wing opposition to the MAPAI government, including MAKI, MAPAM, and *Achdut Ha'avodah*. Their Knesset representatives and their various organs, beginning with *Kol Ha'am* and *Al Hamishmar*, took every opportunity to attack the 'Spanish fascist dictatorship', but many members of the dominant ruling party, MAPAI, also spoke out against any contact with Francoist Spain. One contributing factor to the anti-Franco mood was that in the spring of 1952 the party rejoined the Socialist International. In the upper echelons of the *Histadrut* (which in a few months was to join the International Confederation of Free Trade Unions in Brussels) declarations were often made expressing solidarity with the workers of Spain in their struggle against the oppressive régime. *The Jerusalem Post*, *Davar*, and *Hador* more than once published articles criticizing the Madrid government. In general, the major Jewish organizations in the United

States were hostile to every initiative aimed at rapprochement with the Franco régime.[62]

The pro-Francoist lobby was made up primarily of the Sephardic Jewish communities around the world, particularly those on the Iberian Peninsula and in North Africa. In Israel, too, the Sephardic Jews were the main actors in efforts to persuade the government to change its hostile policy towards Madrid; they hoped that relations with Spain would bolster the Sephardic identity that was threatened in the new state by Ashkenazic hegemony. Notable among these Jews were Eliahu Eliachar (a member of the Constituent Assembly and a Knesset member first for the Sephardi List and later for the General Zionists), Y.R. Molko, and David Siton. Only Sharett's insistence prevented Eliachar from raising the issue of relations with Spain in the Knesset during the very first months of its operation. 'Sharett explained to me repeatedly that such a move was difficult because the leftwing parties would fiercely oppose the establishment of ties with Franco's Spain', Eliachar recalled in his memoirs.[63] Nevertheless, Eliachar talked the matter over with government ministers and members of the Knesset Foreign Affairs and Defence Committee, and formed a group of Knesset members from the right-wing opposition to promote the establishment of relations with Madrid. Knesset members from *Herut* and the General Zionists also expressed criticism, each for different reasons, over the refusal to establish relations with Spain. These critics included the leaders of the General Zionists, Israel Rokach, Peretz Bernstein, Yosef Sapir and Yosef Serlin, as well as their fellow Knesset faction member Simcha Beba, who visited relatives in Barcelona in 1954. Among the *Herut* Knesset members, the main advocates of rapprochement with Spain were Binyamin Arditi, one of the leaders of Bulgarian Jewry in Israel, and Arye Altman. This informal lobby also included, of course, those who hoped to benefit commercially and economically from the development of economic relations with the Iberian Peninsula. The dailies *Herut*, *Ma'ariv*, and *Haboker* began to express, with increasing frequency, the views of the pro-Francoist lobby.

In 1950, when the 'Spanish question' was due to come up at the United Nations again, the Israeli government received a flood of appeals from Sephardic Jewish communities in various states, all urging a change in Israel's policy towards Madrid. Again the Spanish Foreign Ministry, from its offices in the Santa Cruz Palace, used its influence on Sephardic Jews all over the world, this time on a much broader scale than the previous year. The Spanish Jewish communities in Madrid, Barcelona, Tetuan, Tangiers, Casablanca, Rabat, Algiers, Oran, Athens and other cities were mobilized to exert pressure on the Israeli government and Jewish organizations like the World Jewish Congress for Spain's benefit.

In August, the Foreign Ministry in Tel Aviv received two telegrams from the Jewish community in Spanish Morocco, one from Arcila and one from Larache. Both telegrams were drafted in almost identical terms:

> We wish to extend the greatest support to the noble Spanish nation in the United Nations's next General Assembly. [. . .] our gratitude [to Spain] leads us to form this request, which we hope will be granted.

The Jews of Tetuan and Alcazarquivir hastened to follow their compatriots' example.[64] A few days later, an appeal also came from French Morocco. Avraham Banón wrote, from Casablanca, a letter to Foreign Minister Sharett in the name of the Jews of Morocco, almost pleading with Israel to vote in favour of Spain in the United Nations. The writer pointed out the actions taken by Spanish diplomats to save Jews during the Holocaust, and the fact that Spain had opened its gates to Jews following the Second World War. Maimonides, Spinoza, Ibn Gvirol, and Yehuda Halevy, as well as the good treatment enjoyed by the Jews of Spanish Morocco throughout the twentieth century, were all incorporated into this effort to persuade Israel to change its policy on Francoist Spain.[65] The letter had in fact been drafted by Spanish diplomats, with Banón contributing only his signature. Spain's consuls in various places became petition-writers and signature-gatherers among the Sephardic Jews.

The Jews of Tangiers were especially prominent in such appeals, under the pressure of the Spanish authorities. In August 1950, before the United Nations vote, Joe Hassan, the President of the local community, sent a telegram to Prime Minister Ben-Gurion asking Israel to support the cancellation of the United Nations resolutions of December 1946.[66] The President of the Zionist Federation of Tangiers went to meet with Israel's representative in Paris, Maurice Fischer, for precisely the same purpose. In the name of the Jewish community of Tangiers and Spanish Morocco, Yosef Salama entreated the Israeli government to vote in favour of Spain's admission to the United Nations, extolling Franco's treatment of Jews and repeating the dictatorship's familiar claim that Spain had no alternative to Franco, apart from a communist régime. Fischer promised Salama that the position Israel took in the upcoming United Nations

General Assembly meeting would not necessarily be an automatic reiteration of the one it had taken the previous year, and that Israel would re-examine its policy on Spain before participating in another United Nations vote on the subject. Nevertheless, the Israeli representative advised his guest not to entertain any delusions; the best he could hope for was Israel's abstention. Yosef Salama was optimistic, however, and while he was in Paris he also met with members of the Knesset Foreign Affairs Committee. His brother, Isaac Salama, also joined the campaign, offering himself to the Spanish Foreign Ministry as an envoy to Jerusalem.[67] The leaders of the Jewish community and the Zionist Federation of Tangiers sent telegrams in the same spirit to the office of the Prime Minister, Ben-Gurion, to the President of the American Jewish Committee, Jacob Blaustein, and to the President of the World Jewish Congress.

At the same time, another request for a change in Israel's Spanish policy arrived at the office of the Foreign Minister in Tel Aviv, this time from the leaders of the Jewish community in Oran. They, too, had formulated their appeal only after consultation with the Consul-General of Spain. Here again, the grounds given to justify the request were the aid Spain had extended to Jews during the Second World War.[68]

At the same time, a committee of Greek Jews holding Spanish citizenship delivered a letter to the Israeli consulate in Athens asking Israel to support lifting the diplomatic ban on Spain in the United Nations. In their letter, which was addressed to the Prime Minister of Israel, they described how the Spanish government and the vigorous efforts of the Spanish representative in Greece had helped save their lives and property during the Nazi occupation of Greece, when thousands of Jews were being transported to the concentration camps.[69] In reply to this committee of Jews, the head of the West European division, Gershon Avner, wrote that their request would be carefully examined by the government of Israel, which was aware of the assistance Spain had rendered to the Jews during the Second World War. Nevertheless, he emphasized that, by the same token, it could not be forgotten that in that same war Spain had been to all intents and purposes an ally of the régime responsible for the Holocaust of the Jews of Europe.[70] In September a delegation of Sephardic Jews residing in Turkey called on the Israeli consul in Istanbul, Victor Elisar, and appealed to Israel to change its position concerning Spain's admission to the United Nations.

Even the Sephardic rabbinate in remote Colombia sent a request to support Spain's candidacy for United Nations membership. Rabbi Miguel Atias wrote to the Foreign Ministry stating that he had personally witnessed the rescue of Jews by Spanish representatives during the Second World War, and emphasized, in addition, Spain's good treatment of the North African Jews under its jurisdiction.[71]

This great flood of requests from various Jewish communities was judged – correctly – by the Israeli legation in Ankara to be 'part of an overall campaign being waged now by Spain in certain countries [. . .] in order to exert pressure and influence us in this matter'.[72] This assessment was reinforced in the Foreign Ministry as the flow of appeals to Israel from Sephardic Jews increased. At the beginning of 1951, describing the Spanish response to Israel's vote in the United Nations, the head of the West European division wrote decisively: 'The Spanish government has organized pressure on us through Spanish Jews and [Holocaust] survivors all over the world.'[73]

The Spanish Foreign Ministry was highly pleased with this generalized mobilization of Sephardic Jews. The Ministry archives contain various documents praising 'the attitude of fervent patriotism adopted by the Jewish communities of Morocco', and especially Enrique Benarroya, the leader of the Jewish community of Barcelona, 'who is very devoted to Spain, and who has served us admirably on a number of occasions'. The second-in-command at the Spanish foreign office, José Sebastián de Erice, described the appeals from Jews of Casablanca, Tangiers, and Algiers as 'really wonderful'.[74] In Madrid officials believed that all these Jewish appeals to Israel would be enough to change the latter's position, and consequently they turned down offers by Jewish dignitaries from Tangiers and Algeria to visit Israel personally in order to promote Spain's interests.

One man who did go to Israel, in the summer of 1950, was Ignacio Bauer, one of the leaders of the Jewish community in Madrid, who went to deliver a series of lectures designed to change Francoist Spain's image in Israel. Bauer talked about the Jewish communities of Madrid and Barcelona and their freedom to lead a virtually unrestricted religious life, about Spain's efforts to save Jews during the Second World War, and about the scientific endeavours, encouraged by the régime, to conduct research into the history of the Jews of Spain and their contribution to Hispanic culture. This activity was primarily the province of the Arias Montano Institute, established at the height of the Second World War, which published a periodical entitled *Sefarad* under the editorship of Francisco Cantera and José María Millás Vallicrosa.[75]

As the date of the United Nations General Assembly meeting approached, the Spanish consulate in Jerusalem increased its activity – mainly its efforts to discover what approach Israel would take this time. Among other ventures, the Consul tried to establish contact with official representatives of the Foreign Ministry, met with journalists, and strove to obtain from the American Embassy in Tel Aviv a memorandum supposedly presented to it by the Israeli Foreign Ministry which concerned the way Israel would vote on the Spanish issue in the United Nations. The Consul attributed his interest in Israel's position to 'Israel's moral value'. He described 'Spain's special efforts to "buy votes" in the United Nations, a goal on which it is now wasting its last resources'.[76] Once again, Peronist Argentina tried to persuade Israel not to vote against lifting the diplomatic ban on Spain. Its ambassador in Tel Aviv, Pablo Manguel, told the Consul-General of Spain, the Duke of Terranova, that he thought he had managed to talk Israel into abstaining in the new United Nations debate on the 'Spanish question'.[77] The editor of *L'Aurore*, the French-language newspaper published in Jerusalem, had also gathered the impression from his sources in the Foreign Ministry in Tel Aviv that Israel would abstain. On a visit to Jerusalem, Emile Najar, an advisor in the Israeli Embassy in Paris who from an early stage had believed in the need to establish relations with Madrid, told the Duke of Terranova that he had spoken with Sharett about Spain and had tried to convince him of the wisdom of abstaining.[78]

The Spaniards did not rely solely on the efforts of their consulate in Jerusalem. Spain's ambassador in Ankara, Alfonso Fiscowich (who had been Spain's Consul-General in Tunis and, later, in Paris during the Second World War, and whose attitude towards Jews at the time was not always sympathetic), 'implored' his Israeli colleague, Eliahu Sasson, with whom he had developed a warm friendship, to cable an appeal to the Israeli United Nations delegation to abstain from voting against Spain. Fiscowich promised Sasson that his government was seeking possible ways to recognize Israel and to establish diplomatic and economic ties with it, and assured him that Spain's appeal to the Arab states for support in the United Nations General Assembly involved no reciprocal promises that might harm Israel. The Spanish ambassador added, moreover, that it was unbecoming of Israel to make common cause with the Soviet Union and its satellites in the United Nations debate on Spain.[79]

Fiscowich's appeal should be viewed in the light of the special relations that had developed between the two diplomats in Ankara over the preceding six months or so,[80] a connection born of Sasson's personal initiative. Sasson was doing all he could to establish relations between the two states, while wanting at the same time to increase his prestige with the leaders of the Foreign Ministry in Tel Aviv. Sasson visited Fiscowich in March 1950, claiming that he had been directed by his government to create an official but confidential channel of communication with Spain through which to discuss the establishment of normal relations. Fiscowich gave him a speech about Israel's 'moral debt' to Spain for its aid in saving Jews in the Second World War, and about Israel's ungrateful response – its hostile vote in the United Nations in May 1949, preceded by Abba Eban's unjust and inappropriate speech. Sasson explained to him that 'today Israel would not vote the same way as last spring', and attributed the stand Israel had taken at the time to the fact that it had still been in the midst of a war and had not wanted to anger either the United States, from which it received money, or Russia, from which it received arms via Czechoslovakia.[81]

In Madrid, Foreign Minister Martín Artajo gave very serious attention to Sasson's initiative – an initiative of which the Israeli government was completely unaware. Artajo saw Sasson's approach as a sign that Israel's policy towards Spain was changing, and he was ready to conduct talks in Ankara or anywhere else. Artajo informed the Consul-General in Jerusalem, the Duke of Terranova, that in such talks Spain would raise two issues. One was that Israel must immediately send an accredited representative to Madrid – even if only a diplomat stationed in another capital who would visit Madrid briefly for the sole purpose of presenting his letters of accreditation. Spain, for its part, would appoint Terranova as its envoy in Tel Aviv. The other issue was that talks should be initiated to discuss an agreement that would protect Spanish citizens and interests in Palestine, particularly Spanish religious institutions (in Ein Karem, Ramle, and Jaffa), and which would allow Spaniards to make unhindered pilgrimages to the holy places and to practise Catholic rites unrestrictedly in Spanish churches.[82]

Terranova suggested that the talks should indeed be conducted in Ankara rather than Jerusalem, among other reasons so that he could act independently in both sides of the city. He also proposed raising an additional issue in these talks, namely that of compensation for damage caused to Spanish assets in the course of the war in Palestine.[83]

Artajo accordingly gave Fiscowich the green light to conduct talks with Sasson in Ankara on these three demands. All the same, however, being anxious not to injure Spain's good relations with the Arab world, he felt it best not to publicize the existence of any sort of Hispano–Israeli agreement, as long as there was no improvement in Israel's relations with its neighbours (signified, for example, by the conclusion of an Israeli–Jordanian settlement, then being discussed by the representatives of the two states).

At the same time, the President of Israel, Chaim Weizmann, received articles from Madrid bearing the headlines 'Help Spain in the upcoming United Nations Assembly meeting', and 'Help Franco's democratic, anti-communist Spain, in which every citizen, Jewish or not, enjoys complete liberty'. In addition, the booklet *Spain and the Jews*, reissued in the hope of changing Israeli views on the Franco régime, was sent to journalists, media figures, and others.[84]

Obviously, all this extensive diplomacy, the mobilization of Sephardic Jews, and the talks Sasson and Fiscowich conducted in Ankara encouraged Madrid in the belief that this time Israel would not vote against the Franco régime. This conviction may have been nourished, too, by the fact that at the conference of the International Wheat Council, which met in London in June, the Israeli delegate was absent during the vote to admit Spain to the organization. Moreover, after Spain's membership was approved – by a large majority – the Israeli representative congratulated his Spanish colleague.[85]

All Spain's efforts proved to have been in vain, however. Although the Arab League, at the Iraqi government's instigation, decided that the Arab countries would support Spain unreservedly in the United Nations, and Lebanon promised to muster all the votes it could from other countries, Israel resolved to persist in its opposition to lifting the diplomatic boycott on Francoist Spain. In a memo prepared in anticipation of the United Nations Assembly meeting, Emanuel Tsipori of the international organizations division in the Foreign Ministry gave two reasons for continuing Israel's opposition:

1. There has been no change in the Franco régime, which is fascist. Our opposition to its existence is due, among other things, to the close cooperation that existed between Franco and Hitler during the last world war.

2. Our abandonment of the opposing camp would make a great impression, involving much more than just the loss of one vote, for our position

on this matter has great moral importance in the eyes of many delegations, given the special suffering caused to the people of Israel by fascism in Europe. If we show that we are willing to forgive and forget – others will do so all the more easily.[86]

The memorandum offered only one possible justification for abstention, while a vote in favour was not even considered. The justification was that opposition to Franco might anger the majority of Latin American states just when Israel needed their sympathy in the United Nations debate on its own affairs. The main conclusion was that Israel's basic position must remain one of opposition to cancelling the boycott resolutions against Spain. None the less, the memorandum made two additional recommendations. One was not to participate in any special activity in the United Nations beyond the vote itself, and the other was the suggestion that

> in the event that our vote against the proposal to cancel the resolutions should be the one that determines its defeat, we must after all abstain. Since such a possibility exists, it is incumbent upon us to prepare public opinion [in Israel] for it.

In comparison with the unequivocal position Israel had taken just one year previously, here were signs of change and of a certain relaxation of the policy.

Moshe Sharett presented the same position to Ben-Gurion. The Foreign Minister went to New York to attend the debates of the United Nations General Assembly, and after talking with the members of the Israeli delegation he cabled a message to the Prime Minister that the delegation opposed any change in the hostile position on Spain, believing that such a change would deal a heavy blow to Israel's moral status in liberal and left-wing circles, and Jewish public opinion in general. Sharett requested Ben-Gurion's authority to abstain from voting on one of the provisions of the draft resolution, the one concerning the possibility of renewing full diplomatic relations with Spain, and to oppose the draft in its entirety.[87] Ben-Gurion did not give Sharett any new instructions, however. It was not the right time for Israel to alter its position on an issue so sensitive to domestic public opinion since, during the autumn and winter of 1950, Israel was struggling with a serious economic and political crisis. Its foreign currency reserves were dwindling and the regimen of austerity and rationing continued – side-by-side, of course, with a flourishing black market. The government's attempt to shape a new economic programme failed and, in mid-October, Ben-Gurion resigned the premiership. President Weizmann again charged him with the task of forming a new government and, after difficult coalition negotiations, Ben-Gurion presented the new government to the Knesset on 1 November.

In any case, the left-wing opposition took care to remind the government that abstention or a vote in favour of Spain would arouse tough criticism at home. At the beginning of August, Moshe Sneh (MAPAM) said in the Knesset, 'In this Assembly meeting the question of fascist Spain's admission to the United Nations will also be on the agenda. We want an undertaking from the Israeli government that it will strongly oppose such a thing.' The Israeli press also sharpened its anti-Francoist darts as the date of the United Nations vote approached – or such was the impression of the Spanish Consul-General in Jerusalem, who complained in particular of items in *The Jerusalem Post*, a paper 'that has always been notably hostile towards Spain'.[88]

Before the vote, the Consul sent the Foreign Ministry in Madrid his own assessment – a correct one – that Israel would vote against the draft resolution. In analysing the possibilities, the Consul noted that a vote in favour was possible only if the United States put pressure on Israel. In such an event, he believed that Spain would have to recognize Israel at once, and explain to the Arabs that this step merely constituted recognition of an existing fact. If Israel abstained, he advised recognizing Israel and opening an embassy in Tel Aviv which would be separate from the consulate in Jerusalem 'for as long as the problem of Jerusalem remains pending'. If Israel voted against the resolution, the Consul recommended his own transfer from Jerusalem to some other capital and his replacement in Jerusalem by a diplomat of lesser rank, 'because the vote must be seen as very hostile to Spain'.[89] In the end, Israel did vote against the resolution, but Terranova continued to perform his functions as Consul-General in Jerusalem. The reason may have been that Madrid had adopted his attitude that 'we must not abandon the field but keep trying to reconquer it, and make them [the Israelis] change their minds about us'.[90]

The communist invasion of South Korea on 25 June 1950 brought the Cold War to new heights, and accelerated the process of change in Western perceptions of Franco's anti-communist régime.[91] In the United States of the McCarthy period, more and more people were calling for a renewal of relations with Spain. The memory of Franco's sympathy for Nazi Germany was overlaid by the enticing vision of an anti-communist stronghold. In that era before the advent of inter-continental nuclear missiles, Spain's important strategic location at the south-western end of Europe compelled the attention of the Pentagon. At the United States' instigation, the United Nations, too, began to change its policy on Spain in the autumn of that year.[92] On 31 October, the Special Political Committee of the United Nations General Assembly voted on the issue of Spain. By a majority of 37 votes against 10 opposed and 12 abstentions, it was decided to abolish the diplomatic boycott the United Nations had imposed on Spain, which the United States delegate rightly described as a failure in any case.[93]

Israel's representative on the Political Committee, Shmuel Eliashiv, did not merely vote against the draft resolution: he also made a speech in which he repeated the gist of the justifications Abba Eban had presented before the General Assembly the previous year. Eliashiv vindicated the Assembly's 1946 resolution on the grounds that Franco's régime had been established with the aid of Hitler and Mussolini, who wanted 'to establish Nazi and Fascist régimes throughout the world and to liquidate freedom and democracy [. . . and] destroy the Jewish people'. Again the Israeli delegate stressed that although Spain had not participated in the extermination of the Jews, Franco's régime had hoped for Nazi Germany's victory in the war. Nothing had changed in Franco's Spain since the United Nations resolutions of 1946, he said, and therefore there was no reason for the organization to change its attitude towards the régime. Eliashiv repeated the formula that Israel's vote was directed only against Franco's régime and not against the Spanish people, and con-cluded by expressing the hope that Spain would be represented in the United Nations by a democratic government.[94]

Without delay, Martín Artajo urged Terranova and Fiscowich to ascertain the significance of Israel's vote – after all, Madrid had assumed Israel would abstain – and to find out if it was possible to change the vote when the draft resolution on lifting the boycott went to the General Assembly for ratification. Terranova replied from Jerusalem that he had spoken with the Argentine representative, Pablo Manguel, who said that Eliashiv's opposing vote had surprised even some of the officials in the Israeli Foreign Ministry. The Argentine diplomat assured the Spanish Consul that he would try to arrange a meeting for the two of them with the Foreign Ministry

Director-General, Eytan, in order to explain to the latter how unfortunate it was that Israel should forfeit the possibilities of three-way trade between Argentina, Spain, and Israel.[95] At the time, Hispano-Argentine trade relations were already in crisis, with Madrid deeply in debt to Buenos Aires. In Argentina various stratagems to allow Madrid to pay back part of this debt were being discussed, and one of them involved establishing trade relations between the two countries and a third state.

On 4 November, the day after China intervened in Korea, the United Nations General Assembly ratified the cancellation of the diplomatic ban on Spain that it had instituted in 1946. Thirty-eight states voted in favour, 10 against, and 12 abstained. The United States, the vast majority of the Latin American states, and 10 Moslem countries (Egypt, Iraq, Lebanon, Saudi Arabia, Syria, Yemen, Turkey, Iran, Pakistan, and Afghanistan) all supported the resolution. The Soviet Union, Poland, Yugoslavia, Mexico, Uruguay, Guatemala, and Israel were among its opponents. France, Britain, India, Burma, and the Scandinavian countries all abstained.[96] At the opening of the General Assembly session, a spokesperson for the Political Committee said that most of the representatives who had spoken in favour of the resolution in the committee had stressed that it did not constitute an endorsement of the Franco government's domestic policy, but this was probably cold comfort for the opponents of the Francoist régime. The resolution's concrete importance was evident. It paved the way for United Nations members to resume normal diplomatic relations with Spain. In addition, Spain could now join at least the subsidiary agencies of the United Nations, which were open to states that were not members of the organization. Franco's Spain had finally stepped onto the path that would lead it, five years later, to full membership.

According to a number of reports, the fact that Israel had once again voted against Spain greatly displeased the Caudillo. An old Spanish friend of the Israeli representative to the United Nations institutions in Geneva wrote to him a few months later that in his opinion 'you [the Israelis] made a big mistake by voting against Spain in the United Nations in 1950'.[97] The Consul-General, Terranova, was distressed by Israel's vote, and pessimistic about the future of relations with that country. He left Jerusalem after the vote, returning only at the end of January 1951. In contrast to the disappointment occasioned by Israel's vote, Franco had the satisfaction of the Arab countries' favourable vote. That vote could be seen as confirmation of the wisdom of Spain's foreign policy, which had put so much effort into strengthening Spain's ties with the Arab world.

In Spain, the Jews feared that Israel's vote would cause the régime to retaliate against them. The president of the Madrid community, Ignacio Bauer, who revisited Israel at the beginning of 1951, said to journalists:

> Israel's vote against Spain [. . .] was a serious mistake which greatly complicated the situation of the Jews of Spain, particularly the 12,000 Jews who live in Spanish Morocco.[98]

The Francoist dictatorship, however, well aware of the considerable negative impact likely to result from any hostile step against the Jewish community, refrained from such measures.

The Israeli right wing also disapproved of the way Israel had voted on the Spanish question. Members of the General Zionists claimed that Israel would do better to maintain a lower profile in the international arena in matters that did not concern it directly, and that in many cases it should not vote at all, in order to avoid making new enemies. During a Knesset debate on the government's foreign policy, Peretz Bernstein criticized the way Israel had voted, saying that this had been motivated primarily by considerations of internal policy. In his criticisms, Bernstein, a former Minister of Trade and Industry and Knesset member for a party that represented the citrus growers, the industrialists, and business interests, concentrated on the economic aspect of the issue. He emphasized that Spain was Israel's only competitor in its main export, oranges, and that the vote against Spain in the United Nations would prevent any possibility of reaching an agreement with the citrus growers in Spain, 'an agreement that could perhaps have freed the finance minister in future from the necessity of budgeting supports and subsidies for this sector'.[99]

His argument was refuted by Knesset member Zalman Aranne (MAPAI), who said that Israel's vote on the 'Spanish question' constituted additional proof that Israel's foreign policy was independent and uncompromising. Although on the matter of Korea Israel had voted with the United States, it had also voted to admit the People's Republic of China to the United Nations and to expel Nationalist China (Taiwan), as well as against the resolution lifting the boycott on Spain, intended to allow Spain to join the Western anti-communist camp.[100]

In the ensuing months, *Herut* began to publish articles designed to create an atmosphere propitious to establishing relations with Spain. In January 1951, an article appeared under the by-line of A. Guy, the pseudonym used by the writer Abba Ahimeir. The article underlined Spain's role in the rescue of many Jews during the Second World War, comparing its behaviour with that of other countries with which Israel enjoyed friendly relations. Although Abba Eban had attacked Franco's régime for its support of the Nazi régime, Israel maintained amicable relations with Finland, which had been a military ally of the Third Reich; and, after all, 'Franco's Spain gave Jewish refugees a warmer welcome throughout the war than the government of democratic Switzerland'. The article mentioned Spain's tolerant attitude towards the Jews of Spain and Spanish Morocco, the synagogue inaugurated in Madrid in January 1949, and the great impetus the régime had given to research on the medieval history of the Jews in Spain. *Ma'ariv* also published an article by Ahimeir attacking the government of Israel for refusing to recognize the changing international situation and Spain's growing importance in the Mediterranean region. The right-wing intellectual asked whether Sharett thought Franco's régime worse than Stalin's.[101]

The Spanish Consul in Jerusalem quickly forwarded these articles to Madrid, pointing out that this was the first time that a Hebrew-language paper in Israel had presented an extensive picture of Spain's aid to Jews in the Second World War. The Consul saw these articles as the expression of a fledgling movement that favoured revising Israel's policy on Spain.[102]

It is not surprising that Abba Ahimeir was among those who advocated cooperation with Francoist Spain. In November 1936, a few months after the outbreak of the Spanish Civil War, he had published an article in *Hayarden* under the headline 'They Worry about Madrid and We about Jerusalem'. In this article, Ahimeir attacked the leftist circles in Palestine, which worried about 'the well-being of the bolshie-anarchist government somewhere far off in Spain'. He criticized the 'Jewish intelligentsia's hatred for any goy-national movement', and explained, 'The non-Jewish world is alien to us and does not interest us, because we are extremist national Jews'.[103] At the beginning of the 1950s he still took no special interest in the character of Franco's régime, considering it only in terms of whether it was 'good for Jews or bad for Jews'.

In May 1951 *Herut* ran a series of articles by Binyamin Arditi, a Knesset member who was also a board member of the Sephardic

Federation and maintained contact with Spain's Consul in Jerusalem. The articles were devoted to the persecution the Jews of Bulgaria had suffered during the Second World War, and one of them stressed Francoist Spain's assistance in rescuing Jews with Spanish citizenship in Bulgaria and other countries. Arditi emphasized that Jews were indebted to General Franco. Some six months later, Arditi attended the World Congress of Sephardic Jews in Paris as the representative of the Bulgarian community in Israel. Addressing the conference, he expressed thanks to the Caudillo for the hand he had extended to the Jewish people during the Second World War. Arditi also wasted no time in establishing contacts with the Spanish Embassy, and volunteered for any activity acceptable to the Spanish government that would improve its international image.[104]

Following the United Nations vote of November 1950, new ambassadors began to trickle into Madrid, among them those of France and Britain, and within a few months Spain had achieved membership in several subsidiary organizations of the United Nations, such as the Food and Agriculture Organization, the International Civil Aviation Organization, the Universal Postal Union, and the World Health Organization. The vote to admit Spain to the Food and Agriculture Organization took place in New York less than a week after the vote in the United Nations General Assembly on the 'Spanish question'. Forty-five states voted in favour of admitting Spain and only five against. Although the vote was by secret ballot, Madrid assumed that this time, too, Israel had voted against it, together with Mexico, Yugoslavia, India, and Indonesia.[105] By March 1951, the new American ambassador was already present-ing his letters of accreditation to Franco. The international ban on Spain had been breached, although a few more years would pass before Spain achieved full membership in the United Nations, and even then obstacles would still lie in the way of its joining the North Atlantic Treaty Organization (NATO) and, later, the European Common Market.[106] However, as the Spanish monarchist daily *ABC* said a few years later, 'time is working in General Franco's favour'.[107]

The Republican government-in-exile in Paris naturally protested against the November resolution of the United Nations General Assembly, but its voice was scarcely heard any more. The socialist leader Indalecio Prieto, disappointed and defeated, was forced to admit: 'My failure is absolute [. . .] It was I who led my party down the wrong road, who made it trust the democratic governments which did not deserve our trust, as they have just proven.'[108] Israel did not attribute much political importance to the Republican exiles either, and its hostility to the Franco régime did not bring it any closer to the government-in-exile. In December 1950, the Republican government asked Israel to assist it economically by purchasing bonds issued by itself. Fernando Valera, Vice-Premier and Finance Minister of the government-in-exile, approached the Israeli ambassador in Paris with this request. Valera explained that his government required financial support in order to maintain its administrative establishment. A number of Latin American countries had already sent such assistance but it was not enough. His government, he said, would like to receive from Israel a stipend in the amount of $1000 a month, in the form of bond purchases. Valera emphasized, of course, that in order to purchase such bonds, 'it [was] necessary to believe in the triumph of justice and in the re-establishment of the Republic in Spain'.[109]

The Republican request was flatly rejected and the Foreign Ministry gave its ambassador in Paris four reasons for this. First, despite Israel's sympathy for the Spanish Republican government-in-exile, the country was not in an economic situation that would permit it even to consider granting the requested assistance. Second, the government-in-exile had almost no influence within Spain itself. Third, it no longer had any importance in the international sphere, either. At the end of the Civil War it had still enjoyed some influence in a number of Latin American states, but now it no longer had any at all – not even in the more advanced countries of the continent. The sympathy and assistance that it still received there were based more on personal feelings than on political considerations. Finally, even assuming that the Franco régime finally crumbled sometime in the distant future, Israeli officials did not believe the government-in-exile had any chance of taking its place.[110] At the end of 1952, a proposal received by the Israeli embassy in Paris mooting a visit to Israel by the Republican Prime Minister-in-exile was also apparently turned down. Nevertheless, when four Spanish refugees were discovered on an Israeli ship, the Israeli government rejected the idea of turning them over to Franco's Spain, and granted them asylum in Israel.[111]

The dispute in the Foreign Ministry: pressure from below

During the years 1951 and 1952, the Israeli Foreign Ministry attentively followed the rapid process of Spain's integration into the international community, a process that led to Spain's admission into the United Nations Educational, Scientific, and Cultural Organization (UNESCO) in November 1952. Ministry officials also noted with concern Spain's increasingly close ties with the Arab world, reflected in particular by the Spanish Foreign Minister's tour of the Middle Eastern nations in April of that year. The number of people calling for a change in Israel's Spanish policy increased steadily, and a dispute on the subject began to spread inside the Foreign Ministry. This dispute must be understood in the conceptual framework of 'bureaucratic politics', according to which a country's foreign policy is not the sum of the actions of a single, uniform actor (the government) with defined goals or purposes which operates only on the basis of rational criteria. Instead, policy is formed by means of a bureaucratic process in which various governmental bodies and officials take part, often competing and struggling with each other, and arriving at a series of decisions which are not always co-ordinated.

The same two years also saw a change in Israel's attitude towards Germany. At the end of December 1951, the government voted to open direct negotiations with the Federal Republic of Germany on a reparations agreement. In January 1952, the Knesset ratified the government's decision after a stormy debate distinguished by serious disturbances from members of the *Herut* movement, by criticism from the General Zionists (at the time the second largest faction in the Knesset), and by opposition from MAPAM, which viewed this government policy as a ploy to integrate Israel in the Western camp. In March Israeli–German negotiations began in the Netherlands, and in September 1952 Sharett and Konrad Adenauer signed the reparations agreement in Luxembourg.[112] In the wake of this change, advocates of ties with Spain, pointing to the German example, began to demand consistency in Israel's foreign policy – namely, a *Realpolitik* approach to Madrid as well as to Bonn.

In January 1951, Michael Amir, Israel's ambassador to the Benelux countries (Belgium, the Netherlands, and Luxembourg), wrote a polemical letter to the West European division raising the issue of why Israel did not have any kind of diplomatic relations with Germany and Spain when it maintained a consulate in Austria, a country which had been Nazi Germany's active and enthusiastic partner (rather than the victim it had been portrayed), and enjoyed full relations with Poland, a country in which strong anti-Semitic feelings had almost always been the rule. Amir's letter, which condemned 'a fine, moral quixotic line that amounts to tilting against windmills', roused the Director of the division, Gershon Avner, to respond with a detailed presentation of the problems involved in Israel's relations with Germany and Spain. In his letter (already quoted in part in Chapter 2), Avner wrote:

> The problem is difficult, because logic is mostly on your side, while in fact there are complications working strongly in the opposite direction. [. . .] This is not merely a question of deteriorating relations with MAPAM and pre-election propaganda – although that is a factor, too. The central complication, however, does not derive from this. It derives from the fact that all the leaders of our country are members of MAPAI [. . .] and were, in the past, themselves denouncers of Franco's régime. [. . .] It is personally difficult for them today to put all this behind them and to take a step that means accepting the existing situation.[113]

Another letter from Amir led Avner to turn to the Director of the Latin American division, Avraham Darom. Avner held that Israel's policy on Spain should be adjusted to changing international circumstances, given the cancellation of the United Nations's diplomatic ban on Spain and the evident trend towards including Spain in the Western defence network: 'If we are ready to move on the matter of Germany, we have all the more reason to do the same in the case of Spain.'[114] Darom's reply was: 'I share your concern. I have spoken with the Director-General about it.'

Shlomo Ginossar, Israel's ambassador to Rome, also argued that the Israeli attitude towards Spain was unjustified and that the government should adopt a policy reflecting reality and unburdened by sentimental considerations – one that aimed at rapprochement with Madrid. In a letter that Eliashiv Ben-Horin wrote him some months later, saying that there was no objection to the Israeli Consul in Milan maintaining friendly relations with his Spanish colleague, Ben-Horin added: 'We here are not enthusiastic about the policy of boycotting Spain, either.'[115] All these exchanges indicate that the atmosphere in the Foreign Ministry at the beginning of 1951 was already completely different from that which had prevailed only a year and a half earlier. The number of those advocating a reassessment of the position on Spain grew, and they began to speak out more clearly.

A few months passed and nothing changed in Israel's Spanish policy. Amir did not let the matter drop, although he was aware that his views were not shared by the upper echelons of the Foreign

Ministry. In his communications he asked not to be defined as 'an inveterate reactionary', although, he said, 'in the formulation of my views I may ruffle some feathers, and I apologize in advance'. In another letter that he wrote to the Foreign Ministry from Brussels, Amir presented his position in detail. Although Franco had shown sympathy for Hitler's Germany, Amir conceded, he was not an active ally, and even helped many Jews escape the Nazis during the war.

> [Franco's] régime of malice and oppression is not directed especially at the Jews, and we do not orient our political relations according to the internal régime of a country. There is another subsidiary, tactical aspect of the problem. We have adopted a certain policy concerning Germany, and this policy of settling accounts with Germany – which is not easy – must apply only to Germany itself, so that it can achieve its purpose as far as possible. We cannot, in this period, and at the beginning of our political life, set up a general reckoning for all the states that have sinned against us. Against Germany we have an enormous and justified claim which everyone understands. We are not interested in expanding our campaign against other states whose crimes are not as deep or as evident [. . .] Spain, however, throughout that period never carried out any mass murder [of Jews], no wholesale expulsion, even though its press did echo with antisemitic slogans like all the western states during the same time.

Amir added that Israel's policy towards Madrid facilitated Spain's rapprochement to the Arab world, and concluded by asking whether it was right and desirable to abandon the Iberian Peninsula to Arab activity, just when Spain and Portugal were about to be included, directly or indirectly, in the Western defence system, namely NATO.[116]

Following Amir's letter, the head of the West European division again urged his colleague in the Latin American division to reassess the policy on Spain, and consider whether 'it is not appropriate and timely to banish the complexes and change the policy'.[117] The Director-General, Eytan, halted the renewed debate here, once again, and rejected Avner's proposal to publish his letter in order to provoke discussion on the subject.[118] The Director-General settled for passing the letter on to the Foreign Minister.

Eytan's determined stand led the head of the Latin American Division to draft a memo designed to explain why no change should be made in the policy on Spain. Darom justified his view on the basis of five considerations:

1. Since the United Nations resolution to renew diplomatic ties with Spain was passed under pressure from the Western powers, an Israeli initiative in the direction of Spain would be perceived by the Soviet bloc as an abandonment of its 'non-alignment' policy, which was viewed with mistrust in any case.

2. Darom claimed that Spain had no vital interest in establishing relations with Israel at that point. Although Franco would present such relations as a great moral victory, it is doubtful that this accomplishment would, in his eyes, weigh against a possible cooling-off of the relations with the Arab countries that he had been working to build for the past several years. In addition, Spain would have to take into account the possibility that the establishment of relations with Israel would give rise to increased nationalistic unrest in Spanish Morocco.

3. The establishment of ties with Spain would cause disappointment in a number of democratic countries in Latin America that had not recognized the Franco régime, such as Uruguay, Guatemala, and Mexico. On the other hand, it was doubtful that correct relations with Spain would mobilize the Latin American countries most subject to Spain's influence to support Israel's views in matters important to it, notably the problem of Jerusalem.

4. In the economic field, Israel would not enjoy any great benefit from establishing relations with Spain. Madrid could not supply Israel with raw materials or finished products, and certainly not food products, since the Spaniards themselves were half-starved. Israel, in turn, had nothing to sell to Spain.

5. The Jewish community in Spain itself was quite small and under no special pressure from the authorities. Similarly, there was little potential for immigration to Israel from Spain. The community in Spanish Morocco was much larger, of course, but 'up to now there have been no hindrances to the work of the Joint or to emigration to Israel which might justify a change in our policy towards Spain'.

Darom briefly summed up his argument by saying that Israel suffered no real damage from the absence of relations with Madrid, and therefore 'we can afford to follow a policy based on the moral principle of not recognizing the only one of Hitler's creatures that is still alive, as long as no conclusive grounds for changing that policy are produced.'[119] As expected, this memorandum accorded perfectly with the views of the Director-General, who wrote to Darom: 'I completely agree with you, there will be no change in our position on this issue.'[120]

This phase of the debate was concluded by Ya'akov Tsur from Buenos Aires. He agreed that Amir was right in principle, for there was no justification for the anti-Francoist position if Israel based its policy on the principle that it should not interfere in the internal régimes of foreign countries unless Jews were being persecuted there. In his view, however, changing the political line concerning Spain could not bring Israel any advantage and would serve only to 'grease the wheels of anti-Israel propaganda in extreme leftwing circles in the world and particularly in the communist countries.' Accordingly, Tsur recommended that Israel continue its ostracism of the Franco régime, although without being too obvious and without making any unnecessary declarations: 'If we have to vote against Franco, we will, but speeches of explanation and propaganda are, in my opinion, superfluous.'[121]

The Spanish consulate in Jerusalem began to receive reports that a change was developing in the views of a few senior officials in the Israeli Foreign Ministry, and giving rise to internal debate. These reports were relayed primarily through Terranova's contacts with certain Israeli journalists, but the consulate could also sense a change in atmosphere through the increased number of articles and letters to the editor portraying Spain in a favourable light which had begun to appear in Israeli newspapers. This was the case with *Herut*, *Ma'ariv*, *Yediot Aharonot*, *Hamodiah* (the organ of *Agudat Israel*), and the French-language newspapers mentioned earlier (*L'Echo d'Israel*, *L'Aurore*). It was clear to the Spanish diplomats that in many cases these articles were not motivated by sympathy for Spain so much as by the desire to criticize the government's foreign policy. Even in *Davar*, however, the *Histadrut* organ which was controlled by MAPAI, a moderate article appeared in September 1951, written by a spokesperson of the Jewish Agency and describing the Madrid government's cordial treatment of the local Jewish community. 'Our hearts are still not ready to accept the good news about the Franco régime, which did after all lend Hitler a hand in World War II', wrote

I. Klinov.[122] This was the first time – as the consulate hurried to report to Madrid – that an article in a semi-official newspaper expressed praise for the Franco government, rather than criticism alone.[123]

Nevertheless, the media on the whole remained hostile to Francoist Spain. The Spanish legation was particularly annoyed by articles in *The Jerusalem Post*, which had a relatively wide circulation and great influence at the time, and it complained of the 'insulting, violent, and inconsiderate tone of [*The Jerusalem Post*'s] attacks on our country'. The consulate staff wrote letters of protest to the editor of the paper, and Terranova wrote personally to Avraham Darom, the Director of the Latin American division in the Foreign Ministry.[124]

It was not only the changing international attitude towards Spain that began the slow erosion of Israel's position. The two states had started to develop relations – albeit very limited ones – in non-political spheres. Israel began to find itself in contact with Spain in the commercial field, at international conferences and in other frameworks. Citrus-growers in Israel and Spain were in touch over the possibility of developing a co-ordinated marketing policy to avoid competing with each other, and, in mid-1952, representatives from Israel took part in an international conference in Valencia on the subject of citrus problems in the Mediterranean countries. An Israeli paper even remarked that

> there is commercial pressure on the Foreign Ministry to seek an agreement with Spain in order to coordinate the prices and marketing policy of the two states, which are interested in exporting citrus fruit.[125]

The number of Israelis who visited Spain had also increased. In 1949, the Spanish consulate in Jerusalem issued 50 visas to Israelis, whereas by 1950 this number had more than doubled. Although this was still a low figure by any standards, it should be remembered that, at the time, Israel's population was still very small and the country suffered from economic difficulties. Few people travelled abroad at all. The Francoist dictatorship, for its part, with its controversial international image, lack of diplomatic relations with Israel, and economic troubles, was not a particularly attractive tourist destination. Moreover, many Israelis applied for entry visas in Spanish consulates in Europe. Yet despite everything, the number of Israelis travelling to Spain grew steadily: in 1952 the number of Israelis entering Spain was 678, while in the first half of 1953 alone that figure had reached 711.[126] However we interpret this, it seems clear that economic and commercial considerations were gradually beginning to gain prominence among the advantages likely to accrue to Israel from the establishment of diplomatic ties with Spain.

It had also become increasingly clear that the absence of relations with Spain was hurting Israel's chances of creating ties with Portugal, something which Israel now wanted to do. Without a doubt, the only reason Portugal had not yet recognized Israel, Walter Eytan wrote to Ya'akov Tsur, was Israel's negative attitude towards Spain. Binyamin Erlich, who was connected with the Israel Manufacturers' Association and was working unofficially to promote the establishment of ties between Israel and Portugal, wrote to the Foreign Ministry that Portugal refused to recognize Israel on account of its friendship with neighbouring Spain. The fact that Spain maintained good relations with the Arab world, while Israel voted against Spain in the United Nations, led Lisbon to treat Israel coldly.[127]

In addition to a few events sponsored by the Spanish general consulate in Jerusalem to promote cultural connections between the two countries, there was a visit to Israel by the directors of the Arias Montano Institute for Hebrew and Middle Eastern Studies in autumn 1951. The three of them – Professors José María Millás Vallicrosa, Francisco Cantera Burgos, and Federico Pérez Castro – were all fluent Hebrew-speakers and experts on Hebrew literature of the Golden Age. They were described by the Israeli press as 'filled with sincere friendship for the Jewish people and for the young State of Israel, and with a deep love for Hebrew literature. One may see them as a good-will delegation [. . .] on Israeli soil.'[128] It is interesting that the Spanish authorities, always so wary of any step that might draw Arab protest, were not concerned this time about the possible political significance of a visit to Israel by these academics. A year earlier, the Hebrew University in Jerusalem had invited these same professors to participate in the events marking the twenty-fifth anniversary of its foundation, but the Foreign Ministry in Madrid had preferred, for political reasons, not to authorize the visit.[129]

Despite all this, in the autumn of 1951 Israel was still refusing to change its policy on Spain. Gershon Avner did not despair, and continued to press from within for a change. At the end of October, he again urged the Director-General to reconsider the policy towards Spain:

We are moving towards negotiations with Germany. We are moving towards relations with Japan. We have relations with Austria [. . .] It is true that the régime in Spain has not changed, but the régime helped a great many Jews at the time of the world war.[130]

Spain, meanwhile, had not given up on the idea of friendly relations with Israel. Its representatives in various capitals continued to show special interest in their Israeli counterparts. A few days after Israel's second vote against Spain in the United Nations, in the middle of November 1950, the Israeli ambassador in Ankara reported another visit by his Spanish colleague, Fiscowich. Although the close, friendly relations between the two ambassadors had declined, the two continued to meet. According to Sasson, the Spanish diplomat was doing his best to bring about an improvement in Israeli–Spanish relations, and had invited him to visit Spain as a guest of the government. If for any reason Sasson was unable to leave his duties in Turkey, the invitation could be transferred to any other Israeli diplomat. Such a visit, the Spanish ambassador claimed, would permit an accredited Israeli representative to verify at first hand the comfortable circumstances of the Jews of Spain and to discuss the establishment of diplomatic relations with the Spanish authorities. Fiscowich also spoke of his own desire to visit Israel and asked Sasson whether the Israeli authorities would allow him to enter and tour the country and whether Foreign Minister Sharett would agree to meet with him. However, this proposal was unacceptable to the heads of the Foreign Ministry in Tel Aviv, so nothing came of the Spanish initiative.[131]

The Spaniards attributed great importance to the close relationship that developed between Sasson and Fiscowich in the years 1950–52. Madrid officials had the impression, as noted earlier, that Israel had chosen to use its legation in Ankara as a main channel of communication to Madrid, and had directed it to maintain close relations with Spain's representatives in Turkey. Accordingly, they had trouble understanding why Sasson's replacement in Ankara, Maurice Fischer, did not continue his predecessor's tradition of friendly ties with Spain's representatives. After a few months, Fiscowich could no longer conceal his displeasure. He was convinced that Fischer did not understand the role that the government of Israel had allotted to its legation in Ankara. After all, Sasson had said explicitly that his government wanted him to maintain official relations with the Spanish representative in the Turkish capital. When Fiscowich laid all this before Maurice Fischer, the Israeli ambassador was astonished. He wrote to the Foreign Ministry to ask what to do. No less surprised, the Deputy Director-General of the Ministry, Arye Levavi, wrote back:

> Dear Maurice, we were amazed and astounded by your letter [. . .] concerning the Spanish ambassador. There is no doubt that this is an unusual situation and an unexplained development, probably based on a misunderstanding.

Fischer was instructed to continue friendly relations with the Spanish diplomat. He was told, however, that 'it would not be right to reinforce and amplify the Spaniard's assumption that we are maintaining in Ankara a communication link with the Spanish government.'[132] And indeed the Spaniards now realized that Sasson's initiative had been purely personal, carried out without the knowledge of the heads of the Israeli Foreign Ministry.[133]

Spain's ambassadors in Italy and Switzerland, and Spanish diplomats in London and Washington were also friendly with their Israeli colleagues. At the end of 1951, the Israeli Foreign Ministry worked out a clear policy covering meetings between Israeli and Spanish representatives. In no case were such meetings forbidden, but the instructions circulated to Israel's representatives said explicitly that they were to explain

> on every given opportunity that the relation between you is *exclusively personal* [. . .] but he must understand that the time has not yet come for regular relations between the two states, and that meetings between you and the acceptance of an invitation from him – should there be one – have no political significance in terms of the relations between us and Spain.[134]

Martín Artajo's tour of the Middle East

By April 1952, the friendship between Spain and the Arab countries was conspicuous, all the more so because the Western powers' status in the Arab world was declining: Britain, which was blamed for the existence of the State of Israel, was having trouble holding on to the Suez Canal; the French were facing growing unrest in North Africa, particularly in Tunisia; and the United States was already considered Israel's patron, despite its efforts to keep their relations in a low key. While all this was going on, the Spanish Foreign Minister set off on a comprehensive tour of the Middle East.[135]

In his 1952 New Year's speech, Franco had already declared that his country would continue its policy of supporting the Arab states. He mentioned that for hundreds of years Moslems and Christians had lived together on Spanish soil, and he spoke of Spain's historic role in both the Western and Arab worlds. In another speech, delivered by national radio just before Martín Artajo's trip, the Caudillo presented Spain as a shining example of international co-operation – one which had taken upon itself a 'cultural mission' – and he called on the peoples in whom religious feeling throbbed – such as Spain and the Arab countries – to make common cause against atheistic materialism. The central focuses of Spain's activity, said Franco, were on the Iberian Peninsula with Portugal, in Hispanic America and in the Arab world, which had a special place in Spain's heart owing to the historical, spiritual, and blood ties between them.[136]

Martín Artajo defined his trip as a goodwill mission, an occasion to reciprocate the visits by the Jordanian King and ministers of various Arab states, and an expression of gratitude for Arab support in the United Nations and in other international organizations. The visit was also intended to demonstrate that the international boycott on Spain had lapsed, to create the appearance of an active, wide-ranging foreign policy, to ensure continued Arab support in international conferences, particularly for Spain's struggle to join the United Nations as a regular member, to portray Spain as a natural link and mediator between the Middle East and the Western powers, and to pacify Spanish Morocco. Among other things, Artajo wanted to sound out the Arab governments on the Spanish idea of creating a defence alliance among the Mediterranean states, which would include, among others, the Arab and Iberian states – though not, of course, Israel. This alliance against the Soviet threat would complement NATO, from which the Spanish dictatorship was excluded.[137] The importance that Spain attributed to Martín Artajo's trip, and the almost personal commitment that Franco had made to his pro-Arab policy are indicated by the fact that the Generalissimo's only daughter, Carmencita, and her husband, the Marqués de Villaverde, joined the Foreign Minister on the tour.

Martín Artajo's tour, the first visit by a Spanish minister to the Arab countries, lasted three-and-a-half weeks (4 April–29 April 1952) and included six states: Lebanon, Jordan (including a visit to the holy places in East Jerusalem), Syria, Iraq, Saudi Arabia, and Egypt. The Arab capitals gave Martín Artajo an enthusiastic welcome. He, in turn, made speeches about the friendly relations between his country and the Arabs, about 'one blood flowing in the veins of Spaniards and Arabs, who share a single culture and a single destiny'.[138] The Spanish press was, of course, filled with triumphal rhetoric, and every day whole pages were devoted to coverage of the visit. Cinema newsreels showed shots of the various stops on the tour.

Officials in London, of course, were not very happy about the tour, fearing that Spain would try to exploit the difficulties Britain was having with Egypt over the questions of Sudan and the Suez Canal.[139] Israel, too, took a dim view of this new step in Hispano-Arab rapprochement. It was a far cry, however, from this to the note that the Spanish security services passed on to the Foreign Ministry just before the trip, warning of a possible attempt on Martín Artajo's life. That note read:

> given the method used by the English and the Zionists to rid themselves of people who might constitute an obstacle to their plans or create inter-national difficulties for them, [this warning concerns] a possible attempt on the life of the Spanish Minister, to be carried out en route from Beirut–Damascus to Baghdad [. . .][140]

One of Artajo's stops, coinciding with Holy Week, was Old Jerusalem, which he toured privately as a pilgrim, visiting the holy places on foot (these included such places as Golgotha, the Holy Sepulchre, the City of David, the Pool of Shiloah). The Minister was instructed to keep away from all events organized in his honour, mainly to avoid creating misunderstandings concerning Spain's views on the status of Jerusalem. From Jerusalem, Martín Artajo continued on to Bethlehem and then Hebron, where he made a speech intended to explain to his audience that Spain bore no responsibility for the situation in Palestine, since it was not a member of the United Nations and had not taken part in the decisions concerning the fate of this territory in the Middle East.[141]

In the course of the Foreign Minister's tour, and immediately after it, cultural and friendship agreements were signed with Egypt, Syria, and Yemen – thus completing a network of such accords that included most of the Arab countries. Subsequent to the tour, Jordan, Iraq, and Lebanon upgraded their legations in Madrid to embassies. These were the only concrete achievements from the visit – not count-ing, of course, the direct telephone lines between Beirut and Madrid, which Carmencita Franco inaugurated with a telephone call to her father. Nonetheless, the United States, which wanted to improve its standing in the Arab world, may have been impressed by the show of friendship between Spain and the Moslem countries, and assigned even greater importance to the need for a military treaty with Madrid. It is significant that Artajo's departure from Spain coincided almost exactly with the arrival of an American military delegation charged with the task of negotiating with Madrid; many considered this timing as a sign of Spain's intention to increase its bargaining power with the United States using the 'Arab factor'.[142]

One of the things that cast a slight pall on Martín Artajo's visit to the Middle East was Spain's colonial presence in North Africa. Many Arab newspapers, especially in Cairo and Baghdad, called on Spain to leave Morocco if it wanted to remove an obstacle from the path to real friendship with the Arab world.[143] Before Artajo's departure, Abd-el Khalek Torres and a few of his nationalist followers who had been expelled to Tangiers, were allowed to return to Tetuán, the capital of the Spanish protectorate, to resume their party activities, and to publish their newspapers – all to create a more relaxed atmosphere for the visit and to present Franco as a liberal statesman and friend of Islam. At the beginning of February, the Spanish press had published a speech made by the Caliph of Spanish Morocco to his subjects following a visit to Madrid and talks with Franco; the speech included positive remarks about Spain's policy in the protectorate. Martín Artajo was also accompanied by a high-ranking Moroccan officer, General Mohammed ben-Mezzian ben-Cassen, a Moslem who had fought with the Nationalists in the Civil War and had later held various commanding posts in the Spanish army. Although the Secretary-General of the Arab League said that the problem of Morocco could be settled amicably, it was clear to everyone that Spanish rule over Arab territories in North Africa constituted an obstacle to Madrid's relations with the Arabs.[144]

Not everyone in Spain was overjoyed by the display of Hispano-Arab friendship. Some observers expressed doubts about the economic and political basis of such an alliance, particularly in light of the divisions in the Arab world, while others disapproved of co-operation between an eminently Catholic régime and the Moslem world. This sense of uneasiness was bluntly expressed by the Archbishop of Seville, Pedro Segura, in a pastoral letter read in all the churches of his diocese. In it, the Cardinal spoke of 'modern confusion', and explained that excessively close ties with countries holding a religious belief so far removed from Catholicism might cause believers spiritual confusion. Political or military co-operation was legitimate, but it should not entail identification with the moral or religious viewpoints of those countries, said Segura, in a direct reference to Franco's speech on the eve of Artajo's departure for the Middle East. It should be recalled here that the Archbishop of Seville held extreme Catholic views, and did not hesitate to attack either the Falange and its neo-pagan behaviour or certain steps undertaken by Franco himself. His fanatic Catholicism was more than once at loggerheads with the policy of the Holy See. Ten weeks before his attack on Franco's Arab policy, Segura published a strong anti-Protestant pastoral letter in which he explained that the institution of religious freedom in Spain was an intolerable step that would lead to the disintegration of Spain.[145]

The vote in UNESCO

The steady improvement in Spain's international standing continued to encourage the critics of Israel's Spanish policy in the Foreign Ministry. Israel's representative to the United Nations organizations in Geneva, Menahem Kahany, joined those critics when he wrote, in April 1952:

> Whatever the opinion concerning the justification for our attitude towards Spain up to now, don't you think the time has come – if it's not already too late – to sketch new lines that take into account the increasingly important role that Spain is playing in the international arena [. . .]?[146]

Eliahu Sasson also recommended, from Ankara, that Israel re-examine its attitude towards Spain, which was emerging from its isolation as a force to be reckoned with in the Middle East and as a player of strategic importance in the international sphere in general – one valued by the United States, moreover. Sasson's conclusion was: 'We need [. . .] a decision based on reality and [our] interests, not on history alone.'[147]

Once again the leadership checked the growing pressure from the lower ranks of the hierarchy to change the policy. The Director-General of the Ministry wrote briefly to the Foreign Minister, Moshe Sharett: 'In my opinion, we should not change our policy line. Approved?' And the Foreign Minister replied briefly: 'Yes, *for the time being*, no.'[148] Interestingly, Sharett underlined the words 'for the time being'. This indicates that he had already abandoned the strongly hostile attitude towards Spain that he had maintained in 1948 and 1949. However, this reply gave Eytan enough backing to deflect the objections of the critics. A letter was accordingly sent to Israel's representative in Geneva saying that, despite the changes in Spain's international status, there were currently no grounds for changing Israel's policy towards this country.[149] Barely a few months later, the Foreign Ministry would be trying to assess the public's reaction to a softening of the attitude towards Francoist Spain.

During 1952, the gradual process of Spain's integration into the various United Nations agencies continued – a process that would pave the way to membership in the United Nations Organization itself a few years later. On 18 November, Spain's admission to UNESCO was approved by a majority of 44 – including France and Britain – against only four dissenting votes. The 'nays' were Burma, Mexico, Uruguay, and Yugoslavia. This time Israel's representative did not vote against Spain, but joined the six other representatives who abstained: Denmark, India, Luxembourg, Norway, the Netherlands, and Sweden. Membership in the organization was an achievement that added greatly to the Franco régime's prestige. This victory, which was celebrated in Madrid by a special edition of the Falangist daily *Arriba*, aroused a wave of protest from European liberals and socialists (one symbolic expression of protest was the resignation of the well-known Catalonian 'cellist, Pablo Casals, from all UNESCO activity) as well as, of course, in Israel.[150]

To the Israeli Communist Party, Israel's abstention from the UNESCO vote was one more step in Israel's integration into the Western camp. The leader of the party, Meir Wilner, spoke out in the Knesset, attacking Israel's failure to vote against Franco, 'Hitler's pupil and partner', and seeing in that abstention a further proof that Ben-Gurion's government was acting 'as a blind satellite of American foreign policy'.[151]

In February 1953, Knesset member Avraham Berman, of the Left-Wing Faction, addressed a question on this matter to the Foreign Minister. Berman described the protests aroused in Israel and other countries by 'this shameful decision' of UNESCO to admit 'Franco's fascist Spain' as a member. These protests included a declaration by Poland, Czechoslovakia, and Hungary that they would resign from the organization; the resignation of the members of the Norwegian UNESCO committee and of social democrats of various nations from their posts in the institution and its committees; and the sharp protest registered by the Guatemalan parliament. Berman addressed two questions to Sharett. First, did he think that Israel had any place in the same organization with Hitler's ally? Second, how did he explain the Israeli delegation's failure to oppose the admission of Franco's Spain to UNESCO?[152]

This was not the first time that Israel had abstained from voting on Spain's admission to one of the international agencies connected with the United Nations. In May 1951, Spain was admitted to the World Health Organization, and on that occasion, too, Israel's representative abstained from the vote. Mexico was the only country that turned in an opposing vote.[153] At the time, however, almost no protests were heard; the difference in response was largely because Spain's achievement, in terms of prestige and symbolism, was much greater in the case of its admission to the United Nations cultural organization. Another factor worth noting is that the Catalonian Co-ordinating Committee of the Spanish exiles in Paris thought fit to congratulate the Israeli ambassador, Maurice Fischer, on the decision to abstain rather than vote in favour of Spain's admission to UNESCO.[154] In the international climate prevailing at the time, even an abstention was some consolation to the Republican exiles, who were forced to watch as the dictatorship entrenched itself in their homeland.

The draft reply to Knesset member Berman's question, prepared by the head of the Foreign Ministry's United Nations division on behalf of Minister Sharett, revealed new nuances in the attitude to Spain. It said that Israel supported the principle of universality in all matters pertaining to membership in international organizations, and that the Israeli delegation to the United Nations General Assembly had always voted in favour of opening the doors of the organization to all countries that wished it and which had been recognized according to accepted international procedure. Israel had followed this principle when the applications of Libya and Indonesia were under consideration, both of them countries with which Israel had no diplomatic relations. When the question of admitting Spain had arisen at the UNESCO conference, 'we did not see, in accordance with this principle, how we could oppose it, but our special stand on Spain led us to abstain from the vote'. The draft reply also claimed that Czechoslovakia, Poland, and Hungary, which had announced their resignation from UNESCO, had not participated in the organization's activities in the last three years, and it was doubtful that Spain's admission was the main reason for their leaving. It further emphasized that these three communist countries had not taken part in the last conference and had not used their right to vote against Spain's admission. Yugoslavia, in contrast, had voted against Spain's admission, but did not quit the organization – on the contrary, it strengthened its relations with it. Accordingly, Israel saw no reason to withdraw from UNESCO over Francoist Spain's admission.[155]

Sharett gave his reply to Berman's question in the Knesset in July 1953, just five months after it had been presented. 'The government of Israel', said Sharett succinctly, 'sees no reason to give up its place in a comprehensive, universal international organization, participation in which is eminently beneficial to the state of Israel, solely because some other state has joined it.'[156] Sharett's firm reply should be seen in the context of the vigorous anti-Soviet, anti-communist position MAPAI had adopted at the end of 1952, after the revelation of the Prague trials. The 'doctors' trials' in the Soviet Union, disclosed in January 1953, and the temporary severance of diplomatic relations between Israel and Moscow, naturally expedited the growing hostility towards the Soviet bloc.

In a letter to the Israeli ambassador to Washington, the director of the United Nations division described Israel's abstention from the UNESCO vote as

> a big step forward towards the goal [. . . of] opening formal relations with this state [Spain]. That abstention brought down a rain of criticism from all quarters of the population, and despite the logical explanation that was given – that the principle of universality theoretically demanded support – it is clear that the Foreign Ministry was far ahead of public opinion. Under these circumstances, it is inconceivable that a vote for Spain would be accepted by the public at all, and we should not have shrugged off this factor.[157]

The slow process of erosion in Israel's position on Spain must also be associated, as emphasized earlier, with the change in Israel's policy on Germany.[158] At the end of 1952, however, after the reparations agreement had been signed with the Federal Republic of Germany, Israeli public opinion was still in an uproar, and the government was buffeted by heavy criticism from both the Right and the Left. It was clear to the heads of the Foreign Ministry that this was not the right time for an about-face in its attitude towards Spain as well. Israel's representatives in Europe were therefore told that the abstention from the UNESCO vote did not reflect any change in Israel's official policy on Spain.[159]

Francoist Spain, of course, took a positive view of Israel's abstention in UNESCO, and welcomed its support a short time later for the adoption of Spanish as one of the official languages of the United Nations institutions, together with English and French. A speech by the Israeli delegate, Moshe Tov, in the Economic and Social Council (ECOSOC) of the United Nations was praised in Madrid, and printed in *Mundo Hispánico*, the journal of the Instituto de Cultura Hispánica (Institute of Hispanic Culture), which was connected with the Foreign Ministry.

Spain's representatives in Israel reported a changed atmosphere, both in their relations with government officials and in the media and public opinion. In the week that Israel abstained from voting against Spain in UNESCO, the Duke of Terranova presented the accredited envoy, Pedro López García, who had been sent to replace him as Consul-General in Jerusalem, to Dr Avraham Biran, the Interior Ministry official in charge of the Jerusalem district and the Foreign Ministry's representative in the city. Their conversation with Biran, reported Terranova, was very friendly and showed signs of a change in Israel's attitude towards Spain. Biran told the Spanish diplomats that both sides should let bygones be bygones – an allusion to Israel's votes against Spain in 1949 and 1950. Biran also thanked the outgoing Consul-General for his attendance at the funeral of the first President of Israel, Chaim Weizmann, who had passed away a short time before. In his report to Madrid, the Consul also mentioned that, for the first time, he had received an official communication from the Israeli Trade Ministry; that the Spanish professors visiting Israel had been warmly received; and that *Ha'aretz* had begun to run a series of articles by Dr Haim Gamzu praising Spain's treatment of Jews. Finally, he remarked on 'the changed attitude of *The Jerusalem Post* [. . .], which has now offered to publish as many items on Spain as we wish and that are likely to interest its readers'.[160]

4

Israel's Belated Initiative (1953–56)

The idea of a consulate in Barcelona

The year 1953 marked a turning point in Spain's international status. The concordat that it signed with the Vatican in August and the economic–military pact it concluded with the United States a month later, on 26 September, strengthened the position and prestige of the Spanish régime both at home and abroad. The Pact of Madrid, as it was called, made Spain officially an ally of the United States, and consisted mainly of agreements to supply weapons and economic aid to Spain. In return, Spain undertook to allow the United States to build sea and air bases on its territory. According to official United States sources, the magnitude of economic aid (including credit) extended to Spain over the ensuing 10 years came to $1.688 billion, augmented by $521 million in military aid. Although this support was minor compared to what other Western European states enjoyed in the framework of the Marshall Plan, it was to have a far-reaching impact on Spain, which would soon begin an accelerated process of development.

The agreement that Spain signed with the Holy See replaced the 1851 concordat – abandoned during the period of the Republic – and completed the Catholic Church's recognition of the régime. The first clause of this agreement provided that 'the Roman, Apostolic, Catholic religion continue[d] to be the sole religion of the Spanish nation', and that it would enjoy the rights and privileges to which it was entitled by divine and ecclesiastical law – thus reaffirming the inferior status of non-Catholics in Francoist Spain. For some years, the Vatican had been reluctant to identify itself too closely with an arbitrary, oppressive dictatorship. Only when it became clear that the régime was firm and that there was no foreseeable alternative did the Pope bow to growing pressure from the Spanish Catholics and agree to sign an agreement with the Generalissimo. The Franco régime could rejoice in the victory of its foreign policy. The official regularization of its relations with the most important spiritual power and the most important temporal power in the West was a boon to the dictatorship's propaganda. According to some reports, the Generalissimo saw this as the final victory of the Civil War.[1]

For much the same reasons, 1953 was also a watershed in Israel's Spanish policy. Foreign Ministry discussions on the subject became more thorough and more pertinent. The emotional and ideological opposition to relations with Francoist Spain was weakening, and the advocates of an Israeli initiative aiming at reconciliation with Madrid were joined by high-ranking officials like Avraham Darom. 'When I came to the Latin American division in 1953', Joel Barromi was to recount years later,

> I found a state of uneasiness over the growing cooperation between Spain and the Arab countries [. . .] Although political revulsion [towards the Francoist dictatorship] still existed, people felt it was in our political interest to achieve some kind of normalization with a régime that was an existing fact and showed no indication of changing in the near future [. . .] There was a feeling that we were losing out because there was a state that essentially did not have to be anti-Israeli, yet was aligning itself with the Arab countries.[2]

This change of attitude can be attributed to adjustment to Spain's altered international status, to an appreciation of Israel's specific interests, and to the dynamic common to nearly every Foreign Ministry: the desire to universalize the country's foreign relations and to establish diplomatic and consular ties with as many states as possible. This is especially true of a small country that feels it is fighting for its very existence. Accordingly, there was mounting criticism of decision-makers who were ruled by personal affinities rather than pragmatic interests, and who behaved as though the State of Israel had not yet been established.

A confidential memorandum prepared by Darom at the beginning of the year was the basis for a renewed internal debate on Hispano-Israeli relations.[3] This memorandum constituted an updated, methodical review of the advantages and disadvantages of continuing the policy of shunning Spain. The fact that the number of reasons 'obligating and facilitating a *volte-face*' was nearly double the number of 'motives and considerations in favour of maintaining our traditional position' indicates the increased strength of the revisionist trend regarding the policy on Spain. Since the initiation of this internal debate back in 1950, the arguments offered by the proponents of change had grown more sophisticated, and both arguments and proponents had increased in number. The long memorandum that Darom had prepared on the same subject three years previously had contained only four 'possible advantages' that would accrue to Israel if relations were established with Madrid.[4] Two of them concerned the possibility that Spain would persuade the Vatican and a number of Latin American countries to accept a solution more favourable to Israel in the matter of Jerusalem. These speculations were unfounded, since, like the Vatican, Francoist Spain supported the internationalization of Jerusalem in order to protect the Christian holy places, and it would never have tried to persuade any entity whatsoever to adopt a position more amenable to Israel's insistence that Jerusalem was its capital. On the contrary, in 1948 and 1949, as described earlier, Spain urged states in Latin America to make their recognition of Israel conditional on the latter's consent to the internationalization of Jerusalem. In any case, these hypothetical advantages gradually lost their importance – at least from 1953 on – as the Jerusalem issue faded into the background. It would not resurface on the United Nations General Assembly agenda until a decade and a half later, in 1967, when Israel occupied the eastern part of the city.[5]

The principal justification that the new memorandum gave for continuing to boycott Spain was that

> the negative characteristics of Franco's Spain, which made it unacceptable to us in the past, are still present now. The régime in power is the same tyrannical, reactionary régime that was established with the help of the Nazis and the Fascists, and it is following in their footsteps.

This view of the matter reflected no attempt to discover whether any internal changes or developments had taken place in the régime itself since 1939, or at least since the end of the Second World War, but rather focused on the change in its international standing. This justification was a moral and ideological one, and carried greater weight than any other.

Other arguments centred on possible reactions in Israel and abroad to a policy change. Policy-makers feared public censure from Israelis, Diaspora Jews, and 'progressive circles around the world' in the event of reconciliation with Francoist Spain. The anticipated reaction of the communist bloc and its supporters in Israel was also a source of concern. The retreat from the policy of non-alignment that Israel had declared at the beginning of its career as an independent state was drawing sharp criticism from the left-wing opposition, especially the socialist MAPAM, which was the most serious ideological rival of the social-democrat ruling party, MAPAI. Since the outbreak of the Korean War in the summer of 1950, Israel had increasingly identified itself with the Western camp. Although the Cold War had eroded its non-alignment policy, it still preferred to avoid unnecessary conflicts with the Soviet bloc. Rapprochement with Francoist Spain – which meant adopting the West's policy on yet another international issue – might anger Moscow and give the left-wing opposition at home an important propaganda weapon in its battle against the government's foreign policy. This concern demonstrates once more the persistent link between events in the domestic political sphere and the nature and timing of foreign policy decisions.

Further on in his memorandum, Darom discussed Spain's close ties with the Arab world and the possibility that the régime would prefer not to establish relations with Israel for fear of damaging those ties or its relations with the Vatican and with the Moslem population of Morocco. In such a case, the Spaniards were likely to reject an Israeli initiative, and 'we might lose both ways – the government will lose face at home and abroad, and there will be no real gain in the form of political relations.' He also noted that the number of Jews in Spain and Spanish Morocco was small and consequently Israel did not have much 'Jewish interest' there. Moreover, since Spain was not a member of the United Nations, it was less important to Israel than other states, whose membership in the organization gave them an influence on resolutions concerning the Middle East. The force of this argument was doubtful, since at the time the memorandum was written Spain was clearly moving towards inclusion in the subsidiary organizations of the United Nations, and its admission to the mother organization was merely a question of time.

The seven arguments offered in favour of continuing the hostile policy towards Spain were counterbalanced by 13 reasons for a change. The first argument on the pro-change side involved a principle too, albeit one without any moral overtones: Israel's desire to establish diplomatic relations with as many states as possible. According to Darom, it was difficult to justify opposition to Spain when Israel had already signed a reparations agreement with Germany, commenced negotiations with Austria, established a legation in Japan, and strengthened ties with various Third World regimes that were by no means model democracies – Perón's régime in Argentina, for example. The memorandum laid great emphasis on Spain's changed international status and its gradual incorporation into the 'family of nations' since November 1950, when the United Nations General Assembly had resolved to lift the diplomatic sanctions imposed on the régime four years earlier.[6] Following that resolution, foreign ambassadors began to stream back to Madrid, and the United Nations' subsidiary organizations began, one by one, to open their doors to Spain.

At the beginning of 1953, then, Israel was lagging behind these changes in the international arena; as Darom said:

> It should be remembered that when we came out against Spain in the United Nations in 1949, we were acting in accordance with a view prevailing among most of the other delegations; in the meantime, the majority has changed position.

The memorandum noted in particular the improving relations between Washington and Madrid, and the imprudence of adhering to an anti-Francoist policy now practised mainly by the Soviet bloc:

> We cannot swim against the tide. The improving relations between the US and Spain will undoubtedly lead other western countries to follow suit. It will be hard for us to insist on keeping to the sidelines. If we do, we will appear to be avoiding a step that has become inescapable, given our situation between east and west.

In presenting the geopolitical and military argument for ties with Spain, Darom relied in part on an assessment received a few weeks earlier from Col. Chaim Herzog, the former head of army intelligence who was then military attaché in Washington. Herzog predicted – correctly – that despite temporary setbacks in the United Nations, Tunisia and Morocco would soon win independence. This meant the possibility of an Arab threat to Israel's sea connection through 'our only main artery, the Mediterranean Sea'. He warned of a situation in which one side of the Strait of Gibraltar – the entrance to the Mediterranean Sea – would be hostile, its ports closed to Israeli ships or even serving as bases for attacks on Israel's supply lines throughout the sea; while on the other side the Iberian Peninsula comprised two states with which Israel had no diplomatic relations. Describing this possibility as 'fraught with disaster for our country',[7] Herzog had come to two unequivocal conclusions: first, Israel's security situation and its desire to break the blockade around it made relations with Spain imperative; and second, Spain's strategic location in the Mediterranean Sea obliged Israel to do everything possible to prevent a closer association between the Arabs and the Spaniards.

Establishing relations with Spain was also supposed to remove the obstacles in the way of ties with Portugal. Although in May 1948 Israel had refrained from sending an announcement of its new state-hood to either Franco's Spain or Salazar's Portugal, by March 1949 it was already making a distinction between the two dictatorships. Hoping for recognition by Lisbon, it informed the latter of the establishment of the State of Israel and the formation of its first government. Portuguese recognition, however, had been slow in coming.[8] Darom now proposed trying to establish relations with both Iberian states at the same time. Presenting this effort as a step in the development of Israel's Mediterranean policy would reduce the public impact of the Jewish state extending a hand to the Franco dictatorship.

There was also an economic motive. Political ties would facilitate the development of trade and shipping connections and permit co-ordination in cultivating and marketing citrus fruit. Israeli traders in the private sector had already initiated business ties with Spain and were urging the government to make their work easier by establishing formal relations. There were also contacts between government offices – at least between the Ministry of Agriculture and the Spanish government – concerning common interests. Thus, economic interests were joining the pro-Francoist lobby gradually forming in Israel, which also included members of the right-wing and centrist parties, the religious parties, and organizations of Sephardic Jews.

Darom also pointed out that, during the Second World War, Franco's Spain, 'with all its faults', had provided a temporary refuge to Jews fleeing to safety across the ocean; that it encouraged historical and literary research on the Jews of Spain and their medieval cultural heritage, within the framework of the Arias Montano Institute ('the propagandistic intent of this activity goes without saying, but it is undeniably based on deeds'); and that the immigration to Israel of Sephardic Jews from Bulgaria, Greece, and North Africa had 'increased the number of inhabitants in Israel who feel affinity and even sympathy for Spain'. Only limited importance was now attributed to public opinion in Israel and abroad, since in

Israel public opinion was already moving towards reconciliation with Spain, or could easily be prepared for it. World public opinion could be persuaded that rapprochement was mandated by circumstance.

Darom concluded his memorandum with the words:

> Despite hesitations and personal difficulty in deciding one way or another, I agree with many of our people in the legations and the ministry that the time has come to re-examine our position on Spain, and that we should at least investigate the possibility of establishing normal relations with Spain and Portugal.

Interestingly, the memorandum recommended that contact be maintained with the Duke of Terranova, who had been Spain's Consul-General in Jerusalem until the end of 1952 and who had recently been appointed Director of the Division of Religious Institutions at the Foreign Ministry in Madrid. Efforts could be made through him, said the memorandum, to sound out the Spanish Foreign Ministry's attitude. Terranova, who had never been respected or taken seriously while serving as Consul in Jerusalem, suddenly rose in the esteem of some of the Tel Aviv Foreign Ministry officials.

As on previous occasions, senior officials tried to choke off the developing debate. The Foreign Minister, Moshe Sharett, read Darom's memorandum, and promptly wrote to the Director-General of the Ministry that although it was clear that 'eventually we will have to take that step towards Spain, I do not believe the time has come yet.' His justification was that such a step would not give Israel any political benefit but would merely attract criticism from the Israeli public and Diaspora Jews. Sharett rejected the claim that the process of reconciliation with Germany warranted a softened attitude towards Spain as well:

> The compelling consideration in Spain's case is that the Franco régime was a loyal ally of Nazism and Fascism, that is to say, it yearned for their victory and saw its future in a world régime that was built on, among other things, the graves of the Jewish nation, and soaked with [that nation's] blood. The comparisons with Italy, Austria, and Japan, and even Germany, are not appropriate here, since in all those countries new régimes have arisen which have renounced, at least in word and most of them in deed, the bitter tradition of the former régime. Not so with Spain, where the same régime has remained intact without any change in nature or practice within the country.[9]

Sharett's views thus represented a repetition of the arguments of principle that Abba Eban had adduced in his United Nations speech in May 1949. He had, however, added a tactical element as well, in the idea that the time was not right for a change of position and in his acknowledgment that sooner or later such a change would have to be made. The boycott policy no longer existed, and when, a few weeks later, a Philippine Airline (PAL) plane carrying Spanish Foreign Minister Martín Artajo made a stopover in Lod on its way to Manila, Sharett made a point of instructing the Director-General of the Foreign Ministry to send someone from the protocol division over to the airport to greet the Spanish Minister and to ensure that all went smoothly there. An official from the protocol division exchanged greetings with the Spanish Minister, and the two conducted a conversation 'on various non-committal subjects'. No political importance attached to this stopover but, the protocol official said, before boarding the plane 'the minister thanked me very much, and asked me to convey his thanks and greetings to his "colleague"'. Both sides, however, preferred that Artajo's stopover receive no publicity, so that public opinion could not assign it a political significance it did not have. For this reason, the Spaniards had chosen a very early hour of the morning for the visit and Artajo did not leave the airport, to avoid attracting too much attention.[10] During a visit to Brazil in May 1953, in the course of a tour of South America, Sharett met the Spanish ambassador in Rio de Janeiro at a reception held by the Israeli Embassy, and greeted him with warm friendliness.[11]

In the meantime, Foreign Ministry officials continued to explore the issue of whether the Spanish government was still inclined to mend fences with Israel. They tried to find out whether the Spanish government had encouraged the articles appearing in the European press about the Madrid government's tolerant treatment of Jews and Israel's ingratitude in the United Nations towards a state that had helped save Jews in the the Second World War,[12] and they noted particularly that Spanish ambassadors in various capitals around the world continued to treat their Israeli counterparts in a friendly manner. The Spanish ambassador in The Hague displayed special cordiality towards Michael Amir, who reported to the Foreign Ministry: 'During the visit I had the impression there was a delicate, covert apology here, and an attempt to explain the situation and to do something about the relations, or lack of relations, between the two states.'[13] Spain's ambassador in Washington, José Félix de Lequerica, told Rabbi Maurice Perlzweig, one of the leaders of the

World Jewish Congress, of his strong desire to see diplomatic relations established between Spain and Israel, mentioning the Golden Age of the Jews of Spain and Spain's rescue operations during the Second World War. Lequerica – a cynical, opportunistic politician and one-time ambassador to Vichy who had been considered a notorious supporter of the Axis and who treated Jews with reserve – expressed his willingness to do 'almost anything' to put an end to 'the anomalous situation' of the relations between the two states.[14]

The debate in the Foreign Ministry did not cease, and from the end of 1952 Abba Eban, then performing the dual function of Permanent Representative at the United Nations and ambassador to Washington, was one of the main proponents of a policy change. From where he sat, in the country that led both the Western world and the process of rapprochement with Madrid, Israel's Spanish policy appeared 'antiquated and unrealistic'. Eban argued that normalizing Israel's relations with Spain would not imply support for, or legitimization of, the dictatorship installed there: 'Harmful régimes of this kind exist in other states with which Israel maintains normal relations.'[15] Eban wrote to the Foreign Ministry three times, and urged its administrators to work for the establishment of normal relations with Spain and to accustom public opinion to the idea that such a step was vital. Eban, like the other advocates of relations with Spain, stressed the possibility that such a connection would improve Israel's relations with other Latin and Catholic states, the danger that the creation of a Hispano-Arab alliance would pose to Israel, and the immediate practical importance of securing the goodwill of a country which was gradually gaining admittance to international organizations.[16] An example of this 'immediate practical importance' was Spain's vote in favour of Israel at the conference of the United Nations Food and Agricultural Organization held in Rome. On that occasion, Spain was in the minority of states supporting Israel's wish to be considered part of the group of Middle Eastern members of the organization rather than part of the European bloc.[17]

This advocacy by Eban, one of Israel's senior diplomats, bore fruit. It led the Deputy Director-General of the Foreign Ministry, Arye Levavi, to draw up a memorandum that included a recommendation to set up an Israeli consulate in Barcelona as a first step towards establishing normal relations with Spain. This was not the first time that the idea of opening a consulate in Spain as a way of establishing some sort of foothold on the Iberian Peninsula had been mooted in internal debates. The Spanish consulate in Jerusalem had received reports of such discussions from journalistic sources back at the beginning of 1951. In the fall of that year, the Spanish Consul, Terranova, had even suggested to Madrid that it invite Israel to appoint a trade representative with consular powers in Barcelona, but Foreign Minister Artajo rejected the idea. In the summer of 1953, Knesset member Eliahu Eliachar also tried to organize a petition by several Knesset members urging the government to open a consular legation in Spain as a first step towards full diplomatic relations.[18] Only at the end of 1953, however, was an official recommendation to that effect made, with the backing of senior officials in the Foreign Ministry.

Foreign Minister Sharett, for his part, requested data on the volume of shipping and trade between the two countries and the number of countries that maintained consulates in Spain.[19] He was evidently trying to strengthen the economic and commercial arguments, as well as stressing other countries' conduct as a counterweight to the moral and ideological arguments against change before he broached the idea of establishing a consulate in the Catalonian capital to his government colleagues.

By the end of 1953, Ministry officials had finished gathering data on the advantages that Israel would reap by forging ties of some kind with Spain, and a coherent recommendation concerning the appointment of an Israeli consul in Barcelona could be made. The report prepared by Dr Joel Barromi, Head Administrative Assistant in the Latin American division, gave priority to economic considerations, listing three specific justifications for relations: sea connections, air connections, and the expansion of trade. The management of ZIM, the Israeli shipping company, judged that the establishment of regular relations with Spain and Portugal would give the Israeli merchant fleet's activities in the Iberian Peninsula a substantial boost. Its assessment was that, although Israeli ships had so far been treated well and had not suffered from any discrimination, a consular mission would be able to facilitate ZIM's operations in Spain considerably. The report noted that between September 1952 and November 1953, Israeli ships had paid 24 visits to the Iberian Peninsula, 17 of them to Spain.[20] As for air connections, the absence of relations with Spain and Portugal hampered efforts to develop flight routes from Israel to Latin America. El Al, Israel's national airline, had asserted that any flights to Latin America would have to stop over on the Iberian Peninsula, but the lack of ties with those countries ruled out such a possibility.

In the absence of diplomatic relations, commercial ties had not developed very far either. The establishment of political ties was likely to permit the expansion of bilateral trade in various fields. Members of the Israeli Citrus Marketing Board showed interest in various agricultural study courses in Spain. Still more important, however, was the fact that during 1953 Spain began to look like a potential source of arms. Pursuant to Spain's agreement with the United States in September of the same year, the Spanish army was to receive new weaponry and to develop a local arms industry. Israel, accordingly, might some day be able to buy Spanish weapons or outdated military surplus, as Egypt had already begun to do.[21] According to Barromi's report, the Spanish government was also showing interest in developing commercial ties with Israel. A representative of Israel's Discount Bank, in Spain for a visit, had made contact with the Banco Exterior de España, whose principal stockholder was the Spanish government and whose former director was now the Minister of Trade. The Spanish bank had expressed its willingness to sign agreements with Discount Bank and to encourage trade between the two countries.

As to political considerations, the report emphasized first of all Spain's traditional ties with the Arab world – ties that had grown closer since the end of the Second World War as Spain tried to break free from the international isolation imposed on it. Indeed, at the time the memorandum was written, Spain's relations with the Arabs seemed to be at a high point. Following Artajo's tour of the Middle East in April 1952, Spain concluded a series of cultural and friendship agreements with most of the Arab states. King Idris of Libya, Ahmed Shukeiri, the Deputy Secretary of the Arab League, the Iraqi Defence Minister, the Syrian Foreign Minister, and the Saudi Interior Minister all visited Madrid in the following months. In the second half of 1953, Spain's diplomatic legations in Iraq, Lebanon, and Jordan were upgraded to embassies.[22]

In Spanish Morocco, the Moroccan nationalists were allowed greater licence – at least, so long as most of their actions were directed against the French. The Spanish High Commissioner, General Rafael García Valiño, instituted a more flexible policy than that of his predecessor, José Varela, who had passed away in 1951. The Spaniards took advantage of France's growing difficulties in Morocco, sharply denouncing the overthrow of the legitimate sultan, Mohammed ben-Yusuf, his exile to Madagascar in August 1953, and his replacement by a puppet sultan, an elderly, docile cousin by the name of Molai Mohammed ben-Arafa. This last step had been taken without any prior consultation with Madrid, to the Spanish government's open displeasure. Friday prayers in the mosques of Spanish Morocco continued to be recited in the name of the deposed sultan, Mohammed V, in recognition of his status as the true ruler. The anniversary of his coronation, 18 November, was celebrated with great fanfare that year. Franco expressed sympathy for 'the natural aspirations of the Moroccan people', and even encouraged autonomous Moroccan rule in the Spanish sector.

By these actions, Franco gave Spain the appearance of a progressive colonial power and a friend to the Arabs, in contrast to France and Britain, which suffered from their image as hated imperialistic powers. Ironically, in January 1954, the Spanish High Commissioner in Morocco declared that the world was threatened by two dangers: communism and colonialism. The Spanish press also talked of the possibility of co-operation between Spain and the Arabs in their struggle against the control that their 'common enemy', Britain, exercised over Gibraltar and the Suez Canal. However, Franco's policy afforded the Spanish protectorate only temporary immunity against the spreading nationalistic unrest in Morocco. By setting himself up as a defender of Moroccan nationalism against French colonialism, Franco did not leave himself a very wide margin for manoeuvre should France's policy change – and it did change, unilaterally, at the end of 1954, as successive governments in Paris strove to free their country from an irksome colonial burden.

In an attempt to reduce the gap between pompous rhetoric and negligible trade relations, a Hispano-Arab economic conference met in May 1953, in Valencia, attended by delegates from Egypt, Syria, Lebanon, Jordan, and Iraq. In its wake, Spain and Egypt signed a payments agreement. Madrid even considered the possibility that Spain would serve as a storage and transit depot for Arab merchandise destined for export to Latin America, thereby becoming a connecting link between the two blocs of states on which Spain had depended since the end of the Second World War.[23]

Barromi believed that an Israeli overture towards Spain had a chance of succeeding for four reasons. First, Madrid was still interested in appeasing international and Jewish public opinion, although that interest was waning. Second, it wanted to gain influence among Sephardic Jews. Third, it wanted some say over the Christian holy places on Israeli territory and to ensure good conditions for Spanish pilgrims travelling to Israel.[24] Finally, there was a fundamental contradiction between continuing the Spanish colonial régime in Morocco and supporting Arab nationalism. The Israeli diplomat concluded with the usual, though inaccurate, cliché that Franco himself had

> never showed any anti-Semitic tendencies, and does not show open fondness for the Arabs, as shown by the repressive measures he has taken towards Arabs in Morocco at various times. He will decide the question of Israel as every other question, on the basis of cold calculation, without any loyalty.

The Israeli Foreign Ministry believed that Spain wished to keep operating the consulate it had established in Jerusalem back in the mid-nineteenth century, and that Madrid knew that the consulate's continued operation was a function of the legal ambiguity that characterized the status of all the foreign consuls in the city at the time. Accordingly, Israeli officials reasoned that the Spaniards would welcome the opening of an Israeli consulate in Barcelona, since that would put the consular relations between the countries on a mutual basis (Spain also had an honorary consul in Haifa). The fact that opening a consulate was not a conspicuous political step and that it was slated for Barcelona rather than the capital, Madrid, was supposed to make it easier both for Israel to contend with adverse public opinion and for the Spanish government to ignore possible Arab protests.[25] At the time, 23 states operated consulates in Barcelona (over 30 states had diplomatic relations with Spain at that point).

This port city was also presented as the best place to install an Israeli legation because it was the capital of Catalonia – a major industrial and commercial centre where there was considerable interest in developing economic ties with the Middle East. The local Jewish community, then about 2,000 strong and growing, was expected to help the Israeli consulate both with its activities and its relations with the authorities. Other arguments intended to convince the doubtful included the encouragement that the establishment of a consulate would provide to the small community of Spanish Jews and the larger community in Spanish Morocco, and the need to offer consular protection to the hundreds of Israelis who had begun to visit Spain – some of them on diplomatic passports – for holidays, business, or in order to participate in international conventions (the Spanish Consul in Jerusalem exaggerated, however, in saying that

Spain had already become a fashionable destination for Jewish tourism).[26]

Since, at the time, Israeli newspapers of the centre and right wing had already called for the establishment of diplomatic relations with Spain, Barromi's memorandum suggested promoting similar articles in other papers and publicizing the aid that Spain had extended to Jews during the Second World War. In the event of adverse public opinion, Barromi advised that emphasis be laid on the fact that it was a consulate, not an embassy, that was contemplated – although, within the Foreign Ministry itself, the consulate had been presented all along as a first step towards full diplomatic relations between the two countries. Here emphasis should again be laid on the role played by *Herut* and the General Zionists in preparing the ground for a rapprochement with Spain. Their Knesset representatives and their respective organs, primarily the dailies *Herut* and *Haboker*, called on the public to rid itself of socialistic ideological considerations and take into account only 'national interests' of foreign policy and economic needs which demanded the establishment of relations with Spain. The fact that the nature of the régime in Spain was contrary to the accepted political culture of Israel was irrelevant, since it was not Israel's business to interfere in the internal affairs of other countries.

A caustic article appeared in *Herut,* for example, attacking remarks published in the newspaper *Davar* – including one identifying the Franco régime with Hitler's national-socialist régime. The *Herut* article was entitled 'Insolent Attack on Spain'. 'Is the government of Israel working for the Cominform or the Spanish socialists and anarchists?' asked A. Shamai. 'Are we really interested in putting Spain on the side of the Arab League? Surely we have no objective quarrel with Spain' – the same Spain that had saved Jewish lives during the Holocaust and that wielded influence in the Catholic world and in Latin America.[27]

Articles of this type represented an effort to strike at the government's policy, as well as a desire to represent the economic lobbies that were associated with these parties. These groups were joined by many Sephardic notables who touted the 'Golden Age' of Spanish Jews, and Spain's actions on behalf of Jews in the two world wars. Particularly active in this respect were Knesset members Eliahu Eliachar and Binyamin Arditi, as well as David Siton, Yitzhak Molko, and others.[28]

The Deputy Director-General, Levavi, passed Barromi's report on to the Director-General, Eytan, with this comment attached: 'I wholeheartedly recommend opening a consulate in Barcelona in the spring of 1954'.[29] Eytan, a fervent anti-Francoist – as he kept reminding Sharett – was still not to be persuaded. As a means of solving the problem of Israel's relations with the Iberian Peninsula without establishing ties with Spain, he suggested opening a consulate in Lisbon rather than Barcelona.[30] Levavi insisted:

> As a small, isolated Mediterranean nation, we cannot afford, in my view, to ignore forever a well-established reality. A consulate in Barcelona shouldn't make any political waves. The commercial, Jewish, maritime, and other justifications are real ones, and can serve as effective camouflage. In Lisbon we will achieve no real immediate purpose, and are unlikely to approach any more distant aim.[31]

A few days later, six senior officials held a consultation in the Foreign Ministry. All those present supported rapprochement with Spain. Notable among those speaking in favour of the move was Emile Najar, head of the West European division, who for some years had been in touch with Spanish diplomats in an effort to promote a dialogue between Israel and Spain. To underline the issue's urgency, Najar described a conversation he had held with the new Spanish Consul-General in Jerusalem, Pedro López García. The latter had hinted that Israel should make haste if it wanted to improve its relations with Madrid, because 'a time will come when [Israel] will have trouble establishing ties with Spain, owing to the [latter's] close relations with the Arabs.'[32]

Avraham Darom also agreed in principle to the idea of opening a consulate, but asked that such a step not be taken too hastily.

> The government is based on MAPAI, which is an active member of the Socialist International. This organization is still hostile to Franco. Persuading MAPAI will therefore be difficult, and will require some advance preparation.

In MAPAI there was indeed substantial opposition to ties with the Francoist dictatorship. Reuven Barkatt, Secretary-General of MAPAI and a Knesset member, had prepared a document, circulated to all members of the Socialist International, which presented a position sympathetic to the principle of universal membership in the United Nations – with certain reservations. Barkatt explained, for example, that the possible membership of Francoist Spain – a country he described as 'a fascist state' – did not accord with the organization's ideals. Meir Argov, Chairman of the Knesset's Security and Foreign Affairs Committee, and a supporter of non-alignment, did not conceal the repugnance he felt as a socialist at the idea of any contact with Franco. The *Histadrut*, which was also under MAPAI's hegemony, periodically came out with declarations of support for the workers of Spain and their struggle against Francoist tyranny.[33]

Another reason Darom gave for delaying all initiatives concerning Spain was the conflict just then breaking out between Spain and France over Morocco: 'Any step on our part towards Spain may harm our good relations with France. It is imperative to wait until this quarrel dies down.'

During the debate it was pointed out that the Foreign Ministry's proposed budget for the coming financial year already contained provision for establishing a consulate in Barcelona, though stress was laid on the fact that some of the budget items were bound to be cut and that if the ministry wanted to maintain the provision it would have to defend it vigorously. Both Najar and Levavi recommended trying to co-ordinate the opening of a consulate in Barcelona with the opening of a consulate in communist China as a way of minimizing potential left-wing criticism of the softened attitude towards Spain.

Sharett's response was prompt: 'I am in favour of opening a consulate in Barcelona', he wrote, underlining every word. He added that approval would be required from the government, or at least the Ministerial Committee on Security and Foreign Affairs. He rejected the idea of establishing a consulate in China, however. Unlike Spain, Sharett wrote, China offered 'no trade, no visits, no ships'.[34]

It is unlikely that Spain would have welcomed an Israeli proposal to set up a consulate at the beginning of 1954. In the summer of 1953, when the Consul in Jerusalem reported talk he had heard about establishing a consular presence in Barcelona, the Foreign Ministry in Madrid immediately instructed him to take steps to delay any contacts tending in that direction. When, in February 1954, he reported another rumour that he had heard about the possibility of the Jewish Agency opening an office in Spain that would also act as a connecting link between the two states, the Consul was asked to explain to Agency officials that it was not the moment to establish an office in Spain.[35]

A telegram the Spanish Foreign Ministry circulated among its legations in the Middle East said that lately Israel had been making overtures towards Spain, in the context of which various ideas had been mooted, from the institution of an honorary consulate to the establishment of full diplomatic relations. The telegram pointed out that the State of Israel had conducted a hostile policy towards Spain since its foundation and that establishing relations with it would have a negative impact in the Arab world.[36]

Madrid loses interest in Israel

At the beginning of 1953, Pedro López García replaced the Duke of Terranova as Spain's Consul-General in Jerusalem.[37] Unlike the Duke, the new Consul made no intensive efforts to further the cause of diplomatic relations between Spain and Israel. Under López García, the consulate seemed to lose some of the vitality that had characterized its activities in Terranova's time. It also lost its capacity to promote material improvement in relations between the two countries. This was partly because of differences in the personalities of the two Consuls, but officials in the Foreign Ministry (which was moved to Jerusalem in the summer of 1953)[38] attributed the new Consul's behaviour primarily to Madrid's waning interest in forming political ties with Israel. The report prepared by Joel Barromi at the end of 1953, which included the recommendation to establish an Israeli consulate in Barcelona, remarked:

> The previous consul, the Duke of Terranova, has more than once made overtures concerning the establishment of regular diplomatic ties between Israel and Spain. The present consul, López, has so far refrained from taking any clear steps in this direction. This may be an indication of Arab influence in Madrid.[39]

Nevertheless, the Consul did take the trouble to inform the Foreign Ministry that it should make haste if it wanted to establish relations with Madrid, 'because of its increasingly close relations with the Arabs.'[40]

As Israel lost importance in Spain's eyes, various organizations and other entities in Israel made greater efforts to foster rapprochement with Madrid, and articles favourable to Francoist Spain frequently appeared in the Israeli press. The new Consul reacted to most of these friendly manifestations with a mixture of suspicion and hostility, usually declining to encourage them. Behind every one of these initiatives he saw the long arm of the Israeli government – a government seeking credit for diplomatic achievements in a period when its international standing was problematic – even in the case of completely private undertakings or actions by members of the opposition. Apparently unable to grasp the dynamics of democratic political life, this representative of the Francoist dictatorship was prey to various conspiracy theories and negative images of Israel and Jews.

In the fall of 1953, the Israel–Spain Friendship League was established in Tel Aviv. The new organization, founded by a group of right-wing anti-communists headed by the lawyer Rafael Mani, stated its purpose as the creation of an atmosphere more propitious to rapprochement with Spain. In his speech at the foundation ceremony, Mani said:

> I cannot accept the way leagues of friendship with mortal enemies and notorious haters of Zion have blossomed in our midst owing to the presence here of traitors and Diaspora-minded Jews, and to the lack of a handful of honest, openhearted people to declare out loud that only those states showing us peace and good-will deserve close relations; and who more than Spain and its people is worthy in all respects? Spain, after all, was one of the saviors of this country's Jews in World War I, and Franco's government was in fact one of those which saved Jews from extermination by the Nazis [. . .]
>
> For Spain, although devoutly Catholic, strongly wishes to recognize us, and has even sent a distinguished personality of the Spanish people here to us, the Duke of Terranova, who earned considerable credit in the old *Yishuv* in this country back in World War I [. . .]; and how shameful that our government crassly spurned the hand extended to us. Why did it do that? Was not Stalin's régime an ally of Hitler and the Nazis in those days of trouble for all humankind? And if Franco's régime saw fit to protect its country from communism by means of Hitler's régime, did it thereby sin against us? Did Franco's régime soil its hands with the blood of Jews? History will judge Franco favourably for having dared to eradicate communism from his country and for erecting an iron curtain against Stalin's régime.[41]

To express its warm feelings for Spain, the League flew the Spanish flag over the building housing its offices on 12 October, 'Hispanidad Day' – the anniversary of Columbus's arrival in the New World.

The Spanish Consul, reporting back to Madrid on the new League's activities, expressed doubt concerning the real intentions of the League's President, attorney Rafael Mani. Those intentions seemed dubious to him, mainly because Mani and the other leaders of the organization were Ashkenazic, 'something which increases my suspicions concerning their sincerity'.[42] López placed greater trust in another group that was trying to establish a similar organization in Jerusalem since its members were Sephardic and focused on cultural activities. Even so, the Consul offered no encouragement to this group either.

During November and December of that year, the Secretary of the Israel–Spain Friendship League, Moshe Galili, visited Madrid. Although the Spaniards remained unmoved in the face of Israeli friendship initiatives during those months – fearing that Israel was trying to sabotage their relations with the Arabs – Madrid officials did not want to give Galili the impression that no one wished to see him. As one of the heads of Spanish diplomacy wrote, it was, after all, 'impossible to ignore the considerable power of the Jewish people, including Jews in the US, [. . . and even the Arabs] admit that Israel cannot be expected to disappear'.[43] Accordingly, Galili met with middle-ranking Spanish officials, telling them he had come with Sharett's blessing and the knowledge of the Israeli Foreign Ministry. According to him, Israel had renounced the position it had taken in 1949. It desired Spain's mediation in its dispute with the Arab countries and was interested in establishing a branch of the Jewish Agency in Madrid.[44] Galili urged the Duke of Terranova, a good friend of Mani's and currently head of the Spanish Foreign Ministry's Division of Religious Affairs, to encourage pilgrimages to Israel and to work on establishing an Israel–Spain friendship league in Madrid.[45]

This initiative, too, was purely personal and completely un-supported by the senior officials of the Foreign Ministry. They were, in fact, reluctant to co-operate with such a strongly right-wing group. The Spaniards, however – who at first had actually mistaken Galili for Israel Galili, a *Haganah* commander and later one of the leaders of *Ahdut Ha'avodah* – had no way of knowing this, lacking as they did any direct communication channel to the Israeli administration. They saw Galili and other Israelis who made overtures to Spanish diplomats in Europe as semi-official envoys. The Israelis, by contrast, had no intention of seeking Spanish mediation, or of using a minor Finance Ministry functionary such as Galili for political errands. When Arab newspapers printed reports of Galili's 'political mission', a spokesman for the Israeli Foreign Ministry quickly clarified that the Israeli government had not established any contact with the Spanish authorities or with their representatives in any state, nor had it authorized anyone else to do so on its behalf. The Spaniards' interpretation of this was that the failure of Israel's efforts at rapprochement, revealed by the Arab press, had forced the government to deny everything.[46]

None the less, Arab governments were perturbed by the reports of Israel's efforts to move closer to Spain. Spanish diplomats warned that any change in Madrid's attitude towards Israel would damage its relations with the Arabs and endanger their support for Spain in the international arena.[47] Spain's ambassador in Cairo correctly pointed out that 'recognition [of Israel] will be much more serious and spectacular [now] than it might have been had it taken place unobtrusively when the other powers recognized Israel'.[48] Accordingly, Madrid immediately set about reassuring the Arab countries. The ambassador in Cairo was instructed to state that Spain had never thought of establishing relations of any kind with Israel or of acceding to an Israeli request to mediate between Jerusalem and the Arabs.[49]

The reactions of the Spanish Consul in Jerusalem to what was taking place in Israel were clear from his cables concerning an economic conference in the city. The participants in this conference, he said, included 'all the prominent American–Jewish–Masonic figures of banking and finance'. Some of his reports, reflecting the Francoist dictatorship's obsession with freemasonry, informed Madrid of the establishment of an independent Israeli framework for freemasons, and of the 'Judaism–Masonry alliance, whose two components naturally complement each other'. As if this were not enough, he depicted the heads of the Jewish community in Spain as agents of the Israeli government working to further its interests, and warned against Israeli tourists who extended their stay in Spain and began economic activities on its territory. The Consul feared not only Marxist infiltration but also the awakening of a 'Jewish problem' in Spain – a problem suffered by other countries but from which Spain had been free since the end of the fifteenth century, thanks to the wisdom of Ferdinand and Isabella. Accordingly, he recommended keeping a strict eye on the activities of the Jewish communities in Spain, and on the education these Jews gave their children.[50]

During 1954, worrying reports reached Jerusalem concerning Spain's increasingly close relations with the Arab countries and its waning readiness to develop political relations of any kind with Israel. After another visit to Madrid in January 1954, the Deputy Secretary of the Arab League, Ahmed Shukeiri, published a report that Israel had asked to establish diplomatic relations with Spain and that Spain had refused. The Spanish government did not comment, finding it convenient to let the Arabs believe the story. The report also quoted the Spanish Foreign Minister, Martín Artajo, as follows: 'Spain does not desire to establish relations with Israel, and it wants to take all possible steps with the Pope to safeguard the holy places in Palestine'.[51] That year, the Spanish government decided to establish the Institute of Hispanic–Arab Culture in Madrid, as well as the Generalissimo Franco Hispanic–Arab College, which was designed to accommodate up to 100 Arab students and researchers. An exhibition of Spanish products left Barcelona for a tour of the Arab countries.

In April, General Franco met the Secretary-General of the Arab League, Abdul Khalek Hassouna, in Madrid. On the same day, the new ambassador of Iraq presented his credentials to the Spanish dictator. The visit by Hassouna, who presented himself as an admirer of Spain and Franco, highlighted the unresolved problems in Spain's relations with the Arabs. The guest asked to visit Spanish Morocco, and the Spanish press was instructed to use caution in reporting his pronouncements regarding Morocco's future. A major press conference planned for Hassouna in Madrid following his return from Tetuan was cancelled at the very last minute on the orders of the Spanish Foreign Ministry.[52]

None the less, Spain's orientation remained irrevocably pro-Arab. One of the editors of the British *Times* told Israel's press attaché in London that while visiting Spain he had come across 'hostile, extremist' anti-Israeli propaganda. The Spanish Foreign Minister had told him explicitly that 'Spain would vigorously oppose any relations with Israel, since it saw itself as someday heading a major Moslem bloc'.[53] His bluntness may have been due to the fact that he was talking to a journalist, but Spain's interest in Israel and readiness to move towards it had clearly diminished considerably since 1949–50, when Spain had still felt itself to be an international pariah.

Spain's coolness towards Israel was notable on a number of occasions during those months. For example, the Israeli navy was refused permission to cross Spanish territorial waters during exercises in the western Mediterranean.[54] Spain's attitude was even clearer in the realm of sports – a sphere in which politics always plays a part. When the Spanish soccer federation proposed to send the Atlético Madrid team to Israel for a series of games, the Spanish Foreign Ministry vetoed the idea.[55] Moreover, in 1954 the Spaniards

informed Israel that Israeli athletes would not be allowed to participate in the Mediterranean Olympic Games that were scheduled to be
held in Barcelona the following year. This decision provoked a wave
of protests in Israel and the United States. Spain's representatives
argued unconvincingly that Israel had not taken part in the first
Mediterranean games held in Alexandria in 1951, and that Spain was
only inviting the Alexandria participants. Israel encouraged criticism
of Spain's decision in the United States, claiming that it had been
influenced by Arab pressure. Emanuel Celler, a Jewish congressman
from New York who had been publicly sympathetic towards Spain
since meeting with Franco, demanded explanations from Spain's
ambassador to Washington, José María de Areilza. The United States
representative on the international Olympic committee told Spanish
diplomats that Israel had not participated in the Alexandria games
because it was then at war with Egypt but that situation bore no
resemblance to Israel's relations with Spain. In any case, sports and
politics were not to be so blatantly mixed.[56]

Artajo was angered by this criticism. In telegrams to the
ambassador in Washington he argued that although there was no
state of war or outright political friction between the two states,
'Israel [had] no right to ask for anything, since it [had] been in the
front line of Spain's enemies at every international assembly and by
its own wish [did] not have relations with Spain'. Artajo explained
that inviting Israel to Barcelona would lead the Arab countries to
boycott the games, and that Spain owed them preferential treatment
because of their loyal friendship. There was no question of animosity
towards the 'Jewish race', he added, since Spain had helped save Jews
in the world war. Zionism and the State of Israel, however, were
another matter, since they had 'shown hostility towards Spain by
their own choice'.[57]

At the beginning of 1955, Spain's ambassador to Brussels, the
Conde Casa Miranda, who took a friendly view of Israel, explicitly
told ambassador Yosef Ariel, 'We will not make any sort of gesture
now which might hurt the Arabs' feelings, although we have no
illusions as to the military and economic value of the Arab states.'[58]
The Foreign Ministry in Jerusalem began to receive the impression
that Spain's attitude towards Israel had deteriorated considerably.

After the military treaty between Spain and the United States was
signed, Madrid could afford to give its pro-Arab policy an anti-
French and anti-British character. This was clearly reflected in,
among other things, the encouragement the Spanish authorities gave

the Moroccan nationalists who were fighting French rule in Rabat. The Spaniards waged a psychological war against France's Moroccan policy but were careful not to take any overly radical steps, such as declaring the protectorate's Caliph as regent, or the Spanish zone as an independent kingdom. The intention was not to cause an international crisis over Morocco, but to ensure French recognition of Spain's status and rights in North Africa and the Mediterranean, and to enhance Spain's prestige in the eyes of the Arabs. As the Spanish ambassador in Brussels told his Israeli counterpart:

> It's true we have scores to settle with France [. . .] They certainly behave badly towards Spain. But the purpose of our demonstration against the French policy in Morocco was to win the Arab peoples' friendship for Spain. And we've succeeded very well in this. We have quiet in Spanish Morocco, and great sympathy in the Arab world.[59]

In January 1954, the political committee of the Arab League did in fact decide to support Spain's position on Morocco and also on Gibraltar, which Spain had lost at the beginning of the eighteenth century and which is still in British hands today.[60] London worriedly watched both this development and Spain's supply of arms to Egypt during a time when Anglo-Egyptian negotiations over the Suez Canal were in crisis. Since the beginning of 1952, London had repeatedly asked the Spanish government to stop selling war matériel to Cairo. Each time Spain reassured the British that it understood their position and would send no further shipments to Egypt. Yet the shipments continued, and the British could do nothing but protest again.[61] The overthrow of King Farouk by a military coup in July 1952, and the subsequent declaration of a republic, did not damage relations between Cairo and Madrid. On the contrary, the nationalist officers admired General Franco: he had won the Civil War, he had managed to withstand the pressures of the major powers, he had not hesitated to adopt a policy different from that of colonialist France and Britain, and he did not recognize Israel.

The increasingly close relations between Spain and the Arabs led Joel Barromi to compose a new memorandum in the fall of 1954, calling for the speedy establishment of an Israeli consulate in Barcelona. 'Clearly, any further delay may compromise the chances of success in this direction once and for all.'[62] The memorandum was, for the most part, a repetition of the report Barromi had written in December 1953, with a few additions and corrections. Again emphasis was laid on the economic advantages that Israel could gain from relations with Spain. The new memorandum gave still greater weight to Spain's value as a possible source of arms for Israel. It also heavily stressed what had long been a solid fact: 'The present Spanish régime is stronger today than ever before. There is no hope of its overthrow or a change in its character in the near future.' The natural conclusion was, of course, that Israel would have to adjust to this reality quickly, particularly since the Arab countries were trying to make Spain an active partner against Israel. The national unrest in Morocco further highlighted the fact that the absence of an Israeli presence in Spain made assisting the Jews of North Africa difficult.

Sharett wavers

Ben-Gurion's resignation from the premiership in December 1953 put Moshe Sharett into the most senior post in the executive branch. For almost two years – from January 1954 to November 1955 – Sharett played a dual role, as Prime Minister and Foreign Minister. Finally convinced that a consulate in Barcelona was an important first step in the process of normalizing relations with Spain, he now found himself with a golden opportunity to make a breakthrough in this direction. In fact, however, nothing happened. Sharett did not prove a confident, resolute Prime Minister; his leadership was on occasion wavering and timid. More than once he was obliged to out-manoeuvre various members of the government who tried to exploit his weaknesses. These circumstances apparently discouraged him from raising such a controversial issue as forming ties – even if only on the consular level – with Nationalist Spain. When Sharett vacated the Prime Minister's office at the end of 1955, the relations between Israel and Spain were almost exactly where they had been at the beginning of 1954 – 'almost' because in the interim two years had passed, and time was of critical importance. Every postponement of an Israeli initiative, every period of inactivity, diminished the chances that Madrid would look with favour on an approach from Jerusalem. Spain's relations with the Arab world were steadily improving, while Israel had missed the opportunity to secure a foothold on the Iberian Peninsula.

None the less, pressure for a change in the policy on Spain continued in the Foreign Ministry throughout this period. Yosef Ariel, Israel's ambassador to Brussels, was now one of the leading advocates of rapid action. While the heads of the Foreign Ministry in

Jerusalem were discussing the possibility of establishing a consulate in Barcelona, Ariel raised a new idea:

> We should investigate the possibility of sending a diplomatic agent (perhaps in the guise of a consul or consular agent) to Tangier. Tangier is a very important observation station [for events in both North Africa and the Iberian Peninsula].[63]

However, the Foreign Ministry did not adopt this suggestion either.

Israel's representative in Tokyo, Yosef Linton, joined those clamouring for normal relations with Spain. 'We were able to rein in our emotions when we discussed reparations from Germany. Reality dictates that Israel do the same with respect to Franco.'[64] The Latin American division called for speedy action in the direction of Spain, which was 'starting to take on an international importance it [had] not had since perhaps the days of the Armada [in the sixteenth century]'.[65] The division heads recommended that some sort of representative be sent to Spain, even under cover as a journalist or academic, with the task of nurturing cultural and economic relations and stimulating public sympathy. This plan, never implemented in the 1950s, was attempted unsuccessfully by the Foreign Ministry in the mid-1960s, when Ionnathan Pratto was sent to Madrid, supposedly to collect material for historical research. The experiment was repeated with much greater success at the beginning of the 1980s, when Israel sent Shmuel Hadas to live in Madrid. Officially, Hadas was Israel's representative to the World Tourism Organization, which has its headquarters in Madrid. In practice, he was Israel's unofficial ambassador in Spain, where he strove to enlist support in political, economic, cultural, and media circles. Some six years later the two states finally established full diplomatic relations, and Hadas became Israel's first ambassador to Spain.[66]

The year 1954 saw another in the series of mediation attempts that had been initiated by prominent figures in the Spanish Jewish community since 1949. Many of these would-be mediators, as we have seen, made themselves into tools of Francoist diplomacy, in the hope of ensuring the continuation of the dictatorship's tolerant treatment of Jews or furthering personal interests, or else out of a sincere desire to support the State of Israel in general and the Sephardic Jews living there in particular. Enrique Benarroya, a Jewish businessman born in Spanish Morocco and a leader of the Jewish community in Barcelona, asked Israel's representative in Switzerland to apprise Jerusalem of his offer to mediate between the two countries. Benarroya had already tried in the past to bring the two states together and had even earned praise from the Spanish Foreign Ministry for his efforts. He told Israel's representative in Bern that Bechor Shitreet, a MAPAI member and himself a Sephardic Jew who served as Police Minister from 1948 to 1967, had asked him to 'sound out the government of Spain to see whether it would be willing to establish official relations with the State of Israel.' Benarroya met with the Spanish Foreign Minister, Martín Artajo, who – according to Benarroya – had agreed that he could 'try his luck in Israel'.[67]

The Foreign Ministry in Jerusalem was still not enthusiastic about using Jews living in Spain as mediators between the two states, and Benarroya's initiative was scrapped. In his response to the Israeli representative in Switzerland, Director-General Eytan wrote: 'This is not the first Jew to appoint himself a mediator between Spain and us. We do not usually require the services of such people, no matter how good their intentions.' In the same year, the Ministry also rejected similar efforts by Jewish Agency workers and members of the World Jewish Congress.[68]

It was not only the difficulty of making political decisions that delayed action on Spain. A much more prosaic obstacle was financing such action – a problem that led the Foreign Ministry to defer the plan for a consulate in Barcelona time after time. In February 1954, the Director-General was already writing:

> We included that consulate in our draft budget for 1954/55, but it was cut, together with every other new proposal we presented, for reasons of economy. Accordingly, it seems unlikely that such a consulate will open this year.[69]

In October of that year, a day after receiving Barromi's new memorandum, the Deputy Director-General, Arye Levavi – who favoured the idea of a Barcelona consulate – was notified that the plan would have to be shelved once again. He wrote 'regretfully' to Director-General Eytan, insisting that efforts to gain a foothold in Spain must not cease.[70] Eytan's response was to request a re-examination of Sharett's position, and his authorization to include the wherewithal for establishing a consulate in Spain in the Ministry's new budget proposal. Sharett sent back a handwritten, one-word reply: 'yes'.[71] But once again, 'to my great sorrow, the budget controller has cut all our proposals (including the reserve) that exceed the 1954/55 budget, and I fear that in 1955/56, we will not even be able to continue employing the Ministry's current staff'.[72] None the less, if the Prime Minister and Foreign Minister had taken a clear and resolute stand in favour of a consulate in Spain, the budgetary problem could presumably have been circumvented in some way.

As Israel procrastinated over its Spanish policy, various other considerations kept arising that dictated still further postponement of a change. On one occasion it was said that the establishment of relations with Spain might rekindle the public debate over relations with Germany; on another, it was claimed that given the tension between Spain and France over Morocco, a rapprochement with Spain might endanger Israel's good relations with Paris. An additional argument was the great sensitivity of Asian countries such as Burma and India to Israel's position on Spain. The Director-General of the Foreign Ministry was, at the time, under the strong impression – which later proved unfounded – that 'the fact that we have no relations with Spain is a serious political asset in the eyes of the Asian nations, and we must discuss it carefully before coming to any decision'. Eytan wrote to Israel's representative in Tokyo that during his visit to India two years previously he had noted that the official Indian position praised Israel for two things: its recognition of the Beijing government in 1950 and its lack of any kind of relations with Francoist Spain.[73] Later, the elections of the summer of 1955 were on the horizon, and as the ambassador to Brussels told his Spanish counterpart:

> Just now I can't see the prime minister appearing in the Knesset a few months before the elections with a proposal for a radical change in our foreign policy – for example, establishing diplomatic relations with a number of states with which we do not yet have normal relations.[74]

Despite Spain's growing friendship with the Arabs, Foreign Ministry officials had not lost their hope that an Israeli approach to the Franco government might still be greeted with favour. One reason for this was the contradictory messages emerging from Madrid. Manifestations of antipathy were balanced by occasions when Israeli representatives attending international conferences in Spain – such as that of the International Aviation Organization in May 1954 – were given a warm reception. With the régime's encouragement, the leader of the Jewish community in Barcelona published a condolence letter at the death of Israel's president, Chaim Weizmann, which was reprinted by a state news agency. In many parts of Europe Israeli diplomats maintained friendships with Spanish ambassadors, who frequently bewailed the absence of formal ties between the two states, offered their services as mediators, and expressed satisfaction over the gradual development of bilateral trade relations.[75]

Particularly striking were the words that Spain's ambassador to Washington, José María de Areilza, spoke in May 1955 – words which seemed to call for diplomatic ties between Spain and Israel. Although nothing explicit was said, it was enough to arouse a wave of criticism from the centrist and right-wing press in Israel concerning the government's inactivity on this subject. *Ha'aretz* published an editorial criticizing the decision-makers for adhering to the policy of boycotting Spain long after the European nations had abandoned it. This policy had become an anachronism that was due for elimination – particularly since Israel gained nothing from it, the paper argued. *Ma'ariv* published an interview with a Spanish Foreign Ministry official who claimed that his country was interested in diplomatic relations with Israel and was not worried that they would injure its ties with the Arab countries, since, after all, many countries maintained legations in both Israel and in Arab capitals.[76]

Franco, for his part, despite – or perhaps because of – the Jewish state's open hostility since 1949 and the absence of formal relations, continued to take a fairly tolerant line with the small Jewish community in his country, primarily to create a liberal image for the benefit of Western public opinion. Since 1949, Spain had in fact conducted a two-pronged policy. While it was moving closer to the Arabs and gradually losing interest in Israel, it nevertheless maintained its favourable policy towards Jews – though it should be remembered that, like other non-Catholics, Jews were not allowed to practise their religion publicly and they were treated with a certain suspicion typical of ultranationalistic, paranoid dictatorships such as Franco's.

In the summer of 1953, the Caudillo granted a formal interview to the then-head of the Jewish community in Madrid, Daniel François Barukh, a native of Jerusalem with a French passport who, upon arriving in Spain for the first time in 1949, had enlisted in the worldwide Francoist propaganda service, spreading the word that religious tolerance was the rule in Spain, and that no anti-Semitism existed there.[77] During their conversation, Franco mentioned, among other things, the financial assistance he had received from Jews in Tetuan during the Civil War. The authorities gradually allowed the Jews to organize community institutions, to arrange religious services, and to maintain ties with international Jewish organizations. None the less, at the time of the meeting between Franco and Barukh, the Jewish community of Madrid had not yet been formally recognized by the Spanish government. Ignacio Bauer had requested such recognition back in January 1950, but had received no response. In January 1954, Barukh raised the issue with the Spanish authorities – again to no avail.[78] The fact that the leaders of the community were of diverse origins and that most of them were not born in Spain increased the Nationalist régime's suspicions of them. The various rights that the Jewish community enjoyed up to the publication of the 'Law of Religious Freedom' in 1967 were in fact based on purely *de facto* arrangements, since the *Fuero de los Españoles* (the 'Spanish Bill of Rights') had not accorded full equality to all the religions in Spain; Spain was officially a Catholic country.

None the less, in September 1953 – the same month when Spain signed its treaty with the United States – the Jewish community celebrated the new year, *Rosh Hashana*, at the Madrid Hilton, with special holiday festivities officially sanctioned by the authorities. This was the first time since the expulsion of the Jews at the end of the fifteenth century that the Jews of Madrid had said the *Rosh Hashana* prayers in public. Representatives of the government were present, as were representatives of the United States embassy and the American Sixth Fleet, which was visiting Spain at the time. Jews from other cities in Spain also attended. The wide coverage this event received in the international press alarmed the régime, and prompted the fear that Protestants and Moslems would demand the same treatment. As a result, the following year the authorities forbade the *Rosh Hashana* prayers scheduled to be held at one of the hotels in the capital, although in 1955 they again authorized the holiday prayers to take place in a public venue.[79] A new synagogue was built in Barcelona, where the community offices and both the Sephardic and Ashkenazic synagogues had been concentrated in one building since 1954. The Madrid authorities even considered the possibility of extending Spanish citizenship to all the Sephardic Jews in Egypt, to ease their unpleasant situation as stateless people.[80]

Franco made a point of stressing his country's religious freedom, particularly to guests and journalists from the United States and especially the favourable treatment accorded to Jews in Spain. In an interview with a reporter from the *New York Herald Tribune*, Franco said:

Outside the gates of my palace, you can see two Moorish soldiers; they are of the Mohammedan faith, and no one hinders them from worshipping their god. In Madrid there is also a Jewish synagogue, and no one has ever done it harm. There is also such a synagogue in one of the cities of Spanish Morocco, where a third of the residents are Christians, a third are Jews, and a third are Moslems. These peoples have lived side by side very happily for many years. Does this sound to you as though somebody is being persecuted on account of his religious beliefs?

Four years later, in a conversation with the publisher of the American weekly *US News and World Report*, the Caudillo said:

There has never been anti-Semitism in Spain. I deny that absolutely. In the framework of our relations with Germany in the European war, we had difficult times because we defended Jews. Our behaviour caused a sensation in Europe, because when Jews were persecuted, Spain defended them.[81]

One of the leaders of the American–Jewish Committee who visited Madrid in the fall of 1953 returned to the United States with favourable reports, and two of the leaders of the World Jewish Congress who visited Spanish Morocco at the beginning of 1954 did, in fact, receive the impression that the situation of the Jews there was better than that of their brethren in French Morocco. The local Spanish High Commissioner, General García Valiño, was quick to meet with the two Jewish envoys from the US, and made every effort to display friendliness towards the Jews living in the area. However, the guests received the impression that the leaders of the local Jewish community were subject to strict supervision by the authorities.[82] Officials in Jerusalem knew that besides the tolerant treatment of the local Jewish community Madrid continued to show great interest in Sephardic Jews living in Israel, whom it considered likely to assist in disseminating Spanish culture in the Middle East and to further Spain's interests in the area. Relying on statistics published by the periodical *Mundo Hispánico*, the Spanish Foreign Ministry estimated that about half a million Jews in Israel spoke Ladino or Spanish.[83]

On several occasions the conflicting messages issuing from Spain led the research division of the Foreign Ministry to readjust its assessments concerning the chances of establishing ties with Madrid. At the end of 1954 the division compiled a relatively pessimistic report.

> If we were to approach Franco with a proposal to establish diplomatic relations, he would be unlikely to accept immediately, but he might not close the door completely; for Spain – which is still trying to establish itself in the eyes of world opinion – does not ignore the moral weight the creation of ties with Israel would have, the influence of the Zionist movement in the world, of world Jewry in general and America in particular.

Six months later, in mid-1955, the forecast was rosier; Spain was felt to be interested in relations with Israel. The conclusion, then, was that Israel should '"strike while the iron [was] hot" and begin immediate negotiations with the Spaniards [. . .]'.[84] It should be noted that in memoranda composed during that period, virtually no mention was made of moral and ideological considerations; in the Israeli Foreign Ministry such concerns had completely given way to *Realpolitik*, just as they had in the foreign ministries of the other Western states.

The Spanish refusal

During the second half of 1955, pressure grew within the Israeli Foreign Ministry to revise the policy on Spain. Developments in the international sphere strengthened the hand of those advocating a change. First, the nationalist ferment in French Morocco focused attention on the fact that the absence of an Israeli presence in Spain would impede any effort to assist the Jews of North Africa. Sharett in fact sent Israel's ambassador in Paris, Ya'akov Tsur, a confidential request for a report stating that concern for the fate of Moroccan Jews demanded the establishment of ties with Madrid. With the help of such an evaluation, the Prime Minister – then in his last weeks of office – would have a better chance of winning support for a proposal to mend fences with Spain.[85] The ambassador in Paris sent Sharett the desired assessment:

> Consular and diplomatic relations with Spain are likely to take on special importance if the security situation in Morocco continues to deteriorate. There are two situations in which we would be unable to use either the Marseilles port or some other port in the south of France: 1.) if the French government decides to limit or halt outgoing traffic; 2.) If actual war breaks out in the region and the shipping routes between Casablanca and France are disrupted. Under these circumstances, and in the case where the stream of refugees proves greater than the capacity of the ships in the ports

of Morocco, a disorderly mass of refugees may flee into the Spanish zone
and Tangiers (the borders are not strictly guarded) in an effort to cross
the Strait of Gibraltar and reach Spain. The assistance of the Spanish
authorities will be essential, if we want to control this flow, prepare camps,
and arrange for transferring these refugees to Israel. Nor should we ignore
the fact that in the absence of an Israeli legation, the Spanish government
is subject to the exclusive influence of the Arab countries. This means that
eventually the Arabs will have an easy time getting the doors locked
against potential emigrants to Israel. These arguments should be sufficient,
in my view, to convince all those who oppose recognizing Franco.[86]

Nevertheless, Tsur concluded his letter with a pessimistic assessment
of the chances that Spain would agree to relations with Israel at that
point. He thought it doubtful, but believed that talks should be
initiated with the Madrid government all the same. A few weeks later
he recommended the prompt opening of a consulate in the Spanish
capital – not in Barcelona – to ensure an Israeli presence in Madrid.[87]

Spain's ever-growing friendship with the Arab world made establishing channels of communication with the Spanish administration
doubly important. At the beginning of June 1955, King Hussein of
Jordan visited Spain where he was received with great ceremony, just
as his grandfather had been six years previously when he became the
first head of state to visit Madrid since the Civil War.[88] This was the
first of a series of visits that made Hussein the Arab leader most
friendly with Spain, both during the dictatorship and afterwards,
when he remained on close terms with King Juan Carlos I. In any
case, during 1955 the Arabs began to show great sensitivity to any
talk of a possible rapprochement between Spain and Israel, and any
reports to that effect were immediately denied by the Spaniards.

Meanwhile, the non-political advantages to be derived from
relations with Madrid began to figure more prominently. Jerusalem
saw clearly that despite Spain's good relations with the Arabs and the
Arabs' declarations that closer ties with Israel would compromise
Spanish–Arab friendship, the Spaniards were in fact interested in
fostering economic, cultural, and athletic connections with Israel. In
March 1955, the Discount Bank of Israel signed a financial agreement with the Banco Exterior de España. The Consul-General in
Jerusalem advised his government to set up a centre for the dissemination of Spanish culture among Spanish-speaking Jews in Israel,
and in the summer of 1955, despite Arab pressure, a delegation of
Israeli students arrived to participate in the international university

games held in San Sebastián, and was warmly received (the Spanish authorities even prevented the Egyptian delegation from distributing anti-Israeli leaflets). Trade relations between the two countries began to expand.[89]

All these circumstances led the deputy director of the Latin American division, Ionnathan Pratto, to write a new memorandum to the Foreign Minister. This memorandum opened by stressing that the arguments Tsur had raised concerning the possibility that Israel would need Spain's help to bring some of the Moroccan Jews to Israel carried great weight and demanded quick action. It also expressed the hope that the worsening situation in French Morocco would make Spain realize the danger it, too, ran by strengthening Arab nationalist groups and supporting the Arab League. As an additional reason for establishing relations with Spain, the memorandum cited the ties between Spain and the Vatican, which had improved since the two had signed their concordat, and Israel's desire to reach an understanding with the Holy See on a number of issues, including the status of Jerusalem. Pratto predicted that the United States would welcome the establishment of ties between Israel and Franco's anti-communist régime, and said:

> in our political struggle with the Arab world, it is clear that the establishment of diplomatic relations with Spain would constitute a political achievement of the highest importance, likely to enhance our standing in the international arena.[90]

It was Spain's admission to the United Nations, however, that really tilted the balance. The Francoist dictatorship had waged a long battle to gain entry to the United Nations, but for six years the Cold War defeated all efforts to add new members to the organization. The Soviets vetoed the applications of all non-communist states – including Spain – while the West rejected all Moscow's allies. In January 1955, Spain was forced to settle for permanent observer status at the United Nations headquarters in New York. That autumn, however, the two superpowers began to examine a proposal to admit 18 new members into the United Nations all at once, including Spain. Protracted negotiations finally ended with the admission of all the applicants except Mongolia and Japan. On 14 December 1955, the Soviet Union, together with 54 other states, voted to admit Spain to the United Nations. No one voted against the proposal. Only two states abstained, and the representatives of three other states were absent during the vote.[91] Spain's admission to the United Nations as part of a package deal between the two major political blocs took away some of the glory of the Franco régime's victory, and the Caudillo was to remain *persona non grata* in many circles for years to come, but none of this altered the fact that from then on Franco's Spain was recognized as part of the family of nations. The Spanish press described Spain's admission to the United Nations as a rectification of the wrong and injustice done to the country in the past.

When Spain's acceptance by the United Nations was almost a certainty, and Jerusalem felt sure that 'before long [. . . Spain would be] one of those deciding our fate', Israel decided to join the supporters of Spain's candidacy. Having so decided, of course, it tried to make political capital out of the situation. The Foreign Ministry advised some of its ambassadors in Europe to tell their Spanish colleagues in advance how Israel intended to vote and to present that intention as 'a sign of good will on Israel's part'.[92] Israel did indeed vote in favour of Spain's admission a few days later and even congratulated Spain afterwards, as it did most of the other new members who were admitted at the same time. The Foreign Ministry in Jerusalem noted that 'the Spaniards were the first to thank us for our congratulations', and the Director-General added with satisfaction, 'I think they were happy to do so'. Nevertheless, both countries took great care to prevent leaks to the press about the exchange of telegrams between Sharett and Artajo.[93]

Arye Levavi, who as Deputy Director-General of the Foreign Ministry had favoured the establishment of any kind of relations with Madrid, continued to press for ties in his new post as Israeli ambassador to Yugoslavia. His acquaintance with the representative in Yugoslavia of the Republican government-in-exile only strengthened his awareness that the Francoist régime was solid and that there was no point in entertaining the delusion that it could be replaced in the foreseeable future. He claimed that there was no longer any justification for ideological opposition to ties with Spain, since even the Soviet Union and Yugoslavia had begun to make overtures to the Franco régime. As examples, he reported visits by athletes, joint participation in various conferences and, of course, the significance of their vote to admit Spain to the United Nations.[94] Indeed, by the mid-1950s, Soviet diplomats, researchers, and technicians had begun to visit Spain and to take part in international conferences there.[95]

After he had relinquished the Prime Minister's office to Ben-Gurion and returned to the sole function of Foreign Minister, Sharett actually worked much more actively on the problem of establishing diplomatic relations with Spain. In the span of three weeks his personal diary records his attendance at no fewer than four meetings on the subject.[96] In the Foreign Ministry, of course, additional debates took place. On 8 January 1956, the government discussed the future of relations with Franco's Spain, concluding with a decision 'to authorize the Foreign Minister to do whatever necessary for the establishment of normal diplomatic relations with the state of Spain'. The idea of forming ties with Spain aroused dispute among the Cabinet ministers, and presumably some of them opposed the decision. In his personal diary Sharett jotted down only a few words about it: 'In the cabinet meeting arguments about [establishing relations with] Spain.' Because the subject was so sensitive, the Cabinet agreed not to enter the decision in the minutes; it was recorded separately in a document deposited with the Cabinet Secretary, Ze'ev Sharf, for safekeeping. That very week endorsement for an Israeli initiative in Spain's direction was provided by the Spanish socialist Luis Araquistain, a political exile living in Switzerland who, in the time of the Republic, had first been Minister for Labour and then ambassador to Berlin and Paris. During a visit to Tel Aviv he declared: 'Israel should establish diplomatic relations with Spain even if the present régime continues.'[97]

Sharett chose Ya'akov Tsur, one of the main advocates of relations between the two states since 1949, for the task of making a formal application to Spain, and Tsur lost no time in doing so. He informed the Spanish embassy in Paris that the government of Israel was prepared to establish diplomatic ties with Spain. Tsur was on friendly terms with the ambassador, the Conde de Casa Rojas, who had done what he could to save Jews in Romania during the Second World War; but the ambassador happened to be away from Paris, and Tsur did not want to lose time unnecessarily by waiting for his return. Accordingly, he gave the message to the embassy's *chargé d'affaires*.[98]

Officials in Madrid believed the Israeli initiative was prompted by the government's difficulties at home and abroad. Action by the Israeli army against Syrian forces on the north-eastern shore of the Sea of Galilee in December 1955 (an operation which cost the Syrians dozens of wounded and which was designed, among other things, to show Damascus the futility of its new defence pact with Egypt) had scuttled Israel's negotiations to buy arms in the United States, and had given rise to a unanimous vote of censure by the United Nations Security Council. Israel's relations with the Soviet Union had deteriorated since the 'doctors' trial' in Moscow – publicized early in 1953 – and a bomb attack on the Soviet embassy in Israel. Relations with Britain were tense as well, owing to British arms sales to Arab countries. The Spanish Foreign Ministry assumed that Israel was seeking a compensatory foreign-policy achievement in the form of establishing relations with Spain, and that afterwards it intended to mobilize the latter's influence in Latin America. In any case, officials in the African and Near Eastern division warned that responding favourably to Israel's offer would be very damaging to Spain's good relations with the Arab states, and pointed out that Israel had not withdrawn its opposition to the United Nations proposal to inter-nationalize Jerusalem as a way of protecting the Christian holy places. The division's recommendation was therefore to reject the Israeli proposal 'softening our refusal with the excuse that the Spanish government does not consider this to be the right moment for the establishment of the relations called for'[99] – a phrase that Israeli diplomats were to hear from Spanish representatives many times over the following years.

The Director-General of the Spanish Foreign Ministry, Juan de las Bárcenas (Spain's representative in Jerusalem in 1939), agreed with the recommendation but stressed that the refusal must be courteous since at some point Spain would doubtless establish relations with Israel – 'since I doubt the Arabs will erase Israel from the map'. Bárcenas's advice was to justify the refusal by saying that Israel first needed to find a solution to the Middle Eastern conflict.[100] On 22 February, Tsur was visited by the Conde de Casa Rojas who informed him that the Israeli proposal had been turned down. The Ambassador communicated the rejection 'politely, but unmis-takably'. After assuring Tsur that 'Spain [did] not feel negatively about Israel, and there [was] even a sympathetic attitude towards [it]', the Spanish representative explained that the time was 'not yet ripe'. The Spaniards did make the establishment of ties conditional on an improvement in the relations between Israel and its Arab neigh-bours, and on Israel's consent to the internationalization of Jerusalem. Referring to these conditions, which Israel obviously could not accept, Tsur wrote: 'The hint was taken, and no interpreta-tions were required.'[101]

Spain's response should not have surprised Israel, especially since Madrid had received the proposal at a time when it was particularly troubled by the situation in Morocco and its friendship with the Arabs was therefore doubly important. At the beginning of 1956, the Moroccan nationalist ferment spread to the Spanish zone, which hitherto had been known as the 'happy region' (the situation in the Spanish protectorate continued calm for a long time, partly because, in contrast to the high proportion of French living in the French section, there were not many Spanish settlers around to cause tension in relations with the local residents). Spain's support for Moroccan nationalism – as long as it had targeted the French – now boomeranged against Franco. He, however, preferred to blame the failure of his policy on the High Commissioner of Morocco, García Valiño.

A few months previously, France had surprised the Caudillo with a series of swift measures aimed at granting independence to the part of Morocco under its control – a radical change in policy prompted by the realization by officials in Paris that the situation in North Africa was becoming a heavy burden on France. In September 1955, the Sultan Mohammed ben-Arafa, ruling by courtesy of the French, left Morocco, and the legitimate Sultan, Mohammed V, was restored to the throne. In December a Moroccan Cabinet began to function in Rabat, and at the beginning of March 1956 France signed an agreement that granted independence to most of Morocco. These events sparked a wave of strikes and nationalist protests in the Spanish zone, and Franco was obliged to consent to independence for the Sharif kingdom, including the territory under Spanish control, by April 1956. Even Spain's friendly relations with the Arabs could not help the Caudillo maintain control in Spanish Morocco.[102]

This was, of course, a bitter pill for the man who had won military glory in service in Morocco and who, in the past, had proclaimed his country's historical mission in North Africa. The decision to let go of Morocco aroused disapproval in certain circles in Spain and in parts of the army, although it was vital to prevent an expensive and prolonged colonial war, as well as serious damage to Spain's image as a friend of the Arab world. In any case, once Franco had made the decision, he carried it out with full ceremony, inviting the Sultan to come to Madrid to make the official arrangements for ending the Spanish protectorate. The Caudillo wanted to present the abandonment of the protectorate – a step which in fact represented the failure of his Moroccan policy – as a victory, and accordingly put all his propaganda resources into gear and mobilized the masses at his disposal. He himself delivered a speech expressing his happiness at

handing over the Spanish zone to the Sultan, the head of the independent new state of Morocco.[103] However, a few stumbling blocks
remained in the relations between the two states, namely the
Mediterranean coastal cities in the north (Ceuta and Melilla), the
enclave of Ifni on the Atlantic coast in the south, Cabo Jubi, and the
Spanish Sahara (Río de Oro). Spain retained possession of these territories, and they were to overshadow its relations with Morocco for
many years to come.

Spain's rejection of relations with Israel was therefore predictable;
the only surprising thing was that Jerusalem officials had ever
believed that such an initiative had a reasonable chance of success.
Following Spain's refusal, Tsur wrote in his diary that the Spanish
response 'was to be expected' and that he 'did not see much chance of
such an announcement without previous negotiations'; yet Moshe
Sharett already had a possible candidate in mind to head the hypothetical Israeli legation in Madrid. That candidate was David Shaltiel,
who had participated in the effort to save Jews by way of Spain in
1944 and who, having just completed a period as Israeli ambassador
to Brazil, was now awaiting a new appointment.[104] In fact, however,
Spain no longer had any real interest in establishing formal relations
with Israel. It no longer needed Israel's vote in the United Nations,
since it had been a member itself since December 1955. The diplomatic sanctions against it had been lifted some time previously, its
relations with the United States continued to improve, and its friendship with the Arabs was still holding up. Economically, Israel was not
an important potential market for Spanish products, nor was it a
major source of anything that Spain needed.

None the less, as will be seen, Israel persisted in the face of the
Spaniards' explicit rejection, trying again and again to bridge the gap
with Franco's Spain. However, years of unceasing political effort
were to have no effect – certainly not while the Caudillo still lived.
Only a democratic Spain would open up new horizons for Israel.

5

Spanish Hostility (1956–75)

In January 1986, a few days after Spain and Israel announced the establishment of diplomatic relations with each other, Abba Eban spoke out in defence of Israel's May 1949 vote against the United Nations proposal to lift the international diplomatic sanctions on Spain. Eban, distressed by the 'dissemination of imaginary myths about so-called Israeli "guilt" for the absence of these relations [between Spain and Israel] in the past', explained that

> absurdly enough, we knew that even if we had lost our senses and joined those who pardoned Nazism, Spain at the time would never have dreamed of establishing relations with us, since it was completely committed to a pro-Moslem policy.[1]

This view, shared by many, does not accord with the facts. During Israel's first years of statehood, as we have seen, Franco was interested in establishing full, normal relations, largely in the hope that Israel's moral weight and the influence of various Jewish communities – particularly the Jews in the United States – would help him to break the international boycott that had been declared on his régime. Relations with Israel could help Spain integrate more quickly into the family of nations, just as they helped the Federal Republic of Germany some years later.[2] Only Israel's refusal prevented the establishment of relations at the time:

> There is no doubt that in 1949 Franco wanted relations with Israel, since at the time Spain was trying to get the sanctions against it lifted; and if Israel – which was the state of the main victims of World War II and which had in the meantime been admitted to the United Nations – had forgiven Franco's Spain, that act would have helped break down the western countries' resistance to his régime.[3]

Franco did, of course, begin to develop close relations with the

Arab countries even before the State of Israel was founded. Spain's attitude of friendship and co-operation towards the Moslem world was more than a temporary political tactic; it was a consistent policy, linked to Spain's colonial possessions in North Africa and involving a great deal of lip service concerning the heritage Spain shared with the Moslems and Spain's vision of itself as a bridge between the Moslem and Christian worlds. After the Second World War, relations with the Arabs were a way for Spain to break out of the international isolation that had been imposed on it. Yet for all that, Spain was not 'completely committed to a pro-Moslem policy'. Franco always had the sense to leave himself room to manoeuvre, and as long as he could reap advantage from relations with Israel he was prepared to do so, despite his ties with the Arabs. When Israel refused to respond to Spain's overtures, the Francoist régime had the wit to turn its absence of relations with the Jewish state into a political asset – a way of moving closer to the Arabs.

When Israel finally asked Spain to establish diplomatic relations, it was already too late. The historic opportunity had passed, perhaps as early as the autumn of 1953, when Spain signed the economic-military agreement with the United States. That year was a turning-point in the international status of the Francoist régime, which was gaining legitimacy in the Western world. Spain's increasingly diversified ties with Latin America, the Arab world, and the United States, its gradual integration into various international organizations – including the United Nations in December 1955 – all helped strengthen the régime's self-confidence, and it had less and less need of relations with Israel. If Israel erred, it was – as mentioned earlier – by not showing the necessary initiative and alacrity to change its policy on Spain when the other Western countries were doing so. By 1956, when Israel was finally galvanized into action, Spain had already stepped onto the path of accelerated economic development, the régime had become less rigid than it had been 10 or 15 years earlier, and its international position was stronger. The potential benefits of ties with Jerusalem had dwindled considerably.

Israel's attempts at rapprochement and Spain's pro-Arab response

In retrospect it is clear that, by the spring of 1956, relations between the two countries were such that the diplomatic option was no longer practicable. Officials in Jerusalem, however, refused to give up. As

soon as Jerusalem was informed of Spain's explicit refusal to establish ties with Israel, it decided, in the interests of order and efficiency,
to put one person in charge of everything pertaining to relations with
Spain. The person selected for this position was Moshe Tov.[4] In
April, Sharett informed Tov that he was to be sent as an observer to a
meeting of UNESCO's Executive Board in Madrid, charged 'with a
dual mission – to win votes to elect us to a UNESCO commission at
the next annual conference, and to pave the way for diplomatic
communication with the Franco government, since our official
request to it has been rejected.'[5] But Tov returned empty-handed. The
approaches that Israel's representatives in Mexico and Sweden made
to their Spanish colleagues came to nothing. At the same time,
Foreign Ministry officials were discussing the possibility of sending
Diomedes Catroux, a French friend of Israel who was head of the
France–Israel Association at the time, to Spain and Portugal to
investigate the possibility of establishing diplomatic ties with the two
Iberian nations.[6] This plan bore no fruit either.

During the Suez crisis and the Sinai war, Spain generally showed
sympathy for Egypt, a position that allowed it to appear as a friend of
the Arabs, as opposed to 'imperialistic' Britain, France, and Israel.
On 26 July 1956, the President of Egypt, Gamal Abdel Nasser,
nationalized the Suez Canal Corporation, which, under British
and French control, administered the canal. In an interview with
the newspaper *Arriba*, Franco eagerly voiced support for Egypt's
position and criticism for Britain's policy in the Middle East.[7]
Nasser's move, however, endangered the Constantinople convention
of 1888, which all European maritime nations had signed and which
declared that the canal must remain 'open to vessels of all nations'
and 'free from blockade', a right which was suspended only during
the two World Wars.

Nasser nationalized the canal largely in response to the refusal of
the United States, Britain, and the World Bank to assist him in building the Aswan Dam – they were concerned about the economic risk
as well as growing Soviet influence in Egypt. The Egyptian ruler
wanted, among other things, to use the revenues from the canal to
finance the ambitious Aswan project. The international crisis which
had just broken out was compounded, of course, by other factors: the
Arab–Israeli conflict and the Israeli commando raids on Egyptian
territory; British fear of the threat that Nasser and his aspirations to
the leadership of the Arab world posed to Britain's position in the
Middle East; Britain and France's concern about their oil supply; and

the Paris government's anger over Nasser's support for the rebels in Algeria. Prime Minister Anthony Eden saw Nasser as a 'megalomaniacal dictator' and cited the ruinous consequences of the appeasement policy Britain had followed during the 1930s as grounds for a firm stand against Egypt.

The major media in Madrid greeted the nationalization of the canal with enthusiasm. *Arriba, Madrid, Pueblo*, and *Ya* all devoted editorials to Nasser's 'daring step' and the challenge he had set the imperialist powers, using terms that were almost identical to those employed by the Soviet papers during the period. At the mid-August London conference of the principal countries that used the canal, the Spanish delegation, led by Foreign Minister Artajo, tried to defend Egypt's interests and to mediate between it and the Western powers. This diplomatic activity, however, did not satisfy Egypt, which expected more vigorous support from Spain, given their friendship over the past decade, and it certainly caused annoyance in the Foreign Ministries in London, Paris, and Washington.[8]

In the meantime, the tension around the Suez Canal was growing. The canal pilots stopped work and Egypt tried to recruit others to take their places. Several dozen Spaniards were hired to help in the operation of the canal. At the beginning of September, some 60 Spaniards announced their willingness to go 'to defend Egypt from foreign aggression', and observers in London were already evoking the 'Blue Division' which had been sent to assist the *Wehrmacht* in its war against the Soviet Union. Just before the fighting broke out, General Franco told a reporter from the Associated Press news agency that the events in Egypt, like those in Algeria and Morocco, reflected changes in the international sphere and represented a protest against imperialism and colonial oppression.

Following the co-ordinated attack on Egypt, 'the [Spanish] press and radio were clearly biased, and even aggressive' towards Israel, France, and Britain, as the president of the Jewish community in Madrid, Louis Blitz, wrote. At the beginning of November, the Falange organ, *Arriba*, claimed that by the criteria established at the Nuremberg trials, Anthony Eden, Guy Mollet, and David Ben-Gurion could be tried as war criminals. The Falange was very sympathetic to Nasser's régime; after Perón's fall ended the enthusiasm it had showed for Peronism at the end of the 1940s and the beginning of the 1950s, it was ready for another object of admiration. Now it was enamoured of Nasserism, which it saw as the model of a nationalist régime aspiring to social justice.[9]

Before long, however, the Spanish media moderated their support for Nasser; the régime was concerned about its image in the West, and certain circles, particularly in the military forces, were worried about the Soviet Union's growing influence in Egypt and the possibility that Egypt's brand of Arab nationalism might encourage calls for the eradication of the Spanish presence in North Africa, beginning with Río de Oro. The newspaper *ABC* published a number of articles which, although expressing disapproval of the manner and timing of the Anglo-French intervention, nevertheless claimed that the operation would further the interests of the Western bloc, since it had caused the destruction of a great deal of military equipment that the Soviets had sent to Egypt. Some articles also maintained that the Russians in fact wanted to take over Egypt and make Nasser their puppet. Particularly prominent among these articles was one by the retired general Alfredo Kindelán, one of the founders of the Spanish air force in the time of Alfonso XIII and commander of Franco's air force during the Civil War. The decision for a military intervention was not made by irresponsible fools or bloodthirsty sadists, but by talented politicians, Kindelán wrote, reproaching the Falangist *Arriba*. In mid-December, Franco met with both the United States Ambassador in Madrid and the Army Minister, Agustín Muñoz Grandes, in quick succession, and within two days the attacks on 'Western imperialism' disappeared from the papers.[10]

The contours of Spain's Middle Eastern policy, which had been shaped during the years when Alberto Martín Artajo occupied the Foreign Ministry (1945–57), did not change even after Artajo was replaced by Fernando María Castiella. Castiella, it should be noted, had volunteered in 1942 for the 'Blue Division', served on the Russian front, and was decorated by Hitler for his heroism in battle in the Ukraine. Monarchistic in outlook but loyal to Franco, Castiella was more a bureaucrat than a politician. During his term of office (1957–69), Spain's traditional friendship with the Arab countries continued, although the gestures towards the Arabs became less frequent and more selective as Spain was gradually incorporated into the Western camp and political changes took place in the Middle East. In addition, Moroccan independence and the military clashes of 1957–58 in the Spanish enclaves of Ifni and the Western Sahara had left a residue of anti-Moslem sentiment. The Franco régime's pro-Arab policy in the first decade following the Second World War depended on co-operation with conservative, dynastic régimes which appeared to form a barrier to Western liberalism, modern secularism, and communism. But the advent of radical régimes bearing the label of 'national socialism' in Egypt, Syria, Iraq, and Algeria aroused certain misgivings in Spanish officialdom.[11]

None the less, Spain continued to maintain close relations with the Arab countries, and most of the major leaders of the Arab world visited the country during those years. The Franco régime refused to consider any Israeli idea for establishing diplomatic ties so long as the Middle Eastern conflict remained unresolved and Israel did not consent to the internationalization of Jerusalem and the holy places. A few weeks after taking up his duties, Castiella received a report from Spain's ambassador to the United Nations, Lequerica, about a conversation he had had with Abba Eban and Moshe Tov during which the two Israeli ambassadors had expressed Israel's desire for ties with Madrid. Lequerica was in favour of such ties, which in his opinion would be favourable to Spain – especially just then when greater willingness to admit it to NATO was evident. Castiella rejected the idea and a few weeks later he instructed officials to deny the reports of contacts between the two states which were appearing in the Israeli press.[12]

In the autumn of 1958, following the opening of an Israeli consulate in Portugal, *Herut* Knesset member Arditi – a man whom Francoist diplomacy regarded as 'a friend of Spain' and who had visited the country a few years earlier – asked the Foreign Minister about relations with Spain during a Knesset debate. The General Zionists, in their party convention before the Knesset elections, adopted a resolution favouring the establishment of ties with this country. Maurice Perlzweig, head of the World Jewish Congress's division of international relations, also explored the issue during his visits to Madrid in August 1958 and May 1959. Israel's ambassadors in Bogota and Helsinki raised the matter with their Spanish counterparts.[13]

The Spanish Foreign Ministry accordingly sent a circular to all its diplomatic missions reviewing the bases of its Middle East policy. The circular recalled Israel's hostile attitude towards Spain in various international forums at the end of the 1940s and the beginning of the 1950s and contrasted it with the support that the Franco régime had received from the Arab countries. It also mentioned the issue of the Christian holy places. The Spanish diplomats were advised to maintain correct relations with their Israeli colleagues but to avoid any move that might be interpreted as a deviation from their country's established foreign policy.[14]

In January 1959, Castiella visited Damascus, where he was quoted by the press as having said that Spain would never recognize the State of Israel. Upon returning to Madrid, he declared that the friendship between Spain and the Arab countries rested on solid foundations: their historical ties and the links of blood and culture. Moreover, the Arabs appreciated the fact that Spain, together with the Holy See, was the only European state that had not recognized Israel. The Minister quickly added that of course this did not imply a hostile attitude towards Jews, and evoked Spain's behaviour in the Second World War.

Naturally, this blunt declaration of favour for the Arab side vexed the Israelis, who arranged what appeared to be an act of retaliation. When Moshe Tov, a member of Israel's delegation to the United Nations, organized, in co-operation with the Institute of Cultural Relations with Latin America, Spain, and Portugal, a tribute to the Uruguayan ambassador at the United Nations, General José Asensio was invited as the representative of the Republican government-in-exile of Spain.[15]

A few days later, the subject of relations with Spain was discussed in the Knesset again, when Mordechai Nurock of the National Religious Party (MAFDAL) called for the establishment of ties with Madrid. The Foreign Minister, Golda Meir, responded that she applauded the humanity Spain had shown during the Second World War, but that it was untrue to say Israel was 'spurning the hand that Spain [was] extending to us in peace and brotherhood'. Various efforts made to effect a rapprochement had been fruitless, and Spain had erected barriers even to economic and cultural relations between the two countries, for political reasons. Meir mentioned Castiella's statements in Damascus, and expressed hope that the quotations published by the media were not accurate, and that the two states would find a way to establish normal ties.[16]

In May of the same year, in preparation for Golda Meir's tour of Latin America, the Spanish Foreign Ministry sent another circular to all its legations on the American continent, clarifying its position on Israel: recognition of the State of Israel now would deal a blow to 'our Arab friends' and Spain's relations with the Vatican and would put unnecessary obstacles in the way to solving the dispute with Morocco concerning the future of the Spanish enclaves in North Africa. The Israeli political system, the circular went on, was based on ideological principles contrary to those underlying the Spanish régime; Israel had nothing to offer Spain economically and in certain fields it was even a dangerous competitor; in Latin America Israel worked hand-in-glove with left-wing elements and Spanish exiles, launching joint attacks on the Franco régime in various newspapers. For these reasons, Spanish diplomats were to avoid participating in cultural activities initiated by organizations linked with Israel and to refuse courteously any invitations to take part in events organized by Israeli missions to mark visits by dignitaries.[17] During the years 1957–59, the Spanish Foreign Ministry warned against expanding cultural ties with Israel to avoid damaging Spain's good relations with the Arab countries. For the same reason, the Instituto de Cultura Hispánica (Institute of Hispanic Culture) cancelled a planned special edition of the periodical *Mundo Hispánico* which was to be devoted to Sephardic Jews.

In 1958, a representative of the World Federation of Sephardic Communities, Yair Behar Passy, set up an office in Spain. Behar, of Argentine origin, had co-ordinated the undertaking with the Israeli Foreign Ministry and had received permission from the Spanish authorities to stay in Madrid. One of his most important initiatives was the World Sephardic Bibliographical Exhibition, which was inaugurated in December 1959 in the building that housed the national library in Madrid. The inauguration ceremony was attended by the Education Minister, Jesús Rubio, the Director of the Instituto de Cultura Hispánica, Blas Piñar (who in the early 1960s would help found the organization Amistad Judeo-Cristiana, as well as visit Israel), and the President of the Real Academia de la Lengua (Royal Language Academy), Ramón Menéndez Pidal, together with representatives of various Jewish organizations. The latter included the World Jewish Congress, the World Zionist Organization, the Alliance Israelite Universelle, and the World Federation of Sephardic Communities. Cultural and research institutions from 13 states, including Israel (the Hebrew University, Ben-Zvi Institute, the Bezalel Museum, and others), and from the Vatican sent objects worth a total of more than $1 million for display in the exhibition, and some 12,000 people visited it.

From the beginning the Spanish Foreign Ministry, suspicious and cautious as always, was dubious about the idea of organizing such an exhibition, and it made its support conditional on the organizers

taking care that this exaltation of one facet of our own culture does not degenerate into a glorification of those aspects of Sephardic thought which

are fundamentally antagonistic to the spiritual concept of the authentic
Spain . . .

When Iraqi diplomats protested about the 'Zionist propaganda' in
the exhibition, and other Arab sources also voiced concern, Castiella,
solicitous for 'traditional Hispano-Arab friendship', hurried to
assemble the Arab representatives in Madrid and explain to them
that Spain did not intend to recognize Israel, and that the whole
purpose of the event was merely to strengthen the cultural ties
between Spain and Sephardic Jews.[18]

Following the success of the exhibition, Behar and the World
Federation of Sephardic Communities proposed setting up a travelling exhibition of a similar nature that would visit various capitals in
Europe and America. To this end, they asked the Spanish government
for organizational assistance and partial financial support. The
Spanish Foreign Ministry opposed the plan, believing that the previous exhibition had been exploited by 'Jewish and Zionist propaganda' to weaken Spain's position in the Arab world and had created
the mistaken impression that Spain was about to recognize Israel. For
the Foreign Ministry, 'the Sephardic soul was always a double-edged
sword that should be used only when it was certain not to fall into
foreign hands'. In the Santa Cruz Palace, Foreign Ministry officials
warned that the Education Ministry, the Instituto de Cultura
Hispánica, and the Consejo Superior de Investigaciones Científicas,
which were co-operating with Behar, lacked a global vision of the
interests of Spanish foreign policy and therefore might unwittingly
serve the interests of the State of Israel, which differed from those of
Spain.

In the summer of 1962, Behar concluded his mission in Madrid.
Jerusalem decided not to send anyone else to Spain on a permanent
basis, and made do with frequent visits to Madrid by the Consul-
General in Lisbon, Shimon Amir, to keep a channel of communication open with some of the Spanish institutions and the Jewish
community. It was not until four years after Behar's return that the
Israeli Foreign Ministry decided to send another representative to
Spain to create a climate that would be more favourable to Israel. In
the summer of 1966 the veteran diplomat Ionnathan Pratto finished
his post as the director of the division of relations with the Christian
churches, and the Deputy Director-General of the Foreign Ministry,
Arye Levavi, offered him a choice between Malta and Madrid.
Pratto, a native of Florence and the scion of a Sephardic Jewish

family (his full family name was Pratto Villareal Fernandes), chose Madrid. In the course of his diplomatic career, he had served in Peronist Argentina and Castro's Cuba, so he was fluent in Spanish. His past experience in conducting relations with the Vatican and the Christian communities in Israel was also supposed to help him in his new post in Franco's Spain. Since Behar had left Madrid, no one had been posted there by the Israeli Foreign Ministry. This time Levavi wanted to send someone with 'a more serious, though not official, authority'. Pratto went to Madrid with an Israeli diplomatic passport, although not in a diplomatic capacity; he was supposedly on a year's sabbatical to do research. The research subject Pratto had chosen to justify his stay in Spain was the role that the Jews expelled from Spain played in the relations between the Ottoman Empire and the Kingdom of Spain.[19]

Before he left, the Israeli security services checked with their Spanish counterparts to make sure that Pratto's stay in Madrid would not create any problems. Madrid made no objection to his coming. Pratto arrived in Spain in October 1966 and immediately began to develop contacts with prominent members of the Jewish communities in Madrid (particularly the Mazín, Pinto and Lasry families) and in Barcelona; with Spanish intellectuals researching the heritage of the Jews of Spain – mainly at the Consejo Superior de Investigaciones Científicas, such as Pérez Castro and Cantera Burgos; and with journalists, particularly those employed by *ABC* – such as Guillermo Luca de Tena and Luis María Anson – and *Ya* – notably Bartolomé Mostaza. He gradually expanded these ties to include, among others, certain groups in the Catholic Church, especially Opus Dei, some of whose members occupied important posts in the political system of the time, and the heads of the Instituto de Cultura Hispánica, notably the President, Gregorio Marañon, and the Secretary-General, Enrique Sánchez Puga.

Pratto carried out his activities discreetly, eschewing any publicity that might bring Arab pressure to bear on the government of Spain, which was permitting him to stay there on an Israeli diplomatic passport. The only minister Pratto met while staying in Spain was the Minister of Tourism, Manuel Fraga Iribarne, who explained that he personally supported the establishment of relations with Israel, although Franco would not hear of it. Pratto kept in touch with the Spanish Foreign Ministry through his friend José María Moro, the ex-Director of the office of the Foreign Minister, Castiella.

After two years in Spain, Pratto returned to Israel. He could not point to any concrete achievements, although no one had expected that his mission there would actually bring about the establishment of diplomatic relations between the two countries. He should be credited, however, with the creation of an atmosphere that was more favourable to Israel in various circles. At his initiative, for example, several important journalists from Spain visited Israel during those years and, after returning home, they published sympathetic articles on Israel and expressed support for the establishment of diplomatic ties with it (although in the aftermath of the Six-Day War, the Spanish press, particularly that part identified with the Falange, published several virulently anti-Israeli articles). In any case, Jerusalem officials were not interested in long-term action with uncertain benefit at the time. Gershon Avner, Director of the West European division, heard Pratto's report and decided not to advise the ministry leadership to send someone else in his place. From Pratto's return in the summer of 1968, no other Israeli diplomat was sent to stay in Spain for some 12 years.

Towards the mid-1960s, the economic and trade relations between the two states expanded considerably and the Israeli shipping company, ZIM, set up a firm by the name of Astromar in co-operation with the Spanish company Atlas Expreso to encourage Hispano–Israeli trade. A stop in Barcelona was added to ZIM's Haifa–New York line, and it was agreed that every 10 days the ships *Israel* and *Zion* would anchor there to pick up passengers and cargo. In the spring of 1965, however, the government of Spain decided to halt this trend and it limited the anchorage rights of Israeli ships to the ports of Malaga and Palma de Mallorca. The authorities categorized this move as 'a purely administrative measure' but it was mainly the result of heavy pressure exerted by the Arab countries. Apparently, in the wake of the establishment of full diplomatic relations between Israel and the Federal Republic of Germany, the Arabs wished to sabotage any rapprochement between Spain and Israel, while the Madrid government, for its part, wanted to enlist Arab support in its dispute with Britain over the future of Gibraltar. The new limitations on shipping ties with Israel were criticized in Britain and the US, and Spain retracted them.[20] However, it rejected applications by the Israeli airline, El Al, to establish an air link between the two countries.

In the first half of 1970, Israel was hopeful of a possible approach from Spain. Spanish diplomacy had begun to show initiative and activity unlike its conservative behaviour since the Second World

War. The new Foreign Minister, Gregorio López Bravo, began to conduct an eastward-looking policy. At the beginning of that year he went to Moscow to discuss establishing relations with the Soviet Union, the sworn enemy of Francoism, although he continued to work on improving ties with the United States.[21] The new minister – a technocrat and Opus Dei member who had studied in the United States for a time and had held senior economic positions in the past – gave additional evidence of his pragmatism and different style when he met with a representative of Mexico who, more than 30 years after the Civil War, still refused to recognize the Franco government. Jerusalem officials expected López Bravo to show greater responsiveness towards Israel too; but, to their great disappointment, no real change was to take place in Madrid's Middle Eastern policy, as López Bravo himself told President Nasser during a visit to Egypt in January.[22]

In June, the Israeli Foreign Minister, Abba Eban, met with López Bravo in Luxembourg for a brief talk. Eban had been trying to engineer ties between the two countries for 15 years and had cultivated friendships with some of Spain's senior diplomats. Having gone to Luxembourg to sign Israel's first major agreement with the European Community, he tried to link the Community's relations to Spain with its relations to Israel so that Israel's economic interests would not be hurt, while at the same time working to promote relations between Madrid and Jerusalem. Eban achieved his first aim, saying: 'My tactical plan in the EEC had been to ensure that an agreement between the Community and Spain would be resisted by countries friendly to Israel unless there was a parallel agreement with Israel.' And indeed, the Foreign Minister of France, Maurice Schumann, who was advocating the treaty between the Community and Spain, strove to further the negotiations between the Community and Israel.[23] In later years, after Franco's death, Israel would ask its friends in Europe to make Spain's admission to the Community conditional on its prompt establishment of relations with Israel.

None the less, Eban did not manage to bring Israel and Spain together. It is true that his talk with López Bravo was the first meeting at the ministerial level between the two countries, and that López Bravo wanted news of it to appear in the press – perhaps to improve Spain's image in Western public opinion. The meeting achieved nothing concrete, however. Eban told the press that the establishment of relations depended solely on Madrid, since Israel had already expressed its desire for such relations. López Bravo, however, declared that Spain would establish relations with Israel only after a just and lasting peace had been achieved in the Middle East and the problem of the Palestinian refugees had been resolved.[24]

Thus, although in the course of his term as Foreign Minister (1970–73) López Bravo improved Spain's relations with the Soviet Union (achieving a bilateral trade agreement and the opening of a TASS office in Madrid and an EFE office in Moscow), established normal diplomatic ties with East Germany and China, and signed consular agreements with Hungary, Poland, Bulgaria, Romania, and Czechoslovakia, its attitude towards Israel did not change. A series of factors prevented any move in the direction of the Jewish state: pressure from the Arab states, misgivings in the Spanish Foreign Ministry, and opposition from a number of senior figures in the government, beginning with Luis Carrero Blanco, Franco's right hand, who was appointed head of the government in June 1973 (he was murdered in December of the same year by the Basque underground movement, ETA).

During the Yom Kippur War, official Spain's sympathies were again patently with the Arab countries, whose support Spain needed in international forums. At the same time, Morocco, which had received Cabo Jubi in 1958 and Ifni 10 years later, was increasing its demands for the Spanish Sahara, at the border of southern Morocco. Fewer than 75,000 people were living in this arid strip, which measured some 260,000 square kilometers, in the mid-1970s and most of them were nomads. The Moroccans wanted to annex it in order to realize their nationalist aspiration to 'Greater Morocco' and to gain control of the rich phosphate deposits there. Meanwhile, the Polisario underground was waging a struggle for independence against both Spanish colonial rule and Morocco's annexationist ambitions.[25]

Although the Americans had used their bases in Spain to transfer equipment and supplies to Israel during the Six-Day War – with or without the knowledge of the Spanish government – in 1970 Madrid informed the United States administration that in any future conflict between Israel and its Arab neighbours, the United States would no longer be able to use its three air bases on Spanish territory to assist Israel. The Spanish government stated this position again, publicly, in October 1973. During the Yom Kippur War, Spain indeed forbade the United States to use those bases, claiming that they were meant to support the NATO defence system against the Soviet threat, and not to serve as refueling and supply bases for the Middle East. Privately, the United States told Spain that it would use the bases 'only for routine purposes and not in new operations in the Middle East'. The Spaniards understood this to mean that reconnaissance planes flying over the Middle East would continue to refuel in Spain, and suspected that the information gathered by these planes would be passed to Israel. None the less, they preferred not to raise the issue in their contacts with the Americans.[26]

Again, clearly pro-Arab and anti-Israeli articles appeared in the Spanish press. The Jewish community of Madrid, for its part, organized campaigns to donate blood for wounded Israeli soldiers, and young people from Barcelona and Madrid went to Israel to harvest crops in the framework of 'Operation Orange', replacing the Israeli workers who were away at war.[27] Madrid's sympathetic attitude towards the Arab countries in the following months was also attributable to Spain's nearly total dependence on Arab oil for its energy needs. Expressions of gratitude to the Arabs for not cutting off the oil supply to the Iberian Peninsula appeared in Spanish newspapers.[28] However, Spain's pro-Arab line did not earn it any price reductions for its oil; it did not pay even a penny less than other Western consumers.

From 1956 to 1975, Spain continued to support the Arab position in the United Nations General Assembly. Spain's representative in the organization automatically raised his hand for almost every Arab-initiated resolution censuring Israel. In December 1971, Spain supported the call for Israel to withdraw to the 1967 borders, and three years later, in November 1974, it voted in favour of two pro-Palestinian draft resolutions: one stating that the Palestinian people had the right to self-determination and sovereignty, and the other giving the PLO observer status in the United Nations.[29] In the argument over the English version of Resolution 242 (passed by the Security Council in 1967) versus the French version, Spain held by the French one which demanded Israel's withdrawal from *all* the territories it had conquered in 1967. Of all the states of Western Europe, it was, ironically, the Spanish dictatorship which supported the Palestinian people's claim to self-determination most ardently. Occasionally, Spain's support for the Palestinians was even more comprehensive than that of some of the Arab countries. By October 1968, the Spanish Foreign Minister, Castiella, had already raised the issue of the Palestinian refugees in the United Nations General Assembly,[30] and from that moment on, opposition to Israel's policy towards the Palestinians became Spain's main ideological justification for refusing to establish relations with the Jewish state. In this way, the conservative, reactionary dictatorship gave itself a progressive image in the eyes of the Arab and Third World countries, and earned broad support in the United Nations, which allowed it to slow the process of decolonializing its North African possessions – a process that had begun in the mid-1950s. At the beginning of the 1970s, for example, when the non-aligned countries introduced a resolution in the United Nations condemning states that subjugated other peoples, Spain was not included with Israel, Rhodesia, South Africa, and Portugal. Sahara was forgotten for the time being.[31] Only when the Caudillo was already on his death bed did Spain deviate from its usual voting pattern of absolute solidarity with the Arab position in everything relating to the Middle East; this deviation came during the vote on the General Assembly resolution condemning Zionism as a form of racism.

On 17 October 1975 the Third General Assembly Committee passed a resolution declaring that Zionism was a form of racism and a manifestation of racial discrimination, and putting it in the same category as the South African policy of apartheid. The resolution was passed by a large majority, led by the Arab countries, the Third World states, and the communist bloc. Seventy states voted in favour of it, 29 against, and 27 abstained. As expected, Spain was among the supporters of the resolution, which the United States representative described as a deplorable step that encouraged and approved the racist phenomenon known as anti-Semitism.[32] At the time, an extensive international campaign was under way against the Franco régime, following the execution of five guerrilla fighters from the ETA and FRAP organizations at the end of September.[33] This incident was scheduled for debate in the same United Nations committee, and by voting against Israel Spain sought to ensure support for its own position from representatives of the Arab countries and the Third World. The United Nations was also expected to debate the issue of Sahara's future, and the Madrid government was trying to mobilize all possible support for its policy.

It should be noted that in May of the same year Spain, fearing an extended colonial war, had declared its intention of granting Sahara its independence. Morocco raised a protest, but the International Court of Justice ruled on 16 October that Morocco had no territorial sovereignty over Sahara. King Hassan II declared in response that he would send 350,000 Moroccans on the Green March, a peaceful mass march into the disputed territory, organized to speed up the negotiating process that would lead to decolonialization. The march – supported by most of the Arab countries, much to Madrid's chagrin, including Spain's best friends in the Arab world – began on 6 November and was cut short after three days because it had 'achieved its object'. In the middle of the month, the Spaniards announced they would withdraw from the Sahara by the end of February 1976, transferring responsibility for the region to Morocco and Algeria.[34]

Following the Third Committee's adoption of the resolution equating Zionism with racism, the United States administration and some Jewish organizations began to exert heavy pressure on various countries in anticipation of the debate on it in the United Nations General Assembly. President Gerald Ford explicitly threatened to take measures against states voting in favour of the anti-Zionist resolution. Pressure of this kind, particularly by Sephardic organizations, was also brought to bear on the Madrid government, and this time, unlike on previous occasions, it bore fruit.[35] The Spanish Foreign Ministry was in conflict over the position Spain should take in the General Assembly vote. The opposing poles of the debate were represented by the veteran ambassador to the United Nations, Jaime de Piniés – who, hostile to Israel for many years, feared the reaction of the Arab countries and the Third World – and the ambassador in Washington, Jaime Alba, who tried to convey to the Ministry heads the harsh response of Jewish public opinion in the United States and its great influence; he warned of the sanctions that the United States was likely to employ against countries voting in favour of the General Assembly resolution against Zionism. Alba had the upper hand, especially given the feeling in the Santa Cruz Palace that 'the Arab countries do not appear to appreciate sufficiently the Spanish position [concerning the Middle East], which they are now taking for granted.'[36] On 10 November, the General Assembly ratified the text of the anti-Israeli resolution, which Israel's ambassador to the United Nations, Chaim Herzog, tore to pieces in the course of his speech before the Assembly.[37] During the vote, Spain's representative was absent from the hall.

None the less, during the years 1974 and 1975, years when Francoism was dying a slow death, no significant change – such as the establishment of diplomatic relations – could be expected in Spain's attitude towards Israel, particularly since that was the period of the world energy crisis. Moreover, following the October 1973 war many Third World states severed their ties with Israel, which became more isolated in the international arena.

Spanish aid to Jews in Arab countries

Throughout the period studied in this chapter, from 1956 onward, the distinction the Franco régime made between the State of Israel and the Sephardic Jews, particularly those with Spanish citizenship, was clearer than ever. Nasser's nationalization of the Suez Canal in July 1956 triggered a chain of events in Egypt which worsened the situation of Westerners in Egypt in general and of the local Jewish community in particular. Spain's ambassador in Cairo, José del Castaño, asked the Madrid Foreign Ministry to authorize him, on humanitarian grounds, to provide asylum in the embassy to anyone in mortal danger who requested it. Martín Artajo, after consulting with Franco, gave him the requested authorization, on condition that asylum was offered only to those who were indeed in imminent danger. In the autumn of 1950, King Farouk had paid a private visit to Madrid, and during a talk with the former Spanish ambassador to Cairo, Carlos Miranda, he said that his government was considering expelling some 20,000 Jews from Egypt in retaliation for Israel's expulsion of thousands of Arabs from Palestine. In consequence of this talk, the Spanish Foreign Ministry sent instructions to its representatives in Cairo to protect Jewish subjects of Spain if necessary. In any case, by the end of 1956 some 30 Sephardic families had arrived in Barcelona from Egypt. Most of them left for other countries after a few months, with the aid of the Joint, and the rest settled in the Catalonian capital.[38]

Following the joint offensive by Israel, France, and Britain, the Jews of Egypt, a community numbering some 50,000 whom the nationalist régime identified with Israel and Zionism, suffered persecution of every kind: mass imprisonment, denial of citizenship, expulsion, property confiscation, loss of employment, and more.[39] A decree published on 22 November amended the 1950 citizenship law to state that Zionists and those who were not loyal to the state could not receive Egyptian citizenship, and people in this category who already had citizenship were to be divested of it. Of course, the law did not define who was to be considered a Zionist; this was left to the whims of the authorities. The press and radio pursued a campaign of incitement and threats against Jews, and Jews were exposed to various insults in the street. This time, however, no serious incidents of violence against Jews – of the sort seen in 1948 and 1952 – were recorded. The Alexandria harbour and the Cairo airport were full of Jews seeking to leave the country. Jews who left during those months were forced to leave their property behind and to give up their Egyptian citizenship. More than one family left with only the clothes on their backs. All community activity was paralyzed, as were most of the community's health, education, and social-welfare institutions.[40]

While Nasser declared that the reports of Jews being persecuted in Egypt were baseless propaganda and that Jews suffered from no discrimination whatsoever, the Spanish Consul in Alexandria, Carlos de Urgoiti, spoke of a 'campaign of terror' conducted by the police and military authorities and the national militia of Egypt:

> Hebrews [Jews], English, French, and stateless people suffered house searches, confiscation of their property or dismissal from their employment without compensation . . . Very many of them were arrested, beaten and mistreated in all kinds of ways which recall the methods of the Cheka during the era of Red terror in Madrid.[41]

The ambassador in Cairo also refuted the official press's declarations concerning the fraternal relations between Jews and Moslems in Egypt, and the claims of the Interior Minister, Zakaria Mohieddine, to the same effect:

> These declarations . . . do not correspond to the reality of what is happening here; there is no doubt that instructions have been given to force the greatest number of Jews to evacuate this country, a campaign stimulated by the greedy desire to take over their businesses, companies, and enterprises and to give their jobs to Moslem Egyptians.[42]

Among the Jews arrested – whose total number must have exceeded 900 – were four with Spanish citizenship: León J. Israel Modiano, businessman; Jaime Simhon Bousso, clerk; Ester Yahiel Treves, nurse and director of a Jewish charity association; and León G. Carasso, commercial agent in Alexandria for a shipping firm, Naviera de Exportación Agrícola S.A. of Valencia. Among the many hundreds whose property was impounded (businesses, companies, and private houses were seized), another six were Spanish subjects: Mauricio Benzakein Hakun, Dario Israel Modiano, Bondi M. Saporta, Saul Coronel Saragossi, and Máximo and Roberto Braunstein Zaccai. Spanish Embassy officials visited the Jews with Spanish citizenship at the prison, about 20 kilometers away from Cairo, and took care of their needs. The Spanish ambassador's energetic actions prevented additional arrests of Jews with Spanish citizenship, although many of them were harassed on various pre- texts and were occasionally called to report to the police station. The ambassador informed the Egyptian authorities of

> the bad impression that the measures taken against the persons and goods of the aforementioned Spanish subjects had made on the Spanish Government . . . and that the way they had been treated [was] contrary to the excellent relations existing between our countries and to the proofs of friendship recently afforded in relation to the present events.[43]

Despite Spain's involvement in international talks to resolve the Suez crisis, and although it supplied significant quantities of arms to Egypt during the years 1952–56, it was not until March 1957 – when the authorities began to soften their attitude towards Jews – that confiscated assets were restored to the Jews mentioned above, except for those belonging to Bondi Saporta, which were not returned to their lawful owner until a year later.[44]

The leaders of the Jewish community in Madrid sent a letter to Franco in December 1956, asking him to intervene on behalf of their persecuted brothers in Egypt. They requested Spanish aid for all Sephardic Jews, not just those with Spanish citizenship, and for the rest of the Jews too, if possible, as well as asylum in Spain for those Sephardic Jews obliged to leave Egypt. Naturally, all the harassment they suffered made many Egyptian Jews opt for emigration, and the Nasser régime encouraged them to do so. In their letter to the Caudillo, the leaders of the Madrid community recalled Spain's action in saving Jews during the Second World War. Eliahu Eliachar, Vice-President of the World Federation of Sephardic Communities, approached the Spanish Consul-General in Jerusalem, Mariano Madrazo, and asked if Spain would agree to serve as a transit station for Sephardic Jews leaving Egypt, who would later continue on to other destinations. Similar requests to the Spanish government were submitted by the Anglo-Jewish Association, through the Spanish ambassador in London, Miguel Primo de Rivera, and by the World Federation of Sephardic Communities, through the Spanish ambassador in Washington, José María de Areilza.[45]

Areilza recommended acceding to these requests, since 'only a few hundred of those having to leave Egypt would go to Spain', yet 'Spain's gesture in opening its doors publicly to these former members of our nation would be highly appreciated, and would have an incalculably favourable impact' on US public opinion.[46]

Nevertheless, the Foreign Ministry in Madrid thought that the arrival in Spain of a crowd of Jewish refugees might cause a number of political and economic problems; it also had reservations about the possibility that some of the refugees might choose to remain permanently in Spain. Foreign Ministry officials also pointed out that, in 1924, Spain had given the Sephardic Jews in Egypt an opportunity to apply for Spanish citizenship and many had not bothered to exercise this right. The Ministry therefore instructed its representatives to make a strict distinction between Jews with Spanish citizenship, who were to be protected like other Spanish citizens, and other Sephardic Jews, to whom Spain was willing to provide humanitarian assistance, in co-ordination with the United Nations and other powers. In fact, in February 1957, the Spanish government decided to adopt a criterion that would restrict eligibility for assistance to Spanish citizens.[47]

Ambassador Castaño's activity on behalf of Jews with Spanish citizenship was praiseworthy but was to be expected, since these Jews were, after all, citizens of his country. The importance of this activity, therefore, should not be exaggerated, as it has been in a number of recent books. In any case, Israel's ambassador in Paris, Ya'akov Tsur, conveyed to his Spanish colleague, José Rojas y Moreno, Israel's gratitude for the efforts of the Spanish embassy in Cairo to protect the Jews there – 'not only the Sephardic Jews, but in general all those whose race or nationality made them the object of severe persecution'. Since Egypt's lack of diplomatic ties with Britain and France had left no British or French representatives in Cairo, and the United States was afraid to compromise its relations with the Arabs, the Spanish embassy, according to Tsur, was 'the only one that, with a sense of humanity and great courage, had protected and defended the persecuted Jews.'[48]

Nevertheless, no evidence has yet been found that Spain's action was as broad as the Israeli ambassador's words suggest. In contrast, the Spanish government's less generous side is reflected in a more or less contemporaneous decision concerning Sephardic Jews in Libya made by Luis Carrero Blanco, Franco's closest assistant and a blatant anti-Semite. Worried by a series of circumstances following Libya's declaration of complete independence in 1952 which included the Israeli–Arab conflict and the development of relations between Tripoli and the Arab League, the Jews still in Libya (most of them had emigrated to Israel by the mid-1950s) feared that the government would not protect them in times of danger or even renew their passports so that they could leave the country. Some Libyan-born Sephardic Jews, afraid that the situation in Libya would worsen, approached the *chargé d'affaires* in the Spanish embassy in Tripoli, Angel Díaz de Tuesta, with a request for Spanish citizenship. The request was roundly rejected by the Foreign Ministry on the instructions of Carrero Blanco.[49]

In contrast to Spain's limited actions on behalf of Jews with Spanish citizenship in Egypt in 1956 and 1957, the Franco régime made a much more important contribution to helping Jews in distress in the Arab countries during the following years. It assisted the clandestine mass exodus of Jews from Morocco at the end of the 1950s and, in the framework of 'Operation Yakhin' at the beginning of the 1960s, it allowed the organizations helping these Jews emigrate to Israel to use Spanish territory as a transit station. It also assisted Jews to leave Egypt after the Six-Day War.

In post-independence Morocco, particularly after the country joined the Arab League in 1958, Jews were subjected to restrictions and emigration to Israel was limited. President Nasser's visit to Morocco in January 1961 to attend the Casablanca Conference – a conference meant to deal with the Congo crisis, though the participants spent much of their time attacking Israel – aroused strong anti-Jewish agitation. Hundreds of Jews were arrested, and many others were attacked or harassed. The newspapers were filled with hostility towards the 'imperialist Zionist entity'. Many Jews decided to leave Morocco and emigrate to Israel. At that time there were already some 120,000 Moroccan Jews in Israel, with about 200,000 remaining in Morocco.[50]

During the years 1957–61, when the Mossad was smuggling Jews out of Morocco to Israel, one of its main routes was by land, stealing across borders.[51] A central role in this respect was played by Tangiers, a city which had once enjoyed international status, and the two Spanish enclaves in Morocco, the Mediterranean port cities Ceuta and Melilla. The columns of emigrants that reached these three cities were loaded on ferries which took them from Tangiers to British-controlled Gibraltar, or to the Spanish port of Algeciras, and from Ceuta and Melilla to either Algeciras or Malaga. All the emigrants were bound for the transit camp in Marseilles, whence they were eventually moved to Israel. Jews holding valid Moroccan passports were flown directly from Tangiers to Spain. Plans had also been made to smuggle Jews out through Ifni, another Spanish enclave on the Atlantic coast, although these plans were never implemented. Obviously, the co-operation of the British and Spanish consuls in Tangiers was vital for obtaining transit permits. The Spanish consuls in Casablanca and Fez also agreed to issue entry permits to Melilla without informing the Moroccan authorities.

Britain's assistance was the result of an arrangement between the Israeli and British governments. In contrast, the Franco régime's aid to the illegal emigration of Moroccan Jews was not rooted in any formal agreement, but based on an understanding developed in the field between Mossad operatives like Hasdai Doron and the Spanish consuls and governors of the cities of Algeciras, Ceuta, and Melilla. Some of the Mossad emissaries received Spanish passports allowing them to enter Moroccan territory without a visa. Isser Harel, head of the Mossad at the time, later wrote in his memoirs of the understanding that Mossad had come to with the Spanish authorities in these enclaves:

> The thing was achieved without any difficulty. On the contrary, the cooperation of these entities was above and beyond every expectation. Similarly, it was arranged with Spain's local authorities in the Mediterranean ports that they would allow the emigrants to pass without insisting on formalities and official documents . . .

Clearly, in a dictatorship like Franco's, such a thing could not be accomplished without authorization at the highest level. Why did the Spaniards assist this enterprise in a period when their relations with Morocco were already strained? It is difficult to believe that their motives were purely humanitarian. A partial explanation may lie in the residual bitterness that the Spanish leadership retained towards Morocco since the latter's independence and in the light of its claims on the enclaves still under Spanish control. Another reason may have been – as one of the organizers of the operation, Shlomo Havilio, was to admit later – that 'we supplied the Spaniards with various kinds of information'.[52] Either way, 'Spain [deserved] gratitude, since the hasty emigration of Jews from Morocco to Israel and France . . . could rely on the good offices of the Spanish authorities . . . '[53]

During the first half of 1961, however, Morocco and the Arab countries protested that Spain had become a tool of Israel and that it was permitting emigration to strengthen 'the Zionist enemy of the Arab world'. The anti-Spanish campaign was particularly marked at the beginning of that year, following the wreck of the former British ship *Price* (the Mossad's code name for it was *Egoz*) on the night of 10 January. Forty-four of its passengers perished: 42 illegal emigrants – 10 families – the ship's radio operator (who was the Mossad's agent on board), and a Spanish sailor. This mishap publicly exposed not only the story of the clandestine emigration of Morocco's Jews, but also Spain's involvement in it, since the ship, although flying a Honduras flag, had embarked from the Alhucemas bay near Melilla, and its captain, Francisco Morilla Reinaldo, and the two crew members were Spanish.[54] It provided an opportunity for the Moroccan media to renew their demands that Spain transfer Ceuta, Melilla, Ifni, Sahara, and other territories still under its control to Moroccan sovereignty.

A few days after the Six-Day War broke out, the Jewish community in Madrid asked General Franco to take action to protect the Jews in the Arab countries, who were again being pointed out as collaborators and agents in Israel's service and suffering from a new wave of persecution in the name of 'state security'. Similar requests reached the Spanish government from various Jewish organizations, such as the World Jewish Congress and the Jewish-American Committee by way of the Spanish ambassador in Washington, Alfonso Merry del Val, and the Spanish delegation to the United Nations. The Spanish government was, at the time, publishing declarations of support for the Arab position, while its spokesmen called for the return of the Palestinian refugees to their homes and the establishment of peace in the Middle East on the basis of the 1947 United Nations partition resolution; yet it decided to accede to the petitions.[55] Some two weeks after the fighting began, instructions were sent to Spain's legations in Egypt, Lebanon, Libya, Tunisia, and Morocco that when Jews, 'whether Sephardic or not', applied to them for assistance, 'the possibility of exercising the available means of protection should be considered, always with the agreement of the local authorities'. Spanish diplomats were told that, should the Egyptian government be prepared to allow Jews to depart, they were to provide those Jews with whatever documents and help they needed to leave the country. These instructions stressed that Spain's motives were purely humanitarian and that such actions were in no way at variance with Spain's support for the Arab cause.[56]

The remnants of the splendid Jewish community in Egypt, which from 90,000 people on the eve of the Second World War had dwindled to no more than 2,500, were treated with rough cruelty.

Not long after the war began, a few hundred Jews were arrested, comprising most of the men of the community. After two or three days, they were transferred to the Abu-Zaabal prison near the capital. A hysterical, vengeful mob tried to attack them on their way there. In prison, the Jews were brutally mistreated by their guards. The Spanish ambassador in Cairo, Angel Sagaz, petitioned the police, the Interior Ministry, and President Nasser himself to obtain the release of Jews being held in severe conditions, and to obtain permission to leave the country for those Jews who desired it. Sagaz argued that there was no reason to doubt Spanish friendship for the Arab countries, the proof being that Spain had never recognized Israel. He emphasized that for many years Spain had been trying to protect the descendants of the Jews expelled from Spain. Spain understood that the Egyptian authorities had to take measures against certain people during wartime for reasons of security but, the Spanish diplomat added, it knew that the Egyptian authorities had never discriminated against anyone 'for reasons of race or religion'. Accordingly, Spain was willing to offer documents and travel tickets to Jews wishing to leave the country, if the police had no objection to their departure.[57] The ambassador promised that those Jews who left the country would not afterwards become tools for propaganda against the Nasser régime, and would not emigrate to Israel but to countries in Europe and America. Indeed, every Jew who received a Spanish passport was asked not to publicize the situation of the Jews in Egypt and not to emigrate to Israel immediately, in order not to endanger those of their brothers who stayed behind. The Spanish passports issued to Jews were good for only two years, and could not be renewed.

During the years 1967–69, a total of more than 615 families – more than 1,500 Jews – left Egypt with the help of the Spanish government and the energetic efforts of the Spanish ambassador in Cairo, Angel Sagaz. This assistance is not mentioned at all in books on the Jews of Egypt during the twentieth century, although it was revealed by the United States press as early as 1968.[58] In the initial stages, Spain paid all the expenses involved in issuing documents, transferring Jews from prison or from their homes to the airports or seaports, and transporting them abroad. In later stages, HIAS, an aid organization for Jewish emigrants and refugees, arranged for their evacuation and paid their air fare, on Air France planes, to Paris.[59] The Jews who left Egypt were allowed to take only a few possessions with them; they were forced to leave even wedding rings, bracelets, and watches behind. At Sagaz's suggestion, they were able to deposit such valuables at the Spanish embassy in Cairo for transport out of the country in the Spanish diplomatic bag, after which they could reclaim them abroad.[60]

Spain's action earned it the gratitude of Jewish organizations all over the world. The Madrid government's anger was therefore all the greater when, in mid-December 1967, during a debate in one of the United Nations General Assembly committees on the decolonializa-tion of Gibraltar, the Israeli delegate, Arye Ilan, made a speech against Spain intended to explain why Israel was abstaining from the vote of censure against the British occupation of Gibraltar. In his speech, Ilan mentioned the 'Blue Division' which Spain had sent to fight alongside the armies of the Wehrmacht on the eastern front during the Second World War, and ridiculed the notion that a repre-sentative of dictatorial Spain should pretend to teach the committee members the laws of freedom, democracy, and social justice. The Spanish delegate, Jaime de Piniés, responded harshly. He accused Israel of 'Nazi behaviour' and 'aggressive activity' towards its Arab neighbours, and advised it to remember the help Spain had given the Jews during the Second World War. Protest and criticism were not restricted to the pages of the Spanish press. Max Mazín, the president of the Madrid Jewish community, sent a telegram of complaint to the Israeli Foreign Minister, Abba Eban, in which he denounced the 'wounding references' to Spain in the Israeli delegate's speech; Eliahu Eliachar, one of the leaders of the Sephardic community in Jerusalem, asked Abba Eban: 'How did it happen, who needed this, who gave the instructions for an Israeli representative to come out with a sharp anti-Spanish speech?'[61]

During the same period, similar efforts on behalf of Jews in distress were made by Spain's ambassadors in Baghdad and Tripoli but were unsuccessful owing to the opposition of the Iraqi and Libyan authorities. The government of Syria also took a stern line with what it saw as interference in its internal affairs. In 1972, however, follow-ing a request by the head of the Mossad, Tzvi Zamir, to his Spanish counterpart, a few dozen Syrian Jews left Syria through Lebanon with the aid of Spanish documents.[62]

The renaissance of the Jewish communities in Spain

By treating the small Jewish community in Spain with relative tolerance, the Franco régime tried to win the same moral legitimation that it might have been able to achieve from relations with the Jewish state at the end of the 1940s and during the 1950s. Until the mid-1950s, when it became clear that diplomatic relations between Spain and Israel were out of the question, General Franco established a policy allowing the Jews of Spain to conduct a more or less unfettered community and religious life. The Franco régime also encouraged research and cultural activities that made much of the Jewish contribution to medieval Spanish culture. It was not until the 1960s, however, when the régime's gestures towards Sephardic Jews in general and Jews in Spain in particular became more frequent and publicly visible. During that decade a new era can be fairly said to have begun for the Jewish community re-establishing itself on Spanish soil.

The Spanish Foreign Ministry was opposed both to a plan then being mooted to set up an Instituto de Cultura Hispano–Judía (Institute of Judeo-Hispanic Culture) and to any meeting between the leaders of the World Federation of Sephardic Communities and General Franco, fearing that such moves would be exploited to promote the interests of Israeli foreign policy. None the less, in July 1960, the Caudillo met with the heads of the Federation, notably the Sephardic Chief Rabbi of the British community, Salomon Gaón, and the President of the World Federation of Sephardic Communities, Denzil Sebag Montefiore. Others present at the meeting included the Education Minister and Max Mazín, then vice-president of the Jewish community of Madrid, Blas Piñar, Director of the Instituto de Cultura Hispánica, and Professor Pérez Castro. During the meeting, Franco again mentioned the lifeline his country had provided to Jews in the Second World War, and expressed admiration for the way Sephardic communities around the world had preserved the ancient Castillian tongue and Spanish customs. The Caudillo took the opportunity to award medals to Gaón and Montefiore. More important, however, this meeting paved the way for the establishment, about a year later, of the Instituto de Estudios Sefardíes (Institute of Sephardic Studies), which was to conduct research on the Ladino language and the cultural heritage of the Jews of Spain in co-operation with the Consejo Superior de Investigaciones Científicas and the World Federation of Sephardic Communities.[63]

In March 1964, the Caudillo took what can be seen as an important and highly symbolic step when he signed a decree authorizing the establishment of a museum of Spanish Jewish culture in Toledo in the ancient building of the El Tránsito synagogue, which had been built by Shmuel Halevy in the mid-fourteenth century. After the expulsion of the Jews, it had been turned into a church and maintained by one of the religious orders for many years until it was declared a national monument at the end of the nineteenth century. The same decree also established the composition of the Board of Directors that would administer both the museum and the adjoining library. It was to include Professor Haim Beinart (an expert on the history of the Jews of medieval Spain from the Hebrew University in Jerusalem), the president of the Jewish community in Madrid, and representatives of Sephardic organizations around the world.

That summer, a monument to Maimonides was unveiled in Córdoba, in a square named after the city of his burial, Tiberias. The civil governor of the city made a speech lauding the Sephardic Jews' ties to the Iberic homeland of their forefathers, and an international scholarly symposium held in Madrid was dedicated to the cultural heritage of the Sephardic Jews, honouring the figure of Dr Angel Pulido Fernández, the liberal senator who had striven during the first quarter of the twentieth century to promote a closer relationship between Sephardic Jews and their former homeland. This event, which formed part of the festivities marking the twenty-fifth anniversary of the Nationalist régime, permitted the authorities to express goodwill towards Jews. The Spanish postal service issued a stamp showing the courtyard of the Santa María la Blanca synagogue.

Alongside these initiatives, the Jews' community organization expanded, as did their activities in the fields of culture, education, welfare, and provision of religious services. The Jewish Agency had been sending Israeli teachers to the Barcelona community since the second half of the 1950s.[64] In 1964, a Jewish kindergarten was opened in Madrid, gradually developing into a primary school over the following years. The Maccabi youth organization, various social activities, and summer camps offered complementary Jewish educational frameworks.

At the beginning of 1965, Max Mazín and Alberto Levy, the heads of the Jewish communities of Barcelona and Madrid respectively, met with Franco in the El Pardo palace. This meeting was described inaccurately in the United States as the first of its kind between representatives of Spanish Jewry and a Spanish head of state since 1492, when Isaac Abarbanel tried in vain to persuade Ferdinand and Isabella not to expel the Jews. Among other things, Mazín and Levy asked the Caudillo to extend legal recognition to the Jewish community of Madrid and, at last, this community was granted full and explicit formal recognition by the authorities – although still only as a private rather than a public association, and only after it had changed its name from 'La Comunidad Israelita de Madrid' (The Israelite Community of Madrid) to 'La Comunidad Hebrea de Madrid' (The Hebrew Community of Madrid), so that its recognition would not be interpreted as a change in Spain's attitude towards the State of Israel.[65]

That same year, an umbrella organization was founded for the four large Jewish communities – the veteran communities in the coastal cities of North Africa, Ceuta and Melilla, and the revitalized, well-organized ones in Barcelona and Madrid. This organization became Spanish Jewry's representative in contacts with the authorities and joined the World Jewish Congress. None the less, when the Congress asked permission to organize a world conference of Sephardic Jews in Madrid, the Spanish Foreign Ministry, under heavy Arab pressure, refused, and the project was never carried out. As for the umbrella organization of the Spanish communities, it cannot be credited with any real achievements in the ensuing years, apart from the publication of a monthly magazine, *Hakesher*, which became a source of information on what was happening in the Jewish communities.[66]

Gradually the number of Jews in Spain grew. In 1950 the total was estimated at some 2,500; by the beginning of the 1970s it had already risen to over 9,000 (3,500 in Madrid, 3,000 in Barcelona, 1,400 in Melilla, 600 in Ceuta, 600 in Malaga, about 70 in Seville, and a few isolated families in other cities). The two main originating points for immigrants to Spain were North Africa – primarily Morocco, where independence and the incorporation of the Spanish protectorate and Tangiers into the Moslem kingdom had made Jews anxious about the future – and Latin America, where economic crises and constant upheavals in political life led many to abandon the continent in search of better prospects. This trend was particularly marked towards the mid-1970s, following the rise of brutal military régimes in Chile, Uruguay, and particularly Argentina. Latin American Jews were especially drawn to Spain, whose language they knew and which, moreover, had been enjoying an impressive economic boom since the 1960s. The country became even more attractive after Franco's death, when it began the process of democratization.[67]

In general, the Jews of Spain welcomed the June 1967 law guaranteeing religious freedom to the non-Catholic minorities. Extended debates in the upper echelons of the Spanish régime preceded this legislation, which guaranteed religious freedom as one of the basic rights of human dignity; the conservative majority in the

Spanish Church and members of the radical Right tried to defeat it and Franco was forced to exert all his influence to pass it. Among other provisions, the law gave all religions the right to observe religious rituals publicly and not merely privately; it permitted the non-Catholic communities to establish organizations; and it guaranteed equality between the different religions in matters of marriage, burial, and so on. Nevertheless, to the discontent of both Jews and Protestants, all non-Catholic organizations had to be registered and approved by the authorities to ensure that they were closely supervised. Obviously, absolute religious freedom and full equal rights among all religions were impossible in Franco's Spain; they were to be achieved only with the transition to democracy. None the less, as Max Mazín realized, the new law was an important step forward.[68]

On the eve of Rosh Hashana in 1968, the President of the Jewish community in Madrid introduced the community's first rabbi, Baruch Garzón Serfaty, a young man from North Africa who had been ordained only shortly before, in England. In December of that year, Madrid's synagogue and new community centre, *Beit Ya'akov* (Ya'akov House), were inaugurated on Balmes Street. Nine years earlier, in October 1959, when the previous synagogue was opened – still in a private apartment in a residential and office building, in a city centre sidestreet – the inauguration ceremony had been discreet, attended by a police supervisor and, on the censor's instructions, covered only by the international press, not the Spanish press.[69] Now, however, for the first time since 1350, a new synagogue was formally and publicly inaugurated on Spanish soil, with the approval of the authorities. The ceremony was attended by a large crowd, including Jews from all over Spain, representatives of international Jewish organizations, the chief rabbis of Britain and Argentina, Church representatives, senior government officials, and the mayor of Madrid. The new building consisted of a spacious synagogue seating some 700 worshippers, a *mikve*, and halls for social and cultural activities. The opening of this synagogue in effect constituted a sort of unofficial cancellation of the expulsion decree issued by Ferdinand and Isabella in 1492.[70] A few months later, the Jewish community of Barcelona inaugurated new additions to its community centre, and this event, too, was public, attracting a large crowd that included representatives from abroad.

None the less, the authorities tried to restrict activities in the Madrid community centre to the religious sphere and to prevent any event that might be interpreted as expressing sympathy towards the

State of Israel. At the beginning of the 1970s, the police prohibited a public meeting with the retired Israeli general Yosef Avidar. In January 1974, the jurist Dr Natan Lerner, who worked for the World Jewish Congress and Tel Aviv University, arrived in Madrid to lecture on Middle Eastern affairs. About an hour before his lecture at the community centre began, the police informed him that the event could not take place because no permit had been obtained in advance, and they threatened to disperse those present by force. The next day the Jews of Madrid protested to the Justice Ministry, claiming that since the meeting was to take place inside the community centre, no permit was needed under the law of religious freedom. The Justice Ministry rejected their arguments on the grounds that the meeting was not of a religious nature. In contrast, Lerner's lectures on 'Jewish–Christian Friendship' and 'Religious Minorities in Israel' took place as scheduled.[71]

Regardless of the régime's policy towards Jews, the Jewish community was divided within itself during those years. This schism focused mainly on the figure of one of the community's leaders, Max Mazín, a native of Poland, against the background of the increasing influence of Jews originating from Tangiers and Spanish Morocco. Although Mazín resigned his position at the beginning of 1970, his influence remained strong and the conflict continued. Moreover, the Barcelona-based Jewish community council did not function efficiently. Lerner advised the World Jewish Congress to do something about reorganizing this body and transferring its headquarters to the country's capital, and to make every effort to heal the gash in the Madrid community. One of the reasons for the disputes concerning Mazín was the activities he undertook in co-operation with Catholics in his efforts to improve Jewish–Christian understanding.

During the 1960s, partly under the influence of the decisions of the Second Vatican Council and Pope John XXIII's more liberal policy – which signaled a change in the Catholic Church's attitude towards other Christian churches and Jews – a Jewish–Christian dialogue also began in Spain. The fact that the Jewish communities in Spain, unlike the Protestant congregations, did not try to proselytize made it easier for Catholic Church officials to engage in co-operative enterprises. By the end of 1961, the first meeting of this kind took place in Madrid, in the Consejo Superior de Investigaciones Científicas, with the participation of Professor Cantera Burgos, who for years had been striving to improve understanding between members of the two religions, as well as between Spain and Israel; Father Antonio Peral of the Arias Montano Institute; Father Vicente Serrano, representing the Archbishop of Madrid; José María Pérez Losano, the editor of *Ecclesia*; Sister Esperanza Mary, mother superior of the Order of Nuestra Señora de Sión; and Rabbi Salomon Gaón, one of the leaders of the Sephardic community in London.[72] Naturally, in the Spanish Church, part of which was still steeped in its traditional anti-Semitism, some warned against dangerous liberalism and excessive tolerance towards Jews, believing it would lead to a blurring of basic religious truths. Nevertheless, such meetings were increasingly common over the following years.

The organization that had the greatest impact in this respect was the Amistad Judeo–Cristiana (Jewish–Christian Friendship), which was founded by public figures, Catholic clergy, and the leaders of the Jewish community. Its purpose was to fight prejudice and eliminate misunderstandings between Christians and Jews in Spain. The central figures in this organization were Max Mazín, the President of the Madrid Jewish community, and Father Vicente Serrano. Among other things, they met with the Minister of Information and Tourism, Manuel Fraga, in an attempt to ensure that programmes of an anti-Semitic nature would not be transmitted by radio or television, something which had happened in the past, particularly around Easter time. The most striking event organized by the association, however, was in February 1967, a week after the government ratified the draft law on religious freedom: a joint prayer ceremony carried out by a few priests and some of the leaders of the Madrid Jewish community at the Santa Rita Church, before an audience of some 500 people. The liturgy, especially prepared for the occasion, included some excerpts from the Book of Psalms, a prayer for peace from the Jewish prayer book, and a Christian prayer composed by members of the organization.[73]

The association's activities aroused criticism from certain Falangist circles and conservative sectors in the church, which were hostile to Jews ('the people who were guilty of crucifying Jesus'), as well as from representatives of the Arab countries, which viewed such projects as a cover for Zionist activity. Arab pressure led, for example, to the postponement of a lecture on the status of the different religions in Israel that had been organized by Amistad and was to have been given by Jesús María Liaño upon his return from a visit to Israel in the summer of 1965. Nor were the orthodox circles in the Jewish community always delighted by these initiatives which, on the Jewish side, were spearheaded by Max Mazín and Shmuel

Toledano; they expressed concern that the distinctions between the two religions would become blurred. Meanwhile, a similar organization was established in Barcelona in 1967, later followed by one in Seville, in the summer of 1970.

Despite the criticisms, Amistad could take credit for a number of important achievements. As a result of its co-operation with the Education Ministry, during the years 1967–69 some 200 elementary- and high-school textbooks were revised to exclude hostile references to Jews. At the association's initiative, certain definitions in the Spanish dictionary were also corrected to eliminate negative references to Jews and Judaism.[74]

In 1969, Father Vicente Serrano and his colleagues in Madrid founded the Centro de Estudios sobre el Judaísmo (Centre for Studies on Judaism), and about three years later, at the instigation of the Archbishop of Madrid, Cardinal Vicente Enrique y Tarancón, the centre became an official institution of the Church under the name Centro de Estudios Judeo-Cristianos (Centre for Judeo-Christian Studies). The new centre was supposed to enlighten Christians about the origins of their faith by acquainting them with Judaism, the cradle of Christianity.[75]

Spain had thus largely reached a reconciliation with the Jewish people, but the State of Israel was another matter. With Franco's passing, the Jews focused all their hopes on the institutions of the revived Borbon monarchy and on the figure of Don Juan Carlos himself. Before he was even declared king, *el Príncipe* had expressed his sympathy with Jews in general and Sephardic Jews in particular and advocated normalizing relations with the State of Israel.

Epilogue: The Winding Road to Diplomatic Relations (1976–86)

The Caudillo's death and the parallel demise of the Francoist régime opened new horizons for the Jewish community in Spain, which numbered some 11,000 at the time. Only a democratic Spain was able to permit true religious freedom. Article 16 of the Constitution of December 1978 guaranteed unrestricted freedom of religion and worship, subject only to the necessity of maintaining public order.[1] All restrictions were lifted from the non-Catholic minorities in Spain and their status was no longer inferior to that of Catholicism, which ceased to be the state religion. The King and Queen, who played a vital role in the transition to democracy, also made an important contribution to relations between Christians and Jews in Spain, and to reconciling Sephardic Jews with the land of their Iberian fore-fathers. By February 1976, Juan Carlos was already meeting with the heads of the Jewish communities of Madrid and Barcelona, as well as the heads of the Sephardic communities of Britain, the Netherlands, and other European countries. In May of that year – just before the royal couple flew to the United States – Queen Sofía of Spain, who had taken a seminar on religion at the Universidad Autónoma de Madrid, participated in Friday evening prayers at the synagogue in the capital. This ceremony, which was conducted by Rabbi Benito Garzón and received wide coverage on the front pages of both Spanish newspapers and the Jewish world press, was attended by Catholic, Baptist, Lutheran, and Mormon representatives and had great symbolic significance for the creation of a tolerant atmosphere in the new Spain.[2]

Yet there was still no real change in the relations with Israel. In his coronation speech before the Spanish Parliament, after Franco's

death in November 1975, King Juan Carlos spoke of the need to universalize Spain's foreign relations and to normalize its ties with all the
states of the world. In the course of 1977, Spain did indeed establish
diplomatic relations with Mexico, the Soviet Union, and the other
countries of the Eastern bloc.[3] Hopes that relations would also be
established with Israel were soon dashed, however. Spain's pro-Arab
policy was one of the traditions that the Francoist dictatorship
handed down to the new democracy. Under the governments of
Carlos Arias Navarro, Adolfo Suárez, and Leopoldo Calvo Sotelo,
the reluctance to establish full diplomatic ties with Israel continued,
as did the fear of Arab reactions to any rapprochement with the
Jewish state. This maintenance of the status quo can be attributed to
a number of factors, including inertia, concern – at least in the early
years – about the reactions of the extreme Right (*'el Bunker'*), the
small Jewish community's negligible influence on Spain's decision-
makers, and Spain's wish to maintain good relations with the Arab
countries, particularly in light of its problems with Morocco concerning the future of the coastal cities Ceuta and Melilla. The influence of
Arab economic power following the war of October 1973 was also
significant; the oil crisis dealt a heavy blow to the Spanish economy,
which was completely dependent on Middle Eastern oil for its energy
needs, and the Spanish balance of payments suffered, registering a
deficit of more than 4 billion dollars in 1976.[4]

　　None the less, even in the first post-Franco government, one
notable effort was made to bring about the establishment of ties.
That effort was the initiative of the Foreign Minister, José María de
Areilza, who since at least the mid-1960s had been expressing consistent public support for Hispano-Israeli rapprochement. In the
middle of December 1975, Areilza was received at the Zarzuela
Palace by the King, to whom Max Mazín had conveyed, some time
previously, a friendly message from the President of the State of
Israel, Efraim Katzir. At the time, the King was thinking that relations with Israel could be conveniently normalized as part of the
process of universalizing the monarchy's relations in general.[5] It
should be noted, however, that Areilza's initiative did not have Arias
Navarro's approval. The Consul-General in Jerusalem at the time
was a connection of Areilza's, Santiago de Churruca y Plaza, the
Count of Campo Rey. The Consul met with Ionnathan Pratto (who
was again serving as director of the Foreign Ministry's division of
relations with the Christian churches) to inform him that Areilza
believed the time had come to establish relations between the two

states, but not full ones and not immediately. Areilza's proposal was that Israel should first set up a consulate in Spain, but Israel rejected this suggestion. Such ideas had been relevant in the 1950s and 1960s, but Israeli Foreign Ministry officials were no longer willing even to discuss such a level of relations. The Foreign Minister, Yigal Allon, said that Israel wanted full relations at the ambassador level – in other words, all or nothing.

According to Pratto, Areilza agreed after a time to the opening of an Israeli embassy, but would not consent to the appointment of an ambassador – only a *chargé d'affaires*. In Jerusalem, Areilza's plan was not completely clear but the two states began to draw up communiqués of mutual recognition. Pratto and the Director of the West European division, Yeshayahu Anug, together drafted a communiqué approved by Allon which was nevertheless pigeon-holed because the Spanish Prime Minister, Arias Navarro, resisted the idea, as did sectors of the army and the extreme Right. On one occasion, for example, Areilza made statements in a recorded interview on Spanish television favouring the normalization of ties with the Soviet Union, Mexico, and Israel. When he watched the interview that evening, he discovered that the reference to Israel had been deleted. The Arab countries, for their part, were exerting strong pressure. In the end, Areilza did not have enough time to bring about a change in the government's position on Israel. In July 1976, Arias Navarro – who had gradually come to be perceived as an obstacle to the democratization process in Spain – was forced to resign, and Areilza was no longer Foreign Minister.[6] Franco had appointed Arias after the assassination of Carrero Blanco to ensure the continuation of the régime and to perpetuate the values of the Nationalist camp which had won the Civil War. However, the King became increasingly dissatisfied with Arias's inability to deal with the growing power of the opposition in any way except by repressive violence. The King's views became evident when he allowed a senior journalist from *Newsweek* to quote him referring to Arias as 'an unmitigated disaster'.[7]

Juan Carlos sought another politician who would be able to guide the transition to democracy and to cope with pressure from the right-wing '*Bunker*' as well as from the left-wing opposition. He found such a man in the person of Adolfo Suárez, Secretary-General of the 'Movement'. Strangely enough, it was Suárez, a product of the Francoist system, who was able to dismantle it.

The new government, led by Suárez and with Marcelino Oreja as

Foreign Minister, was unwilling to establish diplomatic ties with Israel. Suárez had reportedly been ready to consider such ties at the beginning of his term, and to that end had sent a trusted representative, the journalist José Mario Armero, to the United States to meet with the Director-General of the Israeli Foreign Ministry, Shlomo Avineri. He changed his mind under pressure from his pro-Arab advisors and out of fear that the Arabs would institute an oil embargo or take other retaliatory measures, such as severing diplomatic relations, sponsoring terrorist acts, or backing the claims then being heard in the Organization of African Unity that the Canary Islands were in fact African colonies entitled to independence.[8] Despite the rhetoric about Hispano-Arab friendship, in those years the Arab countries invested much less money in Spain than they did in a number of other European countries which maintained good relations with Israel. However, Suárez was already having enough trouble trying to ensure a calm transition to democracy and so preferred not to raise foreign-policy issues that might exact no small political and economic price – notably the establishment of relations with Israel.[9] At the same time, Israel's policy in the occupied territories, the defeat of the Labour party and the victory of the right-wing Likud in the Knesset elections of May 1977, and the subsequent invasion of southern Lebanon in the framework of 'Operation Litani' in the spring of 1978 were all factors working against the chances of engineering a breakthrough in Hispano-Israeli relations.

In December 1976, the World Jewish Congress convention met in Madrid at the request of the local Jewish community and with the permission of the authorities. The convention was intended to highlight the change that had taken place in Spain's attitude to Jews and to demonstrate support for the process of democratization in that country. At the last moment, however, Rafael Mendizábal, the Undersecretary of the Justice Ministry and a member of the Interministerial Commission on Religious Liberty, cancelled his scheduled participation in the opening ceremony. None of the government ministers met with the convention-goers, and the King did not meet with the President of the Congress, Nahum Goldmann, and other leaders of the organization as planned. The reason was pressure by Arab diplomats, who feared that the event would become a lever in the process of rapprochement between Spain and Israel and made threats of economic retaliation. Jerusalem was angry. Spain's behaviour was perceived as an insult to the entire Jewish people, and a shameful capitulation to Arab pressure. The Foreign Minister, Yigal Allon, condemned this 'insulting behaviour and submission to naked Arab pressure', while Moshe Dayan wrote of 'the slap in the face we received in Madrid'. He saw an 'insult to the Jewish people as a whole in the way Spain behaves toward Israel'.[10]

In the following months, during his many visits to Arab capitals, Marcelino Oreja promised his hosts that Spain was unlikely to normalize relations with Israel in the near future. While visiting Jordan, he even declared that Spain would not establish diplomatic ties with Israel until the latter returned the territories occupied in the 1967 war and recognized the rights of the Palestinian people. Under the current circumstances, Oreja explained, instituting relations with Israel might be interpreted as conferring legitimacy on the occupation of those territories. In April 1977, Suárez met in Washington with the former United States ambassador to the United Nations, Arthur Goldberg, who raised the issue of ties with Israel in the name of the US Jewish organizations. The meeting was conducted in shrill tones, and ended after only 10 minutes with great animosity on both sides.[11]

Adolfo Suárez is best remembered in the Hispano–Israeli connection, however, as the first European Prime Minister to receive the PLO leader Yasser Arafat officially (in September 1979). The embrace Suárez gave Arafat, who arrived in Madrid wearing a military uniform and a gun belt, and the friendship shown towards the Palestinian leader aroused a storm of protest from Jews in Spain and Jewish organizations in other countries, who demanded the speedy establishment of diplomatic ties with Israel to redress the balance. Prominent Jews in the United States even threatened an economic and tourism boycott of Spain. Perhaps in an attempt to soften the bad impression created by Arafat's visit, Oreja made a speech in the United Nations General Assembly explaining that his country in fact recognized Israel's right to exist, since, after all, the United Nations recognized the right of all the states in the region to live in peace within secure and recognized borders. Israel and the American Jews, however, did not see this as a meaningful step forward. Marcelino Oreja met in New York with the heads of the Conference of Presidents of Major Jewish Organizations in the United States, who demanded the prompt initiation of relations with Israel. This talk, too, took place in an acrimonious atmosphere, and after 15 minutes, the Jewish representatives left the room in a rage.[12]

In the ensuing months, Suárez adopted a 'progressive, independent' foreign policy, and his hostility towards Israel deepened. The historic visit of the Egyptian President, Anwar Sadat, to Jerusalem in November 1977, and the signing of the peace treaty between Israel and Egypt about a year-and-a-half later did not bring the desired change in Madrid's position. Spain was now making normalization of its relations with Israel conditional on a 'comprehensive solution' of the Middle Eastern conflict, including the Palestinian problem. Like the countries of the Arab rejectionist front, the Spanish government did not see the treaty as a significant move towards global peace in the region, and it was supported in this view by both the extreme Right and Left, the latter viewing Israel as a tool of American imperialism in the Middle East. A disappointment was also in store for those who hoped that the election of the Sephardic Yitzhak Navon, an expert on Spanish–Jewish folklore, as President of Israel would pave the way to Madrid.

In 1981, Suárez resigned the premiership after almost five years in office. After having guided the transition from dictatorship to democracy, he was both physically and psychologically exhausted. ETA terror, military unrest, the intrigues of his disintegrating party, Unión de Centro Democrático (Union of the Democratic Centre), economic problems, and his declining popularity in public-opinion polls – all these factors took a heavy toll. He was replaced by his deputy, Leopoldo Calvo Sotelo. The new government adopted a more pro-Western orientation than its predecessor. Spain joined NATO, and negotiations for Spain's admission to the European Community gained momentum. At the same time, Madrid initiated contacts with Israel concerning the possibility of establishing diplomatic ties, and by the summer of 1982 Calvo Sotelo and his Foreign Minister, José Pedro Pérez Llorca, were already close to a decision. However, Israel's invasion of Lebanon, the massacre in the Sabra and Shatila Palestinian refugee camps by Israel's Christian allies, and the decision to bring forward the general elections in Spain put an end to these talks.[13]

The absence of relations with Israel was gradually becoming an obvious anomaly, since the only other country with which Spain did not have diplomatic relations at the time was Albania. The situation really became intolerable, however, when democratic Spain began to move towards full integration in the European Community and NATO. Given these circumstances, throughout the first half of the 1980s a number of Western European countries – notably the Netherlands, France, and the Federal Republic of Germany – and many delegates in the European Parliament urged Spain to normalize its relations with Israel, since all the states of the Community, which aspired to a common foreign policy, had diplomatic relations with Israel, and the Community itself maintained trade agreements with it.

In the summer of 1980, Yitzhak Shamir, the Israeli Foreign Minister, and David Kimchi, the Director-General of the Ministry, decided to send the Argentine-born Shmuel Hadas, an experienced diplomat, as an unofficial ambassador to Madrid, where he would work on creating a more favourable feeling towards Israel in the capital. Officially, Hadas served first as Israel's representative to the Conference on Security and Cooperation in Europe, and later as the country's permanent representative in the World Tourism Organiza-tion, a United Nations organization based in Madrid. Hadas soon embarked on a broad range of activities, making contacts with political, economic, cultural, and media groups. In these activities, Hadas relied on the Madrid Jewish community and various organiza-tions that had arisen in Spain at the end of the 1970s, such as the Association for Spain–Israel Friendship which was headed by promi-nent intellectuals like Julio Caro Baroja and Camilo José Cela; the Association for Spain–Israel Cultural Relations; and the Hispano-Israeli Association for the Promotion of Trade and Industry. He initiated or co-ordinated visits by Israeli personalities to Spain – sometimes in the teeth of the Spanish Foreign Ministry's disapproval (for example, the visit by the ex-Defence and Foreign Minister, General Moshe Dayan) – and trips to Israel by Spanish politicians of various parties, journalists, businessmen, intellectuals, artists, and clergymen.[14]

The absence of diplomatic relations was also made more evident by the fact that in other, non-political spheres, ties between Spain and Israel were gradually expanding. The volume of trade between the two states was still negligible and suffered from sharp oscillations, but it was steadily increasing (see table), even though it was clear to all that a real breakthrough in trade relations would be possible only after the establishment of formal ties – as indeed eventually proved to be the case. In 1977, Israel took part for the first time in an agri-cultural exposition in Zaragoza, and continued to do so in the following years. In 1984, Israel was represented at Madrid's big trade fair, and later at the Barcelona international fair as well. Spain even served as a transit station for Israeli goods en route to Morocco.[15]

Tourism and air connections were developing as well. In 1972, the Spanish travel agency Melia opened an office in Tel Aviv and com-

ISRAEL'S FOREIGN TRADE WITH SPAIN
(IN MILLIONS OF DOLLARS)

Year	Imports from Spain to Israel	Exports from Israel to Spain	Trade Balance
1950	0.2	–	–0.2
1960	0.1	0.5	0.4
1970	3.3	10.1	6.8
1975	30.9	15.5	–15.4
1976	19.0	12.8	–6.2
1977	19.8	12.3	–7.5
1978	35.2	16.9	–18.3
1979	47.8	69.7	21.9
1980	39.6	36.7	–2.9
1981	59.1	30.4	–28.7
1982	42.1	28.4	–13.7
1983	124.7	27.0	–97.7
1984	84.2	29.5	–54.7
1985	77.1	29.9	–47.2

Source: Central Bureau of Statistics, *Statistical Abstract of Israel* [Hebrew], 1978, 1979, 1980, 1982, 1983, 1984, 1986.

mercial flights between the two countries were inaugurated at the end of the 1970s. The number of Israelis visiting Spain began to rise rapidly. During the 1980s, tens of thousands of Israeli tourists descended on Spain every year, and the number of Spanish tourists visiting Israel, although still meagre, grew steadily – except in 1982, the year Israel invaded Lebanon. In the summer of 1983, reflecting Felipe González's Socialist government's readiness to improve relations with Israel, the two national airlines, Iberia and El Al, inaugurated a direct, official route between Madrid and Tel Aviv, to the displeasure of some Arab states.[16] Branches of the ZIM shipping company and various Israeli economic concerns, such as Koor, operated in Spain. The press reported co-operation between the Spanish and Israeli security services in the war against terrorism. Cultural relations were also improving, finding expression in academic conferences, tours by orchestras and folkloric, ballet, and theatre groups, the translation of literary works from Hebrew to Spanish and Spanish to Hebrew, and other activities. The Maccabi Tel Aviv basketball team was well-known to Spanish sports fans; it had been competing since 1966 against Spanish teams such as Juventus and Real Madrid in various frameworks.

The rise to power of the Spanish Socialist Party (Partido Socialista

Obrero Español – PSOE) at the end of 1982, after a sweeping victory in the general elections, was the climax of the transition to democracy in Spain, and it also aroused many hopes in Israel. While still in the opposition, prominent party members, including their leader, Felipe González, had advocated establishing relations with Israel, although the party had adopted various resolutions censuring Israel's occupation of the West Bank and the Gaza Strip and the country's shows of aggression towards various Arab countries, particularly Lebanon. It also called on Israel to allow the Palestinians to exercise their legitimate national rights. Nevertheless, González and the Foreign Minister, Fernando Morán, vindicated Israel's refusal to establish relations with Franco's régime at the end of the 1940s. González viewed the lack of relations with Israel as an anachronistic anomaly.

The connection between the Spanish Socialist Party and the Israeli Labour Party, both members of the Socialist International, played an important role. González had been sympathetic to Israel since his visits there in the 1970s as a guest at the Labour Party conventions (in 1971, he was presented to the convention participants anonymously, as the representative of a clandestine sister party). He had been impressed at the time by the kibbutz way of life and the enterprises of *Hevrat Ha'Ovdim* (the *Histadrut*'s economic umbrella organization). At a Tel Aviv press conference in February 1977, González was already promising that if his party won the general elections in Spain it would establish diplomatic relations with Israel. He emphasized the long-standing ties between his party and the State of Israel and the Jews: 'We lay in the same trenches together, we fought together for the same principles. We are tied to the Israeli Labour Party'. This inter-party channel would prove very important in the process of forging relations between the two states. Spain's socialist trade union (Unión General de Trabajadores – UGT) also had a long history of ties with the Israeli *Histadrut*. During the 1960s and the 1970s, *Histadrut* funds had transferred aid to the UGT, and union activists had secretly visited Israel, where they received training in *Histadrut* institutions. *Histadrut* representatives had visited them in Spain even while Franco was still in power. The leader of the UGT, Nicolás Redondo, visited Israel in 1977 and 1983, and signed a broad agreement with the *Histadrut* covering co-operation, youth, and women. In 1983, the UGT conference passed a resolution supporting the establishment of diplomatic relations with Israel.[17]

From 1983 on, continuous but clandestine contacts began between, on one side, the Secretary of the Spanish government, Julio

Feo, the Prime Minister's aide, Juan Antonio Yañez, and the Director of the Africa and Asia Division of the Foreign Ministry, Manuel Sassot, and, on the other, Shmuel Hadas and Knesset member Micha Harish, then head of the international division of the Labour Party. Harish was well acquainted with both González and other senior members of the Socialist Party. As a member of MAPAI's 'Young Guard', Harish had established contacts back in 1965 with young members of the Spanish Socialist party, still operating in the underground. In February 1967, as international secretary of the Young Guard, he participated in the Socialist party convention that took place in a cemetery in Bilbao. At the Labour Party conventions of 1971 and 1977 he again met with González.[18]

Despite González's declaration to Israeli journalists – 'our intention to establish diplomatic relations with Israel is clear and firm. We will do it in the not-so-distant future, but we have not yet set the exact date'[19] – the talks had their ups and downs. The Spanish government had trouble finding the 'right moment', and was deterred by every expression of protest by Arab diplomacy or disapproval by the more radical wing of the Socialist Party, led by the pro-Palestinian Alfonso Guerra, who, for example, in July 1982, supported the call to expel the Israeli Labour Party from the Socialist International because of its support for the invasion of Lebanon. From the end of the 1960s, support for the Palestinian struggle occupied an important place in the world of Spanish left-wing revolutionary symbols, whereas Israel was beginning to appear as a tool of the United States' imperialist policy in the Middle East.[20] The fear of an Arab oil embargo continued – even though in the 1980s the world energy market was characterized by a surplus in the supply of oil, prices were declining, and so was Arab power – together with the fear of possible commercial retaliation, or of terrorist operations against Spain in reaction to a normalization of relations with Israel.

During the same period, González was also exposed to opposing pressure from the Jewish organizations in the United States, as well as public opinion and the media at home. The elections of October 1982 essentially erased the UCD from the political map. The main opposition to the new Socialist government was the Alianza Popular (Popular Alliance). This party and its leader, Manuel Fraga Iribarne, who had visited Israel at the beginning of 1981, loudly and consistently demanded the unconditional establishment of relations with Israel. Such relations, claimed the party's spokesmen, would not conflict with Spain's continued friendship with the Arab world and its support for the Palestinian cause.[21] Many newspapers incessantly debated the question of relations with Israel, and printed articles supporting the establishment of formal ties. According to public opinion polls published by the daily *El País* in 1983, 38 per cent of those surveyed favoured establishing relations with Israel, 15 per cent were opposed, and 47 per cent had no opinion on the subject, or did not answer the question. A year later the newspaper published a similar survey, and its results indicated a rise in the proportion of those favouring ties with Israel: 44 per cent were in favour, 12 per cent were opposed, and 44 per cent preferred not to state an opinion.[22] Caught between these conflicting pressures, González had trouble reaching a decision; he tried gradually to prepare public opinion and the heads of the Arab countries for that inevitable step in the process of universalizing democratic Spain's foreign relations: the establishment of ties with Israel.[23]

The Spanish Socialist Party's gradual adoption of a more pro-Western policy, and a Cabinet reshuffle in the summer of 1985, brought the contacts with Israel into a new phase. The new Foreign Minister, Francisco Fernández Ordoñez, pursued the issue of relations with Israel much more energetically than his predecessor, Fernando Morán, who had always called for some sort of 'compensation' from Israel in the form of concessions in its relations with the Palestinians or an economic obligation to Spain in exchange for establishing relations.[24] But González had to make the decision. The Israeli air force's bombing raid on the PLO headquarters in Tunis in October led to a suspension of talks for a few weeks. Towards Christmas, however, just before Spain joined the European Community, González made his decision, and on 9 January 1986 representatives of the two states agreed on the draft of a joint announcement of the establishment of relations.[25]

A week later, the joint Hispano-Israeli communiqué was published at The Hague (because at the time the Dutch government was taking its turn as president of the European Community, and perhaps also because the Dutch Parliament, when voting for Spain's admission to the Community, had also passed a resolution calling on the Spanish government to regularize its relations with Israel). Two days later, the two Prime Ministers, Felipe González and Shimon Peres, met in the Dutch capital. The ambassadors of the Arab countries in Madrid were invited to a meeting at the Spanish Foreign Ministry, where Spain's Middle Eastern policy was explained to them. Spain's long-standing fear of retaliatory measures by the Arabs soon proved to have been exaggerated, if not completely unfounded: the Secretary-General of the Arab League postponed a scheduled visit to Madrid, Iran and Iraq called their ambassadors home for a while for consultations, and no further measures were taken.[26]

Thus, in the mid-1980s, the gap was finally closed between the well-developed ties that already existed in many fields – economics, trade, tourism, culture, sports, and more – and relations on the diplomatic and political levels, which had been almost frozen by the Spaniards since 1956. Israel had wooed Madrid in one form or another for 30 years, but it was not until 1986 that the cycle that had begun with the birth of the State of Israel finally ended, and the extensive relations in non-political fields received official validation in the form of full, formal diplomatic relations.

Notes

Introduction

1. *Yediot Aharonot* (Tel Aviv), *Ha'aretz* (Tel Aviv), and *The Jerusalem Post*, 20 Jan. 1986.
2. *Ha'aretz*, 24 Jan. 1986, *The Jerusalem Post*, 19 Jan. 1986. Similarly, the day after the establishment of diplomatic relations was announced, the Spanish writer Camilo José Cela wrote: 'We Spaniards have just put an end not to a situation created thirty or forty years ago, but to the wrong step we took five centuries ago.' Quoted in Shmuel Hadas, 'España e Israel: Quinientos años después', *Política Exterior*, Vol. 30 (1992/3), p. 193.
3. On the revival of the Jewish community in Spain in the second half of the nineteenth century and the beginning of the twentieth, see Haim Avni, *Contemporary Spain and the Jewish People* (Hebrew) (Tel Aviv: 1974) Chapter I; Haim Beinart, *The New Jewish Community in Spain: Background, Reality, and Assessment* (Hebrew) (Jerusalem: 1969) pp. 16–21; J.J. Lichtenstein, 'The Reaction of West European Jewry to the Reestablishment of a Jewish Community in Spain in the 19th Century', Ph.D. diss., Yeshiva University (New York: 1962); Manuel Fernandez Rodríguez, 'España y los judíos en el reinado de Alfonso XII', *Hispania*, Vol. 25, No. 100 (1965) pp. 565–84; Julio Caro Baroja, *Los judíos en la España moderna y contemporanea* (Madrid: 1961), Vol. 3; Isidro Gonzalez, *El retorno de los judíos* (Madrid: 1991).
4. From a speech by Abba Eban before the United Nations General Assembly, 16 May 1949. See Documents of the Ministry of Foreign Relations in Israel State Archives; Jerusalem (hereafter ISA), 2424/7a; and United Nations, *Official Records of the Third Session of the General Assembly*, Part II (Lake Success, New York: 1949) p. 500.
5. Shlomo Ben-Ami, *La revolución desde arriba: España 1936–79* (Madrid: 1980) p. 116.

Chapter 1

1. Gideon Rafael, *Destination Peace: Three Decades of Israeli Foreign Policy* (London: 1981) pp. 5–6.
2. Walter Eytan to I. Linton, Israel's minister in Tokyo, 18 Feb. 1954 (Israel State Archives (hereafter ISA), 2385/27). More than a year after the establishment of Israel, José Sebastián de Erice, second in command at the Spanish Foreign Ministry, wrote to the Spanish Consul in Jerusalem: 'We

are still awaiting the announcement [of the establishment of the State of Israel] prior to official recognition . . . that has been sent to other countries'. See Erice to Casares, 2 June 1945 (Archivo del Ministerio de Asuntos Exteriores, Madrid (hereafter AMAE), Leg. R.4784/26). Initially, Israel passed over Salazar's Portugal as well – but by 13 March 1949, when it notified Lisbon of its creation and of the formation of its first government, Israel was already making a distinction between Spain and Portugal. See memorandum by the head of the Latin American division, Avraham Darom (Drapkin), dated 3 April 1950 (ISA 2413/24).

3. Eliahu Elath, *San Francisco Diary* (Hebrew) (Tel Aviv: 1971) p. 118; and idem, *The Struggle for Statehood* (Hebrew) (Tel Aviv: 1982), Vol. 2, pp. 276–8.

4. Netanel Lorch, 'Israel–Spain: The Establishment of Diplomatic Relations' (Hebrew), *Skirah Hodshit* (March 1986) p. 5. The letter was signed by all the democratic parties operating in the Spanish underground, from the right-wing constitutional monarchist party to the left-wing Socialist party.

5. Yosef Ariel to the Foreign Ministry, 19 March 1954 (ISA 2541/13A).

6. 'Franco Is Helping the Arabs' (Hebrew), *Ha'aretz*, 8 March 1948; 'The Beginning of Spanish–Arab Friendship' (Hebrew), *Ha'aretz*, 5 Sept. 1949; AMAE, R.4786/124 (8 March 1949). Concerning the one-sided reports published in Spanish newspapers, see US National Archives, Documents of the Department of State, Record Group 59 (Washington, DC) (hereafter NA), 28 April 1948 (852.00/4-2848) and 12 July 1948 (852.00/7-1248). A collection of press clippings on these subjects can be found in AMAE, R.2804/4. See also the letters of Shimshon Glanzmann from Barcelona to the Jewish Agency (22 Jan. 1949), and from Haim Glanzmann to the Zionist *Histadrut* in the summer of 1949, in the Central Zionist Archive in Jerusalem (hereafter CZA) (S5T/499).

7. See, for example, *Madrid*, 5 Nov. 1948.

8. *Lucha* (Teruel), 12 Jan. 1949. See also his call for a crusade to defend the holy places, which appeared six months earlier in *ABC* and *Ya*, 23 June 1948.

9. Report by Secretary Velarde, 'Los intereses españoles en relación con el problema de Palestina', n.d. (probably Jan. 1949) (AMAE, R.4785/61). Anger and criticism of Israel were also aroused in Spain by the *Hagana*'s bombing, on 5 Jan. 1948, of the Semiramis Hotel in Jerusalem, in the mistaken belief that it was a centre for the Mufti's people. The bomb killed 14 citizens, including the Spanish Consul, Manuel Allendesalazar. See, for example, *Ya*, 9 Jan. 1948.

10. A few years later, the Secretary of the Arab League said that 'Spain supplied arms to the Arabs during the war in Palestine'. *Ha'aretz*, 25 April 1952. See also Erice to the Consul-General in Jerusalem, 24 June 1949 (AMAE, R.4784/26); note concerning the sale of arms to Egypt, 23 Oct. 1948 (AMAE R.4783/46); sale of arms to Syria, Feb. 1949 (R.4786/8); Luis Suárez Fernández, *Francisco Franco y su tiempo* (Madrid: 1984), Vol. IV, p. 261; and Antonio Marquina and Gloria Inés Ospina, *España y los judíos en el siglo XX* (Madrid: 1987) pp. 241–4.

11. *Documents on the Foreign Policy of Israel* (Hebrew) (Jerusalem: 1984), Vol. II, p. 431. Sharett's reply was sent on 20 Feb. 1949. See also Erice to Lequerica, 14 Feb. 1949, and Lequerica to Artajo, 16 Feb. 1949 (AMAE, R.4784/39). Eliahu Eliachar, however, recounts in his memoirs the meet-

ings he held back in 1947 and 1948 with representatives of Francoist Spain in Europe and America, who expressed support for Israel. See *Living with Jews* (Hebrew) (Jerusalem: 1980) p. 346.

12. Fingerhut's letter, which was sent to Dr Yosef Burg, then a delegate to the constituent assembly, was sent on by him two weeks later to the Foreign Ministry (ISA, 2541/13A). See also Arístides Peña to Erice, 10 March 1949. Hirsch's letter was sent on 8 March 1949 (ISA, 2541/13A).

13. Eliachar to Eytan, 20 March 1949 (ISA, 2541/13A); Eliachar, *Living with Jews*, pp. 346–8. Barukh, who continued to try to promote relations between the two countries through the early 1950s, wanted to become Israel's Honorary Consul in Spain. In 1954, Barukh was described by Rabbi Maurice Perlzweig, a leader of the World Jewish Congress, as a wealthy, disreputable character who was bound to the Francoist propaganda service. See secret memorandum from Perlzweig, 27 April 1954 (CZA, Z6/852).

14. In 1950 Ignacio Bauer, one of the Jewish community leaders in Spain, estimated the number of Jews in Spain to be some 2,500 (Avni, *Contemporary Spain*, p. 224; see also *The Jerusalem Post*, 30 Aug. 1950). By the beginning of 1951 his estimate had risen to 3,500 (*Herut*, 10 Jan. 1951). For various statistics, see Caro Baroja, *Los judíos*, Vol. 3, pp. 214–15; and *Jewish Chronicle* (London), 1 April 1949 and 6 Oct. 1950. In Spanish Morocco the number of Jews was much larger, of course (see Juan Bta. Vilar, 'Evolución de la población israelita en Marruecos Español, 1940–1955', *Estudios Sefardíes* 1 (1978), pp. 91–120). On the congenial treatment of the Jews of Spanish Morocco, most of whom aided – willingly or unwillingly – the Nationalists during the Civil War, see 'Minuta de la Dirección de Relaciones Culturales', 22 Nov. 1948 (AMAE, R.2767/70).

15. Nehemia Robinson, *The Spain of Franco and Its Policies towards Jews* (New York: 1952), pp. 9–13; Caesar C. Aronsfeld, *The Ghosts of 1492* (New York: 1979), pp. 42–51; and José Antonio Lisbona, *Retorno a Sefarad. La política de España hacia sus judíos en el siglo XX* (Barcelona: 1993) Ch. 5.

16. Avni, *Contemporary Spain*, p. 226, and *Ha'aretz*, 11 Jan. 1949. See also embassy in Cairo to State Department, 5 April 1949 (NA, 852.012/4-549).

17. AMAE, R.2996/1. The decree itself, the Spanish Foreign Ministry's guidelines, and the list of the Jewish families entitled to benefit from the decree also appear in an appendix to a book by Federico Ysart, *España y los judíos en la segunda guerra mundial* (Barcelona: 1973), pp. 175–91. See also Marquina y Ospina, *España y los judíos*, pp. 237–9; and *Jewish Chronicle*, 14 Jan. 1949 and 25 Feb. 1949.

18. *Sefarad*, Vol. 9 (1949), Fasc. I, p. 259.

19. *Wiener Library Bulletin*, Vol. 3 (1949), p. 39.

20. Aronsfeld, *The Ghosts*, pp. 53–4.

21. Avni, *Contemporary Spain*, p. 225; George Hills, *Franco – The Man and His Nation* (London: 1967), p. 410; and Caro Baroja, *Los judíos*, p. 214.

22. Quoted in Aronsfeld, *The Ghosts*, p. 43. At the beginning of the Civil War, anarchist activists had entered the Barcelona synagogue, but they did no damage. The synagogue ceased to operate for a few months, but reopened with the blessing of the Republican authorities. It closed down when Barcelona fell to the Nationalists.

23. Yitzhak Weissman, *Against the Forces of Evil* (Hebrew) (Tel Aviv: 1968), pp. 136–9; and *Hatzofeh*, 20 Nov. 1946.
24. *Jewish Chronicle*, 3 Feb. 1950. In Spanish Morocco, in contrast, Jews were allowed to conduct their religious worship and community life without hindrance.
25. On the restrictions on freedom of religion in Franco's Spain, see J.W.D. Trythall, *Franco – A Biography* (London: 1970) pp. 192–3; José Amodia, *Franco's Political Legacy* (London: 1977) pp. 188–93; and Benjamin Welles, *Spain: The Gentle Anarchy* (New York: 1965) pp. 177–82.
26. *Jewish Chronicle*, 28 Jan. 1949, p. 9. In the spring of 1948, Haim Glanzmann, a Zionist activist in Barcelona, wrote about the heavy restrictions on non-Catholic religious worship in Spain. See his memorandum, Jerusalem, 1 April 1948 (CZA, KKL5/16227). On the psychological pressure to which the Jews of Spain were subjected under the Catholic, nationalistic dictatorship, see also Rabbi Ephraim F. Einhorn to Ambassador Griffis, 20 July 1951 (NA, 611.52/7-2051).
27. On the Republic, see Raymond Carr, *Spain 1808–1975*, 2nd ed. (London: 1982), Ch. 15; and Gabriel Jackson, *The Spanish Republic and the Civil War 1931–39* (Princeton: 1965). On the religious provisions in the Republican constitution and the debate waged over them, see Jackson, *The Spanish Republic*, pp. 48–51.
28. On the Republic and its attitude towards Jews, see Avni, *Contemporary Spain*, pp. 44–51; Caro Baroja, *Los judíos*, pp. 209–11; Aronsfeld, *The Ghosts*, pp. 37–43; and Lisbona, *Retorno a Sefarad*, Ch. 2.
29. Ricardo de la Cierva, *Historia del franquismo: Aislamiento, transformación, agonía 1945–75* (Barcelona: 1978) p. 16.
30. The British Foreign Office held that as long as a formal state of war continued in Spain and no significant new legislation was passed, most of the rights granted by the *Fuero de los Españoles* could not be exercised, and the law of the local authorities was negligible. On this assessment and Franco's promises of liberalization, see Boeker to Eden, 12 June 1945 (Public Record Office, Foreign Office Papers, London (hereafter FO), 371/49589) and Boeker to Eden, 23 July 1945 (FO, 371/49589).
31. Soriano was sent to Israel on the instructions of the Caudillo himself, according to what the Spanish ambassador to Brussels told his colleague, Yosef Ariel, at the beginning of 1955. The ambassador, Count Casa Miranda, had served as Deputy Minister in the Spanish Foreign Ministry in 1949. Ariel to Foreign Ministry, 2 Feb. 1955 (ISA, 2413/25b). Soriano was already in Jerusalem on 14 April to discuss the status of the Spanish legation in Israel, as well as the question of the supervision of Spanish property in Jerusalem and its environs. *Ha'aretz*, 15 April 1949. On Eytan's meetings with the Spanish envoys, refer to document dated 24 April 1949 in ISA, 2391/28, and author's personal interview with Walter Eytan, 9 June 1986.
32. See Eytan's memorandum, 22 April 1949 (ISA, 2391/28). It should be noted that once back in Spain, despite the failure of his mission, Soriano apparently gave the Foreign Ministry in Madrid a positive report of Israel. Ariel to Foreign Ministry, 2 Feb. 1955 (ISA, 2413/25B).
33. 24 April 1949 (ISA, 2391/28).
34. Walter Eytan, personal interview with the author (Jerusalem, 9 June 1986).
35. On the Republican government and its limited influence, see Javier Tusell

and Alicia Alted, 'The Government of the Spanish Republic in Exile: 1939–1977', in Yossi Shain (ed.), *Governments-in-Exile in Contemporary World Politics* (New York and London: 1991) pp. 145–65; and Alicja Iwanska, *Exiled Governments: Spanish and Polish. An Essay in Political Sociology* (Cambridge, MA: 1981).

36. See letter from the Director of Protocol, M. Simon, to the Director-General, 9 May 1949 (ISA, 2391/28). The news of Huici's impending visit and the possibility that he would be appointed as Spain's representative in Tel Aviv had already been published in January of that year. *Ha'aretz*, 28 Jan. 1949.

37. See handwritten comments on Simon's letter of 9 May 1949 (ISA, 2391/28).

38. 'The Beginning of Spanish–Arab Friendship' (Hebrew), *Ha'aretz*, 5 Sept. 1949; Angel Marvaud, 'L'Espagne va-t-elle reconnaitre Israel?', *Le Monde*, 8/9 May 1949.

39. On the vote that admitted Israel to the United Nations and on Sharett's first speech in that forum, see Moshe Sharett, *On the Threshold of Nations* (Hebrew) (Tel Aviv: 1964) pp. 353–8; and Rafael, *Destination Peace*, p. 19.

40. AMAE, R.4785/43; Suárez Fernández, *Francisco Franco*, p. 318; Marquina y Ospina, *España y los judíos*, p. 241; Silvio Ferrari, 'The Holy See and the Postwar Palestine Issue: The Internationalization of Jerusalem and the Protection of the Holy Places', *International Affairs*, 60, No. II (1984) pp. 261–83; Edward B. Glick, *Latin America and the Palestine Problem* (New York: 1958) pp. 132–4; and John A. Houston, *Latin America in the United Nations* (New York: 1956) pp. 79–81.

41. The Spanish Civil War has given rise to a multitude of secondary sources focusing on different aspects of the war. Among the best general works are: Hugh Thomas, *The Spanish Civil War*, 2nd ed. (London: 1977); Gabriel Jackson, *The Spanish Republic*; and Stanley G. Payne, *The Franco Regime, 1936–1975* (Madison, WI: 1987) pp. 85–228. On the involvement of Nazi Germany and Fascist Italy in the Civil War see: A. Viñas, *La Alemania nazi y el 18 de julio* (Madrid: 1974); J.F. Coverdale, *Italian Intervention in the Spanish Civil War* (Princeton: 1975); and R.H. Whealey, *Hitler and Spain: The Nazi Role in the Spanish Civil War* (Lexington, KY: 1989).

42. Quoted in Payne, *The Franco Regime*, p. 269.

43. On Franco's position in the Second World War, see Paul Preston, *Franco – A Biography* (London: 1993) Chs 14–20; K.J. Ruhl, *Franco, Falange y 'Tercer Reich': España en la segunda guerra mundial* (Madrid: 1986); Denis Smyth, *Diplomacy and Strategy of Survival: British Policy and Franco's Spain, 1940–1941* (Cambridge: 1986); Javier Tusell, *Franco, España y la segunda guerra mundial* (Barcelona: 1995); and D.W. Pike, 'Franco and the Axis Stigma', *Journal of Contemporary History*, 17, No. 3 (July: 1982) pp. 369–407. A concise, useful account can also be found in Shlomo Ben-Ami, *La revolución desde arriba: España 1936–1979* (Madrid: 1980) Ch. 2.

44. Franco's brother-in-law Ramón Serrano Suñer, one of the Falange leaders and Foreign Minister in the years 1940–42, said that the timing of the war was inconvenient for Spain (Carr, *Spain*, p. 710) and he admitted that he had wanted to enter the war only towards the end. In an interview at the end of 1945, he said: 'Yes, I was pro-German and Spain was pro-German

(. . .). Franco and I, and Nationalist Spain behind us, not only banked on Berlin's victory, but wished for it with all our hearts. My plan was to enter the war at the moment of Germany's victory'. Quoted in Max Gallo, *Spain Under Franco: A History* (London: 1973) p. 159.

45. These expansionist ambitions were reflected in, among others, a number of publications issued in Spain during that period, for example, José María de Areilza and Fernando María Castiella, *Reivindicaciones de España* (Madrid: 1941); and José María Cordero Torres, *Misión africana de España* (Madrid: 1941).

46. The issue of Spain's interests in Palestine is discussed in a book published by the Spanish Foreign Ministry at the height of the Second World War, which was supposed to show the historical continuity of Spain's activities in the Holy Land: Fr. Samuel Eijan, *Hispanidad en Tierra Santa* (Madrid: 1943).

47. On this strategy, see the references in note 43, as well as W.N. Medlicott, *The Economic Blockade* (London: 1952), Vol. I, Ch. 15, and the memoirs of the US Secretary of State and the US, British and Argentine ambassadors in Madrid at the time: Cordell Hull, *The Memoirs* (New York: 1948) Vol. II, Ch. 96; C.J.H. Hayes, *Wartime Mission in Spain* (New York: 1945); Samuel Hoare, *Complacent Dictator* (New York: 1947); and Adrián C. Escobar, *Diálogo íntimo con España: Memorias de un embajador durante la tempestad europea* (Buenos Aires: 1950).

48. Quoted in Ben-Ami, *La revolución desde arriba*, p. 98.

49. On the Third Reich's plans concerning Gibraltar, see Norman J.W. Goda, 'The Riddle of the Rock: A Reassessment of German Motives for the Capture of Gibraltar in the Second World War', *Journal of Contemporary History*, Vol. 28 (1993) pp. 297–314.

50. Winston S. Churchill, *The Second World War* (London: 1949), Vol. II, pp. 460, 552, 562. An exaggerated description of Franco's assistance to the Allies can be found in a book by Willard Beaulac, who was an advisor in the US embassy in Madrid during the war: *Franco: Silent Ally in World War II* (Carbondale, IL: 1986).

51. See the books cited in note 43, as well as: Gerald R. Kleinfeld and Lewis A. Tambs, *Hitler's Spanish Legion: The Blue Division in Russia* (Carbondale, IL: 1979); and R. García Pérez, 'El envío de trabajadores españoles a Alemania durante la segunda guerra mundial', *Hispania*, Vol. 170 (1988) pp. 1031–66.

52. On Spain and the United Nations convention, see A. Lleonart and F.M. Castiella Maiz, *España y la ONU (1945–6)* (Madrid: 1978) pp. 28–30; and Robert P. Huff, 'The Spanish Question before the United Nations', Ph.D. diss. (Stanford University: 1966) pp. 8–22.

53. Actually, as a British official cynically remarked, Francoist Spain did not constitute a threat to the peace and integrity of its neighbours – only to those of its inhabitants. Quoted in Florentino Portero, *Franco aislado: La cuestión española (1945–1950)* (Madrid: 1989) p. 64.

54. On the 'Spanish question' at the Potsdam Conference, see ibid., pp. 79–84.

55. Juan Dura, 'U.S. Policy toward Dictatorship and Democracy in Spain, 1936–1953: A Case Study in the Realities of Policy Formation', Ph.D. diss. (University of California, Berkeley: 1979), pp. 102–5; and Portero, *Franco aislado*, pp. 116–17. In fact, the new Foreign Minister, Alberto Martín Artajo, judged correctly that once the echoes of the election campaign had

died away, British interests in the Iberian Peninsula would outweigh the Labour Party leaders' ideological considerations, and British policy towards Spain would not become more severe. And in the event, Prime Minister Attlee and Foreign Minister Bevin did indeed continue their predecessors' policies, justifying this on the grounds that any intervention would merely strengthen the Franco régime and possibly lead to a new civil war.

56. Mallet to Bevin, 6 Aug. 1945 (FO, 371/49589).
57. Huff, 'The Spanish Question', p. 30; Lleonart, *España y ONU*, Vol. I, p. 57.
58. *Foreign Relations of the United States* (1946), Vol. V, pp. 1043–4, 1052–4. On relations between Spain and France in those years, see P.A. Martínez Lillo, *Una introducción al estudio de las relaciones hispano-franceses (1945–1951)* (Madrid: 1985); and P.H. de Garmo, 'Beyond the Pyrenees: Spain and Europe since World War II', Ph.D. diss. (University of California, Davis: 1971).
59. Huff, 'The Spanish Question', pp. 52–3; Lleonart, *España y ONU*, Vol. I, pp. 61–2.
60. US Department of State, *The Spanish Government and the Axis* (Washington, DC: 1946).
61. United Nations Security Council, Official Records, *Report of the Sub-Committee on the Spanish Question* (New York: 1946); Lleonart, *España y ONU*, pp. 84–98.
62. On the way the régime's propagandists presented Spain's position during the Second World War, see Agustín del Río Cisneros, *España, rumbo a la postguerra* (Madrid: 1947); and José María Doussinage, *España tenía razón, 1939–1945* (Madrid: 1949).
63. Quoted in Payne, *The Franco Regime*, pp. 337–8.
64. See Franco's speeches, collected in *Franco ha dicho (1936–1942)* (Madrid: 1947), pp. 252–3, 260–2; and Trythall, *Franco*, pp. 292–3.
65. This attitude is expressed in a fascinating document prepared by Luis Carrero Blanco, Franco's right-hand man, in August, 1945. See 'Notas sobre la situación política', 29 Aug. 1945 (AMAE, R.1911/12). London and Washington knew that Franco's self-confidence depended largely on his belief that conflict between the Western countries and the Soviet Union was coming, and that the friendship of the United States was guaranteed him. See Boeker to Eden, 12 June 1945 (FO, 371/49589).
66. The text of this resolution can be found in Dusan J. Djonovich (ed.), *United Nations Resolutions*, Series I (General Assembly Resolutions), 1946–1948 (New York: 1973) Vol. I, pp. 50–1.
67. For a list of the states and the way they voted, see Huff, 'The Spanish Question', pp. 248–9. The US doubted the wisdom of the resolution, but voted in favour of it.
68. A list of the states and the level of relations they maintained with Spain can be found in ibid., pp. 251–2.
69. Raanan Rein, *The Franco–Perón Alliance: Relations between Spain and Argentina, 1946–1955* (Pittsburgh: 1993) pp. 43–6; Beatriz J. Figallo, 'Un embajador argentino en España, el Dr. Pedro Radío', *Res Gesta* (Rosario) (July, 1987) pp. 97–103.
70. These five countries were Cuba, Guatemala, Mexico, Panama, and Uruguay. On the debate in the United Nations and the different resolutions

that were proposed during its course, see Huff, 'The Spanish Question', pp. 342–67; Lleonart, *España y ONU*, Vol. II, pp. 272ff; Portero, *Franco aislado*, pp. 267–8; and *ABC* (Madrid), 19 Nov. 1947.

71. On reactions in Spain to the United Nations decision, see 'Spain – Annual Political Report for 1947', 26 May 1948 (NA, 852.00/5-2648).

72. A.A. Ben-Asher, *Foreign Relations 1948–1953* (Hebrew) (Tel Aviv: 1957), p. 115; 'Israel among the Nations – The First Hours' (Hebrew), *Ha'aretz*, 23 May 1949; and Raanan Rein, 'Israel and the "Spanish Question" in the U.N. (1949–1955)' (Hebrew), *International Problems, Society and Politics*, Vol. 30, No. 57 (1991) pp. 74–84.

73. See telegrams of 14 May 1949 (ISA, 2413/24).

74. *Documents on the Foreign Policy of Israel* (Jerusalem: 1986), Vol. 4 (May–December, 1949) p. 49. Apparently Sharett hinted at this in his speech in the Knesset on 15 June 1949, as well as on other occasions. See Sharett, *On the Threshold of Nations*, pp. 363–4.

75. Moshe Zack, 'Jewish Motifs in Israel's Foreign Policy' (Hebrew), *Gesher*, 110 (spring, 1984) Vol. 36; Suárez Fernández, *Francisco Franco*, Vol. IV, p. 334; and *Jewish Chronicle*, 10 June 1949.

76. *Ha'aretz* and *Davar*, 15 May 1949; *Al Hamishmar*, 16 May 1949.

77. Rein, *The Franco–Perón Alliance*, Ch. 2.

78. Navon to Foreign Ministry (12 June 1949) (ISA, 4701/1); *Documents on the Foreign Policy of Israel*, Vol. IV, p. 57. Perón later raised the issue of relations with Spain with both Ya'akov Tsur, Israel's first ambassador to Buenos Aires, and the President of the Peronist Jewish Organization (OIA). See Areilza to MAE, 9 Sept. 1949 (AMAE, R.2627/101).

79. *Al Hamishmar*, for example, emphasized that public opinion in Europe 'well remembers how and with whose help Franco won the Civil War, and what the nature of his régime is. Just in the last months, in connection with Spain's difficult economic situation and the increased activity of the revolutionary underground, this country is experiencing a wave of persecution and terrorism'. See 'Money for Franco' (Hebrew), *Al Hamishmar*, 5 May 1949.

80. Casares to MAE, 24 May 1949 (AMAE, R.4784/26).

81. The text of Eban's speech to the United Nations General Assembly (ISA, 2424/7). See also *Davar* and *Al Hamishmar*, 18 May 1949; and A.J. Lleonart, *España y ONU (1948–49)* (Madrid: 1985) pp. 363–5.

82. Huff, 'The Spanish Question', pp. 374–430; and Portero, *Franco aislado*, pp. 332–8.

83. Ben-Asher, *Foreign Relations*; 'Israel among the Nations' (Hebrew), *Ha'aretz*, 23 May 1949. Israel's vote surprised many, since early predictions in Spain and Britain were that Israel would abstain from voting. See Minutes of 12 May 1949 (FO, 371/79697).

84. Navon to Foreign Ministry, 12 June 1949 (ISA 2571/9, 4701/1); Eban to Sharett, 20 May 1949, *Documents on the Foreign Policy of Israel*, p. 57.

85. Fischer to the Foreign Ministry, 29 May 1949 (ISA, 2424/7A); Galíndez to Eban (ISA, 2413/24).

86. A copy of the letter was sent to the Israeli Foreign Ministry by the Israeli legation in Montevideo (4 July 1949) (ISA, 2424/7A).

87. ISA, 2424/7A.

88. *Divrei Ha-Knesset* (protocols of the Israeli parliament), Vol. I, p. 725. Riftin had been an anti-Francoist for many years. See, for example, his

article 'On the War of the Workers of Spain' (Hebrew), *Hashomer Hatza'ir*, 1 Dec. 1936. Articles in *Davar* also hailed 'the important role that young Israel's representative played in unmasking the plans of Franco's manifest friends, and the intentions of his secret associates'. ('At the Close of the Assembly Session' (Hebrew) 19 May 1945).

89. *Ha'aretz* and *Davar*, 19 May 1949; *Arriba* (Madrid), 12 May 1949; *Jewish Chronicle*, 17 May 1949, 18 May 1949, 19 May 1949, and 10 June 1949); *Ya*, 17 May 1949; *ABC*, 17 May 1949.
90. Trythall, *Franco*, p. 243; Hills, *Franco*, p. 407.
91. Bauer to Sánchez Bella, 15 June 1949 (AMAE, R.2328/35). Copies of Bauer's letter and another letter of the same date describing the normal religious and commercial life of the Jews of Madrid were sent to the Spanish embassies in Washington and the Vatican and to the Consulate in Jerusalem for purposes of propaganda.
92. Oficina de Información Diplomática, *España y los judíos* (Madrid: 1949).
93. Lisbona, *Retorno a Sefarad*, pp. 83–4.
94. The most important study on Spain's attitude towards Jews during the Holocaust is Haim Avni, *Contemporary Spain* (Hebrew), an English translation of which was published under the title *Spain, the Jews, and Franco* (Philadelphia: 1982). See also Marquina y Ospina, *España y los judíos*, Chs. 4–5; and Ysart, *España y los judíos*.
95. Weissman, *Against the Forces of Evil*, p. 149.
96. Chaim U. Lipschitz, *Franco, Spain, the Jews, and the Holocaust* (New York: 1984) p. 5.
97. See April, 1954, memorandum by Perlzweig (CZA, Z6/852); ISA, 2424/7A (10 Aug. 1950); Edouard de Blaye, *Franco and the Politics of Spain* (Harmondsworth: 1976) p. 380, n. 6; and Lipschitz, *Franco*, pp. 159, 169–70.
98. Quoted in Avni, *Contemporary Spain*, pp. 205–6.
99. Dina Porat, *The Blue and the Yellow Stars of David: The Zionist Leadership in Palestine and the Holocaust* (Cambridge, MA: 1990) pp. 111–16.
100. On their activities, see Weissman, *Against the Forces of Evil*; Perez Leshem, 'Rescue Efforts in the Iberian Peninsula', in *Leo Baeck Institute Year Book* (1969), Vol. 14, pp. 231–56.
101. Among others, the Spanish Embassy in Washington published, that same year, a five-page pamphlet: Spanish Embassy, *Spain and the Sephardi Jews* (Washington, DC: 1949).
102. Latin American Division to Embassy in Rome, 17 Aug. 1950 (ISA, 2541/13A).
103. Suárez Fernández, *Francisco Franco*, pp. 342–3.
104. Avraham Darom, Director of the Latin American Division in the Foreign Ministry, in a personal interview with the author (Tel Aviv, 16 June 1986).
105. See Darom memorandum, 3 April 1950 (ISA, 2413/24); Tsur to Radai, 26 July 1949 (ISA, 2415/14); Ya'akov Tsur, *Credential No. 4* (Hebrew) (Tel Aviv: 1981), p. 81.
106. Tsur to Foreign Ministry, 21 Sept. 1949 (ISA, 2578/12A); Ariel to Foreign Ministry, 31 Dec. 1953 (ISA, 2541/14A); Tsur to Foreign Ministry, 5 Dec. 1955 (ISA, 2413/25B).
107. S.F.A. Coles, *Franco of Spain: A Full-Length Biography* (London: 1967) pp. 118–19.

108. Eliachar, *Living with Jews*, p. 349.
109. These remarks were made in the course of the Social Democrat conference in Berlin. See Abba Eban, 'Israel Was Right about Spain' (Hebrew), *Ha'aretz*, 21 Jan. 1986.
110. Benny Pollack, *The Paradox of Spanish Foreign Policy* (London: 1987) p. 96; Fernando Morán, *Una política exterior para España* (Barcelona, 1980), pp. 186–7.
111. Abba Eban, *An Autobiography* (Tel Aviv: 1977) p. 144.
112. Eban, 'Israel Was Right about Spain' (Hebrew), *Ha'aretz*, 21 Jan. 1986. Eban was alluding to claims then being made by the foreign minister and Likud leader, Yitzhak Shamir, that it had been a mistake to reject Francoist Spain's advances in 1949. See *The Jerusalem Post*, 20 Jan. 1986.
113. 'Memo on meeting with Dr S. Glanzmann from Barcelona in the organizational division' (Hebrew), 17 Oct. 1949 (CZA, S5T/499).
114. Throughout the 1940s, Madrid showed interest in the future of the holy places, and the policy towards Israel was influenced by the Vatican's views in the matter. A few weeks before Bauer's visit to Fischer, posters appeared all over Madrid calling upon Spanish youths to 'take the cross in the manner of the first Crusade and liberate Jerusalem'. See *Jewish Chronicle*, 10 June 1949.
115. Fischer to Foreign Ministry, 13 Sept. 1949 (ISA, 2541/13A). In the summer of 1950, Bauer visited Israel in a fresh attempt to bring about a Hispanic–Israeli reconciliation.
116. West European division to Fischer, 19 Sept. 1949 (ISA, 2541/13A).
117. Erice a Cárcer (AMAE, R.3147/3).
118. See Spanish translation of the article by Bernard Klingshoffer in *American Jewish Review* (Feb. 1951), AMAE, 4789/43.
119. Tsur, *Credential No. 4*, p. 60.
120. Rein, *The Franco–Perón Alliance*, pp. 46–7; José María de Areilza, *Así los he visto* (Barcelona: 1974) p. 196.
121. Tsur to Foreign Minister, 21 Sept. 1949 (ISA, 2578/12A). For the Spanish Ambassador's version, see Areilza to MAE, 9 Sept. 1949 (AMAE, R.2627/101).
122. Embassy in Buenos Aires to MAE, 11 Nov. 1949 (AMAE, R.784/11); J. Bendahan to Areilza, 17 Feb. 1950 (AMAE, R.2996/1); and B. Figallo, *El protocolo Franco–Perón: relaciones hispano-argentinas, 1942–52* (Buenos Aires: 1992) pp. 103–54.
123. Artajo to the Minister in Amman, 30 April 1949; and circular from Artajo, 30 May 1949 (AMAE, R.4785/78).
124. On the activities of the Spanish Consul in Jerusalem during the First World War, see Shimon Rubinstein, 'Don Antonio de Ballobar – The Forgotten Spanish Consul' (Hebrew), *Ha-Uma* 83–4 (1986) pp. 205–12; *Al Hamishmar*, 12 March 1986; Arthur Rupin, *An Autobiography* (Hebrew) (Tel Aviv: 1968) Vol. II, p. 254; Eliachar, *Living with Jews*, p. 346; I.R. Molko, 'Turning Points in Relations between Spain and the Jews' (Hebrew), *Gesher*, Vol. 58 (1969) pp. 68–74. On Spain's general policy towards the Jews during the First World War, see Avni, *Contemporary Spain*, pp. 34–6, 53–4.
125. *Ma'ariv*, 24 Jan. 1986.
126. The lawyer Rafael Mani, in a speech before the Israel–Spain Friendship League in 1953, extolled Terranova's actions on behalf of the Jews of

Palestine and said that various legends had grown up around him describing him as a sort of envoy of Eliahu the Prophet, who came to Israel's assistance in time of trouble. See ISA, 2413/24B.

127. A.S. Yahuda, *The Defense of the Jews of Palestine during World War I – Memories of My Stay in Spain* (Hebrew) (Jerusalem: 1952) pp. 71–2.
128. Max Nordau, *Zionist Writings* (Hebrew) (Jerusalem: 1962) Vol. 4, pp. 16–19.
129. Colby to Foreign Ministry, 9 Oct. 1953 (ISA, 2413/26).
130. Terranova to MAE, 8 Sept. 1949, and 'nota informativa', 13 Dec. 1949 (AMAE, R.2804/1). Since the establishment of the State of Israel, no new consulates had been opened in those parts of Jerusalem under Israeli control. Israel was unwilling to allow new consulates to operate on the same basis as those which already existed – i.e., without recognizing Israel's sovereignty in Jerusalem. Similarly, the various countries which were not yet represented in the city were themselves unwilling to open consulates recognizing Israel's rule in Jerusalem which would be subordinate to their embassies in Tel Aviv. See *Ha'aretz*, 23 Aug. 1993.
131. Tartakover to Sharett, 18 Aug. 1950; Sharett to Tartakover, 3 Sept. 1950 (ISA, 2413/24); Terranova to MAE, 27 Sept. 1950 (AMAE, R.4786/140).
132. Eliachar, *Living with Jews*, p. 349.
133. Cásares to Erice, 23 May 1949 (AMAE, R.4784/26.
134. See memorandum by Joel Barromi, 20 Dec. 1953 (ISA, 2578/12A).
135. Latin American division to Levavi, 16 Aug. 1953 (ISA, 2413/24B).
136. Confidential memorandum from the Latin American division to Eytan, 2 July 1950 (ISA, 2413/24).
137. Erice to J. Nuñez, Director-General of Trade, 18 Nov. 1948; Director-General of Security to Director-General of Foreign Policy, n.d.; Nuñez to Erice, 22 Nov. 1948 (AMAE, R.4782/83).
138. Wardi to Darom, 27 April 1950 (ISA, 2578/11); answer from Latin American division, 4 May 1950 (ISA, 2578/11).
139. See documents in AMAE, R.2895/214.
140. Terranova to MAE, 25 Feb. 1950 (AMAE, R.2996/1); Terranova to MAE, 31 Jan. 1950 (AMAE, R.4788/67).
141. Consulate in Jerusalem to Erice, 20 June 1950 (AMAE, R.4787/103); Raoul Ami, *Ce que j'ai vu et entendu en Espagne* (Jerusalem: 1950).
142. Colby to Foreign Ministry, 9 Oct. 1953 (ISA, 2413/26).
143. Confidential memorandum from Darom to the Director-General, 3 April 1950 (ISA, 2413/24); 'The Spanish Problem at the Fourth Session of the United Nations General Assembly', Feb. 1950 (ISA, 37/93/A).

Chapter 2

1. Tsur to Foreign Ministry, 21 Sept. 1949 (ISA, 2578/12A).
2. Tsur to Foreign Ministry, 5 Dec. 1955 (ISA, 2413/25B).
3. See his speech in the *ad hoc* committee of the General Assembly on 31 Oct. 1950 (ISA, 2424/7A; *Hador*, 1 Nov. 1950.
4. Sharett to Eytan, 21 Jan. 1953 (ISA, 2413/24B).
5. Ben-Asher, *Foreign Relations*, p. 115; *Israel and the United Nations – Report of a Study Group Set Up by the Hebrew University of Jerusalem* (New York: 1956) p. 177.

6. Avner to Amir, 8 Jan. 1951 (ISA, 2541/13A).
7. Zvi Kullitz, 'Spain' (Hebrew), *Hayarden*, 7 Oct. 1936. Quoted in Yosef Algazy, 'The Civil War in Spain Reflected in the Hebrew Press in Eretz-Yisrael–Palestine, 1936–1939' (Hebrew), unpublished paper (Tel Aviv University: 1977), pp. 4–5. After attending a naval school in Italy from 1933 to 1936, Kullitz emigrated to Israel and published a book entitled *Mussolini, His Personality and His Doctrine* (Hebrew) (Tel Aviv: 1936) which was one long paean to the Fascist leader.
8. *Davar*, 13 Nov. 1936. *Davar*, the *Histadrut* organ, which in fact expressed MAPAI's views, sided unconditionally with the Republic, and published more information on the Civil War than any other Hebrew newspaper.
9. *Davar*, 6 Nov. 1936.
10. Quoted in Algazy, 'The Civil War', p. 43.
11. Ruth Levin, *The Righteous Were with Spain, 1936–1939* (Hebrew) (Tel Aviv: 1987) pp. 49–50.
12. Algazy, 'The Civil War', pp. 21–7.
13. The Israeli Communists usually exaggerated the number of Palestinian volunteers, putting it at 300–500. See, for example, David Diamant, *Combattants juifs dans l'armée republicaine espagnole* (Paris: 1979) p. 70; Israel Centner, *From Madrid to Berlin* (Hebrew) (Tel Aviv: 1966) p. 11; and Levin, *The Righteous*, p. 8. Shmuel Dotan, however, claims that 'in actual fact, those of Palestinian background among the Brigade combatants in Spain did not exceed 160'. See S. Dotan, *Reds – The Communist Party in Palestine* (Hebrew) (Kfar Saba: 1991) p. 245. Salman Salzman, one of the veteran Palestinian combatants in the International Brigades, rejected Dotan's figures and the 'distorted' way (his word) in which Dotan presents the motives that led the Jewish youths to go to Spain (interview with author, Kibbutz Mizrah, 19 Jan. 1994).
14. Centner, *From Madrid to Berlin*, pp. 81, 137. On the volunteers from Palestine, see also Mordechai Avi-Shaul, *A Hebrew Commander in Embattled Spain* (Hebrew) (Tel Aviv: 1945); David Krone, 'Monologue: The Republic Gave Us Everything It Had' (Hebrew), *Iton 77*, Nos. 77–8 (July–Aug., 1986) p. 26; Yaron London, 'The Pasionerim' (Hebrew), *Ha-Ir*, 7 Oct. 1983, pp. 18–19.
15. Yehuda Sluzki, *The History of the Hagana* (Hebrew) (Tel Aviv: 1972) pp. 1103, 1243; David Shaari, *Cyprus Exile 1946–1949: Clandestine Immigration, the Camps, and the Immigrant Society* (Hebrew) (Jerusalem: 1981) pp. 63–4; Ze'ev Vania Hadari, *Refugees Defeating a Great Power* (Tel Aviv: 1985) pp. 205, 418.
16. Weizmann visited Madrid for the first time in July, 1917, on his way to Gibraltar. In the Spanish capital, he met with Max Nordau, one of the founders of the World Zionist Organization, who had taken refuge in neutral Spain during the First World War. In 1932, he returned to Spain where the Socialist Minister of Education of the Republic, Fernando de los Ríos, told him that the government favoured the idea of a national Jewish home in Palestine. In mid-1937, Weizmann's son Binyamin volunteered to join the International Brigades in defending the Republic, but he was unable to reach Spain; he was turned back at the border, and barely escaped imprisonment. Just before and during the War of Independence, Weizmann spoke of the Arab–Jewish conflict in Palestine in terms of the Spanish Civil War, with clearly anti-Francoist overtones. He saw Franco as

a tool of Mussolini and Hitler, and was aware of the anti-Semitic trends in the Nationalist camp. See Norman Rose, *Chaim Weizmann – A Biography* (Hebrew) (Jerusalem: 1986) p. 163; Chaim Weizmann, *The Letters and Papers of Chaim Weizmann*, Series A, Vol. VII, pp. 458–9, 470, 475, 482; Series A, Vol. XVII, p. 434; Series B, Vol. II, p. 690.

17. See A. Eban, *An Autobiography*, pp. 21, 22.
18. Robert St. John, *Eban* (New York: 1972) pp. 50–1, 58.
19. Avraham Darom, interview with the author (Tel Aviv, 16 June 1986).
20. On Jewish volunteers in the Civil War, see Colin Shindler, 'No Pasarán: The Jews Who Fought in Spain', *The Jewish Quarterly*, Vol. 33, No. 3 (1986) pp. 34–41; Diamant, *Combattants juifs;* Josef Toch, 'Jews in the Civil War in Spain, 1936–1939' (Hebrew), *B'Shear*, Vol. 17, No. 6 (1974) pp. 456–66; Diamant, *Combattants juifs;* and Arno Lustinger, *'Shalom Libertad': Les Juifs dans la Guerre d'Espagne* (Paris: 1991). In the interests of historical accuracy, it should be noted that a few Jews also fought on the side of the Spanish Nationalists.
21. Some writers, of course, give larger figures. Volunteers arrived from some 50 countries. Nationalist Spain's official propaganda, too, naturally exaggerated the number of foreigners it claimed came to help the Republic. On the International Brigades, see V.B. Johnson, *The Legions of Babel: The International Brigades in the Spanish Civil War* (University Park, PA: 1967); A. Castells, *Las brigadas internacionales de la guerra de España* (Barcelona, 1972); D. Richardson, *Comintern Army: The International Brigades and the Spanish Civil War* (Lexington, KY: 1983); Michael Jackson, *Fallen Sparrows – The International Brigades in the Spanish Civil War* (Philadelphia: 1994); and H. Thomas, *The Spanish Civil War*, pp. 982–4.
22. Eytan to Linton, 18 Feb. 1954 (ISA, 2385/27).
23. Walter Eytan, interview with the author (Jerusalem, 9 June 1986).
24. See letter from Israel's legation in Mexico, 30 March 1955, and Eytan's reply, 4 May 1955 (ISA, 2413/25B).
25. U.S. Department of State, *Foreign Relations of the United States* (1950), Vol. III, pp. 1563–66. Golda Meir, the Minister of Foreign Affairs from 1956 to 1965, was also sympathetic to the Spanish Republic. See Golda Meir, *My Life* (London: 1975) pp. 127–8.
26. Kedar to Foreign Ministry, 21 June 1950 (ISA, 2413/24).
27. Amir to Foreign Ministry, 3 June 1951 (ISA, 2413/24).
28. Joel Barromi, in an interview with the author (Jerusalem, 2 Dec. 1986).
29. Beinart, *The New Jewish Community in Spain*, p. 11, n. 1, and p. 49; Y.R. Molko, 'Spain and the Jews' (Hebrew), *Tmurot*, Vol. 6 (March, 1965) p. 28.
30. Avraham Darom, interview with the author (Tel Aviv, 16 June 1986). During the March 1951 Knesset debate on demanding reparations from Germany, Knesset member Eliezer Livneh (MAPAI) took the opportunity to emphasize that 'the people of Israel have not forgiven the Spanish people and the state of Spain for the crime of the expulsion and Inquisition'. *Divrei Ha-Knesset* (official records of the Knesset, in Hebrew) (Jerusalem) Vol. 8, p. 1441.
31. See, for example, Haim Hillel Ben-Sasson, 'The Generation of Spanish Exiles Talks about Itself', in his book *Continuity and Variety* (Hebrew) (Tel Aviv: 1984) p. 198.

32. See Eliezer Schweid, 'The Expulsion from Spain and the Holocaust' (Hebrew), *Alpayim*, Vol. 3 (1990) pp. 69–88; and Edward Peters, 'Jewish History and Gentile Memory: The Expulsion of 1492', *Jewish History*, Vol. 9, No. 1 (1995) pp. 9–34.

33. In designating periods of Jewish history, Ben-Sasson defines the Middle Ages as the period from 632 to approximately 1670. The year 1492 does not mark the end of a period. See 'The Jewish Middle Ages – What Are They?' (Hebrew), in *Continuity and Variety*, pp. 359–78.

34. Molko, 'Spain and the Jews'.

35. See ISA, 2413/24B.

36. *Divrei Ha-Knesset*, Vol. 14, pp. 1618–19; Eliachar, *Living with Jews*, p. 350; and Michael Brecher, *The Foreign Policy System of Israel* (London: 1972) p. 153.

37. See memorandum from Darom, 18 Jan. 1953 (ISA, 2413/24B).

38. Tsur to Foreign Ministry, 21 Sept. 1949 (ISA, 2578/12A).

39. On the Arias Montano Institute, see *Ha'aretz*, 9 June 1944; Beinart, *The New Jewish Community*, p. 25; and 'Presentación', *Sefarad*, Vol. I (1941) pp. 3–5.

40. Shlomo Ben-Ami, 'Spain After Franco, Israel and the Jews' (Hebrew), *Gesher*, Vol. 86 (July, 1976) p. 132.

41. Meir Bareli, *Studies in Foreign Policy* (Hebrew) (Tel Aviv: 1975) p. 69; Brecher, *The Foreign Policy System*, p. 245.

42. Cited in Aharon Kleiman, 'Continuity and Change in Israel's Diplomacy' (Hebrew), in B. Neuberger (ed.), *Diplomacy and Confrontation – Selected Issues in Israel's Foreign Relations, 1948–1978* (Hebrew) (Tel Aviv: 1984) p. 49.

43. See memorandum from Darom, 3 April 1950 (ISA, 2413/24). Portuguese recognition was delayed, however, by the absence of relations between Spain and Israel (among other factors). It was not until the end of the 1950s that Israel opened a general consulate in Lisbon, and it was only raised to the status of embassy in 1977. Portugal opened its own embassy in Tel Aviv more than 10 years later.

44. Joel Barromi, interview with author (Jerusalem, 2 Dec. 1986).

45. See Darom's memorandum to Director-General, 13 June 1951 (ISA, 2413/24).

46. Avner to Amir, 8 Jan. 1951 (ISA, 2541/13A). On the government's extreme cautiousness in foreign issues in general, deriving from its concern for public opinion, see Uri Bialer, *Between East and West: Israel's Foreign Policy Orientation 1948–1956* (Cambridge: 1990) Ch. 2.

47. Bialer, *Between East and West*, p. 46.

48. On the negotiations for the reparations agreement, see Israel Foreign Office, *Documents Relating to the Agreement between the Government of Israel and the Government of the Federal Republic of Germany* (Jerusalem: 1953); Shlomo Shafir, *An Outstretched Hand: German Social Democrats, Jews, and Israel 1945–1967* (Hebrew) (Tel Aviv: 1986) Ch. 5; Nana Sagi, *German Reparations: A History of the Negotiations* (Jerusalem: 1980); Nicholas Balabkins, *West German Reparations to Israel* (New Brunswick, NJ: 1971); and Louis Edwin Pease, 'After the Holocaust: West Germany and Material Reparations to the Jews – From the Allied Occupation to the Luxembourg Agreements', Ph.D. diss. (Florida State University: 1976).

49. On the Knesset debate on reparations, see *Divrei Ha-Knesset*, Vol 10, pp.

895–964; and Yitzhak Gilead, 'Public Opinion in Israel on Relations between the State of Israel and West Germany in the Years 1949–1965', Ph.D. diss. (Hebrew) (Tel Aviv University: 1984) Ch. 6. *Herut*'s opposition at the time both reinforced its image as an anti-democratic movement which represented a threat to the Israeli parliamentary system, and intensified MAPAI's hostility towards this right-wing, nationalist party.

50. Nevertheless, the reparations agreement itself necessarily weakened the opposition to ties with Spain, even among staunch anti-Francoists like Walter Eytan. See Eytan's letter to the Israeli representative in Tokyo, 18 Feb. 1954 (ISA, 2385/27) and M. Brecher, *Decisions in Israel's Foreign Policy* (Oxford: 1974) p. 105.

51. *Divrei Ha-Knesset*, Vol. 1, pp. 718–19. On Israel's foreign policy in those years and the attempt to maintain good relations with both the Western and Eastern blocs, see Bialer, *Between East and West*; Brecher, *The Foreign Policy System*; and Walter Eytan, *The First Ten Years – A Diplomatic History of Israel* (London: 1958).

52. The Foreign Ministry could have learned something about the Soviet bloc's possible reaction to the establishment of relations between Israel and Franco from a meeting that took place back in October 1947 during the United Nations General Assembly's discussions at Lake Success, between Eliahu Elath, then an emissary of the political division of the Jewish Agency in the United States, and one of the members of the Polish delegation. The latter told Elath his delegation had heard news of contacts between Jewish Agency representatives and agents of General Franco to discuss the establishment of relations and that Franco had supposedly proposed to support the Zionist struggle if Zionist activists would help improve the dictator's image in the United States. The Polish representative threatened that, if these rumours were true, the fight for the establishment of the State of Israel would not have the support of the Soviet bloc in subsequent sessions of the General Assembly. Elath wrote: 'I denied the rumour absolutely, and expressed my astonishment that the possibility of relations between Franco and us could even be raised'. See Elath, *The Struggle for Statehood*, Vol. 2, p. 278.

53. On Israel's views on the Korean War, see Bialer, *Between East and West*, Ch. 10; Brecher, *Decisions*, Ch. 4; *Israel and the United Nations*, Ch. 11; and Rafael, *Destination Peace*, pp. 25–9.

54. On the relations between Israel and the Soviet Union in those years, see Yosef Govrin, *Israel–Soviet Relations, 1953–1967* (Hebrew) (Jerusalem: 1990); Ya'akov Ro'i, *Soviet Decision-Making in Practice – The USSR and Israel, 1947–1954* (New Brunswick: 1980); and A. Krammer, *The Forgotten Friendship* (Illinois: 1974).

55. Joel Barromi, interview with the author (Jerusalem, 2 Dec. 1986).

56. A general picture of the Spanish economy in the 1940s and 1950s can be found in: J. Clavera *et al.*, *Capitalismo español: De la autarquía a la estabilización (1939–1959)* (Madrid: 1973), Vol. 1; Joan Esteban, 'The Economic Policy of Francoism: An Interpretation', in Paul Preston (ed.), *Spain in Crisis: The Evolution and Decline of the Franco Regime* (Hassocks: 1976); and José Antonio Biescas and Manuel Tuñon de Lara, *España bajo la dictadura franquista (1939–1975)* (Barcelona: 1982), Ch. 1.

57. Edward Malefakis, 'La economía española y la Guerra Civil', in J. Nadal *et*

al. (eds.), *La economía española en el siglo XX – una perspectiva histórica* (Barcelona: 1987) pp. 162–3.
58. Carlos Barciela, 'Crecimiento y cambio en la agricultura española desde la Guerra Civil', in J. Nadal *et al.* (eds), *La economía española*, pp. 258 ff. It was only the generous aid supplied by Peronist Argentina in those years, in the form of grain and meat shipments and credit to pay for them, that saved Spain from widespread famine. See Rein, *The Franco–Perón Alliance*, Ch. 3.
59. For statistics on the significant drop in agricultural yield and the steep rise in food imports, see Higinio Paris Eguilaz, *Diez años de política económica en España* (Madrid: 1949) pp. 43–5, 81–3.
60. Kleiman, 'Continuity and Change', p. 47; Brecher, *Decisions*, p. 104.
61. Eytan to Linton, 18 Feb. 1954 (ISA, 2385/27).
62. Walter Eytan, interview with the author (Jerusalem, 9 June 1986).

Chapter 3

1. Fischer to Avner, 4 Jan. 1950 (ISA, 2541/13A). Avner's reply was sent on 12 Jan. 1950: 'We have no inclination to embark on any relations whatsoever with Spain – commercial or otherwise'. See ISA, 2541/14A.
2. *Ha'aretz*, 24 March 1950, 27 March 1950, 28 March 1950.
3. *Ha'aretz*, 25 July 1951.
4. The memorandum was written on 3 April 1950. See ISA, 2413/24.
5. In July 1950, the Spanish legation in London reported that 24 states, in addition to the Vatican, maintained ambassadors or accredited representatives in Madrid. See J. Lee Shneidman, *Spain and Franco 1949–1959* (New York: 1973) p. 55.
6. José Mario Armero, *La política exterior de Franco* (Barcelona, 1978), p. 56.
7. On United States relations with Spain in those years, see W.R. Gilmore, 'The American Foreign Policy Making Process and the Development of a Post World War II Spanish Policy, 1945–1953: A Case Study', Ph.D. diss. (University of Pittsburgh: 1967); J.W. Cortada, *Two Nations Over Time: Spain and the U.S., 1776–1976* (Westport: 1978); Dura, 'U.S. Policy'; Angel Viñas, *Los pactos secretos de Franco con Estados Unidos* (Barcelona: 1981).
8. Kennan to State Department, 24 Oct. 1947 (NA, 711.52/10-2847).
9. 'Policy Toward Spain', May 1950 (NA, 611.52/6-850).
10. On the pro-Francoist lobby in Washington, see T.J. Lowi, 'Bases in Spain', in H.L. Stein (ed.), *American Civil–Military Decisions, A Book of Case Studies* (Birmingham, AL: 1963), pp. 667–702.
11. Acheson to Connally, 16 Jan. 1950 (NA, 611.52/1-1650).
12. See A.J. Multer, 'The Truth about the Jews in Spain', *Congressional Record*, Proceedings and Debates of the 81st Congress, 2nd session, 24 Jan. 1950; also ISA, 2541/13A.
13. Payne, *The Franco Regime*, pp. 293, 304, 318; Aronsfeld, *The Ghosts*, pp. 42–6; Lipschitz, *Franco*, pp. 16–19; Juan Pablo Fusi, *Franco – A Biography* (London: 1987) pp. 70–1.
14. Lisbona, *Retorno a Sefarad*, pp. 99–100.
15. None the less, 20 years later Franco expressed a completely different view

in a conversation with his cousin and Military Secretary, General Franco Salgado Araujo. He agreed that the Third Reich 'persecuted Jews unjustly', and that it bore the historical responsibility for 'the great crimes committed against those of that race during the war'. Franco justified the shock felt by the world when it found out about the massacre of the Jews, but complained that there were not enough protests against the crimes of the communist governments. See Francisco Franco Salgado-Araujo, *Mis conversaciones privadas con Franco* (Barcelona: 1976) pp. 307–8.

16. Ramón Garriga, *Los validos de Franco* (Barcelona: 1981) pp. 222–8. See also Javier Tusell, *Carrero Blanco. La eminencia gris del régimen de Franco* (Madrid: 1993).

17. See Gregorio Cámara Villar, *Nacional-Catolicismo y escuela. La socialización política del franquismo (1936–1951)* (Madrid: 1984), *passim*.

18. At the beginning of the 1950s, the Jews in Spain were better off than the Spanish Protestants in many respects. Beinart, *The New Jewish Community*, p. 48. Rabbi Efraim Einhorn from Detroit, however, after visiting Spain in the summer of 1951, described the psychological pressure on the Jews of Spain and the covert anti-Semitism which deterred them from emphasizing their Jewish identity in public. See Rabbi E.F. Einhorn to Ambassador Griffis, 20 July 1951 (NA, 611.52/7-2051).

19. On the dispute over Jerusalem's status, see Uri Bialer, 'Jerusalem 1949: Transition to Capital City Status', *Cathedra* (Hebrew), Vol. 35 (1985): 163–91; Motti Golani, *Zion in Zionism: The Zionist Policy on the Issue of Jerusalem, 1937–1949* (Hebrew) (Tel Aviv: 1992); E. Bovis, *The Jerusalem Question 1917–1968* (Stanford: 1971); J. le Morzellec, *La question de Jerusalem devant l'Organisation des Nations Unies* (Brussels: 1979) and M. Brecher, *Decisions*, Ch. 2.

20. On Jordan's position on the question of Jerusalem's status, see, for example, numerous reports in AMAE, R.4784/38 and R.4789/149.

21. 'Carta-encíclica de Su Santidad Pío XII renovando la petición de oraciones para una justa solución de Tierra Santa', 30 Oct. 1948, and 'Por la internacionalización de los Santos Lugares – Carta encíclica de Su Santidad Pío XII de 15 de abril de 1949', 23 April 1949, *Ecclesia* (Madrid). On the Vatican's policy towards Israel and Jerusalem, see Ferrari, 'The Holy See'; Meir Mendes, *The Vatican and Israel* (Hebrew) (Jerusalem: 1983); Walter Zander, *Israel and the Holy Places of Christendom* (London, 1971); L. Rokach, *The Catholic Church and the Question of Palestine* (London: 1987) and A. Kreutz, *Vatican Policy on the Palestinian–Israeli Conflict* (New York: 1990).

22. Bialer, 'Jerusalem 1949', pp. 190–91.

23. At the beginning of 1950, the Foreign Ministry in Tel Aviv became concerned that the Latin American countries would call for a special session of the United Nations to discuss the issues of both Jerusalem and Spain. The head of the Latin American division instructed the Israeli ambassador in Buenos Aires to make every effort to torpedo the possibility of such a meeting, particularly the danger that the two problems would be combined. See Darom to Tsur, 25 Jan. 1950 (ISA, 2424/7A); meeting of Israel's delegation to the United Nations (13 Jan. 1950), *Documents on the Foreign Policy of Israel*, Vol. 5 (Jerusalem: 1988) p. 24. On Latin America and the question of Jerusalem, see Glick, *Latin America*, Ch. 8.

24. On the Franco régime's relations with the Holy See, see Antonio Marquina

Barrio, *La diplomacia vaticana y la España de Franco (1936–1945)* (Madrid: 1983); and Javier Tusell, *Franco y los católicos* (Madrid: 1984).

25. Circulars from Artajo to Spain's representatives in America, 11 June 1949 (AMAE, R.3472/12) and 12 Feb. 1949 (R.4784/39). See also many reports in AMAE, R.3472/14, R.4784/32, R.4784/33, R.4784/34, R.4784/39, and R.4785/43.

26. See, for example, 'Sobre los antecedentes históricos de la custodia de Tierra Santa' (5 June 1948) and 'La presencia histórica de España en Tierra Santa' (16 June 1949), both in *Arriba*.

27. *Ya*, 27 May 1949; Rives to MAE, 8 Sept. 1949 (AMAE, R.3472/14); and Artajo to Consul-General in Jerusalem, 20 Aug. 1949 (AMAE, R.4785/61).

28. Franco's article is quoted in Suárez Fernández, *Francisco Franco*, Vol. IV, p. 310. See also Consejo Superior de Misiones al Director Gral. de Relaciones Culturales, 23 June 1948 (AMAE, R.3472/13); message sent to His Holiness Pius XII by the Conferencia de Metropolitanos, 12 May 1949 (AMAE, R.4784/33); 'Annual Political Report for Spain: An Estimate of the Situation in 1949' (NA, 752.00/1-2650), p. 43; and S.P. Ben Shmuel, 'Spain's Arab Policy' (Hebrew), *Hamizrach Hehadash*, Vol. 19 (spring 1954) p. 165.

29. See Tsur's confidential memorandum (7 May 1950) to the Director-General and a few senior officials (ISA, 2413/24).

30. Eytan to Tsur, 4 June 1950 (ISA, 2413/24).

31. Kedar to Fischer, 21 June, 1950 (ISA, 2413/24).

32. See his letter dated 12 Nov. 1950 (ISA, 2541/13A).

33. María Rosa de Madariaga, 'The Intervention of Moroccan Troops in the Spanish Civil War: A Reconsideration', *European History Quarterly*, Vol. 22 (1992) pp. 67–97; Shannon E. Fleming, 'Spanish Morocco and the Alzamiento Nacional, 1936–1939: The Military, Economic and Political Mobilization of a Protectorate', *Journal of Contemporary History*, Vol.18, No. 1 (1983) pp. 27–42; and Robert A. Friedlander, 'Holy Crusade or Unholy Alliance? Franco's 'National Revolution' and the Moors', *Southwestern Social Science Quarterly*, Vol. 44 (March 1964) pp. 346–56.

34. See Charles R. Halstead, 'A Somewhat Machiavellian Face: Colonel Juan Beigbeder as High Commissioner in Spanish Morocco, 1937–1939', *Historian*, Vol. 37 (Nov. 1974) pp. 44–6; and Charles R. Halstead, 'Un 'Africain' Méconnu: Le Colonel Juan Beigbeder', *Revue d'Histoire de la Deuxième Guerre Mondiale*, Vol. 83 (July 1971) pp. 1–60.

35. Charles R. Halstead and Carolyn J. Halstead, 'Aborted Imperialism: Spain's Occupation of Tangiers 1940–1945', *Iberian Studies*, Vol. 7, No. 2 (autumn 1978) pp. 53–71; Graham H. Stuart, *The International City of Tangiers*, 2nd. ed. (Stanford: 1955) Ch. II.

36. On Spain's relations with the Arab world in those years, see 'Aspects of Spain's Arab Policy', 3 Dec. 1951 (NA, 752.00/12-351); María Dolores Algora Weber, 'La Liga Arabe ante "la cuestión española" en las Naciones Unidas: 1946–1950', in *Congreso Internacional sobre el Régimen de Franco: 1936–1975* (Madrid: 1993), Vol. II, pp. 387–400; Pollack, *The Paradox*, Ch. 4; and Shannon Fleming, 'North Africa and the Middle East', in James W. Cortada (ed.), *Spain in the Twentieth Century World* (Westport, CT: 1980), pp. 121–54.

37. Madrid Embassy to State Department, 26 July 1948 (NA, 852.20210/7-2648); Griffis to State Department, 13 Sept. 1948 (NA, 752.82/9-1348); Cairo Embassy to State Department, 25 Feb. 1949 (NA, 752.83/2-2549; and Ruiz de Cuevas to MAE, 4 Nov. 1948 (AFF, Leg. 137/390).

38. Ben-Shmuel, 'Spain's Arab Policy', p. 163; Consulate-General (Tetuan) to FO, 4 Feb. 1947 (FO, 371/61523); Andrews to FO, 8 Sept. 1948 (FO, 371/73336); Marriott to FO, 8 Sept. 1948 (FO, 371/68382); Hanky to FO, 10 Jan. 1951 (FO, 371/96169); Franco Salgado Araujo, *Mis conversaciones*, p. 227.

39. 'The Beginning of Spanish–Arab Friendship' (Hebrew), *Ha'aretz*, 5 Sept. 1949; Manuel Espadas Burgos, *Franquismo y política exterior* (Madrid: 1988) p. 211.

40. Francisco Franco, *Discursos y mensajes de S.E. el Jefe del Estado a las Cortes Españolas, 1943–1961* (Madrid: 1961) p. 102.

41. *Ha'aretz*, 29 Dec. 1946; 'Informe sobre envío de una misión cultural al próximo oriente', 20 Feb. 1947 (AMAE, R.2800/17).

42. Maffitt to State Department, 22 Feb. 1948 (NA, 852.00/2-2248); Emmons (Madrid) to State Department, 16 July 1948 (NA, 752.90B/7-1648).

43. Suárez Fernández, *Francisco Franco*, Vol. 4, pp. 344–5. On the Spanish protectorate in Morocco, see Victor Morales Lezcano, *España y el norte de Africa: el protectorado en Marruecos (1912–1956)* (Madrid: 1986); and Miguel Martín, *El colonialismo español en Marruecos 1860–1956)* (Paris: 1973).

44. *Ha'aretz*, 19 Sept. 1947.

45. *Ha'aretz*, 19 Sept. 1947; Suárez Fernández, *Francisco Franco*, Vol. IV, pp. 206–7; Dieguez to MAE, 15 Aug. 1949 (AMAE, R.2697/28); Troutbeck to FO, 13 Sept. 1949 (FO, 371/75315). Abdallah answered his Arab critics thus: 'Russia expresses antagonism towards Franco, just as it does to me. That's why Franco and I are effective and necessary to our countries. I am going to Spain because I want to see Franco, whom Russia hates, as it hates me'. *Ha'aretz*, 5 Sept. 1949.

46. *Ha'aretz*, 6 Sept. 1949; *Times*, 6 Sept. 1949. The Jordanian king's visit was extensively covered in the Spanish press. See, for example, *ABC*, 6–10 Sept. 1949. On the visit, see many reports in AMAE, R.2697/28, as well as Suárez Fernández, *Francisco Franco*, Vol. IV, pp. 343–4; 'Annual Political Report for Spain: An Estimate of the Situation in 1949', pp. 42–3 (NA, 752.00/1-2650); Abdallah, King of Jordan, *My Memoirs Completed: 'Al-Takmilah'* (London: 1978) pp. 60–1.

47. An outstanding example of the successful functioning of the propaganda apparatus could be seen during the visit of Eva Perón, wife of the President of Argentina, in June 1947. On that visit and the way it was exploited by the régime for purposes of propaganda, see Raanan Rein, 'The Visit of the Young Lady: The Franco–Perón Alliance and Evita's Trip to Spain', *Zmanim* (Hebrew), Vol. 10, No. 38 (1991) pp. 80–91.

48. Shneidman, *Spain*, p. 57; 'General Franco and the Arab Countries', an article translated into Hebrew from the French newspaper *Le Monde* and reprinted in *Ha'aretz*, 14 Oct. 1949.

49. Artajo to the High Commissioner in Tetuan, 26 Aug. 1949, Varela to Artajo, 28 Aug. 1949, and Artajo to Varela, 30 Aug. 1949 (AMAE, R.2697/28); Howard to FO, 15 Sept. 1949 (FO, 371/75315).

50. 22 Sept. 1949 (NA, 852.00/9-2249).

51. *The Times*, 20 Sept. 1949; 29 Sept. 1949 (NA, 852.00/9-2949).
52. José Mario Armero, *La política exterior*, p. 54.
53. 11 Aug. 1949 (NA, 852.00/8-1149); Ben-Shmuel, 'Spain's Arab Policy', p. 165; *Ha'aretz*, 24 Oct. 1947 and 5 Sept. 1949.
54. Artajo to High Commissioner in Tetuan, 22 March 1950 (AMAE, R.4786/123); 'nota verbal' to the United States Embassy, 25 Jan. 1951 (AMAE, R.4789/39).
55. Balfour to FO, 25 July 1951 (FO, 371/96170); 'Aspects of Spain's Arab Policy', 3 Dec. 1951 (NA, 752.00/12-351).
56. Ruiz de Cuevas to MAE, 13 March 1948 (AMAE, R.4783/73); *Arriba*, 17 Jan. 1948, and 17 and 21 Sept. 1948; *Informaciones*, 12 July 1948, 26 Aug. 1948; Memorandum of Conversation on the Relations of Lebanon with Spain, 13 May 1948 (NA, 711.52/5-1348); Emmons to State Department, 30 Sept. 1948 (752.90B/9-3048); report dated 18 March 1949 (852.00/3-1849); A. Hourani and N. Shehadi (eds), *The Lebanese in the World: A Century of Emigration* (London: 1992).
57. Rein, *The Franco–Perón Alliance*, p. 48; Arístegui to MAE, 3 May 1947 (AMAE, R.4781/73); Bárcenas to Artajo, 13 March 1950 (AMAE, R.4786); Balfour to FO, 25 July 1951 (FO, 371/96170).
58. For statistics on Spain's trade with these countries in 1934, see Ben-Shmuel, 'Spain's Arab Policy', p. 157.
59. Ibid., p. 165.
60. 'Annual Economic Review: Spain 1951', 6 May 1952 (NA, 852.00/5-652). The complete list can be found in Rein, *The Franco–Perón Alliance*, p. 200. For figures on Spain's foreign trade in 1948–50, including trade with several Arab states, see 'Spain – Annual Economic Report for 1949', 6 March 1950 (NA, 852.00/3-650); 'Spain – Annual Economic Report for 1950', 30 March 1951 (NA, 852.00/3-3051).
61. Tsur to Foreign Ministry, 21 Sept. 1949 (ISA, 2578/12A).
62. On the opposition of Jewish organizations in the United States, see, for example, Sharett to Ben-Gurion, 24 Sept. 1950, in *Documents on the Foreign Policy of Israel* (1950), Vol. 5, p. 554; NA, 852.51/5-1949; 'Statement of the National Association of Jewish Center Workers', 8 June 1950 (NA, 611.52/8-1650); Rabbi E.F. Einhorn to Ambassador Griffis, 14 July 1951 (NA, 611.52/7-2051); *New York Times*, 8 April 1951; Zabala to Lojendio, 7 Aug. 1950 (AMAE, R.3439/26).
63. Eliachar, *Living with Jews*, p. 348.
64. The telegrams were passed from the Latin American division to the Minister's office on 31 Aug. 1950. See ISA, 2424/7A; Yahuda Leon Jalfon, Pte. del Alto Tribunal Rabínico de Tetuán to Ben-Gurion, 28 Aug. 1950 (AMAE, R.4787/188); High Commissioner in Tetuan to MAE, 1 Sept. 1950 (AMAE, R.3147/3).
65. Banón to Sharett, 1 Sept. 1950 (ISA, 2578/11). A copy can be found in AMAE, R.4787/188. See also Gómez Acebo to MAE, 5 Sept. 1950 (AMAE, R.4787/188).
66. M. Mitchell Serels, *A History of the Jews of Tangiers in the Nineteenth and Twentieth Centuries* (New York: 1991) pp. 167–8. See also Joe Hassan's telegrams, 28 Aug. 1950 (AMAE, R.4787/188); and Ruiz de Cuevas to MAE, 21 Sept. 1950 (AMAE, R.3147/3).
67. Fischer to Sharett, 24 Sept. 1950 (ISA, 2541/13A); Ruiz de Cuevas to MAE, 21 Sept. 1950 (AMAE, R.3147/3); and Isaac Salama to Erice, 23

Sept. 1950 (AMAE, R.4787/188).

68. See ISA, 2541/13A, of which a copy can be found in AMAE, R.2578/11; Santa Pola to MAE, 15 Sept. 1950 (AMAE, R.3147/3); Antequera to MAE, 19 Sept. 1950 (AMAE, R.3147/3). Concerning the appeal by the leader of the Jewish community in Algiers, see General Consulate in Algiers to MAE, 12 Sept. 1950 (AMAE, R.4787/188).

69. Their letter of 26 Aug. 1950 was sent by the Israeli Consul to the Foreign Ministry (ISA, 2541/13A). A copy can be found in AMAE, R.4787/188. On the extermination of the Jews of Greece, see Daniel Carpi, 'The Jews of Greece in the Period of the Holocaust, 1941–1943' (Hebrew), *Ialcut Moreshet*, Vol. 3 (1981) pp. 7–39.

70. ISA, 2541/13A. For a copy, see AMAE, R.3147/3. See also Romero Radigales to MAE, 4 Oct. 1950 (AMAE, R.3147/3).

71. See Rabbi Atias's letter, 30 Oct. 1950 (ISA, 2578/11); Alfaro to MAE, 20 Nov. 1950 (AMAE, R.4786/140).

72. ISA, 2424/7A.

73. Avner to Amir, 8 Jan. 1951 (ISA, 2541/13A).

74. Undersecretary of the MAE to Undersecretary of the Prime Minister's office, 20 Sept. 1950 (AMAE, R.3147/3); Erice to Aguirre de Cárcer (AMAE, R.3147/3); Erice to Arístides Peña, 31 Aug. 1950 (AMAE, R.3147/3); and Erice to San Lucar, 3 Oct. 1950 (AMAE, R.4787/188).

75. *The Jerusalem Post*, 30 Aug. 1950; Terranova to MAE, 30 Aug. 1950 (AMAE, R.4787/188).

76. Latin American Division to Director-General, 2 July 1950 (ISA, 2413/24). See also Latin American Division to Director-General, 3 Nov. 1950 (ISA, 2413/24); and Terranova to MAE, 26 Sept. 1950 (AMAE, R.4786/140).

77. Terranova to MAE, 6 Oct. 1950 (AMAE, R.4787/188); Suárez Fernández, *Francisco Franco*, Vol IV, p. 444.

78. Terranova to MAE, 1 Sept. 1950 and 21 Sept. 1950 (AMAE, R.4787/188). Najar also promised Enrique Benarroya, one of the leaders of the Jewish community in Barcelona, to work towards persuading Israel to change its voting pattern on the Spanish question. See Arístides Peña to Erice, 30 Aug. 1950 (AMAE, R. 4787/188).

79. Sasson to Rafael, 2 Nov. 1950 (ISA, 2578/11) .

80. Sasson to Research Department, 19 Feb. 1956 (ISA, 2413/24B); Fiscowich to MAE, 20 Jan. 1953 (AMAE, R.4995/99).

81. Fiscowich to MAE, 3 March 1950 (AMAE, R.4787/89). On Sasson's service in Ankara, see Amikam Nachmani, 'Middle East Listening Post: Eliahu Sasson and the Israeli Legation in Turkey, 1949–1952', *Studies in Zionism*, Vol. 6, No. 2 (Autumn, 1985) pp. 263–85.

82. Artajo to Consul-General in Jerusalem, 13 March 1950 (AMAE, R.4787/89).

83. Terranova to MAE, 17 March 1950, ibid.

84. See ISA, 2413/24; Muskat, 'Spain and Its Treatment of the Jews', pp. 146–7.

85. San Lucar to MAE, 28 June 1950 (AMAE, R.4787/188).

86. See memorandum of 22 Aug. 1950 (ISA, 2424/7A). The memorandum also appears in *Documents on the Foreign Policy of Israel*, Vol. 5 (1950), pp. 488–9. On the position of the Arab states, see Arístegui to MAE, 21 June 1950, and embassy in Beirut to MAE, 27 Jan. 1950 (AMAE, R.3147/3).

87. Sharett to Ben-Gurion, 24 Sept. 1950, in *Documents on the Foreign Policy*

of Israel, Vol. 5 (1950) p. 554.

88. *Divrei Ha-Knesset*, Vol. 6, p. 2420; Terranova to MAE, 30 Oct. 1950 (AMAE, R.4787/4).
89. Consulate-General in Jerusalem to Erice, 20 June 1950 (AMAE, R.4787/103); Latin American Division to Director-General, 3 Nov. 1950 (ISA, 2413/24).
90. Terranova to MAE, 27 Sept. 1950 (AMAE, R.4786/140).
91. The Caudillo, for his part, tried to take quick advantage of the change occurring in the United States, and suggested sending Spanish forces to the Korean front. Ben Ami, *La revolución desde arriba*, p. 113.
92. On the change in United States policy towards Spain in the years 1949–1950, see Shneidman, *Spain*, pp. 48–55; Viñas, *Los pactos*; Gilmore, 'The American Foreign Policy Making Process'; and Dura, 'U.S. Policy'.
93. Huff, 'The Spanish Question', pp. 444–53; Portero, *Franco aislado*, pp. 399–401; *Ha'aretz*, 2 Nov. 1950.
94. For the text of Eliashiv's speech, see ISA, 2424/7A; *Hador*, 1 Nov. 1950. Just before Israel's vote in the United Nations, the Foreign Ministry tried to obtain documents that the United States State Department had published on aid that Fascist Italy and Nazi Germany had given Franco in the Civil War, perhaps in order to reinforce the moral opposition to Franco's régime. See director of the Latin American division to the US division, 25 Oct. 1950 (ISA, 2578/11).
95. Suárez Fernández, *Francisco Franco*, Vol. 4, pp. 444–5.
96. *Ha'aretz*, 5 Nov. 1950; Shneidman, *Spain*, pp. 55–6; Huff, 'The Spanish Question', pp. 455–64; Portero, *Franco aislado*, p. 401.
97. Kahany to Foreign Ministry, 1 April 1952 (ISA, 2413/24).
98. *Herut*, 10 Jan. 1951.
99. *Divrei Ha-Knesset*, Vol. 8, p. 867.
100. Ibid., p. 865.
101. *Herut*, 28 Jan. 1951; *Ma'ariv*, 2 Jan. 1951.
102. Utray to MAE, 30 Jan. 1951 (AMAE, R.4789/43)
103. Quoted in Algazy, 'The Civil War', p. 8.
104. *Herut*, 11 May 1951; Binyamin Arditi, *The Jews of Bulgaria in the Years of the Nazi Regime, 1940–1944* (Hebrew) (Holon: 1962) p. 313; *Jewish Chronicle*, 2 Nov. 1951; 'Nota informativa de prensa israelí' and Cárcer to MAE, 12 Nov. 1951 (AMAE, R.2996/1).
105. 'Nota', 10 Nov. 1950 (AMAE, R.2631/19); 'Nota', 31 Oct. 1951 (AMAE, R.2633/51); Shneidman, *Spain*, pp. 57, 73–4; Blaye, *Franco*, p. 173. The World Health Organization accepted Spain as a member in May of 1951. This time the Israeli delegate abstained from the vote. See Kahany to Foreign Ministry, 1 April 1952 (ISA, 2413/24).
106. It was not so much the dictatorial nature of the Franco régime that kept Spain out of NATO as the stigma of its cooperation with Hitler, since neighbouring Portugal, also ruled by a dictator, was allowed to join. See Crozier, *Franco: A Biographical History* (London: 1967) p. 444.
107. Carr, *Spain*, p. 715.
108. Quoted in Ben-Ami, *La revolución desde arriba*, p. 133. On the reactions of Giral and Alvarez del Vayo, see Propper de Callejon to MAE, 10 Nov. 1950 (AMAE, R.2439/52).
109. Fischer to Avner, 17 Dec. 1950 (ISA, 2541/13A).
110. Ben-Horin to Israeli Minister in Paris, 1 Jan. 1951 (ISA, 2541/13A).

111. Latin American Division to Meroz (Ankara), 6 Nov. 1952 (ISA, 2578/12A); *Divrei Ha-Knesset*, Vol. 12, p. 3196; *Ha'aretz*, 10 July 1952.
112. On the negotiations between Israel and Germany, see Shlomo Shafir, *An Outstretched Hand*, Ch. 5; Sagi, *German Reparations*; Balabkins, *West German Reparations*. On the turbulent Knesset debate, see *Divrei Ha-Knesset*, Vol. 10, pp. 895–964; Yitzhak Gilead, 'Public Opinion in Israel', Ch. 6.
113. Avner to Amir, 8 Jan. 1951 (ISA, 2541/13A).
114. Avner to Darom, 5 Feb. 1951 (ISA, 2578/11); Avner to Amir, 6 Feb. 1951 (ISA, 2541/13A).
115. Ben-Horin to Ginossar, 6 Feb. 1951 (ISA, 2541/13A); Ginossar to Avner, 2 Nov. 1950, in *Documents on the Foreign Policy of Israel*, Vol. 5 (1950), pp. 616–17.
116. See Amir's letter, 3 June 1951 (ISA, 2413/24). This document also appears in *Documents on the Foreign Policy of Israel*, Vol. 6 (1951), pp. 360–61.
117. Avner to Darom, 8 June 1951 (ISA, 2578/11).
118. See handwritten note, 11 June 1951, attached to Amir's letter of 3 June 1951 (ISA, 2413/24).
119. Darom to Eytan, 13 June 1951 (ISA, 2413/24).
120. Eytan to Darom, 15 June 1951 (ISA, 2413/24).
121. See Tsur's letter, 2 July 1951 (ISA, 2413/24).
122. *Davar*, 7 Sept. 1951.
123. Terranova to MAE, 13 Sept. 1951 (AMAE, R.4788/67)
124. *The Jerusalem Post*, 17 and 26 Nov. 1951; Terranova to MAE, 17 Nov. 1951, 3 Dec. 1951 (AMAE, R.4789/89).
125. Eytan to Tsur, 4 June 1950 (ISA, 2413/24); United Nations division to Kahany, 15 April 1952 (ISA, 2413/24); *Ha'aretz*, 25 July 1951.
126. Terranova to MAE, 27 Sept. 1950 (AMAE, R.4786/140); 'Estadísticas de entradas de viajeros en España, años 1951, 1952 y primer semestre de 1953' (AMAE, R.3189/21).
127. Eytan to Tsur, 4 June 1950 (ISA, 2413/24); Ehrlich to Foreign Ministry, 4 Oct. 1951 (ISA, 2578/11).
128. *Hatzofeh*, 9 Oct. 1951; *Yediot Aharonot*, 26 Oct. 1951.
129. Secretario del CSIC to Director Gral. de Relaciones Culturales, MAE, 4 April 1950, 25 Oct. 1950 (AMAE, R.2895/214).
130. ISA, 2413/24.
131. ISA, 2541/13A; Sasson to Research Division, 19 Feb. 1956 (ISA, 2413/24B); Fiscowich to MAE, 9 Feb. 1951 (AMAE, R.4789/76).
132. Fischer to Foreign Ministry, 2 Nov. 1953 (ISA, 2541/14A); Levavi to Fischer, 17 Nov. 1953 (ISA, 2413/25A).
133. Fiscowich to MAE, 17 June 1953 (AMAE, R.4995/99) and 23 Dec. 1953 (AMAE, R.4993/31).
134. See letters to Israeli envoys in Bern and Rome (ISA, 2541/13A). The emphasis on the words 'exclusively personal' appears in the original.
135. Although Spain remained officially neutral in the conflict between Egypt and Britain, during those months the Falange newspapers unequivocally sided with Egypt; it also showed sympathy for Iran in the latter's disagreement with London. See 'Spain: Annual Review for 1951', 21 Jan. 1952 (FO, 371/101997). Spain embarrassed France around the same time by using its influence in Latin America to win support for the Arab countries' bid to put Tunisia's demand for independence on the debating agenda of

the United Nations General Assembly. See Rockwell to State Department, 11 July 1952 (NA, 652.00/7-1152).

136. *Ha'aretz*, 2 Jan. 1952; Shneidman, *Spain*, p. 96.
137. FO, 'Minutes', 23 April 1952 (FO, 371/102009); 'Tenemos la llave del Mediterraneo occidental', *Pueblo* (27 March 1952); Rockwell to State Department, 11 Aug. 1952 (NA, 752.00/8-1152).
138. *Ha'aretz*, 15 April 1952. On Artajo's trip, see the many reports in AMAE, R.3106/13 and R.4987/108. For the wide coverage in the Spanish press, see, for example, *ABC*, 4–30 April 1952.
139. Balfour to FO, 10 Jan. 1952 and 22 Jan. 1952 (FO, 371/102009).
140. 'Nota informativa de la Dirección Gral. de Seguridades', 6 March 1952 (AMAE, R.4987/108).
141. Terranova to MAE, 17 April 1952 (AMAE, R.4987/108); Furlonge to FO, 21 April 1952 (FO, 371/102009); *Ha'aretz*, 14 April 1952.
142. 'Spain: Annual Review for 1952', 16 Jan. 1953 (FO, 371/107668); *Time*, 28 April 1952, p. 21; Shneidman, *Spain*, p. 97; *Le Monde*, 6–7 April 1952; as well as *Ha'aretz*, 28 April 1952.
143. *Ha'aretz*, 15 April 1952; Crocker to State Department, 23 April 1952 (NA, 652.871/4-2352); Baghdad Embassy to State Department, 30 April 1952 (NA, 652.86/4-3052).
144. Balfour to FO, 25 March 1952 (FO, 371/102009); Wesley Jones to State Department, 5 Feb. 1952 (NA, 652.71B/2-552).
145. *Le Monde*, 15 June 1952; *The Tablet* (London), 15 Nov. 1952; Rockwell to State Department, 11 July 1952 (NA, 652.00/7-1152); Suárez Fernández, *Francisco Franco*, Vol. 5, pp. 90–2; Marquina Barrio, *La diplomacia vaticana*, Ch. 6.
146. Kahany to Foreign Ministry, 1 April 1952 (ISA, 2413/24).
147. Sasson to Foreign Ministry, 27 April 1952 (ISA, 2413/24).
148. Eytan to Sharett, 14 April 1952, Sharett to Eytan, 13 May 1952 (ISA, 2413/24).
149. United Nations division to Kahany, 20 May 1952 (ISA, 2413/24).
150. Ben-Ami, *La revolución desde arriba*, p. 115; *Arriba*, 20 Nov. 1952; Suárez Fernández, *Francisco Franco*, Vol. 5, p. 115; Shneidman, *Spain*, p. 107. In October the Socialist International, at its session in Milan, had already condemned the plan to admit Spain to UNESCO, and called on all its members to try to derail the process.
151. *Divrei Ha-Knesset*, Vol. 13, pp. 374–5, 586.
152. *Divrei Ha-Knesset*, Vol. 14, p. 1866. The question was filed in the Foreign Ministry on 11 Feb. 1953 (ISA, 2392/7).
153. Kahany to Foreign Ministry, 1 April 1952 (ISA, 2413/24); Shneidman, *Spain*, p. 74.
154. See therein letter to Fischer, which was sent to the Foreign Ministry on 7 Dec. 1952 (ISA, 2541/13A).
155. Draft reply prepared on 20 March 1953 (ISA, 2392/7).
156. *Divrei Ha-Knesset*, Vol. 14, p. 1866; *Ha'aretz*, 9 July 1953.
157. Kedron to Eban, 13 Jan. 1953 (ISA, 2413/24B).
158. 'The acceptance of reparations from Germany itself somehow weakens everyone's opposition to contacts with Franco', Walter Eytan wrote to the Israeli representative in Tokyo at the beginning of 1954 (ISA, 2385/27).
159. Latin American division to Meroz, 6 Nov. 1952 (ISA, 2578/12A).
160. Terranova to MAE, 14 Nov. 1952 (AMAE, R.4797/61); Moshe Tov, *El*

murmullo de Israel – historial diplomático (Jerusalem: 1983) pp. 299–311; and see articles by Gamzu in *Ha'aretz*, 1 Aug. 1952, 5 Aug. 1952, 5 Sept. 1952, and 12 Sept. 1952.

Chapter 4

1. On the Madrid Pact, see 'Semi-Annual Review of Spain's Foreign Relations and Domestic Political Situation', 1 Feb. 1954 (NA, 652.00/2-154); Viñas, *Los pactos secretos*; Dura, 'U.S. Policy'; Gilmore, 'The American Foreign Policy Making Process'; and Lowi, 'Bases in Spain'. On the concordat with the Vatican, see Rockwell to State Department, 4 Sept. 1953 (NA, 652.65A/9-453); Spanish Government, Oficina de Información Diplomática, *The Concordat between Spain and the Holy See* (Madrid: 1953); Tusell, *Franco y los católicos*, pp. 229–82; S.G. Payne, *Spanish Catholicism* (Madison, WI: 1984), Ch. 7; and Isidro Martín, *El concordato español de 1953* (Madrid: 1954).
2. Author's interview with Joel Barromi (Jerusalem, 2 Dec. 1986).
3. See memorandum, 18 Jan. 1953 (ISA, 2413/24B).
4. See Darom's memorandum, 3 April 1950 (ISA, 2413/24).
5. Officials in the Research Division of the Foreign Ministry expressed doubt, even after Franco signed the concordat with the Vatican, as to Spain's ability to help Israel persuade the Holy See to change its views on Jerusalem. A memorandum prepared on 27 Dec. 1953 explained: 'It is difficult to imagine that Franco, as the ruler of a Catholic country like Spain, would be willing to put himself in jeopardy by raising the issue of internationalization with the Vatican, that he would be willing to mediate in a matter so delicate and predestined to failure'. Spain was, however, judged capable of influencing the views of a number of Latin American countries (ISA, 2578/12A).
6. On the United Nations' policy towards the Franco régime in the years 1946–50, see A. Lleonart, *España y ONU*, 4 vols (Madrid: 1978–86).
7. Herzog's confidential letter was written on 22 December 1952 and sent from Washington to Israel by courier on the 26 December.
8. This feeling, prevalent in the Israeli Foreign Ministry during those years, requires an examination exceeding the scope of this book. Salazar probably had his own reasons for deciding not to establish relations with Israel, although those reasons were doubtless reinforced by the fact that his Iberian neighbour had no relations with Israel either.
9. Sharett to Eytan, 21 Jan. 1953 (ISA, 2413/24B).
10. Lotan to Eytan, 22 Feb. 1953 (ISA, 2413/24B); Artajo to Consul-General in Jerusalem, 19 Feb. 1953, and López García to Artajo, 20 Feb. 1953 (AMAE, R.2849/19).
11. Prat de Nantouillet to MAE, 11 May 1953 (AMAE, R. 4997/45).
12. See, for example, George Bilainkin, 'Spanish–Israeli Relations', *Jewish Chronicle*, 16 Jan. 1953.
13. Amir to Foreign Ministry, 2 June 1953 (ISA, 2541/14A).
14. See Perlzweig's memorandum (ISA, 2541/13A). On Lequerica and his position in the Second World War, see Payne, *The Franco Regime*, pp. 336–7; and Avni, *Contemporary Spain*, pp. 80, 100, 105–6.
15. Eban to Foreign Ministry, 26 Dec. 1952 (ISA, 2413/24).

16. See Eban's letters of 9 Feb. 1953 and 29 May 1953 (ISA, 2413/24B).

17. Israel's minister in Brussels to Foreign Ministry, 31 Dec. 1953 (ISA, 2541/14A); Casa Miranda to Artajo, 7 Jan. 1954 (AMAE, R.5002/37).

18. Utray to MAE, 9 March 1951 (AMAE, R.4792/45); Terranova to MAE, 25 Oct. 1951, and Artajo to Consul-General in Jerusalem, 30 Oct. 1951 (AMAE, R.4792/45); López García to MAE, 2 July 1953 (AMAE, R.4995/100).

19. Sharett to Eytan, 8 July 1953 (ISA, 2578/12A).

20. See Barromi's memorandum, 20 Dec. 1953 (ISA, 2578/12A). At the end of the 1950s, Spain refused, for political reasons, to accede to ZIM's request to institute a regular call at the port of Algeciras instead of at Gibraltar. Madrid did not even allow the Spanish postal services to use the Israeli company's ships. See Marquina and Ospina, *España y los judíos*, p. 287.

21. On Spanish arms sales to Egypt, see, for example, AMAE, R.4783/46, R.4786/8, R.4792/136, and R.4987/24. In March 1953, Spain's embassy in Paris granted entry visas to two Israeli officers and an official of the Ministry of Trade. This trio was in Europe on a military purchasing trip, and asked to visit Spain in order to explore possibilities there for buying equipment to meet the Defence Ministry's needs. See Rojas y Moreno to MAE, 3 March 1953 (AMAE, R.4994/38).

22. 'Spain: Annual Review of 1953', 1 Jan. 1954 (FO, 371/113024).

23. Ben-Shmuel, 'Spain's Arab Policy', pp. 166, 168–170; *Le Monde*, 22 Jan. 1954 and 24 Feb. 1954; 'Semi-Annual Review of Spain's Foreign Relations and Domestic Political Situation', 1 Feb. 1954 (NA, 652.00/2-154), and Witman to State Department, 23 Nov. 1953 (NA, 652.71B/11-2353).

24. Only a few months earlier, on 27 April 1952, Spain's interest in the holy places had been demonstrated once again with the establishment of an association of 'Friends of the Holy Land' to commemorate 500 years since the birth of the Catholic sovereigns. This association, presided over by General Franco himself, included among its objectives the following: 'to arouse in Spain a sense of responsibility and devotion to the Catholic holy places in the Holy Land (. . .) and to act in accordance with the wishes of the Pope to guarantee rights and to preserve the safety and soundness of the holy places, worship in them, and access to them'. See Latin American Division to Ministry of Religion, 12 Oct. 1952 (ISA, 2578/12A).

25. This assessment was shared by the Spanish consulate in Jerusalem, but the Foreign Ministry in Madrid was not enthusiastic about the possibility of an Israeli consulate in Spain, and instructed its Consul to try to delay any Israeli initiative aiming at the establishment of a consulate in Spain. See MAE to López García, 23 July 1953 (AMAE, R.3858/11).

26. *Yediot Aharonot*, 30 Sept. 1953; López García to MAE, 8 Dec. 1953 (AMAE, R.4993/31).

27. *Herut*, 1 Feb. 1954.

28. See, for example, *Haboker*, 16 Oct. 1953, and 15 July 1956; López García to MAE, 8 Sept. 1954 (AMAE, R.5002/37). For what representatives of the opposition said on the subject in the Knesset, see, for example, *Divrei Ha-Knesset*, Vol. 8, p. 867; Vol. 14, pp. 1618–19; Vol. 17, p. 996.

29. Levavi to Eytan, 23 Dec. 1953 (ISA, 2578/12A). Arye Levavi had no sympathy whatsoever for the Franco régime; during the Civil War, one of his friends had been killed in the International Brigades while fighting for

the Republic against the Nationalist forces. At the time, he was unaware of Spain's assistance in saving Jews during the Second World War. And yet, for pragmatic reasons, he supported the establishment of relations with Spain (Levavi in interview with the author, Jerusalem, 25 Jan. 1994).

30. See handwritten memorandum, 28 Dec. 1953 (ISA, 2578/12A).
31. Levavi to Eytan, 28 Dec. 1953 (ISA, 2578/12A).
32. See the summary of the meeting, held on 26 Jan. 1954 (ISA, 2413/24B).
33. On Barkatt's memorandum, see *Israel and the United Nations*, p. 279. On Argov's position, see Perlzweig's memorandum, 27 April 1954 (ISA, 2541/13A). On the *Histadrut*'s protest, see Fried to State Department, 2 April 1951 (NA, 752.00/4-251).
34. See Sharett's response in handwriting on the back of Shack's memorandum, 30 Jan. 1954 (ISA, 2413/24B).
35. MAE to Consul-General in Jerusalem, 23 July 1953 (AMAE, R.4995/100); López García to MAE, 2 Feb. 1954 (AMAE, R.5002/37); and Director-General of Foreign Policy to Consul-General in Jerusalem, 26 March 1954 (AMAE, R.5002/38).
36. Circular, 20 Jan. 1954 (AMAE, R.5002/37).
37. The Consul's son, Pedro López Aguirrebengoa, arrived in Israel in 1986 as Spain's first Ambassador to the State of Israel. On his memories of Israel in the 1950s, see *Ha'ir*, 18 April 1986.
38. Eytan, 'The Struggle', p. 17; Brecher, 'Jerusalem', p. 289.
39. The memorandum was drafted on 20 Dec. 1953 (ISA, 2578/12A).
40. See summary of the consultation on Spain that took place on 26 Jan. 1954 (ISA, 2413/24B). Officials in the Foreign Ministry gradually came to share an unfavourable view of López García. The Deputy Director-General, Arthur Lourie, spoke of 'that consul's hypocrisy' (memorandum of 28 Oct. 1955, ISA, 2413/24B). The Latin American division wrote that same day that 'despite the friendly attitude displayed by the Spanish consul in Jerusalem, we have reason to know that he is not one of Israel's friends, and we should therefore respect him but suspect him' (ISA, 2413/24B). López García ended his functions as Consul-General of Spain in Jerusalem at the end of 1956.
41. Founding speech of the Israel–Spain Friendship League (ISA, 2413/24B). See also Mani to Sharett, 6 July 1953, ibid.
42. López García to MAE, 21 Oct. 1953 (AMAE, R.4993/31).
43. Nota del Director de Mundo Arabe y Próximo Oriente, 2 Dec. 1953 (AMAE, R.4993/31).
44. Informe de Barandica, 16 Dec. 1953 (AMAE, R.4993/31).
45. Nota de Terranova, 27 Nov. 1953 (AMAE, R.4993/31).
46. *Ha'aretz*, 29 Jan. 1954; *Herut*, 29 Jan. 1954; López García to MAE, 30 Jan. 1954 (AMAE, R.5002/37).
47. See reports from Cairo, Tripoli, and Baghdad in AMAE, R.5002/37.
48. Santa Cruz to MAE, 18 Feb. 1954 (AMAE, R. 5002/37).
49. MAE to Santa Cruz, 30 Dec. 1953 (AMAE, R.4993/31).
50. López García to MAE, 6 Nov. 1953 (AMAE, R.4994/38); López García to Artajo, 17 March 1954 (AMAE, R.4435/34).
51. *Ha'aretz*, 28 Jan. 1954.
52. *Ha'aretz*, 25 April 1954; *ABC*, 24, 26, and 28 April 1954; Santa Cruz to Artajo, 26 May 1954 (APG, Leg. 20). Similarly, when Shukeiri visited Spanish Morocco and made a few declarations that grated on the ears of

the Spaniards, the Madrid government reacted the same way, cancelling a planned meeting with Franco at the last minute.

53. Research division to Latin American division, 12 May 1954 (ISA, 2541/13A).
54. Desio to MAE, 29 May 1954, and MAE to ambassador in Rome, 8 June 1954 (AMAE, R.5006/28).
55. Nota, 17 Oct. 1953 (AMAE, R.4993/31).
56. *Ha'aretz*, 18 May 1955; Israel's Embassy in Washington to the Foreign Ministry, 22 Sept. 1955 (ISA, 2413/24B); nota de la O.I.D., 2 June 1955, and embassy in Washington to MAE, 3 June 1955 (AMAE, R.3853/12).
57. Artajo to Areilza, 7 May 1955, and 3 June 1955 (AMAE, R.3853/12).
58. Ariel to Foreign Ministry, 2 Feb. 1955 (ISA, 2413/25B). When, in the summer of 1955, the Israeli government press office invited the London correspondent of the Falangist paper *Arriba* to visit Israel, Spain rejected the proposal after Foreign Minister Artajo consulted Franco himself in the matter.
59. Ariel to Foreign Ministry, 19 March 1954 (ISA, 2541/13A).
60. 'Spain: Annual Review for 1954', 13 Jan. 1955 (FO, 371/117860).
61. 'Semi-Annual Review of Spain's Foreign Relations and Domestic Political Situation', 4 Aug. 1954 (NA, 652.00/8-454).
62. Barromi's memorandum was composed on 26 Oct. 1954.
63. Ariel to Foreign Ministry, 26 Jan. 1954 (ISA, 2578/12A).
64. Linton to Eytan, 1 March 1954 (ISA, 2541/14B).
65. See memorandum by Alexander Dotan, 2 May 1954 (ISA, 2413/24B) .
66. On Pratto's mission, see author's interview with Pratto (Jerusalem, 23 Jan. 1994), and Lisbona, *Retorno a Sefarad*, pp. 279–80. On Hadas's mission, see Hadas, 'España–Israel'; and Fernando Morán, *España en su sitio* (Barcelona: 1990) p. 177.
67. It is not clear whether Shitreet did indeed make such a request, and whether he did it on his own initiative. The Foreign Ministry apparently knew nothing of it, at least to judge by the Director-General's reaction to Benarroya's proposal. See Tolkowski to Director-General, 6 July 1954 (ISA, 2541/14B).
68. Eytan to Tolkowski, 13 July 1954 (ISA, 2413/24B); Foreign Ministry to Meir Grossman, a Jewish Agency administrator, and to L. Bernstein of the Israeli branch of the World Jewish Congress (ISA, 2578/12A).
69. Eytan to Linton, 18 Feb. 1954 (ISA, 2385/27); Najar to Ariel, 5 April 1954 (ISA, 2541/14A).
70. Levavi to Eytan, 27 Oct. 1954 (ISA, 2578/12A).
71. Eytan to Shack, 30 Oct. 1954 (ISA, 2578/12A); Shack to Sharett, 1 Nov. 1954 (ISA, 2578/12A).
72. Eytan to Avnon and Avnon to Eytan, 4 Nov. 1954 (ISA, 2578/12A).
73. West European division to Ariel, 28 Jan. 1955 (ISA, 2541/13B); Eytan to Najar, 26 Jan. 1955 (ISA, 2541/13B); Eytan to Linton, 18 Feb. 1954 (ISA, 2385/27).
74. Ariel to Foreign Ministry, 2 Feb. 1955 (ISA, 2413/25B).
75. See reports by Israel's representatives in Belgium, Switzerland, Italy, Turkey, and Greece (ISA, 2541/14B); *Herut*, 2 May 1954; *Hatsofeh*, 6 Oct. 1953; *The Jerusalem Post*, 20 Oct. 1953.
76. *Ha'aretz*, 18 and 19 May 1955; *Ma'ariv*, 1 July 1955; review by Research Division, 19 May 1955 (ISA, 2413/24B); López García to MAE, 24 May

1955 and 21 June 1955; Artajo to heads of mission in Arab countries, 2 June 1955, and to the ambassador in Washington, 2 June 1955 (AMAE, R.3853/12).

77. *Ha'aretz,* 6 Oct. 1953; *Hatzofeh,* 6 and 8 Oct. 1953; Lisbona, *Retorno a Sefarad,* p. 158. In a letter to Artajo dated March 1955, Barukh wrote: 'In any program to advance Spain's prestige abroad, I beg your Excellency to rely on my services, my loyalty, and my affection'. See also Lequerica to Artajo, 8 Nov. 1953 (APG, Leg. 20).

78. Ministerio de la Gobernación to Director Gral. de Política Exterior, 7 April 1954; and Barukh to Jefe Superior de la Policía de Madrid, 30 Jan. 1954 (AMAE, R.4785/95).

79. Review by research division, 23 Sept. 1955 (ISA, 2541/13B); *Ha'aretz,* 13 Sept. 1953; *Jewish Chronicle,* 21 Oct. 1955; Bárcenas to Director Gral. de Seguridad, 21 Aug. 1954 (AMAE, R.4785/95); Shneidman, *Spain,* p. 139; Lisbona, *Retorno a Sefarad,* pp. 158–64.

80. Avni, *Contemporary Spain,* p. 225; review by research division, 23 Sept. 1955 (ISA, 2541/13B).

81. *Ha'aretz,* 17 Aug. 1951, and 18 May 1955.

82. See Perlzweig's memorandum, following his visit to Morocco (ISA, 2541/13A); Harman to Foreign Ministry, 18 Feb. 1954 (ISA, 2578/12A); *Haboker,* 2 Oct. 1953.

83. See review by Research Division, 19 May 1955 (ISA, 2413/24B); Marquina y Ospina, *España y los judíos,* p. 259.

84. See review by Research Division, 19 May 1955. Eliahu Eliachar, who visited Spain in 1955 in his capacity as Vice-President of the World Federation of Sephardic Communities, was asked by Sharett to investigate unofficially the possibility of establishing relations between the two countries, and was given the impression that for Spain it was already out of the question. See Eliachar, *Living with Jews,* pp. 351–2.

85. Sharett to Tsur, 27 Sept. 1955 (ISA, 2541/13B).

86. Tsur to Sharett, 7 Oct. 1955 (ISA, 2413/24B).

87. Tsur to Sharett, 8 Nov. 1955 (ISA, 2413/24B); Ya'akov Tsur, *Paris Diary* (Hebrew) (Tel Aviv: 1968) p. 197.

88. On Hussein's visit to Spain, see AMAE, R.3872/19; *Arriba,* 10 and 19 June 1955; *Ya,* 7–9 June 1955; *Hoja del Lunes,* 6 and 13 June 1955.

89. See review by Research Division, 23 Sept. 1955 (ISA, 2541/13B); *Christian Science Monitor,* 13 Sept. 1955.

90. The memorandum was delivered to Sharett's office on 24 Oct. 1955 (ISA, 2413/24B).

91. On Spain's admission to the United Nations, see AMAE, R.3305/4, R.3305/8, and R.4278/22; and Shneidman, *Spain,* pp. 138–9.

92. Tsur to Sharett, 8 Nov. 1955 (ISA, 2413/24B); Tsur, *Paris Diary,* p. 197; Foreign Ministry to legations in Ankara and Rome, 4 and 9 Dec. 1955 (ISA, 2541/13B); Bertrán de Lis to MAE, 28 Nov. 1955, and Artajo to permanent observer in the United Nations, 30 Nov. 1955 (AMAE, R.3305/8).

93. Eytan to Tsur, 21 Dec. 1955 (ISA, 2413/25B); Sharett to Artajo and Artajo to Sharett, 17 and 19 Dec. 1955 (AMAE, R.4278/22); López García to MAE, 18 Jan. 1956 (AMAE, R.5522/32).

94. Levavi to Eytan, 23 Dec. 1955 (ISA, 2413/24B); Levavi's interview with the author (Jerusalem, 25 Jan. 1994).

95. Ben-Ami, *La revolución desde arriba,* pp. 160–1; Suárez Fernández, *Franco*

y la URSS (Madrid: 1988).

96. On 22 Dec. 1955, the subject came up during a conversation with the Director-General of the Foreign Ministry in Jerusalem (Moshe Sharett, *Personal Diary* (Hebrew) (Tel Aviv: 1978), Vol. 5, p. 1313). On 5 Jan. 1956 it came up during a discussion among MAPAI leaders (ibid., p. 1327). On 8 Jan. 1956 the government debated the subject of establishing relations with Madrid (ibid., p. 1328). On 18 Jan. 1956, Sharett spoke with Walter Eytan about the possibility of setting up an Israeli legation in Madrid (ibid., p. 1336).

97. Sharf to Sharett, 9 Jan. 1956 (ISA, 2413/24B); Sharett, *Personal Diary*, p. 1328; Shack to Sharett, 9 Jan. 1956 (ISA, 2413/24B); *Davar*, 6 Jan. 1956; López García to MAE, 18 Jan. 1956 (AMAE, R.5522/32).

98. Tsur, *Paris Diary*, pp. 225–6; Diez to MAE, 27 Jan. 1956 (AMAE, R.5522/32). Moshe Tov, in a conversation with the author (Kiryat Ono, 24 June 1986), criticized the government for approaching the Spaniards through the Embassy in Paris rather than at a higher level, and Tsur for talking to a *chargé d'affaires* rather than the Ambassador himself. Yosef Ariel, the Ambassador in Brussels, believed that the application should have been made through him, since the Spanish Ambassador in Belgium was very friendly to Israel and supported the establishment of relations between the two countries wholeheartedly. Ariel was also told this in the Spanish embassy in Brussels. See Ariel to Foreign Ministry, 12 April 1956 (ISA, 2413/25B), and 4 July 1956 (ISA, 2541/13B).

99. Informe de la Dirección General de Africa y Próximo Oriente, and López García to MAE, 2 Feb. 1956 (AMAE, R.5522/32).

100. See his handwritten comment on the document in the preceding note.

101. Tsur, *Paris Diary*, p. 226; Rojas y Moreno to MAE, 30 April 1956 (AMAE, R.5522/32). A few months later, officials of the Spanish Embassy in Brussels told the Israeli Ambassador: 'It's not true that we refused; we made certain conditions'. When the Israeli diplomat replied that the conditions were such that Israel would clearly not be able to accept them, the Spaniards returned, 'That doesn't matter. When conditions are posed, there is always the possibility of negotiating, and they did not have to be interpreted as a refusal'. See Ariel to Foreign Ministry, 19 July 1956 (ISA, 2541/14B).

102. Franco Salgado-Araujo, *Mis conversaciones*, p. 168; Fleming, 'North Africa', pp. 137–8. On the Spanish protectorate in Morocco up until independence in 1956, see Morales Lezcano, *España y el norte de Africa*; Martín, *El colonialismo español*; Antonio Marquina Barrio, *España en la política de la seguridad occidental* (Madrid: 1986) Ch. 7.

103. Francisco Franco, *Pensamiento político* (Madrid: 1975) p. 779; Franco Salgado-Araujo, *Mis conversaciones privadas*, pp. 170–3; Suárez Fernández, *Francisco Franco*, Vol. 5, ch. 6; Trythall, *Franco*, pp. 244–6; Payne, *Politics and the Military*, pp. 441–2; Shneidman, *Spain*, pp. 141–6; José Luis de Arrese, *Una etapa constituyente* (Barcelona: 1982) p. 52. In the course of his talks with Foster Dulles in Washington in April, 1956, Martín Artajo said: 'Our army fought for years in Morocco, creating blood ties, later sentimental ones. All the Generalissimo's authority was needed to talk of independence (for Morocco), which many – especially the military – viewed with apprehension' (AMAE, R.3599/41).

104. Sharett, *Personal Diary*, p. 1372.

Chapter 5

1. *Ha'aretz,* 21 Jan. 1986.
2. In the mid-1970s, after Franco's death, the German foreign minister, Hans Dietrich Genscher, advised his Spanish colleague, José María de Areilza, to work towards normalizing relations between Spain and Israel in the framework of Spain's overall European policy. Relations with Israel, as Genscher knew from the German experience, were likely to ease Spain's integration into Europe; see Ben-Ami, 'Spain after Franco', p. 132. Relations between Spain and Israel resembled those between Germany and Israel in another particular as well. There had been a time when the Federal Republic had been interested in establishing diplomatic relations with Israel, and the latter was unwilling for domestic reasons. Ten years later the tables were turned: now Israel was interested in relations, whereas the Bonn government hesitated, initially deterred by Arab pressure, before entering into full relations. See Brecher, *Decisions,* p. 105.
3. Joel Barromi, interview with the author (Jerusalem, 2 Dec. 1986).
4. Najar to Ariel, 23 April 1956 (ISA, 2541/13B).
5. Sharett, *A Personal Diary,* p. 1382.
6. Tsur to Foreign Ministry, 29 Nov. 1956; and Ilsar to Director-General, 2 Dec. 1956 (ISA, 2541/13B).
7. Shneidman, *Spain,* p. 166.
8. See AMAE, R.4294/14, R.4294/15; and Suárez Fernández, *Francisco Franco,* Vol. 5, pp. 295–300.
9. Louis Blitz to Tsur, 25 Nov. 1956 (ISA, 2520/7); *New York Times,* 5 Nov. 1956; Trythall, *Franco,* p. 247; Fleming, 'North Africa', p. 134; Arrese, *Una etapa constituyente,* pp. 54–5, 122–123; Payne, *Politics and the Military,* pp. 443–4.
10. *The Times,* 21 Nov. 1956; Shneidman, *Spain,* p. 167.
11. Fleming, 'North Africa', p. 140. On how the irregular Moroccan forces were driven back when they invaded Ifni and the Western Sahara, see Welles, *Spain – The Gentle Anarchy,* pp. 239–44.
12. Lequerica to Castiella, 9 April 1957, and circular to all Arab countries, 23 July 1957 (AMAE, R.5522/32).
13. *Herut,* 19 Nov. 1958; Balenchana to MAE, 19 Nov. 1958 (AMAE, R.5522/32); MAE to ambassador in Helsinki, 11 Nov. 1958 (AMAE, R.5965/41); Marquina y Ospina, *España y los judíos,* pp. 287–91.
14. Circular, 11 Nov. 1958 (AMAE, R.5965/41).
15. Marquina y Ospina, *España y los judíos,* p. 283.
16. *Divrei Ha-Knesset,* Vol. 26, pp. 1050–51; *Ha'aretz,* 11 Feb. 1959; Balenchana to MAE, 11 Feb. 1959 (AMAE, R.5965/41).
17. Circular, 14 May 1959 (AMAE, R.5522/32).
18. *Ha'aretz,* 27 Nov. 1959; Welles, *Spain,* pp. 180–1; Marquina y Ospina, *España y los judíos,* pp. 291–4; Lisbona, *Retorno a Sefarad,* pp. 259–62.
19. The information on Pratto's mission is taken from interviews the author held with Arye Levavi (Jerusalem, 25 Jan. 1994) and Ionnathan Pratto himself (Jerusalem, 23 Jan. 1994). Pratto did indeed gather material for historical research during his stay in Madrid, and at the beginning of 1994 submitted a manuscript on the subject for publication in Italy.
20. *Jewish Chronicle,* 22 Jan. 1965, 9 April 1965; *Herut,* 7 and 8 April 1965.
21. López Bravo's *Ostpolitik* is treated by J. Lee Shneidman, 'Eastern Europe

and the Soviet Union', in J.W. Cortada (ed.), *Spain in the Twentieth Century World*, pp. 169–73.

22. *Yediot Aharonot*, 18 Nov. 1969; *Ha'aretz*, 28 Jan. 1970; *Jewish Chronicle*, 6 Feb. 1970.

23. Eban, *An Autobiography*, p. 482.

24. For the statements by López Bravo and Eban after the meeting, see *Ha'aretz*, 30 June 1970, 1 July 1970, 10 July 1970; Ministerio de Asuntos Exteriores, Oficina de Información Diplomática (O.I.D.), *España–Israel* (Madrid: 1986) pp. 31, 186–7.

25. On the conflict over the Western Sahara, see Francisco Villar, *El proceso de autodeterminación del Sahara* (Valencia: 1982); Ramón Criado, *Sahara: Pasión y muerte de un sueño imperial* (Paris: 1977); Juan B. Vilar, *El Sahara español* (Madrid: 1977); Morán, *Una política exterior*, pp. 215–40.

26. Fleming, 'North Africa', pp. 142, 145; James W. Cortada, *Two Nations Over Time – Spain and the United States, 1776–1977* (Westport, CT: 1978), p. 264.

27. Lisbona, *Retorno a Sefarad*, p. 280.

28. Natan Lerner of the World Jewish Congress, 'Report on a Visit to Spain' (Tel Aviv: 23 Jan. 1974) p. 4.

29. Fleming, 'North Africa', pp. 142–3; Roberto Mesa, *Democracia y política exterior* (Madrid: 1988) pp. 163, 239.

30. O.I.D., *España–Israel*, p. 26.

31. Suárez Fernández, *Francisco Franco*, Vol. VIII, p. 198.

32. *Ha'aretz*, 19 Oct. 1975.

33. On this affair see Pedro J. Ramírez, *El año que murió Franco* (Barcelona: 1985).

34. Fleming, 'North Africa', pp. 146–8.

35. Eliachar, *Living with Jews*, pp. 355–6.

36. Quoted in Lisbona, *Retorno a Sefarad*, p. 276.

37. Herzog's speech appears in his book, *Who Stands Accused?* (Hebrew) (Tel Aviv: 1979) pp. 13–23.

38. Nota para Su Excelencia el Generalísimo, 13 Sept. 1950 (AMAE, R.2631/19); Lisbona, *Retorno a Sefarad*, p. 173.

39. On the Sinai/Suez war, see W.R. Louis and R. Owen (eds), *Suez 1956: The Crisis and Its Consequences* (Oxford: 1989); W. Scott Lucas, *Divided We Stand: Britain, the U.S. and the Suez Crisis* (London: 1991); Michael B. Oren, *The Origins of the Second Arab–Israeli War: Egypt, Israel and the Great Powers, 1952–1956* (London: 1992). On the situation of the Jews in Egypt at the time, see Bat-Yeor, *Jews in Egypt* (Hebrew) (Ramat Gan: 1974), pp. 134–6; *American Jewish Year Book* (hereafter *AJYB*), Vol. 58 (1957) pp. 398–403; *AJYB*, Vol. 59 (1958) pp. 395–8; Michael M. Laskier, *The Jews of Egypt, 1920–1970* (New York: 1992) pp. 252–64; Joseph B. Schechtman, *On Wings of Eagles: The Plight, Exodus, and Homecoming of Oriental Jewry* (New York: 1961) pp. 196–202.

40. Although the Nasser régime's policy towards Jews was indeed severe, it is a considerable exaggeration to liken it to the policy of persecuting Jews in Nazi Germany, as the World Jewish Congress and the American Jewish Congress have done. See World Jewish Congress, *The Persecution of the Jews in Egypt: The Facts* (London: 1957); and American Jewish Congress, *The Black Record: Nasser's Persecution of Egyptian Jewry* (New York: 1957).

41. Urgoiti to Artajo, 24 Nov. 1956 (AMAE, R.5571/46).
42. José del Castaño to MAE, 10 Dec. 1956 (AMAE, R.4667/18).
43. Ibid.
44. See reports from Cairo by José del Castaño (AMAE, R.4491/94, R.4667/18, R.5571/46).
45. Carta de la Comunidad Israelita de Madrid a Franco, 19 Dec. 1956 (AMAE, R.4665/49); Madrazo to MAE, 8 Dec. 1956 (AMAE, R.4667/18); Primo de Rivera to Artajo, 2 Jan. 1957, and Areilza to Artajo, 30 Jan. 1957 (AMAE, R.4667/18); Eliachar, *Living with Jews*, pp. 354–5.
46. Areilza to Artajo, 30 Jan. 1957 (AMAE, R.4667/18).
47. Director-Gral. de Política Exterior to Consul in Jerusalem, 22 Dec. 1956 (AMAE, R.4491/94). This view was shared by the Spanish Consul-General in Jerusalem. See Madrazo to MAE, 8 Dec. 1956 (AMAE, R.4491/94).
48. Rojas y Moreno to Artajo, 8 Jan. 1957 (AMAE, R.4540/19).
49. Legation in Tripoli to Artajo, 7 Nov. 1956; Carrero to legation in Tripoli, 19 Nov. 1956; and Director Gral. de Política Exterior to Minister in Tripoli, 23 Nov. 1956 (AMAE, R.6170/34). On the situation of the Jews of Libya in the 1950s and the problem of passports, see Renzo de Felice, *Jews in an Arab Land: Libya, 1835–1970* (Hebrew) (Tel Aviv: 1980) pp. 293–304; Schechtman, *On Wings of Eagles*, pp. 126–47.
50. *New York Times*, 14, 22, and 24 Jan. 1961.
51. On the situation of the Jews of Morocco in those years, see Michael M. Laskier, 'Zionism and the Jewish Communities of Morocco: 1956–1962', *Studies in Zionism*, Vol. 6, No. 1 (spring 1985) pp. 119–38; idem, 'Secret Aliya from Morocco: Government Policy as an Element in Jewish–Muslim Relations, 1956–1961' (Hebrew), *Peamim*, Vol. 63 (1995) pp. 132–59.
52. Isser Harel, *Security and Democracy* (Hebrew) (Tel Aviv: 1989) p. 306; *Ha'aretz*, 13 Oct. 1991; Samuel Segev, *Operation 'Yakhin' – The Secret Immigration of Moroccan Jews to Israel* (Hebrew) (Tel Aviv: 1984); Agnes Bensimon, *Hassan II et les Juifs* (Hebrew) (Tel Aviv: 1993) pp. 87–93; *El País*, 29 Dec. 1988, 2 Jan. 1989.
53. Ben-Ami, *La revolución desde arriba*, p. 179.
54. On the wreck of the *Egoz*, see Segev, *Operation 'Yakhin'*, pp. 174–89; *New York Times*, 13 Jan. 1961.
55. Suárez Fernández, *Francisco Franco*, Vol. 7, p. 406.
56. Cited in Lisbona, *Retorno a Sefarad*, p. 199.
57. Cited in Ysart, *España y los judíos*, pp. 154–5. See also Lipschitz, *Franco*, pp. 186–9. On the arrest of Jews immediately following the outbreak of the Six-Day War, see Bat-Yeor, *Jews in Egypt*, pp. 138–9; Laskier, *The Jews of Egypt*, pp. 290–4.
58. See, for example, *New York Times*, 26 Jan. 1968.
59. For the testimony of one of the Jews rescued from Egypt with Spain's help, see Lipschitz, *Franco*, pp. 151–6.
60. Ibid., p. 189.
61. *Jewish Chronicle*, 27 Dec. 1967; Eliachar, *Living with Jews*, p. 335; Lisbona, *Retorno a Sefarad*, p. 202.
62. Lisbona, *Retorno a Sefarad*, pp. 206–10.
63. Beinart, *The New Jewish Community*, p. 33; *Ha'aretz*, 8 July 1960; *Jewish Chronicle*, 8 July 1960; Marquina y Ospina, *España y los judíos*, pp. 297–303; Lisbona, *Retorno a Sefarad*, pp. 261–3.
64. Irona and Yitzhak Emanuel, 'On a Mission in Barcelona' (Hebrew),

Betfutzot Hagola, 18/19 (winter 1962) pp. 122–4; Aronsfeld, *The Ghosts*, p. 56; *AJYB*, Vol. 63 (1962) pp. 320–1.

65. 'Not Since 1492', *Newsweek*, 8 Feb. 1965, p. 51; *Jewish Chronicle*, 19 March 1965; *AJYB*, Vol. 68 (1967) pp. 337–8.

66. *AJYB*, Vol. 68 (1967) pp. 337–8; Avni, *Contemporary Spain*, p. 226; *Ha'aretz*, 26 Jan. 1956.

67. Beinart, *The New Jewish Community*, pp. 28–9; Ionnathan Pratto, 'Spain' (Hebrew), in Ya'akov Tsur (ed.), *The Diaspora: Western Europe* (Hebrew) (Jerusalem: 1976) pp. 224–5; Institute of Jewish Affairs, *The Jewish Communities of the World* (New York: 1971) pp. 109–10; *AJYB*, Vol. 74 (1973), p. 425.

68. Avni, *Contemporary Spain*, pp. 229–30; *Jewish Chronicle*, 3 March 1967; *Ha'aretz*, 5 Dec. 1966 and 21 Feb. 1967; Aronsfeld, *The Ghosts*, pp. 58–9.

69. 'First in 467 Years', *Time*, 19 Oct. 1959, pp. 53–4; Lisbona, *Retorno a Sefarad*, pp. 165–6. The inauguration of the synagogue in 1959 aroused unease at the Spanish Foreign Ministry, which, gripped by the suspicion characteristic of dictatorships, feared that an overly tolerant attitude toward the Jewish community would arouse displeasure in the Arab world, with which Spain's friendship had already become part of diplomatic tradition. 'The inauguration of the synagogue in Pizarro Street, which has been held without regard to the applicable legal norms, is a typical example of Jewish tactics, which seek on the one hand to keep gaining ground by establishing facts, and on the other hand to exaggerate for the benefit of international public opinion the importance of the positions attained, attributing to them a significance they are far from having. The concrete fact that concerns us [here] must be considered to form part of the vast plan for rehabilitating Judaism in Spain, undertaken some time ago by international Jewry, and whose connections with the foreign policy of the State of Israel are clear.' Quoted in Lisbona, p. 166.

70. Beinart, *The New Jewish Community*, p. 36; Pratto, 'Spain', p. 226; *Ha'aretz*, 18 Aug. 1968, 17 Dec. 1968; *AJYB*, Vol. 74 (1973), p. 425.

71. Natan Lerner, 'Report on a Visit to Spain', Tel Aviv, 23 Jan. 1974, and 'Report on a Jewish–Christian Symposium in Spain', Tel Aviv, 27 April 1975.

72. *Jewish Chronicle*, 15 Dec. 1961.

73. *Jewish Chronicle*, 10 January 1964, 22 January 1965, and 3 March 1967.

74. *Jewish Chronicle*, 30 July 1965, 3 Dec. 1971.

75. *Ha'aretz*, 28 Feb. 1967, 2 March 1967, and 26 April 1967; Aronsfeld, *The Ghosts*, p. 57; Lisbona, *Retorno a Sefarad*, pp. 249–55; Marquina y Ospina, *España y los judíos*, p. 304; *AJYB*, Vol. 74 (1973), p. 428.

Epilogue

1. Ramón Tamames, *Introducción a la constitución española* (Madrid: 1980) pp. 36–8.

2. Aronsfeld, *The Ghosts*, pp. 62–3; *AJYB*, Vol. 78 (1978) pp. 386–7. Two other noteworthy meetings that the king held in his palace during the same period were with Yitzhak Navon, in October, 1976, and with the Sephardic chief rabbi of Israel, Ovadia Yosef, in December, 1977.

3. José Mario Armero, *Política exterior de España en democracia* (Madrid:

1989) pp. 57–9, 60–1.
4. Fleming, 'North Africa', pp. 145–6.
5. J.M. de Areilza, *Diario de un ministro de la Monarquía* (Barcelona: 1977) pp. 19–20.
6. Author's interview with Ionnathan Pratto; *Ha'aretz*, 18, 19 Jan. 1976, 3 Feb. 1976, 5, 9 and 16 March 1976.
7. On Arias Navarro's government, see Paul Preston, *The Triumph of Democracy in Spain* (London: 1986) Ch. 3.
8. Armero, *Política exterior*, pp. 61–2.
9. On Suárez's governments and his difficulties with the democratization process, see Preston, *The Triumph of Democracy*, Chs. 4–6.
10. *Ha'aretz*, 1, 2, 6, 7, 8, and 28 Dec. 1976; *The Jerusalem Post*, 6 and 9 Dec. 1976; *Jewish Chronicle*, 10 and 17 Dec. 1976; *AJYB*, Vol. 78 (1978) p. 387; and Aronsfeld, *The Ghosts*, pp. 63–5.
11. O.I.D., *España–Israel*, p. 50; Marquina y Ospina, *España y los judíos*, p. 315; Lisbona, *Retorno a Sefarad*, pp. 312–13.
12. *Davar*, 14, 16, and 17 Sept. 1979; O.I.D., *España–Israel*, pp. 57–8; Marquina y Ospina, *España y los judíos*, pp. 317–19; Lisbona, *Retorno a Sefarad*, pp. 321–6.
13. *Ma'ariv*, 20 Jan. 1986; Hadas, 'España e Israel', pp. 199–200; Marquina y Ospina, *España y los judíos*, pp. 320–1; Mesa, *Democracia*, p. 241; Armero, *Política exterior de España*, pp. 150–1.
14. On Hadas's activities, see *Ha'aretz*, 9 March 1986; Hadas, 'España e Israel', pp. 197 ff.; Fernando Morán, *España en su sitio* (Barcelona: 1990) pp. 177–8; Lisbona, *Retorno a Sefarad*, pp. 333–8.
15. *Ma'ariv*, 10 Dec. 1985. In the years 1985–1990, Israeli exports to Spain increased sixfold, and in 1987 they reached the $100 million mark for the first time. See *Ha'aretz*, 3 Dec. 1991.
16. Syria, for example, expressed displeasure over the beginning of regular Iberia flights on the Madrid–Tel Aviv route, and over the visit to Israel by the Spanish President of the Senate, José Federico de Carvajal. See *Ma'ariv*, 9 June 1983; *Davar*, 28 July 1983; and *Ha'aretz*, 16 Aug. 1983. Jordan, too, whose request to institute regular flights on the Amman–Madrid route had been turned down, was piqued. See Morán, *España en su sitio*, p. 181. In 1984, 36,152 Israeli tourists visited Spain, and 23,254 did so in 1985. See *Ma'ariv*, 16 Sept. 1986.
17. *Ha'aretz*, 31 July 1975, 26 March 1976, 24 Feb. 1977, and 23 Sept. 1981; *Davar*, 24 Feb. 1977, 19 and 21 Jan. 1986, 25 Jan. 1987, and 'The Workers Anticipated the Politicians' (Hebrew), 2 Dec. 1991; and O.I.D., *España–Israel*, pp. 122 and 172.
18. *Al Hamishmar*, 22 Jan. 1986; *Davar*, 19 Jan. 1986, and 'González and Harish: Not Just a Diplomatic Connection' (Hebrew), 2 Dec. 1991.
19. *Ha'aretz*, 31 Aug. 1984.
20. Morán, *España en su sitio*, p. 171; Mesa, *Democracia*, p. 238.
21. On the party's declarations concerning Israel during the years 1980–85, see O.I.D., *España–Israel*, pp. 143–50; *Ma'ariv*, 12 Jan. 1984 and 29 Oct. 1984; *Ha'aretz*, 8 and 11 Jan. 1984.
22. *Ma'ariv*, 8 Aug. 1983 and 8 Dec. 1983; Hadas, 'España e Israel', p. 203.
23. Morán, *España en su sitio*, pp. 173–83.
24. Armero, *Política exterior de España*, pp. 213–14. Some years later Morán was distressed that his government had not demanded some sort of gesture

from Israel towards the Palestinians in exchange for establishing relations. See Morán, *España en su sitio*, p. 172.

25. *Ha'aretz,* 19 Jan. 1986; Hadas, 'España e Israel', p. 202; Armero, *Política exterior de España*, p. 216. At the same time, the Spanish government drafted a communiqué in which it emphasized its traditional friendship with the Arab states, its opposition to the continued occupation of the Arab lands seized in June 1967, its opposition to any change in the status of Jerusalem and to the policy of Jewish settlement in the occupied territories, and its support for the Palestinian people's right to self-determination.

26. The Spanish intellectual Roberto Mesa, who, like the heads of the Spanish Communist Party, was against establishing relations with Israel, criticized the Arabs' passive response to Spain's political move. See Mesa, *Democracia*, pp. 167, 248. When relations were established with Israel, the PLO's legation in Madrid was raised to the level of an embassy.

Sources and Bibliography

I. *Primary Sources*

Archives

Archivo del Ministerio de Asuntos Exteriores (AMAE), Madrid.
Archivo de la Presidencia del Gobierno (APG), Madrid.
Central Zionist Archives (CZA), Jerusalem.
Israeli State Archives (ISA), Jerusalem.
National Archives, Records of the Department of State (NA), Washington, D.C.
Public Record Office, Foreign Office Papers (FO), London.

Printed documents, speeches, and official publications

American Jewish Congress, *The Black Record: Nasser's Persecution of Egyptian Jewry* (New York: 1957).
Central Bureau of Statistics, *Statistical Abstract of Israel* (1976–1986) (Hebrew) (Jerusalem).
Divrei Ha-Knesset (official records of the Israeli parliament, in Hebrew) (Jerusalem: 1948–75).
Documents on the Foreign Policy of Israel (1948–1952) (Jerusalem: 1984–93).
Franco, Francisco, *Franco ha dicho (1936–1942)* (Madrid: 1947).
— *Textos de doctrina política. Palabras y escritos de 1945 a 1950.* (Madrid: 1951).
— *Discursos y mensajes de S.E. el Jefe del estado a las Cortes Españolas, 1943–1961* (Madrid: 1961).
— *Pensamiento político de Franco* (Madrid: 1975). 2 Vols.
Institute of Jewish Affairs, *The Jewish Communities of the World* (New York: 1971).

Sharett, Moshe, *On the Threshold of Nations* (Hebrew) (Tel Aviv: 1964).

Spanish Embassy, *Spain and the Sephardi Jews* (Washington DC: 1949).

Spanish Government, Oficina de Información diplomática, *España y los Judíos* (Madrid: 1949).

— The *Concordat Between Spain and the Holy See* (Madrid: 1953).

— *España–Israel* (Madrid: 1986).

United Nations, *Official Records of the Third Session of the General Assembly* (Lake Success, NY: 1949).

United Nations, Security Council, *Report of the Sub-Committee on the Spanish Question* (New York: 1946).

U.S. Department of State, *The Spanish Government and the Axis* (Washington DC: 1946).

— *Foreign Relations of the United States* (1945–57).

World Jewish Congress, *The Persecution of the Jews in Egypt: The Facts* (London: 1957).

Memoirs

Abdallah, King of Jordan, *My Memoirs Completed: 'Al-Tekmilah'* (London: 1978).

Areilza, José María de, *Así los he visto* (Barcelona: 1974).

— *Diario de un ministro de la Monarquía* (Barcelona: 1977).

Arrese, José Luis de, *Una etapa constituyente* (Barcelona: 1982).

Avi-Shaul, Mordechai, *A Hebrew Commander in Embattled Spain* (Hebrew) (Tel Aviv: 1945).

Centner, Israel, *From Madrid to Berlin* (Hebrew) (Tel Aviv: 1966).

Churchill, Winston S., *The Second World War* (London: 1949).

Eban, Abba, *An Autobiography* (Tel Aviv: 1977).

Elath, Eliahu, *San Francisco Diary* (Hebrew) (Tel Aviv: 1971).

— *The Struggle for Statehood* (Hebrew) (Tel Aviv: 1982).

Eliachar, Eliahu, *Living with Jews* (Hebrew) (Jerusalem: 1980).

Escobar, Adrián C., *Diálogo íntimo con España: Memorias de un embajador durante la tempestad europea* (Buenos Aires: 1950).

Franco Salgado-Araujo, Francisco, *Mis conversaciones privadas con Franco* (Barcelona: 1978).

Gondi, Ovidio, *Las batallas de papel en la casa de cristal (ONU: los años decisivos)* (Mexico City: 1971).

Hadas, Shmuel, 'España–Israel: Quinientos años después', *Política Exterior*, Vol. 30 (1992/3) pp. 191–206.

Harel, Isser, *Security and Democracy* (Hebrew) (Tel Aviv: 1989).

Hayes, Carlton J.H., *Wartime Mission in Spain, 1942–1945* (New York: 1945).

Herzog, Chaim, *Who Stands Accused?* (Hebrew) (Tel Aviv: 1979).

Hoare, Samuel, *Complacent Dictator* (New York: 1947).

Hull, Cordell, *The Memoirs* (New York: 1948), 2 Vols.

Krone David, 'Monologue: The Republic Gave Us Everything It Had', *Iton 77* (Hebrew), Nos. 77–78 (July–August 1986) p. 26.

Leshem, Perez (Fritz Lichtenstein), 'Rescue Efforts in the Iberian Peninsula', in *Leo Baeck Institute Year Book*, Vol. 14 (1969), pp. 231–56.

Meir, Golda, *My Life* (London: 1975).

Morán, Fernando, *España en su sitio* (Barcelona: 1990).

Nordau, Max, *Zionist Writings* (Hebrew) (Jerusalem: 1962).

Rafael, Gideon, *Destination Peace: Three Decades of Israeli Foreign Policy* (London: 1981).

Rupin, Arthur, *An Autobiography* (Hebrew) (Tel Aviv: 1968).

Sharett, Moshe, *A Personal Diary* (Hebrew) (Tel Aviv: 1978).

Tov, Moshe, *El murmullo de Israel – historial diplomático* (Jerusalem: 1983).

Tsur, Yaacov, *Paris Diary* (Hebrew) (Tel Aviv: 1968).

— *Credential No. 4* (Hebrew) (Tel Aviv: 1981).

Weissman, Yitzhak, *Against the Forces of Evil* (Hebrew) (Tel Aviv: 1968).

Weizmann, Chaim, *The Letters and Papers of Chaim Weizmann* (New York: 1979).

Yahuda, A.S., *The Defense of the Jews of Palestine during World War I – Memories of my Stay in Spain* (Hebrew) (Jerusalem: 1952).

II. Secondary Sources

Algazy, J., 'The Civil War in Spain as Reflected by the Hebrew Press in Eretz–Yisrael–Palestine, 1936–1939' (Hebrew). Unpublished paper (Tel Aviv: 1977).

Algora Weber, María Dolores, 'La Liga Arabe ante "la cuestión española" en las Naciones Unidas: 1946–1950', in *Congreso Internacional sobre el Régimen de Franco* (Madrid: 1993), Vol. II, pp. 387–400.

Ami, Raoul, *Ce que j'ai vu et entendu en Espagne* (Jerusalem: 1950).

Amodia, José, *Franco's Political Legacy: From Dictatorship to Facade Democracy* (London: 1977).

Arditi, Binyamin, *The Jews of Bulgaria in the Years of the Nazi Régime, 1940–1944* (Hebrew) (Holon: 1962).

Areilza, José María de, and Fernando de Castiella, *Reivindicaciones de España* (Madrid: 1941).

Armero, José Mario, *La política exterior de Franco* (Barcelona: 1978).

— *Política exterior de España en democracia* (Madrid: 1989).

Aronsfeld, C.C., *The Ghosts of 1492. Jewish Aspects of the Struggle for Religious Freedom in Spain, 1848–1976* (New York: 1979).

Avni, Haim, *Contemporary Spain and the Jewish People* (Hebrew) (Tel Aviv: 1975).

Balabkins, Nicholas, *West German Reparations to Israel* (New Brunswick: 1971).

Barciela, Carlos, 'Crecimiento y cambio en la agricultura española desde la guerra civil', in J. Nadal *et al.* (eds), *La economía española en el siglo XX – una perspectiva histórica* (Barcelona: 1987).

Bat-Yeor, *Jews in Egypt* (Hebrew) (Ramat Gan: 1974).

Beaulac, Willard, *Franco: Silent Ally in World War II* (Carbondale, IL: 1986).

Beinart, Haim, *The New Jewish Community in Spain: Background, Reality, and Assessment* (Hebrew) (Jerusalem: 1969).

Ben-Asher, A.A., *Foreign Relations 1948–1953* (Hebrew) (Tel Aviv: 1957).

Ben-Ami, Shlomo, *La revolución desde arriba: España 1936–1979* (Madrid: 1980).

— 'Spain after Franco, Israel and the Jews', *Gesher* (Hebrew), Vol. 86 (1976) pp. 131–5.

Ben-Sasson, Haim Hillel, *Continuity and Variety* (Hebrew) (Tel Aviv: 1984).

Bensimon, Agnes, *Hassan II et les juifs* (Hebrew) (Tel Aviv: 1993).

Ben-Shmuel, S.P., 'Spain's Arab Policy', *Hamizrach Hehadash* (Hebrew), Vol. 19 (1954) pp. 153–71.

Bialer, Uri, *Between East and West: Israel's Foreign Policy Orientation, 1948–1956* (Cambridge: 1990).

— 'Jerusalem 1949: Transition to Capital City Status', *Cathedra* (Hebrew), Vol. 35 (1985) pp. 163–191.

Biescas, José Antonio and Manuel Tuñón de Lara, *España bajo la dictadura franquista (1939–1975)* (Barcelona: 1982).

Blaye, Edouard de, *Franco and the Politics of Spain* (Harmondsworth: 1976).

Bovis, E., *The Jerusalem Question, 1917–1968* (Stanford: 1971).

Brecher, Michael, *The Foreign Policy System of Israel* (Oxford: 1972).

— *Decisions in Israel's Foreign Policy* (Oxford: 1974).

— 'Jerusalem', in B. Neuberger (ed.), *Diplomacy and Confrontation – Selected Issues in Israel's Foreign Relations, 1948–1978* (Hebrew) (Tel Aviv: 1984).

Cámara Villar, Gregorio, *Nacional-Catolicismo y escuela. La socialización política del franquismo (1936–1951)* (Madrid: 1984).

Caro Baroja, Julio, *Los judíos en la España moderna y contemporánea* (Madrid: 1961), 3 Vols.

Carpi, Daniel, 'The Jews of Greece during the Holocaust, 1941–1943', *Yalkut Moreshet* (Hebrew), Vol. 31 (1981) pp. 7–39.

Carr, Raymond, *Spain 1808–1975* (London: 1982) (2nd edn).

Castells, A., *Las brigadas internacionales de la guerra de España* (Barcelona: 1972).

Cierva, Ricardo de la, *Historia del franquismo: aislamiento, transformación, agonía 1945–1975* (Barcelona: 1978).

— 'The Nationalist Army in the Spanish Civil War', in R. Carr (ed.), *The Republic and the Civil War in Spain* (London: 1971).

Clavera, J., et al., *Capitalismo español: de la autarquía a la estabilización* (Madrid: 1973), 2 Vols.

Coles, S.F.A., *Franco of Spain: A Full Length Biography* (London: 1955).

Cordero Torres, José María, *Misión africana de España* (Madrid: 1941).

Cortada, J.W., *Two Nations over Time: Spain and the US, 1776–1977* (Westport: 1978).

Coverdale, J.F., *Italian Intervention in the Spanish Civil War* (Princeton: 1975).

Criado, Ramón, *Sahara: Pasión y muerte de un sueño imperial* (Paris: 1977).

Crozier, Brian, *Franco: A Biographical History* (London: 1967).

De Garmo, P.H., 'Beyond the Pyrenees: Spain and Europe since World War II'. Ph.D. diss. (University of California: Davis, 1971).

Diamant, David, *Combattants juifs dans L'Armée Republicaine Espagnole* (Paris: 1979).

Dothan, Shmuel, *Reds – The Communist Party in Palestine* (Hebrew) (Kfar-Saba: 1991).

Doussinage, José María, *España tenía razón, 1939–1945* (Madrid: 1949).

Dura, Juan, 'U.S. Policy toward Dictatorship and Democracy in Spain, 1936–1953: A Case Study in Realities of Policy Formation'. Ph.D. diss. (University of California, Berkeley: 1979).

Eijan, Samuel, *Hispanidad en Tierra Santa – actuación diplomática* (Madrid: 1943).

Emanuel, Irona and Yitzhak, 'On a Mission in Barcelona', *Betfutzot Hagola* (Hebrew), 18/19 (Winter, 1962) pp. 122–4.

Espadas Burgos, Manuel, *Franquismo y política exterior* (Madrid: 1988).

Esteban, Joan, 'The Economic Policy of Francoism: An Interpretation', in P. Preston (ed.), *Spain in Crisis: The Evolution and Decline of the Franco Régime* (Hassocks, Sussex: 1976).

Eytan, Walter, *The First Ten Years – A Diplomatic History of Israel* (London: 1958).

Felice, Renzo de, *Jews in an Arab Land: Libya, 1835–1970* (Hebrew) (Tel Aviv: 1980).

Fernández Rodríguez, Manuel, 'España y los judíos en el reinado de Alfonso XII', *Hispania*, 100 (1965) pp. 565–84.

Ferrari, Silvio, 'The Holy See and the Postwar Palestine Issue: The Internationalization of Jerusalem and the Protection of the Holy Places', *International Affairs*, Vol. 60 (1984) pp. 261–83.

Ferrer Benimeli, José A., 'Franco y la masonería', in Josep Fontana (ed.), *España bajo el franquismo* (Barcelona: 1986).

Figallo, Beatriz J., 'Un embajador argentino en España, el Dr Pedro Radío', *Res Gesta* (Rosario, Argentina) (July 1987) pp. 97–103.

— *El protocolo Franco–Perón: relaciones hispano–argentinas, 1942–52* (Buenos Aires: 1992) pp. 103–54

Fleming, Shannon, 'North Africa and The Middle East', in James W. Cortada (ed.), *Spain in the Twentieth-Century World* (Westport: 1980).

— 'Spanish Morocco and the Alzamiento Nacional, 1936–1939: The Military, Economic and Political Mobilization of a Protectorate', *Journal of Contemporary History*, Vol. 18, No. 1 (1983) pp. 27–42.

Friedlander, Robert A., 'Holy Crusade or Unholy Alliance? Franco's "National Revolution" and the Moors', *Southwestern Social Science Quarterly*, Vol. 44 (1964) pp. 346–56.

Fusi, Juan Pablo, *Franco – A Biography* (London: 1987).

Gallo, Max, *Spain under Franco* (London: 1973).

García Perez, R., 'El envío de trabajadores españoles a Alemania durante la segunda guerra mundial', *Hispania*, Vol. 170 (1988) pp. 1031–66.

Garriga, Ramón, *Los validos de Franco* (Barcelona: 1981).

Gilead, I., 'Public Opinion in Israel on Relations between the State of Israel and West Germany in the Years 1949–1965' (Hebrew). Ph.D. diss. (Tel Aviv University: 1984).

Gilmore, W.R., 'The American Foreign Policy Making Process and the Development of a Post World War II Spanish Policy, 1945–1953: A Case Study'. Ph.D. diss. (University of Pittsburgh: 1967).

Glick, Edward B., *Latin America and the Palestine Problem* (New York: 1958).

Goda, Norman J.W., 'The Riddle of the Rock: A Reassessment of German Motives for the Capture of Gibraltar in the Second World War', *Journal of Contemporary History*, Vol. 28 (1993) pp. 297–314.

Golani, Motti, *Zion in Zionism: The Zionist Policy on the Issue of Jerusalem, 1937–1949* (Hebrew) (Tel Aviv: 1992).

González, Isidro, *El retorno de los judíos* (Madrid: 1991).

Govrin, Yossef, *Israel–Soviet Relations, 1953–1967* (Hebrew) (Jerusalem: 1990).

Hadari, Ze'ev Vania, *Refugees Defeating a Great Power* (Hebrew) (Tel Aviv: 1985).

Halstead, Charles R., 'A Somewhat Machiavellian Face: Colonel Juan Beigbeder as High Comissioner in Spanish Morocco,

1937–1939', *Historian*, Vol. 37 (1974) pp. 46–66.

— 'Un "Africain" Méconnu: Le Colonel Juan Beigbeder', *Revue d'Histoire de la Deuxième Guerre Mondiale*, Vol. 83 (1971) pp. 1–60.

Halstead, Charles R. and Carolyn J. Halstead, 'Aborted Imperialism: Spain's Occupation of Tangiers 1940–1945', *Iberian Studies*, Vol. 7, No. 2 (1978) pp. 53–71.

Hills, George, *Franco – The Man and His Nation* (London: 1967).

Hourani, A., and N. Shehadi (eds), *The Lebanese in the World: A Century of Emigration* (London: 1992).

Houston, John A., *Latin America in the United Nations* (New York: 1956).

Huff, Robert P., 'The Spanish Question Before the U.N.'. Ph.D. diss. (Stanford: 1966).

Israel and the United Nations – Report of a Study Group Set Up by the Hebrew University of Jerusalem (New York: 1956).

Iwanska, Alicja, *Exiled Governments: Spanish and Polish. An Essay in Political Sociology* (Cambridge, MA: 1981).

Jackson, Gabriel, *The Spanish Republic and the Civil War 1931–39* (Princeton: 1965).

Johnson, V.B., *The Legions of Babel: The International Brigades in the Spanish Civil War* (University Park, PA: 1967).

Kleinfeld, G.R., and Lewis A. Tambs, *Hitler's Spanish Legion: The Blue Division in Russia* (Carbondale, IL: 1986).

Klieman, Aharon, 'Continuity and Change in Israel's Diplomacy', in B. Neuberger (ed.), *Diplomacy and Confrontation – Selected Issues in Israel's Foreign Relations, 1948–1978* (Hebrew) (Tel Aviv: 1984).

Krammer, A., *The Forgotten Friendship* (Illinois: 1974).

Kreutz, A., *Vatican Policy on the Palestinian–Israeli Conflict* (New York: 1990).

Laskier, Michael M., *The Jews of Egypt, 1920–1970* (New York: 1992).

— 'Zionism and the Jewish Communities of Morocco: 1956–1962', *Studies in Zionism*, Vol. 6, No. 1 (1985) pp. 119–38.

Levin, Ruth, *The Righteous Were with Spain, 1936–1939* (Hebrew) (Tel Aviv: 1987).

Lichtenstein, J.J., 'The Reaction of West European Jewry to the Reestablishment of a Jewish Community in Spain in the 19th

Century'. Ph.D. diss. (Yeshiva University, New York: 1962).

Lipschiz, Chaim U., *Franco, Spain, the Jews, and the Holocaust* (New York: 1984).

Lisbona, José Antonio, *Retorno a Sefarad. La política de España hacia sus judíos en el siglo XX* (Barcelona: 1993).

Lorch, Netanel, 'Israel–Spain: The Establishment of Diplomatic Relations', *Skirah Hodshit* (Hebrew) (March 1986) pp. 3–11.

Louis, W.R., and R. Owen (eds), *Suez 1956: The Crisis and Its Consequences* (Oxford: 1989).

Lowi, T.J., 'Bases in Spain', in H.L. Stein (ed.), *American Civil–Military Decisions. A Book of Case Studies* (Birmingham, AL: 1963), pp. 667–702.

Lleonart y Amselem, A.J., *España y ONU*, 4 Vols (Madrid: 1978–86).

Lucas, W. Scott, *Divided We Stand: Britain, the U.S. and the Suez Crisis* (London: 1991).

Madariaga, María Rosa de, 'The Intervention of Moroccan Troops in the Spanish Civil War: A Reconsideration', *European History Quarterly*, Vol. 22 (1992) pp. 67–97.

Malefakis, Edward, 'La economía española y la Guerra Civil', in J. Nadal *et al.* (eds), *La economía española en el siglo XX – una perspectiva histórica* (Barcelona: 1987).

Marquina, Antonio, *La diplomacia vaticana y la España de Franco (1936–1945)* (Madrid: 1984).

— *España en la política de la seguridad occidental* (Madrid: 1986).

Marquina, Antonio, and Gloria Inés Ospina, *España y los judíos en el siglo XX* (Madrid: 1987).

Martín, Isidro, *El concordato español de 1953* (Madrid: 1954).

Martín, Miguel, *El colonialismo español en Marruecos (1860–1956)* (Paris: 1973).

Martínez Lillo, P.A., *Una introducción al estudio de las relaciones hispano-francesas (1945–1951)* (Madrid: 1985).

Medlicot, W.N., *The Economic Blockade* (London: 1952).

Mendes, Meir, *The Vatican and Israel* (Hebrew) (Jerusalem: 1983).

Mesa, Roberto, *Democracia y política exterior* (Madrid: 1988).

Mitchell Serels, M., *A History of the Jews of Tangiers in the Nineteenth and Twentieth Centuries* (New York: 1991).

Molko, Y.R., 'Turning Points in Relations between Spain and the

Jews', *Gesher* (Hebrew), Vol. 58 (1969) pp. 68–74.

— 'Spain and the Jews', *Tmurot*, Vol. 6 (Hebrew) (March 1965) pp. 28–30.

Morales Lezcano, Victor, *España y el norte de Africa: el protectorado en Marruecos (1912–1956)* (Madrid: 1986).

Morán, Fernando, *Una política exterior para España* (Barcelona: 1980).

Nachmani, Amikam, 'Middle East Listening Post: Eliahu Sasson and the Israeli Legation in Turkey, 1949–1952', *Studies in Zionism,* Vol. 6, No. 2 (1985) pp. 263–85.

Oren, Michael B., *The Origins of the Second Arab–Israeli War: Egypt, Israel and the Great Powers, 1952–1956* (London: 1992).

Paris Eguilaz, Higinio, *Diez años de política económica en España* (Madrid: 1949).

Payne, Stanley G., *The Franco Régime, 1936–1975* (Madison, WI: 1987).

— *Spanish Catholicism* (Madison, WI: 1984).

— *Politics and the Military in Modern Spain* (Stanford: 1967).

Pike, D.W., 'Franco and the Axis Stigma', *Journal of Contemporary History,* 17, No. 3 (1982) pp. 369–407.

Pollack, Benny, *The Paradox of Spanish Foreign Policy* (London: 1987).

Porat, Dina, *The Blue and the Yellow Stars of David: The Zionist Leadership in Palestine and the Holocaust* (Cambridge, MA: 1990).

Portero, Florentino, *Franco aislado – La cuestión española (1949–1950)* (Madrid: 1989).

Pratto, Ionnathan, 'Spain's Jewry', in J. Tsur (ed.), *The Diaspora: Western Europe* (Hebrew) (Jerusalem: 1976), pp. 219–30.

Preston, Paul, *The Politics of Revenge: Fascism and the Military in Twentieth-Century Spain* (London: 1990).

— *The Triumph of Democracy in Spain* (London: 1986).

Ramírez, Pedro J., *El año que murió Franco* (Barcelona: 1985).

Rein, Raanan, *The Franco–Perón Alliance: Relations between Spain and Argentina, 1946–1955* (Pittsburgh: 1993).

— 'The Visit of the Young Lady: The Franco–Perón Alliance and Evita's Trip to Spain', *Zmanim* (Hebrew), Vol. 10, No. 38 (1991) pp. 80–91.

— 'La negativa israelí: Las relaciones entre España e Israel

(1948–1949', *Hispania* (Madrid), Vol. 172 (1989) pp. 659–88.

Richardson, D., *Comintern Army: The International Brigades and the Spanish Civil War* (Lexington, KY: 1983).

Río Cisneros, Agustín del, *España rumbo a la posguerra* (Madrid: 1947).

Robinson, Nehemia, *The Spain of Franco and its Policies Toward the Jews* (New York: 1952).

Ro'i, Yaacov, *Soviet Decision-Making in Practice – The USSR and Israel, 1947–1954* (New Brunswick: 1980).

Rokach, L., *The Catholic Church and the Question of Palestine* (London: 1987).

Rose, Norman A., *Chaim Weizmann – A Biography* (Hebrew) (Jerusalem: 1990).

Rubinstein, Shimon, 'Don Antonio de Ballobar: The Forgotten Spanish Consul', *Ha-Uma* (Hebrew), Vols. 83/84 (1986) pp. 205–12.

Ruhl, K.J., *Franco, Falange y 'Tercer Reich': España en la segunda guerra mundial* (Madrid: 1986).

Sagi, Nana, *German Reparations: A History of the Negotiations* (Jerusalem: 1980).

Schechtman, Joseph B., *On Wings of Eagles: The Plight, Exodus, and Homecoming of Oriental Jewry* (New York: 1961).

Schweid, Eliezer, 'The Expulsion from Spain and the Holocaust', *Alpayim* (Hebrew), Vol. 3 (1990) pp. 69–88.

Seguev, Samuel, *Operation 'Yachin' – The Secret Immigration of Moroccan Jews to Israel* (Hebrew) (Tel Aviv: 1984).

Shaari, David, *The Cyprus Detention Camps for Jewish 'Illegal' Immigrants to Palestine, 1946–1949* (Hebrew) (Jerusalem: 1981).

Shafir, Shlomo, *An Outstretched Hand: German Social Democrats, Jews, and Israel 1945–1963* (Hebrew) (Tel Aviv: 1986).

Shindler, Colin, 'No Pasarán: The Jews Who Fought in Spain', *The Jewish Quarterly*, Vol. 33, No. 3 (1986) pp. 34–41.

Shneidman, J. Lee, *Spain and Franco 1949–1959* (New York: 1973).

Sluzky, Yehuda, *The History of the Hagana* (Hebrew) (Tel Aviv: 1972).

Smyth, Denis, *Diplomacy and Strategy of Survival: British Policy and Franco's Spain, 1940–1941* (Cambridge: 1986).

St John, Robert, *Eban* (New York: 1972).

Stuart, Graham H., *The International City of Tangiers* (Stanford:

1955) (2nd edn).

Suárez Fernández, Luis, *Francisco Franco y su tiempo* (Madrid: 1984), 8 Vols.

— *Franco y la URSS* (Madrid: 1988).

Tamames, Ramón, *Introducción a la constitución española* (Madrid: 1980).

Thomas, Hugh, *The Spanish Civil War* (London: 1977) (2nd edn).

Toch, Josef, 'Jews in the Civil War in Spain, 1936–1939', *Ba-Sha'ar* (Hebrew), 17, No. 6 (1974) pp. 456–66.

Trythall, J.W.D., *Franco – A Biography* (London: 1970).

Tusell, Javier, *Franco y los católicos* (Madrid: 1984).

Tusell, Javier, and Alicia Alted, 'The Government of the Spanish Republic in Exile: 1939–1977', in Yossi Shain (ed.), *Governments-in-Exile in Contemporary World Politics* (New York: 1991).

Tusell, Javier, and G. García Queipo de Llano, *Franco y Mussolini: la política española durante la segunda guerra mundial* (Barcelona: 1985).

Vilar, Juan B., *El Sahara español* (Madrid: 1977).

Villar, Francisco, *El proceso de autodeterminación del Sahara.* (Valencia: 1982).

Viñas, Angel, *Los pactos secretos de Franco con Estados Unidos* (Barcelona: 1981).

Welles, Benjamin, *Spain: The Gentle Anarchy* (New York: 1965).

Whealey, R.H., *Hitler and Spain: The Nazi Role in the Spanish Civil War* (Lexington, KY: 1989).

Ysart, Federico, *España y los judíos en la Segunda Guerra Mundial* (Barcelona: 1973).

Zack, Moshe, 'Jewish Motifs in Israel's Foreign Policy', *Gesher* (Hebrew), Vol. 110 (1984).

Zander, Walter, *Israel and the Holy Places of Christendom* (London: 1971).

Personal interviews

Joel Barromi (Jerusalem, 2 Dec. 1986); Avraham Darom (Drapkin) (Tel Aviv, 16 June 1986); Walter Eytan (Jerusalem, 9 June 1986);

Arye Levavi (Jerusalem, 25 Jan. 1994); Ionnathan Pratto (Jerusalem, 23 Jan. 1994); Salman Salzman (Kibbutz Mizra, 19 Jan. 1994); Moshe Tov (Kiryat Ono, 24 June 1986).

Newspapers and Periodicals

ABC
Al Hamishmar (Hebrew)
American Jewish Yearbook
Arriba
Davar (Hebrew)
Dvar Hashavua (Hebrew)
El País
Ha'aretz (Hebrew)
Haboker (Hebrew)
Hador (Hebrew)
Ha'ir (Hebrew)
Hatzofeh (Hebrew)
Yediot Aharonot (Hebrew)
Informaciones
Herut (Hebrew)
The Jerusalem Post
Jewish Chronicle
Kol Ha'am (Hebrew)
Le Monde
Ma'ariv (Hebrew)
Madrid
New York Times
Newsweek
Pueblo
The Times
Time
Ya

Index

International Diplomacy Titles

Germany and Israel
A Study of Moral Debt and National Interest in International Relations
George Lavy
In 1952, the Federal Republic of West Germany concluded a treaty with Israel whereby the Germans had to pay three billion Deutschmarks in compensation for the Holocaust. However, the Israelis felt that Germany owed Israel a moral as well as a financial debt, and thus expected further aid and protection.

This book examines the grounds which motivated Germany to grant aid to Israel and the change in their relations as the German economy flourished and gained influence in world affairs.

208 pages   1996
0 7146 4626 1 cloth
0 7146 4191 X paper

Futile Diplomacy III
The United Nations, The Great Powers, and Middle East Peacemaking 1948–1954
Futile Diplomacy IV
'Operation Alpha' and the Failure of Anglo-American Coercive Diplomacy in the Arab-Israeli Conflict 1954–1956
Neil Caplan

These two volumes provide a careful and balanced behind-the-scenes account of the intricate diplomatic activity of the period between the first and second Arab–Israeli wars. Exploiting a range of available archive sources as well as extensive secondary sources, they provide an authoritative analysis of the positions and strategies which the principal parties and the would-be mediators adopted in the elusive search for a stable peace.

The text of each volume comprises both analytical-historical chapters and a selection of primary documents from archival sources.

Volume III 392 pages 1997
0 7146 4756 X cloth
Volume IV 440 pages 1997
0 7146 4757 8 cloth

Futile Diplomacy I
Early Arab Zionist Negotiation Attempts 1913–31
Volume I   277 pages   1983
0 7146 3214 7 cloth

Futile Diplomacy II
Arab–Zionist Negotiations and the End of the Mandate
Volume II 358 pages   1986
0 7146 3215 5 cloth

Envoy to Moscow
Memoirs of an Israeli Ambassador, 1988–1992
Aryeh Levin
The personal memoir of Aryeh Levin, Israel's first Ambassador to Russia since the severance of relations between the two countries in 1967.

Aryeh Levin's four-year tenure as Ambassador to Moscow coincided with great upheavals in the life and times of both Israel and Russia. He was witness to the momentous events that led to the collapse of the Soviet empire and was instrumental in facilitating the immigration of almost half a million Jews to Israel.

440 pages   1996
0 7146 4597 4 cloth
0 7146 4248 7 paper

A China Diary
Towards the Establishment of China–Israel Diplomatic Relations
E Zev Sufott
From his unique vantage point as the key Israeli in the proceedings, E. Zev Sufott offers a fascinating depiction of the clandestine contacts and exchanges between China and Israel which led to the establishment of diplomatic relations. He gives readers a peep behind the bamboo curtain, at the internal processes of China's decision-making and its implementations in the foreign policy arena.

152 pages   1997
0 7146 4721 7 cloth
0 7146 4271 1 paper

Jordan in the Middle East, 1948–1988
The Making of a Pivotal State
Edited by Joseph Nevo and Ilan Pappé
These essays assess Jordan's position in the Middle East in the light of its long quest for legitimacy, both as a state and as a Hashemite monarchy.

320 pages   1994
0 7146 3454 9 cloth